A Translation Theory of Knowledge Transfer

A Translation Theory of Knowledge Transfer

Learning across Organizational Borders

Kjell Arne Røvik

OXFORD
UNIVERSITY PRESS

OXFORD
UNIVERSITY PRESS

Great Clarendon Street, Oxford, OX2 6DP,
United Kingdom

Oxford University Press is a department of the University of Oxford.
It furthers the University's objective of excellence in research, scholarship,
and education by publishing worldwide. Oxford is a registered trade mark of
Oxford University Press in the UK and in certain other countries

© Kjell Arne Røvik 2023

The moral rights of the author have been asserted

All rights reserved. No part of this publication may be reproduced, stored in
a retrieval system, or transmitted, in any form or by any means, without the
prior permission in writing of Oxford University Press, or as expressly permitted
by law, by licence or under terms agreed with the appropriate reprographics
rights organization. Enquiries concerning reproduction outside the scope of the
above should be sent to the Rights Department, Oxford University Press, at the
address above

You must not circulate this work in any other form
and you must impose this same condition on any acquirer

Published in the United States of America by Oxford University Press
198 Madison Avenue, New York, NY 10016, United States of America

British Library Cataloguing in Publication Data

Data available

Library of Congress Control Number: 2022950958

ISBN 978–0–19–883236–2

DOI: 10.1093/oso/9780198832362.001.0001

Printed and bound in the UK by
Clays Ltd, Elcograf S.p.A.

Links to third party websites are provided by Oxford in good faith and
for information only. Oxford disclaims any responsibility for the materials
contained in any third party website referenced in this work.

Preface

An obvious but often downplayed point in the research literature is that the antecedent of innovations in organizations is the capacity to imitate and learn from other organizations. So, what is the content of this capacity? Why do some organizations often succeed while others often fail to transfer and exploit knowledge from other organizations? These are the key questions that will be highlighted and answered throughout this book. During the last four decades, much empirical research and theorizing efforts have been undertaken to improve our understanding of these knowledge transfer puzzles. This book develops a fresh reframing and a new theory of the subject. It is a theory that has the potential to help us better understand and explain variations in knowledge transfer successes across organizational borders. The theory conceptualizes knowledge transfer between organizations as acts of translations, resembling the translation of language and texts.

I have attempted to make transparent in the book the step-by-step processes through which this new theory has been generated—from the first step, which is a review of the extensive existing literature on the subject, via the introduction and use of metaphors and insights extracted from two external domains of translation studies, and to the generation of an inventory of more precise arguments and propositions that constitute the translation theory of knowledge transfer.

The theory that is outlined should be conceived of as a ceiling that I do hope can serve as a floor for other researchers. It should be interpreted, criticized, inspire empirical research, be tested and refined—and become the source to new insights.

I am grateful for comments on the book proposal from three anonymous OUP reviewers and for comments on earlier drafts from Hege Andersen, Bjørn Tore Blindheim, Joep Cornelissen, Barbara Czarniawska, Hanne Gabrielsen, Gunnar Gjelstrup, Hanne Foss Hansen, Tor Hernes, Frank Holen, Erik Juel, Hanne Kathrine Krogstrup, Dag Øyvind Madsen, Søren Obed Madsen, Turid Moldenæs, Nanna Møller Mortensen, Tor Paulson, Hilde Marie Pettersen, Trish Reay, David Strang, and Eleanor Westney. Their comments have clearly added to the quality of this work. I offer a special thanks to James Morrison for providing me with his excellent editing service. Finally, I express my admiration and thanks to the two most important girls in my life—my wife Heidi and my daughter, Regine—for still providing me with discussions, ideas, caring, and love.

Contents

List of Figures vii
List of Tables viii

1. Knowledge Transfer and the Quest for the X Factor 1

I. THE STATE OF THE ART

2. What We Do and Do Not Know: A Review of the Knowledge Transfer Literature 23

II. IN SEARCH OF A NEW THEORY

3. Antecedents of a Translation Theory of Knowledge Transfer 67

III. THE THEORY

4. Reframing Knowledge Transfer as Acts of Translations 105
5. Revealing the Rules of Knowledge Translation 145
6. Reimagining That Translators and Translations Make a Difference 178

IV. IMPLICATIONS FOR KNOWLEDGE TRANSFER PRACTICES

7. Translation Competence: Implications for Knowledge Transfer Practices 213

References 250
Index 299

List of Figures

3.1 Generic model of parallel transfer structures in outer and target domains   77
3.2 Summing up: Salient features of two source domains   99
4.1 Knowledge transfers as acts of translation: Overview   142
5.1 A typology of translation rules: Key concepts and how they are related   177
7.1 Links between translators' knowledge of contexts and outcomes of knowledge transfers   243

List of Tables

2.1 Summary: Seven reviewed knowledge transfer research fields　59
6.1 Summary: Six cases illustrating the role of translators in knowledge transfers　208
7.1 Appropriate translation rules under various scope conditions　245

1
Knowledge Transfer and the Quest for the X Factor

Introduction

This book zooms in on the challenges of transferring and sharing knowledge across organizational borders. Knowledge transfer refers to the processes through which actors and units exchange, receive, and are influenced by the experience and knowledge of others, and it can manifest itself through changes in the knowledge bases or performance of recipients (Argote et al., 2000; van Wijk et al., 2008). Three observations and one main ambition have inspired this book. The first observation is the increased importance of effective knowledge transfer for a wide range of critical organizational success variables. The second is the observation (actually, a number of observations) that effective knowledge transfer is very challenging; such processes sometimes succeed, but they frequently fail. The third observation is that despite extensive research efforts, we still lack theories with high explanatory power to account for the huge variations in knowledge transfer successes, as well as research-based means to guide actors involved in knowledge transfer processes.

Partly in response to these observations, the aim of this book is to outline a new theory that (re)conceptualizes knowledge transfer between organizations as acts of translation, resembling the translation of language and texts. This theory has the potential to improve our understanding of why knowledge transfer processes sometimes succeed and sometimes fail, and also has the potential to inform practitioners involved in knowledge transfers about appropriate actions. The theory points towards translation competence as the key organizational capacity required in knowledge transfers.

Let us first take a closer look at the three above-mentioned observations.

Knowledge transfer and organizational success

The capacity of an organization to transfer and exploit knowledge from other organizations is a key to its competitiveness, progress, and survival.

This insight sheds light on the complex relation between imitation and innovation (Strang and Meyer, 1993). Although society celebrates the innovating organization ("the lone genius") and its inventions (Sevòn, 1996; Perry-Smith et al., 2015), newness and an organization's capacity to innovate are, in fact, often linked directly to its capacity to imitate and learn from other organizations' practices and ideas.

Knowledge transfer capacity affects a number of critical organizational performance variables. Many studies have found that the capacity to identify, transfer, and exploit knowledge from other organizations is an antecedent and key input for a focal organization's capacity to innovate and improve performances (Cohen and Levinthal, 1990; Song et al., 2018). For example, it has been shown that knowledge search and transfer capacity has been a prerequisite for focal organizations' development of new technology (Santoro et al., 2017; Flor et al., 2018), new products (Alexander and Childe, 2013), new patents (Zeng et al., 2019), and has led to improved overall organizational performance, such as increased returns on investments (Patel, et al., 2015) and sales growth (Kohtamäki et al., 2019). The connection between knowledge transfer and competitiveness is often illustrated with reference to the expansion of large multinational corporations, a phenomenon that largely reflects how knowledge can be transferred relatively smoothly across borders *within* such organizations, which regularly creates huge competitive advantages (Westney, 1993; Zander and Kogut, 1995; Jensen and Szulanski, 2004; Riusala and Smale, 2007).

Other studies have indicated that knowledge transfer capacity even affects organizational survival rates. For example, Agarwal et al. (2004) found that among entrepreneurial ventures, *spin-out* organizations (entrepreneurial ventures of ex-employees in parent organizations) had an edge over other entrants in terms of survival, which reflected the existence of corridors of knowledge transfers from the parent organizations to the spin-outs. Winter et al. (2012) studied a group of franchising organizations and the extent to which they were able to transfer and replicate exactly knowledge from their parent organization (the franchisor) about the franchising concept. The authors found that the franchising organizations that most accurately transferred and replicated the franchising concept had significantly higher chances of staying in business and surviving than those franchisees that were less accurate. Tavares (2020) studied organizational survival among 24.163 newly created establishments (spin-outs) from preestablished parent firms in Portugal from 2003 to 2008. The parent firms had the option of transferring workers from the parent organization to the new establishments. The study showed a significantly higher survival rate among establishments with high versus establishments with low levels of employees recruited from the parent organizations. Tavares interpreted the variations in survival rates as being mostly caused by variations in knowledge transfer effectiveness. Firm knowledge, which was embodied in the parent firm workers, was effectively transferred to the new establishments through internal recruitment of workers from parent firm, thus increasing the establishments' survival chances. Ingram and Baum (1997) studied the effects of chain affiliation on individual hotels in the Manhattan hotel industry from 1890 to 1980. They found that, under most circumstances, chain affiliation improved the survival chances for the individual hotels. The researchers ascribed much of this survival effect to effective transfer of operating knowledge from the chain to the affiliated component hotels.

Relevance beyond business organizations

Most of the knowledge transfer literature stems from studies of market-exposed business-firms seeking competitive advantages. In a literature review of knowledge transfer and organizational learning with relevance to public sector organizations, Rashman et al. (2009) concluded that "there is an over-reliance on the private sector as the principal source of theoretical understanding and empirical research" and "a tendency to assume by default that the context was the private sector firm, and that 'the firm' is synonymous with organization" (pp. 486–487). However, knowledge transfers across various borders are decisive for most types of organizations and have impacts on a wide range of outcome variables, beyond business firms and their competitive edge. For example, knowledge transfer also includes the transfer of models of political organizing between nation-states. Efforts to promote and spread democracy to countries where models and practices of democracy are insufficient or absent can be conceived of as a giant knowledge transfer project. These efforts are premised on a strong notion that democracy is the preeminent form of political organizing and governance of nation-states (Ober, 2008). Although the spread of practices and models of democracy has a long history that can be traced back to the American Revolution of 1776 and the French Revolution of 1789, the period since the late 1960s has seen a dramatic increase in attempts to spread this model to the world's nation-states (Whitehead, 1996; O'Loughlin et al., 1998). The so-called "third wave" of democratization began in Sothern Europe in the early 1970s (Gunther et al., 1995) and diffused to Latin America in the 1980s (Hagopian and Mainwaring, 2005). The end of the Cold War in 1989 and the disintegration of former communist Eastern Europe saw the start of extensive attempts to export democracy to East European countries (Schraeder, 2003). These processes were also propelled by the European Union, which demanded democratic governance in exchange for the East European countries becoming members of the European Union (EU) (Olsen, 2002).

However, spreading democracy with the aim of reproducing this ideal in institutions and governance practices in nation-states—often ones that have meager democratic traditions—is probably among the most challenging knowledge transfer processes one can imagine.

In addition to political organizing, we also have observations of the importance of transfer and translations of models of administrative organizing for the shaping of nations-states' public administration. A seminal work here is Eleanor Westney's study of the dramatic transformation of Japan's public administration during the Meiji period (1868–1912) (Westney, 1987). These changes reflected the Meiji leaders' ambition to modernize the country's public administration, inspired by foreign models and as part of a national project that aimed to put Japan on equal footing with the West. The Meiji agents systematically collected information about the practices and the principles of organizing the postal system, the police, and the press in various Western countries. Some features of the Western models were selected and then creatively mixed with Japanese bureaucratic traditions. These knowledge—and translation—processes materialized in a new and radically transformed public administration that observers have assessed as being even more modern than that of its Western counterparts.

Today, many public sector organizations base the development of their services on benchmarks from other comparable organizations and on transferred knowledge about good or best practices. An example is the public education sector, which during the past 25 years has experienced a rationalized and very powerful knowledge transfer turn that aims to improve children and students' learning performances and achievements. Initiated and coordinated by strong international actors such as the Organisation for Economic Co-operation and Development (OECD), the EU, and the IEA (International Association for the Evaluation of Educational Achievements), the rationalized knowledge management system comprises large-scale organizing and routinization of the production, distribution, and implementation of knowledge about effective educational practices (Røvik, 2014). This system entails regular international surveys (such as the Pisa test) that offer big data on matters such as the learning environment and students' performances in various subjects. It also includes the use of clearing houses, which are institutions established for providing evidence-based information about the effects of education programs, policies, and interventions, and have been founded in many Western countries over the last three decades (Slavin, 2008). Clearing houses are designed to identify good educational practices and to compile, analyze, synthesize, shape, and disseminate evidence-based knowledge—especially to professionals, politicians, and the media. The core idea—that public services and practices must be based on identified, gathered, analyzed, and disseminated knowledge about evidenced best practices—is now widespread and represented in most public sectors, such as healthcare (Andersen et al., 2014), social care (Macdonald, 2000), public transportation (Terry, 2000), and urban policy (Harrison, 2000).

The architecture of knowledge transfers

How can knowledge that is developed and used within certain organizational contexts be moved to other organizational contexts and lead to desired organizational outcomes, such as increased competitiveness and survival rates in business firms, as well as more democratic governed nation-states and more modern and effective public administrations? Knowledge transfer is an eclectic concept that covers a lot of variation. However, such variations are all versions of an underlying common knowledge transfer architecture that contains five main elements. These are (a) source organizational context, (b) practices and knowledge to be transferred, (c) borders (or barriers) between source and recipient units, (d) recipient organizational context, and (e) mediators. These elements, and how they are combined, vary greatly between different contexts and knowledge transfer processes. For example, sources and recipients can be separate and independent organizations, as well as separate but internal units belonging to the same organization. Further, the concept of borders entails all kinds of knowledge flow hindrances between sources and recipients. Knowledge transfer always involves some kinds of border crossing and friction. Borders are sometimes minor, such as in processes of intraorganizational knowledge sharing among workers co-located in one organizational unit (Tell et al., 2017). On the other hand, interorganizational knowledge transfers between independent organizations often involve crossing far more challenging borders. The barring effects may increase with increased geographical, cultural, and institutional distance between sources and recipients.

Another element that has significant empirical variance is mediators; that is, those actors involved in transferring knowledge from sources to recipients. Knowledge transfer can be indirect, which means that it is carried out by mediators who are distanced both from the source and the recipient organization (Sahlin-Andersson and Engwall, 2002). Among the typical indirect mediators are consultants (Ostroff, 1999; Wright, 2019), business media (Barros and Rüling, 2019), academics (Grandi and Grimaldi, 2005), and management gurus (Collins, 2019). For example, authors of popular management books are often distant mediators who attempt to convey success formulas from certain organizations to a broad audience of potential recipients (Furusten 1999). Numerous books and articles, most of them published in the 1970s and 1980s, urge Western organizations to learn from Japanese practices of management and organizing (Drucker, 1971; Ouchi, 1981; Pascale and Athos, 1981), while other examples include biographies about famous leaders and their management principles (Novak, 1986; Isaacson, 2011).

Direct knowledge transfer means that source-based and recipient-based actors are more involved in the mediation processes. A well-known example came from the setup of Japanese companies' subsidiaries in the United States in the 1980s (Froin et al., 1999). In some of these cases, the Japanese strategy was to reproduce their management system and production technology with great exactitude in their American transplants (Pil and MacDuffie, 1999). To implement this strategy, the Japanese parent organizations staffed the subsidiaries with a high proportion of Japanese managers and workers who interacted directly with the American employees and instructed them about the parent company's production system (Adler, 1999; Westney and Piekkari, 2020). This often involved linguistically constrained contexts, so the transfer of knowledge was frequently conducted through nonverbal communication, such as showing work movements and real-time demonstrations of how machines and tools should be used (Sunaoshi et al., 2005). The intense effort of direct knowledge transfer knowledge from the Japanese parent organizations is undoubtedly an important factor that explains the successes of many of their subsidiaries in the United States throughout the 1980s and 1990s, especially within the motor vehicle industry (Helper et al., 1999).

The above examples show that certain knowledge transfers vary greatly within the overall common architecture of five elements and can thereby offer very different conditions for transfer processes.

Transfer successes and failures

While knowledge transfers across organizational borders are extremely important for organizations' healthiness, they are not at all straightforward processes with predictable outcomes. Two keywords—*variations* and *complexities*—sum up insights from a large number of observations of knowledge transfer processes. There are many obstacles to effective knowledge transfer, which can come to expression in huge variations in processes and outcomes. In fact, knowledge transfer initiatives often succeed, such as when knowledge is transferred smoothly from a source unit and fully implemented in a recipient unit, sometimes leading to performance improvements and long-lasting competitive advantages. One of the best known, thoroughly researched, and frequently cited knowledge transfer successes is related to the establishment of the above-mentioned Japanese subsidiaries in the United States during the 1970s and 1980s (Florida and Kenney, 1991; Westney and Piekkary, 2020). However, a main finding from empirical studies is the huge variations in processes and outcomes of knowledge transfers across organizational borders (Gupta and Govindarajan, 1994; 2000; Szulanski, 1996; Davenport et al., 1998; Alavi and Leidner, 1999; 2001; Dixon, 2000; Bouncken and Kraus, 2013; Oyemomi et al., 2016; Tell et al., 2017). For example, Davenport et al. (1998) studied 31 knowledge transfer projects in 24 large organizations from various industries and based in different countries. They defined and measured transfers success and failure in relation to four success indicators: (1) growth in the resources attached to the project (people, money, etc.); (2) growth in the volume of knowledge gained and used; (3) survival, which is the likelihood that the project would survive and become a (more) enduring organizational initiative; and (4) evidence of financial return stemming from the transferred knowledge. The researchers classified 18 of the 31 projects as successful. Almost all of the 18 knowledge transfer projects that were classified as successes fulfilled all four criteria. In some of these cases, the knowledge transfers led to major organizational transformations. Five of the 31 projects were classified as failures, while eight projects were at such an early phase that their outcomes could not be evaluated. Another example: Tidd and Thuriaux-Alemán (2016) studied the transfer, adoption, and effectiveness of a research-based innovation management—practices in a sample of 292 organizational units in different industries and countries. Overall, they found significant variations in adoption and usage rates. They also found that usage of the innovation management practices was associated with positive innovation outcomes.

However, knowledge transfer initiatives frequently fail. There are six common indications of transfer problems and failures in organizations. First, such problems often manifest themselves as deficient information in focal (adopting) organizations about potential useful knowledge residing in other organizations. Sometimes an organization can identify a desired practice in another organization, but is not able to fully understand and codify it

(Mansfield, 1985; Strang and Still, 2006). This is a serious challenge for knowledge transfers, especially in cases where the desired practice is premised on context-specific and tacit knowledge (Dhanaraj et al., 2004). The less an adopting organization understands the logic behind a well-functioning practice in another organization, the more challenging it becomes to recreate the practice at home.

The second expression of problems is cases where transfer of knowledge is not initiated, because organizations sometimes do not even discover eminent practices and knowledge that is already present in their *own* organization. For example, in 1992 the American Productivity and Quality Center (APQR) established the International Benchmarking Clearinghouse (IBM), which is an organization designed to search for and transfer global best practices to their prominent and successful member organizations. However, while searching for global best practices outside their own walls, the member organizations—which themselves conducted the benchmarking processes in close cooperation with IBM—were surprised to discover good practices and their appurtenant knowledge base within their own organizations. The discovery was surprising because this had been a hidden secret for the leaders. O'Dell and Grayson (1998), who analyzed this case, summed up the lesson succinctly as follows: "The grass was greener in their own back yard, and they did not even know it" (p. 5).

A third indication of knowledge transfer problems comes to expression in slow or reduced speed of transfer processes (Davidson, 1980; Mansfield and Romeo, 1980). Identified and desired knowledge sometimes move slowly across organizational borders, and even among members within an organizational unit (Zander and Kogut, 1995; Prusak, 1997). In a comparative study of in-house knowledge transfer among a group of IBM member organizations, Szulanski (1994; 2000) provided evidence for this argument. He found that even among the best organizations, it took an average of 27 months to transfer acknowledged and desired knowledge from a part in the organization where it was practiced to other parts of the organization. Such findings also indicate that the notion of high-speed knowledge transfer *within* organizations (for example, within multinational corporations), but not *between* them, needs to be problematized and modified.

A fourth manifestation of transfer problems is instances of missing implementation of transferred knowledge. New knowledge is sometimes discovered, transferred, and even formally adopted by a recipient unit, but then not materialized in new practices (Drago, 1988; Szulanski, 2000; Griffith et al., 2005; Li and Hsieh, 2009). Studies of the development, transfer, and usage of innovations within healthcare (meaning evidenced new knowledge) provide illuminating examples. From healthcare research comes a rich and almost constant supply of new, evidenced knowledge about what should be considered best practices in healthcare. Every year, approximately 10,000 new randomized trials are included in MEDLINE (Chassin, 1998), which is the bibliographic database of life sciences and biomedical information. However, studies have revealed a divide between the supply of evidenced knowledge and practice in healthcare. In the Netherlands and the United States, approximately 30–40 percent of patients are not treated according to present scientific evidence (Schuster et al., 1998; Grol, 2001), while approximately 20–25 percent of healthcare practices are assessed as unnecessary and/or as potentially harmful (Grol and Grimshaw, 2003). A fascinating aspect of these insights from the healthcare sector is that the professionals do not change their healthcare practices according to available new knowledge, even though there are strong professional norms among healthcare personnel to act rationally and be open-minded to new evidence-based knowledge in their fields (Ferlie et al., 2005). Such observations of gaps between available knowledge and practice correspond with similar observations in neo-institutional organization theory about transferred new knowledge and ideas that lead to change of talk in the recipient organization, but leave core practices unchanged (Meyer and Rowan, 1977; Brunsson, 1989; Westphal and Zajac, 2001; Bromley and Powell, 2012; Snellman, 2012; Stål and Corvellec, 2018). Neo-institutional scholars have theorized the logic behind such decoupling as one of seeking legitimacy in broad institutional environments by formally adopting new ideas, thus signaling adherence to widely admired values, such as science, evidence, and progress, while simultaneously seeking effectiveness and efficiency by protecting in-house existing and complex practices that work well from being changed in accordance with the externally legitimized ideas (Bromley and Powell, 2012; Boxenbaum and Jonsson, 2017).

A fifth indication of transfer problems stems from observations of inappropriate transformations of the transferred practices/knowledge throughout the transfer processes. Desired practices and the appurtenant knowledge about them are sometimes transformed during the transfer processes in such ways that they do not work in the recipient units. This can occur because the transfer process has led to transformations that have destroyed fine-tuned inherent causal mechanisms. As mentioned above, Winter et al.'s (2012) study of the spread of a francizing organization illustrates this point. They found that the units that most accurately replicated the actual franchise concept had significantly higher chances of succeeding, in the sense of staying in business, than those units that were less accurate and transformed the concept. In another study, Blakely et al. (1987) researched the dissemination and adoption of seven social innovations programs within the education sector and the criminal justice sector. They found that the more the adopting organization modified and changed the original programs, the less likely it was that they would work as intended. These findings correspond with views known from the fidelity camp (Bauman et al., 1991) and their arguments for the need to remain true to the original, or prototype, when transferring knowledge across organizational borders. According to the proponents of high fidelity, altering evidenced knowledge such as a social improvement program is a transfer failure that reduces its effectiveness (Calsyn et al., 1977; Forgatch and DeGarmo, 2011).

The sixth, and probably the ultimate indication of knowledge transfer failure, is cases where new knowledge is transferred to a recipient organization and then implemented and materialized in new organizational practices but does not work and leads to gaps between expected and actual results (Acemoglu et al., 2008; Askim et al., 2008; Røvik, 2011; Pyun and Lallemand, 2014). Although such outcomes may sometimes be caused by the abovementioned mechanism of low-fidelity transfer, this is only one of several possible reasons why implemented new knowledge does not work. In fact, the opposite argument is frequently raised; that is, that transfer failures sometimes are expressions of too little adaptations of what is transferred to the context of the recipient organization (Cummings and Teng, 2003). Anyway, the research literature contains numerous observations and analyses of instances where new and implemented knowledge fails to work in practice (Pressman and Wildavsky, 1973; Elmore, 1979; Xue et al., 2005; Skogan, 2008; Ren, 2019).

Simple models—complex processes

As illustrated above, there are huge variations in processes and outcomes of knowledge transfer efforts. Even more challenging than revealing such variations is understanding and explaining why they occur. Variations in outcomes often reflect complexities in transfer processes that are very hard to trace, theorize, and model. This insight stands in contrast to widely held views that knowledge transfers are rather simple processes. As stated by Szulanski (2000), current conceptions of knowledge transfers, which also dominate research, portray such processes as rather straightforward, instantaneous, and almost costless. A corresponding notion is that difficulties in knowledge transfers are deviations from what is standard, normal, and expected.

Where do such notions stem from? An important source is the signal–transmission metaphor. This is somewhat surprising because this metaphor, which is imported from information theory, has become an underlying model in most research on knowledge transfer across organizational borders. This theory, which was initially formulated by Claude Shannon (1948) and Shannon and Warren Weaver (1949), and detailed and refined in many later works (Cole, 1993; Pierce, 2012), depicts communication between units as mainly one-way processes and conceptualizes the basic elements in such processes as source (sender), channel, message, noise, and recipient. Shannon and Weaver's theory has informed many research fields, primarily studies of signal transference in technical systems, but also biology and life science (Cobb, 2015) and the social sciences (Leydesdorff, 2021). Within organization theory, it has been widely used to conceptualize and structure knowledge transfer studies, although often without referring explicitly to Shannon and Weaver. However, the signal transmission metaphor also has disadvantages, in that it limits the conceptualization of the complexities of organizational border-crossing knowledge transfer processes. The technological context within which Shannon and Weaver developed their ideas—which was telephone companies and concern with the engineering aspects of electronic communication—has made its mark on the theory, in the sense that it is more suitable for understanding electric signal transmission than human communication. Within this theory, knowledge transfers are mainly conceptualized as one-way directional processes with an active source and sender (that is, a central broadcasting point that initiates and adds all the power to the process) and a passive recipient. However, this is an overly simple conceptualization of knowledge transfer across organizational borders. For example, it does not account for insights from knowledge transfer research and especially studies of absorptive capacity, which show that recipient organizations—and not the source—are often the active parts that search for new knowledge and initiate knowledge transfer processes (Cohen and Levinthal, 1989; 1990; Song et al., 2018). Further, the insight that recipients are not passive receivers, but instead are interpretative systems that may reject and/or transform received knowledge, also complicates simple signal transmission images of knowledge transfer processes. Another feature of the signal transmission model is the notion of high-speed and almost automatized one-directional transfer processes from source to recipient. However, several knowledge transfer studies depict such processes as much more messy, time-consuming (Westney, 1987), and laborious (Szulanski, 1996; 2000) for the involved organizations.

There are many antecedents to the complexities that lead knowledge transfer processes to deviate severely from simple images of signal transmission models. One is the *coordination challenges*. A knowledge transfer across organizational borders is often better depicted as a complex ecology of loosely organized actors, often with divergent interests and aims, than as straightforward one-way signal transmission processes. Thus, knowledge transfers usually comprise many and often relatively loosely coordinated and time-consuming processes. Such processes are often driven by various and shifting groups of actors, who may be involved in different phases of the transfer. For example, some actors can be source-based and mainly involved in early phases, while others are recipient-based and involved in later stages. Increasing the number of involved actors increases the potential for a transfer logic resembling the "whispering down the lane" game, which increases the likelihood that the transferred knowledge will be distorted (Andersen and Røvik, 2015).

A second source of complexity is *knowledge access challenges*. An organization's motivation to acquire knowledge from external sources is usually premised on observations of other organizations' successful achievements, such as their high-quality products and/or high returns. However, a classic challenge that is pertinent to such situations is revealing the factors and trajectories underlying other organizations' achievements; that is, the knowledge and practices that generate the observed results (Røvik, 2014). This is sometimes rather easy, but can often be very difficult, especially when the task is to understand and recreate the causes behind the good and desired practices (Argote and Ingram, 2000). The secrets of the winners are usually hard to trace (Røvik, 2002). This often reflects the corresponding (third) *challenge of divergent interests*: simply, what a knowledge seeker and potential recipient organization wants to know about a desired practice, a potential source organization may want to protect and keep as a secret (Granstrand, 2000). In addition, potential recipients' problems with gaining knowledge sometimes reflect that even source-based actors involved in the performance of the desired practice are not able themselves to fully overview, understand, and communicate in precise terms the decisive factors that account for the quality of the practice (Lippman and Rumelt, 1982). Anyway, knowledge access problems are a defining feature of knowledge transfer processes and a stable source of complications, such as slow speed of the transfer, and, correspondingly, to stable high chances for spread of low-fidelity and distorted versions of desired practices.

Difficulties—or "stickiness" (von Hippel, 1994; Szulanski, 1996; 2000; Szulanski and Capetta, 2003)—such as those mentioned above, are intrinsic parts of knowledge transfer processes. They can be identified, analyzed, and to some extent handled, but never be totally avoided. These are important reasons why knowledge transfer processes frequently deviate from simple images of signal transmission models.

In addition to the dominating signal transmission images, there is also another important source for the notion of relatively straightforward knowledge transfer processes. These are the widely held popular images that knowledge transfer is becoming increasingly simple. Such images are often premised on arguments about an ongoing communication revolution, with social media and other communication technologies inevitably and interactively connecting people, organizations, and ideas in intense information flows, leading to an almost unhindered and rapid global distribution and adoption of knowledge and best practices (Santoro and Bierly, 2006; Turkina and Van Assche, 2018). However, numerous observations have indicated that such flows still involve a great deal of friction. For example, many knowledge transfer studies have shown that the most valuable knowledge—that is, knowledge that constitutes lasting competitive advantages—is often almost nonmigratory in nature and is the hardest type of knowledge to transfer and exploit (Hu, 1995; Nonaka and Takeuchi, 1995). Such observations highlight an important point: to be able to understand and explain variations in outcomes of knowledge transfer processes, one must first acknowledge that complexity is an inherent feature of such processes (Szulanski, 2002).

Theories of knowledge transfers

As argued above, the complexities of knowledge transfers lead to variations. While involved practitioners are tasked with scrutinizing the difficulties and handling the problems, a main research challenge is to reveal, understand, and explain the sources to variations. Since the early 1990s there has been a dramatic increase in research into the role of knowledge for the prosperity of contemporary organizations. This has spawned a large number of studies of knowledge-related issues in general, such as knowledge economy (Neef 1997; Aghion et al., 1998; Adler 2001; Powell and Snellman, 2004), knowledge management (Alavi and Leidner, 2001; Hislop et al., 2018), knowledge creation (Nonaka and Takeuchi 1995; Nonaka and Reinmoeller, 2002; von Krogh et al., 2000), and studies of knowledge transfer across organizational borders in particular (Nelson and Winter, 1982; Mowery et al., 1996; Szulanski, 1996; 2003; Argote and Ingram, 2000; Gupta and Govindarajan, 2000; Fleming, 2001; Argote, 2015).

More than three decades of intense research has generated a multitude of insights. For example, we know much more now than we did 30 years ago about characteristics of knowledge that are easy versus those that are harder to transfer. We also have far more insights about factors that facilitate versus hamper transfer across organizational borders. Overall, the research has revealed the importance of taking contexts into account in order to understand outcomes of knowledge transfer processes. Another important contribution from this research is that it has created (and partly imported from other disciplines) a multitude of images and concepts that are applied to understand knowledge transfers, such as knowledge source, encoding, knowledge repository, channel, knowledge networks, transfer barriers, stickiness, and decoding. These conceptualizations have obviously added elements to the development of a distinct scientific language, which makes it possible for researchers (and also for practitioners) to communicate more precisely about knowledge transfer challenges. The next chapter reviews the knowledge transfer literature in more detail.

However, despite considerable research efforts, a lot remains to be done when it comes to understanding and explaining causes behind variations in trajectories and outcomes of knowledge transfer processes. We have still not seen—and will probably *never* see—a variable that resembles "the big X factor"; that is, an independent variable with very high explanatory power across most organizational contexts and knowledge transfer processes. Most quantitative designed studies of factors hypothesized to explain variations in such processes and outcomes have produced relatively modest significant correlations and explanatory power.

Another feature of the knowledge transfer literature is a shortage of research-based action or instrumental models; that is, models and insights that can guide practitioners' decisions about how to organize and conduct knowledge transfer processes (Røvik, 2016; 2019). There are two main antecedents to this condition. Firstly, it reflects the fact that knowledge transfer research has hitherto been able to explain only a rather small portion of the variations in outcomes of knowledge transfers. Thus, the lack of answers to the question of why knowledge transfer processes and outcomes vary translates into a shortage of research-based answers to the "how to" question; that is, how to cope with and reduce the variations. Secondly, the shortage of instrumental models reflects that authors of published knowledge transfer studies (and of organization and management studies in general) often put minimal effort into deducing the implications for practice and practitioners of their findings (Bartunek and Rynes, 2010). This observation connects to the intensifying debate regarding how and to what extent organization and management theory can be relevant for practitioners (Kieser et al., 2015; Cooren and Seidl, 2020).

Left with the pragmatic ambition of improving understanding and explanations of variations, it is time to revisit the dominant theories of knowledge transfer. A striking common feature of the prevailing knowledge transfer theories is that almost all of them were launched in the burgeoning days of knowledge transfer studies, two and three decades ago. This includes the knowledge-based theory of the firm (Kogut and Zander, 1992; 1993); the theory of creation and utilization of knowledge reservoirs (Argote, 1999; Argote and Ingram, 2000); the theory of knowledge transfer stickiness (Von Hippel, 1994; Szulanski, 1996; 2000); the SECI-theory (socialization, externalization, combination, and internalization) of knowledge creation and distribution (Nonaka and Takeuchi's (1995); the theory of absorptive capacity, introduced by Cohen and Levinthal (1989; 1990); network-based theories of knowledge transfer (Burt, 1992; Nohria et al., 1992; Hansen, 1999); and theories of the importance of distance between source and recipient organizations, such as geographical distance (Porter, 1990), cultural distance (Kedia and Bhagat, 1988; Kogut and Singh, 1988), and institutional distance (Kostova, 1999).

Thus, contemporary knowledge transfer research, which is comprehensive and multifaceted, has, as Thomas Kuhn (1970) put it, the typical characteristics of being in "a normal science period"; this means a period of regular work of researchers (such as observing, testing, reporting, and slowly accumulating details) within already settled theories and paradigms. The normal science period undoubtedly generates streams of new insights, although a lot of the variation in transfer processes and outcomes remains unexplained. Thus, one strategy for vitalizing research about knowledge transfer across organizational units is to *retheorize* the subject; that is, to reconceptualize and reframe (Cornelissen et al., 2021) and thereby stimulate new streams of empirical research.

Toward a translation theory of knowledge transfer

This book develops a translation theory of knowledge transfer, which offers a reframing and reconceptualization of dominating contemporary understanding of knowledge transfer between organizations. The translation theory of knowledge transfer has the potential to explain why the outcomes of knowledge transfer processes vary so much, as well as the potential to guide practitioners' deliberate actions and interventions to improve chances of successful transfers of knowledge. This theory is inspired by insights from two different schools of thought. One is the "sociology of translation" (Serres, 1982; Latour, 1986) and the so-called *Scandinavian institutionalism* in organization theory (Czarniawska and Joerges, 1996; Czarniawska and Sevón, 2005; Sahlin and Wedlin, 2008), which focuses on the translation and transformation of practices and ideas as they travel in time and space. The second source of inspiration is *translation studies* (Holmes, 1972; Bassnett and Lefevere, 1998; Snell-Hornby, 2006). This interdisciplinary school of thought, which was established in the early 1970s, is concerned with the study of communication across various borders; that is, translations at large, including both literary and nonliterary translations.

Three core arguments

The translation theory of knowledge transfer outlined in this book is founded on three interconnected arguments:

1. *Knowledge transfers between organizational sources and recipients can be conceptualized as acts of translation.*
2. *Translation of knowledge (practices and ideas) is a rule-based activity.*
3. *Translations make a difference; the way translations are performed may explain outcomes of knowledge transfer processes.*

Each of these arguments is outlined briefly below.

Reframing knowledge transfers as acts of translations. Although there are different forms of organizational theories, a key common feature of most theorizing is the (re) conceptualization of various organizational phenomenon (Cornelissen et al., 2021). A knowledge transfer process can be thought of and conceptualized as a series of translation acts. Knowledge transfer is a kind of mediation between a source and a target (recipient) organizational unit. Attempts to transfer knowledge from source to target units are usually driven by an ambition to be *inspired* by or, even more ambitiously, to *recreate* certain observed and desired practices and/or results in the target organization. As an act of translation, knowledge transfer involves two critical phases. The first phase is *de-contextualization*, which involves translating a desired practice in a particular organizational context into an abstract representation (for example, images, words and texts). The second critical phase is *contextualization*, which is the translation from an abstract representation of a desired practice in a source context to a concrete practice embedded in formal structures, cultures, routines, and individual skills in a recipient context. When contextualizing, a translator faces two main concerns, which are sometimes contradictory. The first is to avoid missing the essentials of the desired practice in the source context, which, in translational terms, is an argument for foreignizing. The second is to avoid missing the essentials of the recipient context and therefore not making the necessary adaptations that would enable the knowledge construct to fit into this context. This is an argument for domestication as a translation strategy.

Reframing knowledge transfer as acts of translation involves a strong focus on the roles of the mediating actors, such as managers, consultants, expatriates, repatriates, and ordinary employees. Within the translation theory frame, such actors are conceptualized as translators. The mediating actors can be located in the source, in the recipient, or in external organizations. Within a translation theory frame, such mediating actors are conceived of as influential *translators* who are partly involved in identifying and translating representations of (desired) source practices, and partly involved in translating images and representations to new practices in recipient units.

Revealing the modes and rules of knowledge translations. While it is well known that translators regularly shape and put their marks on the transferred knowledge, less is known about how they do this. Do such translation processes have any rules and regularities? Based on empirical studies and inspired by insights from the above-mentioned two schools of thought, I outline a typology of the translation modes and rules in use in knowledge transfer processes. The concept of *translation mode* refers to the specific aim and strategy that can drive a knowledge transfer process. I identify three such modes. The first, *the reproducing mode*, sometimes echoes a deliberate replication strategy, with organizations aiming for a competitive advantage by systematically mimicking (adopting and replicating) others' innovations or best practices. The second, the *modifying mode*, is rooted in a pragmatic approach to knowledge transfer and is characterized by translators' awareness of the challenges of balancing competing concerns of replication and adjustment. The third, the *radical mode*, is expressed in the inclination of translators to consider themselves relatively unbound by source context versions when creating recipient versions. Each translation mode is characterized by the application of specific translation rules, in all four, which refers to more or less explicit guidelines for the appropriate translation of knowledge.

The conceptualization of the repertoire of translation modes and the appurtenant rules are central elements in the translation theory of knowledge transfer.

Reimagining the idea that translators and translations make a difference. A lot of the research about knowledge transfer across organizational borders is characterized by what Szulanski (1996) termed a "barrier approach," which is the underlying notion that flows of knowledge from source to recipient are facilitated or hindered by factors such as organizational structures, physical distance, differences between cultures and nations, and so on. Such barriers can block, halt, or distort knowledge flows and can be expressed in "stickiness," which is the failure of new knowledge to fit in with the needs and/or the problems to be solved in the recipient unit.

Research into various knowledge barriers has clearly added to the understanding of the factors that influence knowledge transfers. From a translation perspective, however, two interrelated characteristics that underlie much of the theorizing about barriers remain problematic. The first is the object, or "thing" image of the knowledge flowing between units. The second is the *transfer* image of the knowledge flow. This image of how knowledge flows evokes associations to physical objects that are moved between locations without being transformed. The object image of the knowledge and the transfer image of the knowledge flows, when combined with a focus on barriers to flows, may lead to a static approach to understanding variations in outcomes of knowledge transfer processes. The barriers, rather than the ways in which practices and ideas are translated during the transfer process, are assumed to determine outcomes. As such, the transfer process itself plays a minor role in understanding outcomes. From a translation perspective, the flow of knowledge from source to recipient is not just transfer, but also a two-phased translation process of de-contextualization and contextualization. Permeating this approach is the notion that *translation performance*—that is, how various actors (translators) based on their knowledge of contexts apply translation rules when de-contextualizing practices and contextualizing ideas—may be just as decisive for outcomes of knowledge transfer processes as the effects of researched knowledge barriers. Translators have the potential to shape and reshape knowledge throughout the transfer process (Mukhtarov, 2014). Thus, they also have the potential to cope with and overcome "stickiness," or instances where knowledge transfers are hindered by various knowledge barriers (Szulanski, 1996; Szulanski et al., 2016). For example, stickiness, as an initially perceived mismatch between a new knowledge construct and a recipient organization, can be translated and transformed into a match, leading to successful adoption. As I argue and show in this book, translators and their translations are often the key factors that explain outcomes of knowledge transfer processes, both successes and failures. This implies that we must tap deep into the micro-processes of translations in order to understand better their logics and to show how insights in these logics can be transformed to guidelines for practitioners involved in knowledge transfers.

Implication for knowledge transfer practice

The translation theory has the potential to not only improve analysis and understanding of knowledge transfer processes, but also to guide deliberate interventions in such processes. In other words, the theory developed in this book is also an action-oriented, or *instrumental*, theory that has implications for practitioners involved in knowledge transfers. The argument that a translation theory can guide practitioners' interventions in knowledge transfer processes rests on the premise presented above, that the way translators perform translations of practices and ideas may have an important impact on the outcomes of knowledge transfer processes. Thus, a key concept for understanding variations in outcome of knowledge transfer processes is *translation competence*. This concept, which will be presented and discussed thoroughly in Chapter 7 of this book, refers to the involved actors' knowledge about how to translate practices and ideas to achieve desired ends in knowledge transfers. I argue that there are two critical features of translation competence in knowledge transfers: (a) the translators' knowledge of source and recipient organizational contexts, and (b) the translators' knowledge of and ability to apply the most appropriate translation rules under various conditions.

Structure of the book

The book is structured in four main parts and seven chapters. After this introductory chapter comes Part I, which contains a review of existing knowledge transfer works (Chapter 2). The review aims to answer two main questions: (a) What factors are theorized as (possible) explanations of variations in processes and outcomes of knowledge transfers between organizations? (b) What do we know from empirical studies about the theorized factors' explanatory power? In addition to conclusions regarding what we know about these subjects, Chapter 2 also highlights some important blank spots in this literature.

Part II ("In Search of a New Theory") presents and discusses the antecedents of the translation theory of knowledge transfer. The theory is constructed on ideas borrowed from fields outside the field of knowledge transfer studies. The two main sources of inspiration for the theory are translation studies (a research field established in the early 1970s and concerned with literary and nonliterary translations) and the Scandinavian/French school of organizational translation (Chapter 3).

Part III, the main part of the book, presents and elaborates the three core arguments of the theory. Chapter 4 reframes knowledge transfer as acts of translation and concentrates on two key translation processes: decontextualization and contextualization. Chapter 5 reveals the modes and rules of translations and develops a typology of three translation modes and four appurtenant rules. Chapter 6 outlines and illustrates empirically the third core argument that translators and translations make a difference. The influence of translators on processes and outcomes is illustrated through six knowledge transfer cases, each taking place in different contexts: the United States, Norway, Denmark, China, United Kingdom, and India.

The last part (Part IV) discusses the implications of the theory for practitioners, especially for actors involved in knowledge transfer processes. The core concept that is outlined and discussed here is *translation competence*, which refers to actors' knowledge of and (more) deliberate use of translation modes and rules (Chapter 7). The chapter also focuses on whether and how translation competence can be nurtured and organized.

PART I
THE STATE OF THE ART

2
What We Do and Do Not Know

A Review of the Knowledge Transfer Literature

Introduction

As shown in the introductory chapter, knowledge transfer across organizational units varies considerably in terms of processes and outcomes: There are successes as well as failures. But what do we know from research about the expressions of and causes behind such variations? To shed light on this and related questions, this chapter reviews a broad selection of the knowledge transfer literature, with attention to how the overall questions of the book have been addressed and answered in this literature. The translation theory of knowledge transfer that I outline over the next chapters builds on, extends, and partly challenges insights from the knowledge transfer literature.

When searching the literature for answers about how and why knowledge transfers across organizational units vary in processes and outcomes, one must first recognize that the knowledge transfer literature is huge and multifaceted. While there were still relatively few knowledge transfer publications in the late 1980s, the early 1990s saw an explosion in the interest of this theme, leading to rapid growth in research and publications. Using queries from various databases, Kumar and Ganesh (2009) estimated that the total number of knowledge transfer publications was 145 in 1996, reached 1000 in 2003, 2000 in 2005, and 3000 around 2007. Obviously, the growth in knowledge transfer research and literature reflects the simultaneous emergence of the knowledge-based view (KBV) of organizations. Although not a theory, KBV is a widely shared acknowledgment among researchers and practitioners that knowledge has become the most strategically important resource of modern organizations (Barney, 1991; Grant, 1996; Alavi and Leidner, 2001).

Although the literature is multifaceted, it contains a perceivable pattern in terms of certain main approaches to the question of what are the critical variables in knowledge transfers. Thus, it is possible to discern seven relatively distinct research traditions, each embracing a certain approach to understanding why variations in knowledge transfer processes and outcomes occur and each with an appurtenant relatively distinct body of literature.

These seven approaches will be referred to as research traditions that study the influence on knowledge transfer processes and outcomes of (1) formal organizational structure, (2) absorptive capacity, (3) social networks, (4) geographical distance, (5) cultural distance, (6) institutional distance, and (7) characteristics of the transferred knowledge.

I review the research literature from each tradition in relation to two main questions:

- What factors are theorized as (possible) explanations of variations in processes and outcomes of knowledge transfers across organizational borders?
- What do we know from empirical studies about their (the theorized factors') explanatory power?

I include in the review of each tradition the following: (1) Contributions widely conceived of as foundational works. (2) Works that have initiated or reported from central debates and/or controversy issues within the tradition. (3) Other works that review the traditions' research literature. (4) High-quality empirical studies. Although some works cross over two or more of the seven research traditions, the literature is remarkably tradition-distinct.

I first review each of the research traditions and in the order they are presented above. I then sum up the state of the art by compiling and comparing the traditions. Finally, I point at implications for a translation theory of knowledge transfer.

Formal organizational structure and knowledge transfer

Many organizational characteristics may hamper or facilitate knowledge transfer and sharing across organizational units (Van Wijk et al., 2008). The transfer literature has concentrated on some certain characteristics; among these is the effects of the formal organizational structure. The formal structure constitutes the overall architecture of the organization, as depicted in organizational charts. The main dimensions of a formal structure are the vertical structure (the hierarchical coordination system) and the horizontal structure (the formal specialization in various types and numbers of units that are located at the same vertical level of the organization) (Gulick, 1937; Egeberg and Trondal, 2018; Christensen et al., 2020). The general concept of *border*, which is frequently referred to in knowledge transfer studies, is often operationalized as boundaries established by formal structures—internally between units within an organization and externally between independent organizations. A common insight within this stream of research is that formal organizational structure influences upon knowledge transfer processes and comes to expression in an overarching main pattern where knowledge flows easily and is shared among members *within* an organizational unit, while transfers across formal organizational borders are usually stopped, distorted, or delayed (Blau and Scott, 1963; Gupta and Govindarajan, 1994; Dougherty and Corse, 1995; Willem and Buelens, 2009; McEvily et al., 2014; Christensen et al., 2020). However, although influential, research indicates that formal organizational structures do not *determine* knowledge transfer processes.

The three main features of formal organizational structure are formalization, vertical differentiation, and horizontal differentiation. The formal organizational structure is constituted and constitutive (Hage, 1980; Ranson et al., 1980), which means that it is more or less deliberately chosen, and that it is supposed to influence and reduce variations in various organizational processes, including processes of knowledge transfer and sharing (Røvik et al., 2021). Here follows a brief review of suggestions and findings about to what extent and how the three most central elements of formal organization structure influence processes of knowledge transfer and sharing.

Formalization

Formalization is both a process and a variable. Many attempts to define the concept as process (for example Hage and Aiken, 1967; Hage, 1975; Schminke et al., 2000) can be synthesized as follows: Formalization is the process by which an organization's tasks, rules, routines, and duties are specified and expressed in written and explicit form. When conceived of as a variable, formalization refers to the degree to which an organization's tasks, rules, routines, and duties are formalized (Pertusa-Ortega et. al., 2010), and the degree to which members de facto behave according to the formalized expectations (Fredrickson, 1986).

Formalizations is the classic formal structure variable, deliberately described by Max Weber in his theory of bureaucracy (Weber, 1924). Weber conceptualized formalization as a key to standardize processes and increase clarity and predictability on roles and responsibilities. However, assumptions in the later literature are more negative about the possible effects of formalization on knowledge creation, transfer, and sharing. Formal rules are associated with control, which may restrict the creation and diffusion of knowledge

(Mintzberg 1979; Von Krogh, 1998; Vlaar et al., 2006). In addition, formal rules are supposed to preprogram tasks and behavior (Schminke et al., 2001), thereby limiting degrees of freedom for members to communicate informally and to develop and exchange knowledge (Chen et al., 2010). Conversely, absence of formalization is associated with increased flexibility, more informal and intense interpersonal communication, and improved conditions for knowledge creation and diffusion (Wang and Ahmed, 2003). Notwithstanding, the literature also contains arguments in favor of formalization as means to enhance knowledge creation and diffusion. Formalized rules and routines are often based on experience and learning about appropriate ways of handling various tasks and conditions (Becker, 2004), including creation and transfer of knowledge (Pertusa-Ortega et. al., 2010). Thus, it is argued that formalized rules can be conceived of as reservoirs of experience-based learning, likened genetic material (Nelson and Winter, 1982), and may function as guidelines for decisions to generate, transfer, and integrate new knowledge (Feldman and Pentland, 2003; Kern, 2006).

While there is a comprehensive literature on the role of formalization in the creation of knowledge, there has been much less research interest in clarifying the extent to which formalization influences upon the transfer of knowledge across organizational borders. There are some empirical studies of the subject. However, when seen in comparison, the findings diverge. Consider the following examples: Forrester (2000) studied how a Japanese and an American automotive firm disseminated product and production innovations from innovation teams throughout the various units of their organizations. She found that the U.S. firm lacked a formal dissemination system. The spread of the innovations was more ad hoc and based on personal and informal networks. Therefore, the transfer across the whole organizations was rather random and slow. Contrary, the Japanese automotive firm applied a strictly organized disseminating system that consisted of a set of formal procedures for spreading the innovations across the whole organization. In addition, all units were supposed to adopt the innovations without questions. The formal transfer procedures led to fast transfer and adoption of the innovations throughout the organization. In another study of factors influencing the knowledge sharing and entrepreneurial orientation within 232 Canadian firms, De Clercq et al. (2013) found—contrary to their expectations—that a high degree of formalization increased trust and moderately facilitated knowledge sharing across internal organizational units. However, results from other studies do not confirm the positive effects of formalization on knowledge transfers: In a study of 146 Taiwanese firms, Chen and Huang (2007) found that less formalization moderately increased social interaction and slightly favored knowledge sharing across organizational borders. In a study of two large European companies with 13,600 and 15,000 employees, respectively, Willem and Buelens (2009) found no empirical support for their proposition that knowledge sharing varied with the degree of formal coordination. With data from 164 large Spanish firms, Pertusa-Ortega et al. (2009) studied the influence of a selection of formal structure variables on various aspects of knowledge performance. One of their hypotheses was that high levels of formalization have a positive association with knowledge performance, meaning that formalization will improve the dissemination and implementation of knowledge in processes, products, and services. However, regression analysis could not confirm their hypothesis.

In conclusion, this means that there are divergent views as well as mixed empirical findings about the effects of formalization on knowledge transfers across organizational borders.

Two other concepts—vertical and horizontal differentiation and integration—are often used in analysis of organizations' formal structure architecture. While vertical differentiation and integration refers to the locus of decision-making authority and the number of layers in the vertical structure (Pugh et al., 1968), horizontal differentiation and integration means the formal division of the organization into subunits (Hage, 1965).

Vertical differentiation

The vertical—or hierarchical—dimension of an organization's formal structure refers to the numbers of vertical layers in the organization. The vertical structure can also influence knowledge transfer. Borders between vertical layers are potential hindrances both for downward and for upward communication (Katz and Kahn, 1978). The common tendency is for members belonging to the same vertical level to interact and share more information and knowledge than with members located at other levels (Blau and Scott, 1962; Egeberg and Trondal, 2018). In principle, there are two opposite ways to intervene in vertical structures—with potential consequences for knowledge transfers. One is to relayer, which means to increase the number of vertical layers, for example as means to reduce top leaders' span of control (Hersey and Blanchard, 1969). The other is to delayer, that is, to reduce the numbers of hierarchical levels and thus compressing the organization's "height" (Worthy, 1950; Drucker, 1988; Keuning and Opheij, 1994), for example as means to shorter communication paths (Kettley, 1995) or to make the organization "leaner" and more effective (Downs, 1995). While relayering may delay and distort knowledge transfer and sharing, delayering may have the opposite effect: increasing speed of transfer and more knowledge sharing.

Surprisingly, there are few empirical studies of the effects on knowledge transfers of changes in the vertical formal organizational structure. In a survey of delayering trends in 2964 organizations across three countries, Littler et al. (2003) found that while "improving decision-making" was the main motive behind delayering reforms, "improving internal communication" across vertical layers was a much lower ranked motive. However, while only 40 percent of the delayered organizations reported that they had achieved improved decision-making, approximately 60 percent of those who stated that "improving internal communication" was the motive behind their delayering efforts reported that they had achieved this objective.

In the research literature, the concept of vertical hierarchical structure and the concept of centralization are often used rather interchangeably. Centralization refers to the locus of decision-making authority within an organization (Van de Ven and Ferry, 1980). High versus low centralization depends on whether the decision-making power is concentrated at the top of the hierarchy or distributed to lower levels of the organization. Centralization is frequently presented as a variable of organization structure and as a feature of the organization hierarchy (Hall, 1987; Tsai, 2002; Willem and Buelens, 2009; Ciabuschi et al., 2011). This may be a source to confusion because degree of centralization/decentralization in an organization does not necessarily indicate how its formal hierarchical structure looks like. However, it is included in the review of this stream of literature since it is often defined as a structural variable and presented together with other such variables.

The main suggestion put forward by many researchers is that while the centralization and concentration of decision-making power at the top of the hierarchy is supposed to hinder knowledge transfer and sharing, decentralization of such power to local organizational units is likely to have the opposite effect (Zaltman et al., 1973; Tsai, 2002; Riege, 2005). It has been argued that centralization means control, which may restrict knowledge flows (Chen and Huang, 2007), while decentralization means autonomy and broadened communication channels (Cardinal, 2001). There has been much research interest in trying to clarify to what extent and how degree of centralization influence upon transfer and sharing of knowledge. Most of the hypothesis that drives the research efforts are in favor of decentralization as a suggested source to increased knowledge transfer and sharing. While centralization may hinder lateral communication and knowledge flow (Souitaris, 2001), decentralization is supposed to mobilize and involve more individuals in decision-making and knowledge creation processes (Ouchi, 2006), and ease the transfer and exchange of knowledge (Lee and Choi, 2003; Kasper et.al., 2008; Pertusa-Ortega et. al., 2010). Notwithstanding, the literature also contain suggestions in favor of centralized structures as possible means to speed up knowledge transfer and sharing. For example, centralized hierarchical authority can be instrumental and a necessary force to facilitate knowledge transfer across internal organizational borders. Ghoshal and Bartlett (1990) argue that lateral knowledge transfer between subsidiaries in Multinational corporations MNCs can depend on whether headquarters engage and initiate transfer processes. Especially, the involvement of centralized hierarchical authority may be important in phases of implementation of transferred knowledge (Ciabuschi et al., 2011; Björkman et al., 2012).

As illustrated above, suggestions diverge about the possible effects of centralization on knowledge transfer—and so do results from empirical studies. Some studies report no significant effects of centralization/decentralization on knowledge transfer and sharing (Ghoshal et al., 1994; Frost et al., 2002; Willem and Buelens, 2009). Others have revealed modest positive effects of decentralization. Among these are Gupta and Govindarajan (2000), Tsai (2002), Chen and Huang (2007) and Ciabuschi et al. (2011). For example, Tsai (2002) studied knowledge transfer in a large multiunit organization consisting of 24 business units. He found that while centralization had a significant negative effect on knowledge transfer and sharing, decentralization, which facilitated informal lateral relations had a significant positive effect on the same variable. Ciabuschi et al. (2011) studied 169 dyadic knowledge transfer projects in 23 MNCs. They revealed that centralization had negative effects—both on transfer efficiency (speed and cost of transfer) and on transfer effectiveness (degree to which transferred knowledge are implemented). However, some studies report positive effects of centralization. Cardinal's (2001) study of innovativeness in 57 pharmaceutical firms found—contrary to common suggestions—a modest positive effect of centralized coordination on firms' capacity to develop radical innovations. Caimo and Lomi (2015) studied knowledge transfer and sharing among members of top management teams and corporate consultants in an international multiunit industrial group. They found that knowledge embedded in task-advice relations were unlikely to be transferred and shared across business units—unless high degree of centralization, that is, the involvement and support from the central hierarchy of the organization.

In sum, the results from these and other studies support a conclusion that effective structures for knowledge transfer and sharing are not simply decentralized or centralized.

Horizontal differentiation and integration

The horizontal differentiation of an organization refers to the division of tasks and how they are organized and performed by a various number and types of subunits. A widely held and strong notion is that the borders between horizontally organized and more or less autonomous subunits are barriers that hinder and limit knowledge transfer and sharing (Ostroff, 1999; Argote et al., 2000; Tsai, 2002; Mohamed et al., 2004; Cordon-Pozo et al., 2006; Gulati, 2007; Christensen and Lægreid, 2008; Willem and Buelens, 2009; Lægreid and Rykkja, 2015; 2022; Wanberg et al., 2015; Christensen et al., 2016; Costumato, 2021). Surprisingly, many publications that focus on the challenges of transferring, sharing, and coordinating across horizontal borders are not concerned with documenting the eventual barring effects of horizontally organized units. The existence of such effects are often assumed, and the studies concentrate on researching various means to increase cross-unit information flows and coordination.

However, there are empirical studies of how horizontally differentiated structures work—and they tend to paint a nuanced picture of the effects on knowledge transfer and sharing. Wanberg et al. (2015) studied the influence of formal horizontal structure and of disciplinary specialization on members' knowledge transfer and sharing practices in two communities of practice (CoPs) within two large multinational construction and engineering companies. CoPs were designed with members from different divisions and disciplines and were used as means to encourage knowledge transfer and sharing across organizational units. The researchers used statistical network-analyzing techniques to map knowledge-sharing connections within the two groups. Results showed that, in one CoP, the used channels for sharing knowledge largely reflected the members' background from certain organizational units, while relatively few new channels across units were established. In contrast, members of the other CoP had developed fine-grained new unit-crossing transfer and sharing channels—in addition to established intra-unit channels, which still were used. The researchers concluded like this: "Formal organizational structure does not produce dichotomous outcomes in which knowledge sharing is siloed or not. Rather, silos must be evaluated in terms of the degree of constrains, which is a continuum" (Wanberg et al., 2015: 127). Christensen and Lægreid (2008) studied the extent to which civil servants in Norwegian governmental ministries and agencies experienced challenges of coordinating across horizontally located organizational units. 1856 civil servants from 18 ministries responded in a survey and assessed their experiences with cross-unit coordination. Results showed that 38 percent of the respondents reported that the horizontal coordination between units within their ow policy were "good," while 47 percent reported "mixed"—and 15 percent reported "bad" experiences. On the average, civil servants in the ministries are more satisfied with the horizontal coordination than are their colleagues in agencies. This means that the civil servants in the ministries, those that normally are responsible for assessing the need for, and for initiating, cross-unit coordinating efforts, are more satisfied than their colleagues in the agencies, who normally are those to be "coordinated." These and other studies indicate that formal structures that separate between horizontally located organizational units are semipermeable borders, which means that they influence processes of knowledge transfer and sharing in complex ways; neither simply block them nor let them flow unhindered.

As mentioned above, there have been many suggestions, shared by practitioners and students of organizations, that horizontal integration can be an effective means of increasing and speeding up the flow of knowledge throughout an organization (Lawrence and Lorsch, 1967; Galbraith, 1973; Ghoshal and Gratton, 2002). There are, in principle, two ways to increase horizontal integration. One is to reduce the number of horizontally organized subunits, either by removing some or by merging two or more of them. Organizational mergers are often motivated by ambitions of reducing costs and/or creating values through increased knowledge transfer and sharing (Hunt and Downing, 1990; Bresman et al., 1999). Horizontal integration is supposed to speed up knowledge transfer within the integrated organization and is a main reason for the establishment of multinational corporations (Kogut and Zander, 1993; Gupta and Govindarajan, 2000; Minbaeva, 2007). However, studies have observed that the formerly formal borders between previously separate organizations often still limits knowledge transfers, even after the mergers. Such observations sometimes reflect that organizational cultures in the previously separate units are still "alive" after the mergers and decelerate knowledge flows across the old organizational borders (Chatterjee et al., 1992; Olie, 1994). It can also reflect a lack of trust across the old borders (Stahl and Sitkin, 2005) or, as Empson (2001) found, that knowledge transfer was hindered by notions among one of the merging units' members that, compared to the units they had merged with, their knowledge base differed fundamentally in terms of quality.

The other main type of horizontally integration is coordinating across existing borders of subunits. Well-known means for such cross-border coordination are project groups, project teams, and task forces (Lawrence and Lorsch, 1967; Ghoshal et al., 1994), cross-functional teams (McDonough, 2000; Mohamed et. al., 2004; Majchrzak et al., 2012), communities of practice that cross borders between subunits (Carayannis et al., 2011; Wanberg et al., 2015), hybrids of networks and hierarchy (Lægreid and Rykkja, 2015), and the organizing of integration roles for boundary-spanners (Nonaka et al., 2006) and "trans-specialists" (Postrel, 2002; Kim and Anand, 2018). A number of studies have been motivated by the suggestion that horizontal integration—of various kinds—will speed up knowledge sharing and transfer. However, findings from empirical research are mixed. For example, while some studies report significant positive effects on cross-border communication and increased knowledge sharing caused by various horizontal coordination initiatives (Ghoshal et al., 1994), others reveal only modest effects (Willem and Buelens, 2009) or report inconsistent findings (Ancona and Caldwell, 1992).

Absorptive capacity and knowledge transfer

In their 1988 paper on technology transfer, Kedia and Bhagat coined the term "absorptive capacity." However, the construct is widely attributed to Wesley Cohen and Daniel Levinthal and their three founding papers from the late 1980s/early 1990s (1989; 1990; 1994). They defined absorptive capacity (AC) as "the ability of a firm to recognize the value of new, external information, assimilate it, and apply it for commercial ends" (Cohen and Levinthal, 1990: 128). According to Cohen and Levinthal, the AC construct is made up of the ability to identify, assimilate, and exploit knowledge from various environmental sources. Acknowledging that most innovations in organizations stem from borrowings from other organizations, Cohen and Levinthal (1990) presented the absorptive capacity construct as a theory of knowledge transfer across organizational borders. As such, absorptive capacity is supposed to be both a barrier and an enabler: While low levels of AC can hinder, high levels can facilitate knowledge transfers and increase the chances of desired outcomes. Gupta and Govindarajan (2000) succinctly formulated the belief in the potential of absorptive capacity to explain variations in outcomes of knowledge transfers: "Even when exposed to the same environment and even when there are insignificant differences in the desire to acquire new knowledge, individuals and organizations may differ in their ability to recognize the value of new information, assimilate it, and apply it to commercial ends" (p. 476).

For more than 30 years, the AC construct has strongly influenced theoretical debates and empirical organizational research—and especially research on knowledge transfer and innovation (Lane et al., 2006; Song, et. al., 2018;

Zou, et al., 2018). The clearest expression of the influence is the enormous research literature it has generated since it was launched in 1989 (Volberda et al., 2010; Sakhdari, 2016; Apriliyanti and Alon, 2017). Cohen and Levinthal's seminal 1990 paper has been cited more than 46,500 times, and AC has been the main topic in more than 15,000 articles published in more than 900 different peer-reviewed journals. As Volberda et al. (2010: 932) noted, the huge and still expanding literature is also an expression of high absorptive capacity within the field of organizational research itself to adopt and exploit the relatively new concept. However, despite being widely held as one of the most promising advances in organizational research, there is growing scholarly awareness of some serious problems with the AC construct (Lane and Lubatkin, 1998; Lane et al., 2006; Song et al., 2018). The identified challenges are of two kinds, which are highly interconnected. The first is ambiguities concerning the antecedents and the content of the construct. The antecedents and content uncertainties feed into the second kind, which is ambiguities about the effects of absorptive capacity.

Antecedents of absorptive capacity

A fascinating feature of the 30-year history of AC is that, simultaneously with numerous research reports about the construct's great advantages and documented effects, a parallel debate has intensified about what AC really is. There are ambiguities regarding the antecedents of AC, the meaning of the term "capacity," and the content of AC and how it works.

Ambiguities of antecedents. The literature contains assumptions about the antecedents of the AC mechanism that have been expressed with varying degrees of clarity. A central insight is that organizations are dependent upon prior related knowledge in order to identify, assimilate, and use new knowledge (Bower and Hilgard, 1981; Cohen and Levinthal, 1990: 129). Therefore, it is supposed that organizations need to have invested in and be knowledgeable about the domain where the new knowledge emerge in order to increase the capacity to identify and assimilate it. This insight feeds into two different assumptions about the nature of AC. One is that the development of absorptive capacity means accumulation over time of domain-specific and specialized knowledge (Pavlou and El Sawy, 2006; Roberts et al., 2012). Thus, AC resembles a radar that becomes increasingly attuned against specific signals from certain domains while simultaneously leaving out others and becoming increasingly specialized. However, a contrary assumption is that developing absorptive capacity means learning how to learn (Estes, 1970), which means increasing the capacity to assimilate knowledge from *different* domains: "Unlike learning by doing, which allows firms to get better at what they already do, absorptive capacity allows firms to learn to do something quite different" (Lane et al., 2006: 836). Due to the assumption that AC depends on prior related knowledge and that it accumulates over time, it has been hypothesized that AC will vary with an organization's age; that is, the older the organization, the more absorptive capacity the organization accumulates (Rao and Drazin, 2002; Huergo and Jaumandreu, 2004). However, empirical studies have not been able to verify this hypothesis (Mowery et al., 1996; Zou et al., 2018).

A second notion is that an organization's absorptive capacity has both organizational and individual antecedents. The most researched and highlighted organizational antecedent is organizations' research and development (R&D) investments and efforts (Cohen and Levinthal, 1989; Lane et al., 2001; Jansen et al., 2005). In addition, the AC literature has identified organizational routines (Lewin et al., 2011; Chalmers and Balan-Vnuk, 2013), management characteristics (Volberda et al., 2010), rewards and HRM systems (Minbaeva et al., 2014), and certain formal structure arrangements (Chen and Chang, 2012) as typical organizational antecedents of AC. Cohen and Levinthal (1989) explicitly stated that organizations' absorptive capacity also has individual antecedents, which means that the level of AC depends partly on the individual members' prior knowledge, memory capacity, and capacity to discover and make sense of new knowledge emerging in various external domains. Based on insights from cognitive theory, Cohen and Levinthal (1990) argued that the development of an individual's memory and stock of knowledge is self-reinforcing. When the individual encounters new knowledge, it can be overlooked, but it can also be recorded into the individual's memory by creating connections with preexisting, already memorized concepts and knowledge. However, the interplay between organizational and individual antecedents of organizations' AC is complex, poorly understood, and underresearched (Lane et al., 2001; Foss, 2011; Martinkenaite and Breunig, 2016; Tian and Soo, 2018).

Asset versus capability. In addition to debates about the antecedents of absorptive capacity, there are also debates and ambiguities about the term "capacity." While AC from certain angles appear as an organizational asset, it is conceived from others as a capability. Conceptualized as an asset, AC refers to "the level of relevant prior knowledge possessed by the focal unit" (Roberts et al., 2012: 628). The underlying assumption is that absorptive capacity equals the stock of knowledge that the organization owns and controls (Helfat and Peteraf, 2003) and which is a function of prior investments in R&D (Lane et al., 2006).

While the early conceptualizations were influenced by the AC-as-asset perspective and centered around R&D issues (Gebauer et al., 2012), later contributions have criticized this approach for being static (Roberts et al., 2012). On the contrary, recent contributions often view AC as a capability; that is, the extent of an organization's ability to identify, assimilate, and exploit external knowledge. The capability to absorb can be established as sets of routines for identifying new knowledge and for combining, sharing, processing, and exploring it (Lewin et al., 2011; Van der Heiden et al., 2016; Enkel et al., 2018). The quality of absorptive capacity routines varies and depends upon several factors, such as the appropriateness of the routines in relation to the knowledge absorption challenges, how well the routines are communicated to the members, and the quality of the training of members in choosing correct routines and to use them in practice.

In addition to the conceptualization of AC capability as routines, the concept of *dynamic capability* has been introduced to define key features of an organization's absorptive capacity (Zahra and George, 2002; Lichtenthaler 2009). Dynamic capability is defined as the organization's "ability to integrate, build, and reconfigure internal and external competencies to address rapidly changing environments" (Teece et al., 1997: 515) and as "the capacity of an organization to purposefully create, extend, or modify its resource base" (Helfat et al., 2007: 4). The dynamic capability view differs from the asset view in that it stresses the capability that (some) organizations have to combine and reconfigure their resources and to constantly change and renew their knowledge base. Thus, the concept "dynamic" refers to "the capacity to renew competences so as to achieve congruence with the changing business environment" (Teece et al., 1997: 515).

The ambiguous contents of absorptive capacity

While many studies have concluded that organizations' absorptive capacity is an important source to successful knowledge transfers, there is still a lot of ambiguity and confusion about the content of AC and how it works. Bluntly, while many AC studies report positive effects, it often remains unclear exactly how and to what extent organizations' absorptive capacity has caused the effects. The main reason for the ambiguities is the multi-dimensional character of the AC construct. Cohen and Levinthal (1990) identified three dimensions in their conceptualization of absorptive capacity: recognition of the value of new external knowledge, assimilation of the knowledge, and exploitation of it for commercial ends. The ambiguities of the content concern two aspects of the AC construct. The first stem from uncertainties about what dimensions absorptive capacity consists of, while the second concerns uncertainties about how the involved dimensions are interrelated and work in knowledge absorptive processes.

Uncertainties about the AC dimensions

There have been many scholarly attempts to revise Cohen and Levinthal's (1990) original three-dimensional AC construct of recognition, assimilation, and exploitation. The endeavors encompass suggestions for minor revisions (such as relabeling, clarifications, and elaborations of Cohen and Levinthal's conceptualization), as well as major revisions, such as introducing new dimensions and/or withdrawal of other researchers' dimensions. Due to space limitations, this chapter offers only a brief review of suggested revisions. Heeley (1997) argued for a reconceptualization of the AC construct to encompass the three dimensions of external knowledge acquisition, intra-organizational knowledge dissemination, and technical competence. While the first equals Cohen and Levinthal's concepts of acquisition, the other two differ in substance compared to Cohen and Levinthal's concepts of assimilation and exploitation. Liao et al. (2003) introduced the dimension of organizational *responsiveness* as an elaboration and potential substitute of Cohen and Levinthal's exploitation dimension. They indirectly criticized the AC construct for being underdeveloped in terms of how and to what extent organizations have the capability to *act* in response to acquired and assimilated knowledge. The most comprehensive and formative revision of the AC construct was introduced by Zahra and George (2002). In their version of the construct, they retained Cohen and Levinthal's (1990) three dimensions, but reconceptualized AC to contain two main parts: potential and realized absorptive capacity. Potential AC encompasses acquisition and assimilation. Realized AC contains two dimensions: transformation and exploitation. The new dimension that they introduced, transformation, was defined as "a firm's capability to develop and refine the routines that facilitate combining existing knowledge and the newly acquired and assimilated knowledge" (Zahra and George, 2002: 190). Thus, through transformation, new knowledge can be rejected or assimilated and added to the organizational stock of knowledge—or it can be transformed in processes where existing knowledge and acquired knowledge are mixed and subsequently lead to new services/products.

In a widely cited paper, Todorova and Durisin (2007) criticized Zahra and George for their theorizing about the transformation dimension and their claim that it is the next step after assimilation. Todorova and Durisin argued that transformation is an alternative to assimilation, rather than a necessary next step after it. When new knowledge fits well into existing knowledge and cognitive schemes, it has increased chances of being assimilated. In such cases, there is less need for transformation of the new knowledge. However, in cases where acquired new knowledge does not resonate well with the established stock of knowledge and cognitive maps, processes are likely to be released to transform and modify the new knowledge to establish an acceptable fit. Thus, according to Todorova and Durisin, assimilation and transformation are conceived of as *alternative* dimensions and steps. In a more recent contribution, Song et al. (2018) argued that an organization's absorptive capacity contains three dimensions. The first is absorptive effort, which refers to investments made by an organization that facilitate searching, identifying, and acquiring external knowledge. The second dimension is absorptive knowledge base, which refers to the organization's accumulated stock of knowledge that facilitate understanding, recombining, and transformation of external knowledge. The third is absorptive process, which refers to routines and practices for diffusion and knowledge sharing *within* an organization.

The interconnectedness of AC dimensions

As indicated above, it remains unclear what dimensions are involved in generating organizations' absorptive capacity. In addition, it remains unclear how the dimensions relate to each other and, thus, how and to what extent certain versions of interconnectedness are associated with various levels of absorptive capacity (Camisón and Forés, 2010). Many studies have assumed a logic of sequentiality in the ways that the dimensions of absorptive capacity are related and activated. For example, Todorova and Durisin (2007) argued that the relationship between the dimensions assimilation and transformation follows a sequential order, where assimilation comes first, and where certain characteristics of the assimilated knowledge determine whether transformation is activated or not. Zahra and George's (2002) conceptualization of knowledge acquisition and assimilation as potential absorptive capacity, and transformation and exploitation as realized absorptive capacity, clearly indicate a logic of sequentiality where the two potential dimensions predate and forerun the two realized dimensions. However, this notion of a certain sequence logic contrasts with suggestions in early AC studies where organizations' R&D investments and their current stock of knowledge were supposed to define and predate processes of search and assimilation. When compared, these different suggestions indicate that notions of unidirectional sequences of action chains across the AC dimensions do not account for the inherent complexities in the ways absorptive capacity works. Zahra and George (2002) are aware of that: They argue that potential and realized AC play separate yet complementary roles in the AC mechanism. For example, this means that a high level of potential AC does not necessarily lead to innovations, and neither does high levels of realized AC. This indicates that the AC dimensions are intertwined and connected in complex logics of mutual dependency and simultaneity. These logics, which remains poorly understood, are decisive for how AC works in practice.

The extent to which AC works does not depend solely on the intra-organizational relatedness of the AC dimensions. Lane and Lubatkin (1998) introduced an interorganizational perspective on AC and the concept of relative absorptive capacity. They criticized AC contributions for suggesting that an organization, by means of its absorptive capacity, has equal opportunities to gain knowledge and learn from all other organizations. However, Lane and Lubatkin argued that the ability to identify, transfer, and learn from another organization's practices and knowledge depends on whether the two organizations have matching attributes, which refers to the degree of similarity on variables, such as organizational structure, knowledge base, and knowledge processing routines. The greater the similarity among each of the three dimensions (acquisition, assimilation, exploitation) of the source and the knowledge seeking/recipient organization, the more effective the absorptive capacity of the recipient.

Lane and Lubatkin's theory of relative absorptive capacity breaks with a central feature of the AC literature. Although the construct of absorptive capacity is presented as a theory of how learning and innovations are based on knowledge transfers from external sources to a focal organization (Cohen and Levinthal, 1990: 128), most AC studies have focused almost exclusively on the knowledge seeking/receiving unit. Thus, what is left out is attention towards how an organization's absorptive capacity is influenced by the external source organization(s), features of the knowledge to be transferred, and the relationships between the source and the knowledge seeking/recipient units.

Ambiguities of outcomes

In their first seminal articles, Cohen and Levinthal (1989; 1990) argued that an organization's level of absorptive capacity is clearly associated with its chances of identifying and transferring valuable knowledge from external sources, exploiting it, and achieving desired outcomes. In other words, a suggestion that the level of absorptive capacity is a key independent variable to explain variations in outcomes of knowledge transfer processes (Escribano et al., 2009; Farell et al., 2019). Numerous attempts have been made to trace AC effects on outcomes of knowledge transfers. In their review of the AC literature, Song et al. (2018) found that more than 50 outcome measures have been used in empirical AC studies. Many studies have tried to trace effects of AC on innovations, using various measures, such as new products (Stock et al., 2001; Xie et al., 2018), new patents (Fabrizio, 2009), and technology development (Keller, 1996). In addition, many studies have sought to reveal the effects of AC on overall organizational performance, such as sales growth (Kohtamäki et al., 2019), returns on sales and assets (Kostopoulos et al., 2011), green innovations (Galbreath, 2019), and resilience (Gölgeci and Kuivalainen, 2020).

Although many studies have reported positive effects of absorptive capacity on outcomes, there are still unresolved puzzles that lead to ambiguities concerning how and to what extent AC really has effects on various outcome variables. There are three main reasons for these ambiguities.

The first is ambiguities that stem from the multidimensional character of the AC construct. It generates two main uncertainties when assessing research that reports about the effects of AC—summarized in a *what* and a *how* question. The "what" question concerns remaining uncertainties about what dimensions are actually involved in shaping the absorptive capacity. The "how" question refers to uncertainties about the interconnectedness of the dimensions: the logics of the coworking of involved dimensions when absorptive capacity is generated. When these challenges remain unresolved, it is partly due to a tendency among researchers to conceive of AC as a unidimensional construct rather than a multidimensional one (Bierly et al., 2009). According to Lane et al. (2006), this tendency reflects the reification of the AC construct, which means that it has become taken for granted, and thus, that researchers "increasingly fail to specify the assumptions that underlie their use of it" (p. 834).

The second reason for cause-and-effect uncertainties related to absorptive capacity stems from operationalization challenges. Links are sometimes loose between conceptualizations and operationalizations of this construct. For example, Mowery et al. (1996) criticized attempts to measure AC in terms of R&D investments and intensity. In addition, the same measures are sometimes used as indicators of absorptive capacity (cause) in some studies and as indicators of outcomes (effects) in others. For example, Cohen and Levinthal (1989) used organizations' spending on R&D as measure of outcome in their operationalization of absorptive capacity, while this variable in their theory was conceived of as a central element of organizations' assimilation capability (Lane et al., 2006), and thus, an element of potential absorptive capacity.

The third reason why considerable uncertainty remains about how absorptive capacity works—and the outcomes it generates—can be traced back to research methods. While researchers' efforts to theorize the AC construct strive to conceptualize highly complex processes, survey and quantitative methods are the dominant and almost exclusive methods in empirical AC research. However, such methods are often inappropriate for gaining deeper insights into this construct's *sui generis*. For example, dynamic capability (the notion that an organization can develop the ability to "learn how to learn" and be able to constantly renew its competencies to develop innovations) is a key concept in the AC literature. In practice, dynamic capability entails extremely complex processes, such as mobilization and mixing of organizations' knowledge bases, memory systems, individual cognitions, personal skills, etc. Thus, to gain thorough knowledge into these processes, they need to be studied as such; that is, by qualitative process study methods. However, as Lichtenthaler (2009) showed, studies and measures of absorptive capacity as a dynamic capability are, for the most part, survey-based and quantitative. Easterby-Smith et al. (2008) stated that the progress of research on AC since 1990 has been disappointing and that the lack of development mainly "result[s] from the dominant use of research methods which are more relevant for testing, rather than developing, theory. If so, then new ideas and perspectives are far more likely to be added if qualitative methods are used to examine absorptive capacity" (p. 485). However, some new process-based AC studies have been published recently, among them Sjödin et al. (2019) and Horvat et al. (2019).

Social networks and knowledge transfers

A third body of literature within knowledge transfer research is social network studies. A central assumption is that characteristics of the social networks that connect actors, organizations, and fields can explain variations in knowledge transfer processes and outcomes. Wasserman and Faust (1994) defined a social network as "a finite set or sets of actors (e.g. people, organizations or other social entities) and the relation or relations defined on them" (p. 20). Phelps et al. (2012) provided a more complex conceptualization, defining a social network as "a set of nodes—individuals or higher level collectives that serve as heterogeneously distributed repositories of knowledge and agents that search for, transmit, and create knowledge—interconnected by social relationships that enable and constrain nodes' efforts to acquire, transfer and create knowledge" (p. 1117). The underlying assumption in social network analysis is that the exchange of ideas and knowledge is embedded in social relationships and that such relationships matter in terms of transfer outcomes (Contractor and Monge, 2002; Kilduff and Brass, 2010). A key feature of networks is repeated and lasting exchange relationships between the network's actors (Podolny and Page, 1998) that provide capacity and capability for knowledge transfer.

Network analysis is an interdisciplinary field that includes very different disciplines and research agendas, such as macroeconomics and studies of economic growth (Aghion et al., 1998), demography and studies of changes in populations (Heckathorn and Cameron, 2017), healthcare and epidemiological studies (Pescosolido and Levy, 2002), and mapping of social structures in sociology (Parsons, 1951), organization theory (Scott and Davis, 2003)—and in social anthropology. One of the first researchers to apply network theory in empirical studies was the British anthropologist J.A. Barnes, who conducted fieldwork in a small Norwegian fishing village in the early 1950s. One day, while resting his eyes on a fishing net in a boathouse, the idea struck him that it visualized the whole social structure of the village he was studying:

> The image I have [of the village's social structure] is of a set of points, some of which are joined by lines. The points of the image are people, or sometimes groups, and the lines indicate which people interact with each other… A network of this kind has no clear externally boundary, nor has it clear-cut internal division, and certainly there are clusters of people who are more closely knit together than others.
>
> (Barnes, 1954: 43–44)

This brief review zooms in on insights from the usage of the social network construct in studies of knowledge transfer across organizational borders. This large and still expanding stream of publications took off at the turn of the twenty-first century (Phelps et al., 2012; Marchiori and Franco, 2020). Several of the most influential publications from this early phase broadly analyzed how social networks—or "social capital"—are antecedents of organizations' access to knowledge (Granovetter, 1973; Nohria et.al., 1992; Hansen, 1999; Dyer and Nobeoka; 2000; Tsai, 2001; Adler and Kwon, 2002; Reagans and McEvily, 2003), and important means for the creation, transfer, and utilization of knowledge (Powell et al, 1996; Powell, 1998; Nahapiet and Ghoshal, 1998; Tsai and Ghoshal (1998); Baum et al., 2000; Gupta and Govindarajan, 2000; Lee et al., 2001; Inkpen and Tsang, 2005).

Four capabilities of networks are especially important when assessing how they may influence knowledge transfer processes across organizational borders.

Sensor capability. Social networks can sometimes function as an organization's sensor system that spans different parts of the environment, increasing the chances of discovering interesting knowledge. Thus, social networks can be effective in making organizations aware of new practices and knowledge earlier than organizations that must rely on information through formal transfer channels (Nahapiet and Ghoshal, 1998; Ardichvili and Cardozo, 2000; Puhakka, 2006). Tsai (2001) found that early recognition of new knowledge from external sources co-varied with organizational actors' positions in various networks.

Knowledge-creation capability. More than mere channels through which knowledge "just flows," networks are sometimes also fabrics for the creation of knowledge (Cross et al., 2001; Know, 2001; Inkpen and Tsang 2005; Nieves and Osario, 2013; Faems et al., 2020). For example, this capability of networks is observed in research-intensive industries where scientific and technological developments happen so quickly and breakthroughs are so pervasive and often so destructive for existing technologies and solutions that single organizations rarely possess the requisite capacity to innovate on their own (Powell and Brantley, 1992; Huggins et al., 2012). In such cases, rather than the single organization, the locus for creation of new knowledge and innovations are often networks that knit actors with various competencies and from various organizations.

Storing capability. Knowledge can be stored in networks, then accessed, and used later (Olivera, 2000, Jasimuddin and Zhang, 2011). Powell et al. (1996) provided an example of this in a study of interorganizational collaborations in biotechnology industry, concluding: "Sources of innovation do not reside exclusively inside firms; instead, they are commonly found in the interstices between firms, universities, research laboratories, suppliers, and customers. Consequently, the degree to which firms learn about new opportunities is a function of the extent of their participation in such activities" (Powell et al., 1996: 118).

Transfer capability. Social networks are potential channels for transferring knowledge between actors and organizations. It has been assumed and shown that some social networks and some types of knowledge are especially effective vehicles for transferring and sharing of context-specific and complex knowledge (Uzzi, 1996; Fritsch and Kauffeld-Monz, 2010). Social networks, consisting of frequently interacting actors connected with strong ties, are better suited for transferring complex knowledge (Hansen, 1999). Transfer of context-specific and tacit knowledge is often facilitated by direct and repeated contact between actors who trust each other (Axelsson and Johanson, 1992; Von Hippel, 1994; Dima and Vasilache, 2015).

Two dimensions of social networks

A key concept in network analysis of knowledge transfers is social capital, which is defined as the aggregate of resources that are embedded within, available through, and derived from the networks of relationships possessed by an individual or organization (Nahapiet and Ghoshal, 1998: 243). Thus, social capital encompasses both the networks and the value of the knowledge, which are created and/or transferred within them (Ganguly, 2019). The social capital and the involved networks can be described and analyzed in terms of the structural and the relational dimension. The central structural feature is the focal actors' position, or localization in a network. Focal actors' position determines connections to all other actors and parts of the whole network (Burt, 1992). Cohesion is the central concept when featuring the relational dimension. Cohesion refers to the degree of mutual interaction, socialization, and closeness between two actors (Granovetter, 1992). In the remainder of this section, I present frequently applied structural and relational theoretical constructs in network studies, and then present an overview of main research findings about the extent to which and how social network characteristics affect knowledge transfer processes and outcomes.

Structural and relational constructs

The structural and relational constructs applied in network analysis are developed with reference to three network levels: the single node level, the dyadic level, and the whole network level.

The node level. A node is a single point in a social network. A network consists of a number of nodes that are connected by various numbers of links. A node is an actor: It can be one or more individuals, a unit in an organization, an organization, or a nation. A key variable in determining a node's influence in a network is *centrality*, which refers to a node's localization/position in relation to the center of the network. *Network constraint* is another frequently used variable to analyze single node actors' position in networks. A network can be closed and thus constrained, in the sense that all nodes are strongly interconnected with each other (Burt, 1992). It is suggested that a node's embeddedness in closed networks provides social capital, but also redundant knowledge and limited access to new ideas and knowledge. However, a node's influence in a network does not depend solely on its central location; it can also depend on whether the actor/node plays the role of a connecting point between two or more separated networks. Sociologist Ronald

Burt (1992; 2004) developed the theory of structural holes within or between networks, stressing the strategic importance of connecting points. A structural hole exists in social networks when parts of a network or two or more networks are not connected with direct links (ties). Actors that operate by the edge of networks and bridge separate networks are supposed to be in a strategic position with access to new ideas and knowledge (Gargiulo and Benassi, 2000; Kwon et al., 2020). The knowledge-gaining advantages of such a brokerage position are conceptualized as *betweenness centrality* (Freeman, 1977), which means the extent to which a node lies on the path between two or more separate networks and can therefore control the transfer of knowledge across the networks.

The dyadic level. A dyad in network analysis refers to the social relationships between two individuals. The key relational construct is *tie strength*, which depicts the degree of closeness between two actors (Granovetter, 1973). The strength of a tie is indicated through the frequency, intensity, and duration of the interaction. The higher the tie strength, the higher the closeness felt between involved actors (Gillath et al., 2017). While strong ties are supposed to facilitate trust and the transfer of high fidelity and tacit knowledge (Granovetter, 1973), weaker ties are supposed to lead to less constraints on actors and to benefit access to new ideas and knowledge (Hansen, 1999).

The whole network level. Researchers sometimes zoom in on the whole network and on "the overall distribution of the presence and absence of connections" (Carpenter et al., 2012: 1334) in such networks. A frequently applied structural construct at this level is *network density*, which conceptualizes the frequency and the intensity of interactions among all nodes within a network. It is defined as the ratio of all ties between nodes that are *actually present* in a network—to the number of *possible* ties between the nodes. Thus, density is a measure of the overall level of connectedness among members in a network (Provan et al., 2007). Another construct applied to analyze whole networks is *centralization*, which refers to the extent to which one or a few nodes are considerably more connected than others.

Network characteristics and knowledge transfer outcomes

This section offers a brief overview of what we know from studies of the extent to which social network characteristics influence knowledge transfer processes and outcomes. The insights are presented with reference to studies of three *structural elements* (characteristics of nodal position, ego network (that is, the local network of one single node), and the whole network) and the main *relational element*, which is tie strength.

Effects of network node position
A substantial amount of research has been carried out to examine effects on knowledge transfer processes and outcomes of a node's centrality in a social network. Studies at the intra-organizational level indicate that high network centrality of an organizational unit is associated with increased access to new knowledge and improved chances for transfer and adoption of knowledge (Tsai and Ghoshal, 1998; Phelps et al., 2012; Ortiz et al., 2021). A foundational work here is Tsai's study (2001) of firms in three businesses. While revealing a connection between units' network centrality—and access to, transfer and adoption of knowledge—Tsai also found that this connection was moderated by the units' absorptive capacity. Studies at the interorganizational level have found associations between (focal) organizations' network position and knowledge transfer outcomes. The number of links (ties) to prior knowledgeable adopters is associated with the focal organization's network position (Still and Strang, 2009; Marchiori and Franco, 2020) and can lead to variations in knowledge transfer success. However, research about the effects of network position on knowledge transfer processes and outcomes are ambiguous. Studies provide conflicting evidence (Phelps et al., 2012: 1138) and the causal mechanisms used to explain the association are mostly assumed (Reagans and McEvily, 2003).

Effects of ego networks
The concept of ego network refers to the "nearest," or local, network of one single actor (node). Much research has been conducted to clarify how and to what extent features of ego networks influence outcomes of knowledge transfer processes. Despite these efforts, results are partly inconsistent. The lines of inconsistency run between suggestions and findings about the role of structural holes in ego networks, and the role of closed and tight ego networks. Some researchers suggest that structural holes in ego networks is a main source for organizational innovations, in that it facilitates access to and transfer of diverse new knowledge to the focal organization (Burt, 1992; Hansen, 1999; Wu et al., 2020). However, other researchers have suggested that organizational innovations are contingent upon network closure. Closed networks have characteristic features of many and direct links between members, which facilitate the sudden diffusion of thick, tacit, and high-fidelity knowledge (Ahuja, 2000; Maleszka, 2019). Phelps et al. (2012) summed up the inconsistency of these suggestions as follows: "Structural

holes and network closure are inversely related, implying the information benefits of structural holes must come at the expense of cooperative benefits of closure and vice versa" (p. 1145).

Effects of whole network
Network effects on knowledge transfer processes and outcomes can also be traced at the whole network level. Whole network studies go beyond studies of single nodes and ego networks and try to catch the overall pattern of links among all nodes in a bounded population (Kilduff and Brass, 2010). For example, a whole network can consist of three or more organizations where individuals and units are linked by many types of connections and flows (Kilduff and Tsai, 2003; Provan et al., 2007). There are few studies from this overall network level in general, and even fewer that especially study the influence of whole networks on knowledge transfers. Despite the small number of studies, it is widely suggested that network density—that is, the actual type and degree of connectedness among actors—has an influence on knowledge transfer processes and on the rate of adoption of innovations within whole networks (Cowan and Jonard, 2004; Provan et al., 2007; Bodin and Crona, 2009). A foundational work here is J. Singh's study (2005) of diffusion of innovations within a sample of regional interorganizational U.S. networks. Using data of patent citation as dependent variable, he initially found that intra-organizational diffusion was stronger than interorganizational diffusion of innovations. However, the interpersonal whole network that connected various organizations was important in determining the observed pattern of knowledge diffusion. The existence of links among members were associated with increased knowledge flows. Link lengths were especially important: While multiple and direct (short) links were associated with innovation diffusion, few and indirect (long) links were associated with opposite effect.

Social relational network element: Effects of tie strength
One of the most researched subjects in network analysis is the effects of social tie strength. It refers to the frequency, duration, and affective attachment of the relationship between network actors. However, results from these research efforts are somewhat contradictory. On one hand, a lot of research indicates that increasing tie strength increases the likelihood of enhancing levels of trust (Putnam, 1993; Ring and Van de Ven, 1994) and thus enhancing knowledge exchange between network members (Uzzi and Lancaster, 2003; Levin and Cross, 2004; Mishra and Mishra, 2013). Strong ties are associated with improved conditions for knowledge creation (Tsai and Ghoshal, 1998) and for the sudden and efficient transfer of tacit knowledge (Hansen, 1999;

Ganguly et al., 2019). On the other hand, several studies have indicated negative effects of strong ties on organizations' capacity to create and transfer knowledge and innovations. Some researchers have found that strong ties and high levels of trust are associated with reduced motivations to innovate (Yli-Renko et al., 2001). Others have pointed to weak ties as being more efficient than strong ones for spanning structural holes and gaining new ideas and knowledge (Granovetter, 1973; Hansen, 1999). There are also research that indicates few effects of strong versus weak ties to explain the passing of sensitive information across organizational borders (Stevenson and Gilly, 1991). Thus, Centola (2018) took a different stand, arguing that the spread of ideas, knowledge, and behaviors is no longer dependent upon either strong or weak ties due to the emergence of the web society and internet, which has established highly effective digital transfer channels beyond social relationships.

Distance

A large body of literature concentrates on how a certain aspect of the relationships between source and recipient units—the distance—affects knowledge transfers. Much of this research has centered on illuminating three aspects of distance: geographical (proximity), cultural, and institutional distance. These are conceived of as three distinct research traditions.

Geographical distance and knowledge transfer

Proximity in knowledge transfer studies refers to the spatial distance between source and recipient units. There is a lot of uncertainty about the effects of physical distance on knowledge transfer processes and outcomes. Much of this uncertainty stems from problems with isolating effects of geographical distance from effects of cultural distance. It is hard to account for cultural and contextual differences, which often co-varies with physical distance. The methodological challenges and the meager supply of evidence have stimulated the emergence of two contrastive views about geography and knowledge transfer: the pro-proximity view and the "death of distance" view.

Pro-proximity. The main pro-proximity argument is that knowledge flows faster and is more effectively shared among co-located actors and organizations than among geographically dispersed ones. These arguments are often backed by empirical observations and theories about patterns of innovations. A defining feature of innovations is geographical concentration, which means that they are likely to occur at certain places where people and resources are co-located, and where ideas and knowledge are exchanged due to geographical proximity. Arguments about the importance of geographical closeness between actors to propel innovations have been emphasized both in early and in later contributions to innovation theory. An early contribution came from Schumpeter (1934), who observed that having innovators who were geographically co-located and therefore easily shared ideas and knowledge was an important condition that could lead to bundles of interconnected innovations concentrated in space and time An example is the development of the steam locomotive in Great Britain during the early nineteenth century (Torre, 2008). This major innovation almost simultaneously led to series of technical complementary innovations (such as steel retails that could carry heavy locomotives) due to rapid knowledge sharing among geographically concentrated actors, such as engineers, businesspeople, retailers, and politicians.

Early insights about the importance of geographic proximity between innovators are continued as antecedents of later observations and theories of business clusters. This concept, introduced by Michael Porter (1990), refers to a geographic concentration of interconnected organizations and actors—such as producers, suppliers, researchers, and other relevant institutions in a particular area. There is a lot of evidence for the success of clusters to promote innovations by gathering various resources within a limited geographical area (Cooke, 2001; Massey and Wield, 2003). Most evaluations emphasize that the main driving force behind high innovation rates in clusters is the speed and quality of the knowledge exchange, which take takes place through networks formed by co-located actors and institutions (Edquist, 1997; Langen, 2002; Owen-Smith and Powell, 2004; Claver-Cortés et al., 2017). These insights have laid the groundwork for innovation policies and strategies at the international level, such as the OECD's innovation policy initiatives (Lundvall and Borrás, 2005), as well as at the national level (Kuhlmann, 2001) and the regional level (Cooke et al., 1997; Tödtling and Trippl, 2005). The popularity of "clustering" comes to expression in a worldwide diffusion of this idea, leading to various versions and conceptualizations, such as innovation poles (Taddeo et al., 2017), technological districts (Rosiello et al., 2015), technological parks (Claver-Cortés et al., 2017), science parks (Massey and Wield, 2003), industrial parks (Sosnovskikh, 2017), and technopoles (Castells 2014).

Death of distance. The agglomeration-inspired innovation theorists' main argument about the need for geographic proximity in order to speed up innovations has, since the mid-1990s, been challenged by researchers who question the basic premise in this argument, which is that geographic closeness is decisive for effective knowledge exchange between potential innovators. The most succinct phrasing of those thoughts, coined by Cairncross and Cairncross (1997), is "the death of distance," suggesting that new developments of digital communication technologies and new travel habits have meant that geographical distance may no longer be a limiting factor for people and organizations' ability to exchange knowledge.

Although geographical distance still counts as a transfer barrier, it obviously means less than it did only two or three decades ago. Research indicates that the new communication technology has dramatically increased long-distance contacts and knowledge sharing across organizational borders and also across clusters (Breschi and Malerba, 2001; Pinch et al., 2003). Even more interesting is the changing *content* of long-distance communication. It is increasingly possible to communicate hard facts as well as "thick" and tacit knowledge, and even emotions—a phenomenon that Bunnell and Coe, (2001) characterize as "the de-territorialisation of closeness." Modern communication technology has the potential to unify the traditional strong connection between place and presence. Actors can now be present and participate in work processes at several places simultaneously without being co-located (Urry, 2004). Thus, communication technology has made it possible to untie the connection between place and time (Hernes, 2014). It is possible to exchange knowledge and co-work from different places in real time. This is well known, for example, from co-operation within epistemic communities, which are networks of individuals who almost entirely communicate by modern communication technology and, in principle, from locations all over the world (Håkanson, 2005).

In sum, we are left with two highly contrastive approaches to the question of what geographical distance means for knowledge transfer and sharing. One approach stresses that geographical closeness is the key to knowledge exchange and innovations, while the other proclaims that geography no longer matters for human communication. The pragmatic interpretation is that physical distance still does matter, but far less than it did before the communication revolution. However, it is hard to find evidenced insights about where, when, how, and to what extent physical distance influences upon knowledge transfer processes and outcomes. Undoubtedly, it reflects the methodological challenges of isolating and measuring the pure effects of geographic proximity. However, there are some studies that manage to document such effects and, albeit modestly, support the suggestion that physical distance does influence knowledge transfer (Arundel and Geuna, 2001; Torre, 2008; Ensign et al., 2014; Vlajcic et al., 2019; Bignami et al., 2020). It has been argued that the inherent knowledge transfer models underlying the two views of the importance of physical distance—indirect transfer by the use of modern communication technology, and direct transfer through face-to-face interactions—are two means suited for transfer of different types of knowledge. Whereas communication technology is appropriate for long-distance transfer of codified knowledge, tacit and noncodified knowledge is much more vulnerable for long-distance travels and are therefore more effectively exchanged in direct physical meetings (Lundvall 1988; Gertler 2003; Ambos and Ambos 2009). However, this argument is challenged by scholars who have observed a line of development where modern communication technology is increasingly suited to help overcome the effects of geography and to be present from various places and distances. Thus, such technologies are increasingly used to produce and exchange noncodified and tacit knowledge (Amin and Cohendet 2004; Hsu et al., 2007).

Cultural distance and knowledge transfer

In addition to geography, the effects of distance on knowledge transfer across organizational borders have also been studied in terms of cultural distance. The concept of culture refers to the common values, beliefs, assumptions, and customs of a group of people (Schein, 1990; Hofstede, 2001). Culture shapes the ways in which individuals within the group interpret and understand reality, and consequently, shapes their actions. Thus, culture influences upon the interpretation of, and receptivity toward, messages and knowledge coming from other cultures. Cultural distance, in terms of how different/similar source and recipient cultures are, is conceived of as an important variable to understand processes and outcomes of knowledge transfers (McDermott and O'dell, 2001; Carrillo et al., 2009; Srivastava et al., 2020; Fu et al., 2022). Increased cultural distance between source and recipient is believed to increase the potential of distortions of messages and problems of knowledge transfers (De Long and Fahey 2000; Boh et al., 2013; Shenkar et al., 2020).

Knowledge transfer research has mainly been concerned with theorizing and studying the effects of the *national* cultures in which source and recipient units are embedded. Two seminal papers, both published in 1988, laid important foundations for the stream of literature that focuses upon knowledge transfer across national cultures (Kedia and Bhagat, 1988; Kogut and Singh, 1988). Kedia and Bhagat (1988) and Westney (1987) were among the first to conceptualize and enhance the role of national cultures, and especially, to theorize conditions under which cultures facilitate or hamper cross-national knowledge exchange. Kedia and Bhagat's point of departure is the notion that cultures co-varies more or less systematically with nations and that borders between nations represent potential barriers to knowledge transfers. They proposed that the effectiveness of knowledge transfers decrease with increased national cultural differences between source and recipient. They also argued that transfer between two nations will be most culturally affected when one of them is an advanced industrialized nation and the other is a developing country. Kedia and Bhagat focus especially on the transfer of technology and argued that the effectiveness of such transfer across national cultures varies with characteristics of the technology: whether it is product-embodied (that is, the transfer of physical products, like advanced computer components), process-embodied (for example, the transfer of patent rights of a scientific process and engineering details about how to operate the technology), or person-embodied (experience-based knowledge shared among source practitioners about appropriate ways to use the technology). Central to their theory is the proposition that transferring personal- and process-embodied knowledge of technologies is more difficult than transferring product-embodied knowledge across units located in different nations, because cultural differences between nations play greater roles in such transfers.

Kogut and Singh (1988) studied the influence of national cultures on foreign organizations' entry modes to investments in the United States. The two main analyzed types of entry modes are *acquisition* (the purchase of sufficient stock in an existing company to gain control) and *joint venture* (a cooperative enterprise by two or more organizations in a common and separate organization, which otherwise retain their separate identities). Acquisition is the most complicated and risky mode and can involve the integration of existing foreign management and the alignment of structures, routines, and practices across national and organizational borders. Thus, successful acquisitions may require the foreign investing organization to obtain thorough knowledge about the organization that is a candidate to be acquired (Meschi and Métais, 2015). Joint ventures are less complicated, partly because they do not presuppose integration with a foreign organization, and because responsibility can be assigned to local partners. Kogut and Singh (1988) argued that cultural differences between foreign investing organizations' home country and the United States (where the investments take place) influence the managers' perceptions of the revenues, costs, and degree of uncertainty of alternative entry modes. Thus, Kogut and Singh's article has an underlying notion of national cultures as potential barriers to knowledge transfers. They suggest that the greater the distance in national culture between the investing organizations' home country and the country where the planned investment will take place, the more difficult it will be for the investing organization to obtain and interpret knowledge about a foreign investment project and the country and culture it is embedded in. Therefore, they also suggest that the greater the cultural distance between the investing organization's home country and the country of entry, the more likely it is that the organization will choose joint venture over acquisition as entry mode. Both Kedia and Bhagat (1988) and Kogut and Singh (1988) used the work of Hofstede (1984) to operationalize and study national cultural variations. Hofstede conceptualized and mapped national cultures according to a four-dimensional framework: (1) weak versus strong uncertainty avoidance, (2) individualism versus collectivism, (2) small versus large power distance (that is, the extent to which the less powerful actors in a nation accept or reject an unequal distribution of power as a "normal state"), and (4) masculinity versus femininity. Analyzing data from 128 foreign entries into the United States, Kogut and Singh found clear variations in preferred entry modes between investing organizations from different nations. Data support their hypothesis that increased cultural distance between the countries of the investing organization and the country of entry (in this case, the United States), leads to increased propensity to avoid acquisition and choice of joint venture as entry mode; and, on the contrary, decreased national cultural distance increases the propensity for choice of acquisition.

Criticism has been raised towards cultural distance research. Some critics argue that the concept of national culture lacks construct clarity (Tung and Verbeke, 2010; Shenkar et al., 2020), while others have revealed flaws in the way the concept has been used in empirical knowledge transfer studies (Shenkar, 2001; Selmer et al., 2007). In addition, there are studies that report only a modest effect (Beugelsdijk et al., 2018), or almost no effect (Maseland et al., 2018), of national cultural distance on processes of knowledge transfer across organizational and national borders.

Institutional distance and knowledge transfer

In a widely cited work, Tatiana Kostova (1999) challenged the fruitfulness of the concept of cultural distance to indicate nation-level barriers to knowledge transfer. Instead, she proposed a reconceptualization of cultural distance in terms of the institutional distance between source and recipients' home countries. She developed the construct of *country institutional profile* (CIP) to capture key elements of the national environment that influence knowledge transfer processes. To operationalize the institutional distance construct,

Kostova leaned on Scott's "three pillars" of institutions; that is, the regulative, cognitive, and normative pillars (Scott, 1995). The regulative dimension refers to existing laws and formal rules and regulations within a country (Dikova and Van Witteloostuijn, 2007). Kostova argued that the probability of implementing a practice that has been transferred across national borders depends greatly on the extent to which it fits in with the recipient country's laws and formal rules. For example, it has been observed that national regulations influence investing organizations' choice of entry modes (Chao and Kumar 2010). The cognitive dimension refers to notions and beliefs that are widely shared by people in a specific country. The more the cognitive pillars of source and recipients' home countries differ, the more challenging it becomes for recipient actors to recognize, interpret, understand, and assess the transferred practice (Khalil and Marouf, 2017). The normative component refers to the dominant values and norms in the population in a given country. The more that norm and value systems differ between the source and recipients' home countries, the more challenging are the processes of implementing a transferred practice. Kostova's concept of institutional distance is multidimensional and complex. It includes three dimensions of institutional theory: economic institutionalism, organizational institutionalism, and comparative institutionalism.

In sum, Kostova argued that institutional distance—that is, the difference between the country institutional profiles of the source and recipient's home countries—is a barrier that accounts for a lot of variations, including variations in knowledge transfers of practices across national borders. Among studies of transfer of practices across national borders that explicitly apply the institutional distance construct are Kostova, 1999; Jensen and Szulanski, 2004; Ho et al., 2018. The institutional distance—construct has generated a strand of literature (e.g Delios and Beamish, 1999; Kostova and Roth, 2002; Xu and Shenkar, 2002; Malik, 2013; Beugelsdijk et al., 2017; Fortwengel, 2017; Aguilera and Grögaard, 2019; Jackson and Deeg, 2019; Kostova et. al., 2020). Overall, many of these studies have found that increasing institutional distance at the country level is associated with increased chances for negative organizational performance. Institutional distance is also associated with effects on survival rates. For example, increasing institutional distance is especially associated with decreasing chances for survival of foreign market entries (Kostova et al., 2020). However, there are certain unresolved theoretical and methodological challenges with the institutional distance construct. Its multidimensional and very inclusive character may create a sense of a "catch-all" concept that is more or less a substitute for the concept of country (Kostova et al., 2020). While it is a multidimensional concept, researchers frequently treat it as a unidimensional construct. Thus, operationalization and measures of the constructs varies substantially, which makes it difficult to compare studies and findings (Hutzscenreuter et al., 2016).

Knowledge characteristics and knowledge transfers

A seventh stream of research has concentrated on features of the knowledge itself as antecedents of variations in knowledge transfer processes and outcomes. The key variable is knowledge ambiguity, which is the degree to which the content of the knowledge to be transferred is clear and the involved actors in the adopting organization fully understand how it works in other organizations and how it can be used in practice (Hedlund and Zander, 1993; Crossan and Inkpen, 1995; Foos et al., 2006). The concept of causal ambiguity, which is attributed to Lippman and Rummelt (1982), refers more specifically to instances with irreducible uncertainty about which factors have caused observed superior (or inferior) results. Thus, within this stream of research, knowledge ambiguity is conceptualized as a main barrier for organizations that aim to imitate other organizations (Reed and DeFillippi 1990; Simonin, 1999).

Much of the research on knowledge ambiguity has centered on the dichotomous concepts of tacit and explicit knowledge. Tacit is noncodified knowledge and is therefore hard to transfer and acquire, while explicit knowledge is codified and easier to transfer. A defining characteristic of tacit knowledge is that it cannot be adequately articulated by verbal means. The coining of the concepts of tacit and explicit knowledge is credited to Michael Polanyi—first mentioned in his 1958 book *Personal Knowledge* and elaborated in later works (1962; 1967). An important forerunner for these concepts was outlined in a paper by Gilbert Ryle (1945), who distinguished between two types of knowing: to "know that," which is the intellectual knowledge of propositions, and "know how," which is detailed and often tacit knowledge about how to carry out certain tasks. While explicit knowledge often stems from logical deductions and the formulation of propositions, tacit knowledge is generated through actors' daily experience and their involvement in practical problem-solving activities (Polanyi, 1967; Lam, 2000), and by observations and imitations of others (Kikoski and Kikoski, 2004). Therefore, tacit knowledge is, by definition, localized knowledge because it emerges and is applied within a specific context (Nonaka and Takeuchi, 1995; Brown and Duguid, 1991; Muniz et al., 2022). Tacit knowledge can be embedded in specific organizational units (Nelson and Winter, 1982), or in networks, and/or be embodied as personalized knowledge in certain actors (Wah, 1999).

A frequently expressed notion within this stream of literature is that tacit knowledge is often of higher value than explicit knowledge. While explicit knowledge, stored and expressed in manuals, for example, can offer step-by-step guidelines for how to implement new technology and/or how to plan and orchestrate the accomplishments of various organizational tasks, tacit knowledge is often decisive for whether or not the new technology and the explicitly designed routines and procedures will work in practice (Wagner and Sternberg, 1987). Another argument for the higher value of tacit knowledge refers to competitive advantage. While explicit knowledge is relatively easy to share, tacit knowledge is harder to acquire, and is therefore (sometimes) the secret to a successful practice, which protects competitive advantage (Berman et al., 2002). A third and common argument appreciating tacit knowledge is that such knowledge developed and used by organizational members to solve specific problems is often the antecedent of *new* knowledge and innovations in organizations (Leonard and Sensiper, 1998; Seidler-de-Alwis and Hartmann, 2008).

Knowledge transferability

There is a strong and unifying notion within this stream of research that tacit knowledge is harder to transfer and acquire than explicit knowledge. This notion is premised on three main arguments.

First, there is the challenge of codifying, which is transforming tacit knowledge into explicit knowledge, and avoiding the loss of crucial elements of the knowledge base during such translations (Teece, 1977; 1981). The limiting factor is language and grammar. The domain of words often lacks the richness and precision necessary to explicate the tacit elements of knowledge. The literature offers ambiguous answers to the question of whether tacit knowledge is codifiable or not. Some scholars are skeptical and have argued that attempts to explicate the tacit dimension can lead to unsatisfying reductionism, leaving out the essentials (Alavi and Leidner, 2001; Okafor and Osuagwu, 2006; Yugin et al., 2011; Hanafizadeh and Ghamkhari, 2019). Even more skeptical was the philosopher Bernard Williams, who claimed, "reflection can destroy knowledge" (Williams 1985: 148). Others are more optimistic. For example, one of the four modes of Nonaka and Takeuchi's (1995) model of "knowledge conversation" is "externalization." This mode encompasses various means to make tacit knowledge communicable while retaining as much of the tacit knowledge in the explicit version as possible. The challenges of how to explicate tacit knowledge have been discussed in many other work (see, e.g., Novak and Gowin, 1984; Wilson, 2001; Milton, 2007; Hanafizadeh and Ghamkhari, 2019).

Second, the nonmigratory character of tacit knowledge sometimes reflects organizations' interests in protecting the basis of their competitive advantage. Tacit knowledge, as far as it adds to competitiveness, can be of high strategic significance since it is difficult to transfer and difficult for competitors to reveal and acquire (Barney, 1991; Zander and Kogut, 1995; Lado and Zhang, 1998; Borges et al., 2019). However, organizations, such as multinational corporations, will often also have a strategic interest in explicating tacit knowledge that has been developed in certain units within the organization, and then scale it up and diffuse it to other units within the organization, in order to effectively exploit the gained knowledge to strengthen the competitive advantage towards other organizations (Tsai, 2001). This is referred to as "the leveraging dilemma" (Coff et al., 2006), which means that explicating and up-scaling od tacit knowledge within an organization may reveal the tacit knowledge—the "secrets"—for external competitors, which would make it more imitable (Rivkin, 2001). In such cases, the advantage of the formerly tacit knowledge may decrease and even be lost. As Coff et al. (2006) argued, there are no simple solutions to this dilemma.

Third, on average, transferring and acquiring tacit knowledge usually takes more efforts and resources and is therefore far more costly than transferring explicit knowledge. To reveal and acquire ambiguous knowledge often presupposes the gradual buildup of trust and of shared understanding across organizations (Szulanski et al., 2004), and it often requires enduring close—even face-to-face—interactions (Halldin-Herrgård, 2000; Becerra et al., 2008). Therefore, as far as knowledge-searching organizations consider search costs, they may decide to quit or limit efforts to acquire the tacit secrets behind other organizations' successful practices.

Evidence or not?

The ways certain knowledge properties (such as the degree of ambiguity/clarity) influence the possibility of transferring the knowledge is a fairly well-researched theme. However, as Hedlund and Zander (1993) and Simonin (1999) observed in the 1990s, and which remains the case today, relatively few empirical studies have linked knowledge properties to its transfer across organizational borders. Findings from these studies are somewhat mixed in relation to prevailing theories and suggestions. Some examples are provided below.

Zander and Kogut (1995) studied the internal transfer and external competitors' imitation of 44 major Swedish innovations taking place after 1960, all of which had achieved a major share of world markets. The authors hypothesized that the more codified and therefore more easily communicated and understood the innovation, the shorter the times to internal transfer to other organizational units, and also the time to external competitors' imitation. Their data supported the suggestion about the internal transfer: The degree of codification had a significant impact on the speed of transfer of the innovations to units within the corporations. Surprisingly, however, the degree of codification did not determine rates of competitors' imitation of the innovations. To illustrate and gain a deeper understanding of what they had observed at an aggregate level, the authors closely examined information from three innovations. One of these was an example of a highly codified innovation based on rather uncomplicated manufacturing processes. However, the codified character of this innovation's knowledge base did not speed up competitors' imitation rates. Competitors' nonadoption of internally codified knowledge sometimes reflects the source organization's capacity to maintain secrecy towards external competitors (Ahmad et al., 2014). The two other examined innovations were both based on complicated and noncodified knowledge. However, the tacit nature of this knowledge did not prevent these innovations from being rapidly imitated by competitors. Zander and Kogut suggested an explanation of these surprising findings by introducing the concept of "common knowledge": "Imitation may be possible even if the innovator's manufacturing knowledge remains proprietary. The importance of manufacturing varies by innovations. In some industries, the key capability is knowledge of the customers' needs; knowledge of how to manufacture may be 'common' among competitors" (Zander and Kogut, 1995: 80).

Based on data from 147 large and medium-sized U.S. organizations, Simonin (1999) studied the simultaneous effects of knowledge ambiguity and its antecedents on technological knowledge transfer. Contrary to Zander and Kogut (1995), he found that increased degrees of knowledge ambiguity led to increased problems for imitating organizations. Simonin also found that tacitness was the most typical antecedent of knowledge ambiguity. Dhanaraj et al. (2004) studied transfers of tacit and explicit knowledge between 140 international joint ventures (IJVs) and their foreign parent organizations. They found that strong relational embeddedness between parents and their appurtenant IJVs facilitated transfer of tacit knowledge, while it did not affect the transfer of explicit knowledge. They also hypothesized that transfer of tacit and of explicit knowledge from their foreign parents would have a positive impact on the IVCs' performance. Surprisingly, while data supported the suggested positive effect of explicit knowledge on performance, the expected corresponding positive effect of tacit knowledge transfer on the joint ventures' performance was not found.

State of the art and the road ahead

Together, the seven reviewed research fields, with their relatively distinct bodies of literature, cover the main approaches in knowledge transfer research over the last four decades. This research has brought forward new theories and concepts, as well empirical-based insights, which have improved our understanding of how and why knowledge transfers across organizational units vary in processes and outcomes. In this section, I first distill and compare the contributions from the reviewed research fields and then introduce how the translation theory outlined over the subsequent chapters relates to insights from these fields.

State of the art

Table 2.1 contains a brief summary and comparison of the seven reviewed research fields—and related four characteristics. The first is the unifying theoretical assumptions that underlie each field. The second is the central independent variable. Each of the seven research fields concentrate on one or a few key variables that are supposed to be the main explanatory factors to variations in knowledge transfer processes and outcomes. The third characteristic highlights some of the most consistent findings from empirical research, and the fourth highlights the mixed findings and critique that have been raised against research from the various fields.

All seven of these theories are constructed around an image of a main barrier that may either prevent, distort, and decelerate knowledge flows, or enable and propel them. In six of the seven research fields—the design of formal organizational structure, the absorptive capacity, features of the social network, and three versions of distance between source and recipient (geographical, cultural, and/or institutional)—the barriers are conceptualized as organizational properties. In the seventh knowledge research field, focusing on knowledge features and especially on the extent to which it is ambiguous, the barrier is a property of the transferred knowledge. The

Table 2.1 Summary: Seven reviewed knowledge transfer research fields

	Formal organization structure and knowledge transfers	Absorptive capacity (AC) and knowledge transfers	Social networks and knowledge transfers	Geographical distance and knowledge transfer
Unifying theoretical assumption	Formal structure can channel and sometimes determine knowledge transfers, and can therefore be the source of variations in knowledge transfer processes across organizations.	Recipient organizations' level of absorptive capacity can be decisive for variations in knowledge transfer processes.	Social networks within and between organizations—and the actors' position within them—can be decisive for variations in knowledge transfer processes.	Geographical distance between organizations (and individuals) can affect and be the source of variations in knowledge transfer processes.
Central independent variable with barring/facilitating effect	Formal organization structure. (Horizontal and vertical structure.)	Absorptive capacity, (that is, the ability of an organization to recognize the value of new, external information, assimilate it, and exploit it for commercial ends).	Features of the social network (that is, actors' network position, tie strength, density and connectedness).	Geographical distance.

Continued

Table 2.1 Continued

	Formal organization structure and knowledge transfers	Absorptive capacity (AC) and knowledge transfers	Social networks and knowledge transfers	Geographical distance and knowledge transfer
Consistent findings	1. Borders between vertical layers of formal structure are potential hindrances for upward and downward knowledge transfers. 2. While delayering is associated with increasing knowledge transfer and sharing, relayering is associated with the opposite effect. 3. Borders between horizontally organized units are potential hindrances for horizontal knowledge transfers. 4. While horizontal integration is associated with increased knowledge transfer and sharing, horizontal differentiation is associated with the opposite effect.	1. High levels of AC are associated with increased chances of transfer, adoption and exploitation of new knowledge. 2. Studies have found associations between high levels of AC and certain transfer outcomes, such as the generation of new products, new patents, technology development, and overall organizational performance.	1. High network centrality of an organizational unit is associated with increased access to the knowledge base of successful prior adopting organizations. 2. Network actors that span structural holes between networks have increased chances of detecting and gaining new knowledge. 3. The more that actors are connected with many, direct, and lasting social ties, the better the conditions for transfer of tacit, complex and "thick" knowledge.	Geographical closeness, as is typical in various kinds of business clusters, is associated with increased knowledge exchange and increased chances for the emergence of innovations.

| Mixed findings/critique | 1. Results from studies of the effects of formalization on knowledge transfers and outcomes are inconsistent. 2. Results from studies of the effects of organizational centralization/decentralization on knowledge transfers and outcome are inconsistent. | While many studies have reported the effects of AC, it is often unclear whether the effects are caused by AC. This is due to three aspects of the construct and of AC research: 1. The construct's multidimensional character, which is often treated as a unidimensional construct. 2. Loose links between conceptualizations and operationalization of the AC construct. 3. Claimed causal links between AC and effects are often assumed, not examined and showed. | 1. Results from research about effects of actors' network position on knowledge transfer processes and outcomes are ambiguous 2. Results from studies of the role of closed networks (strong ties) versus the role of more open networks (weaker ties) with structural hole-spanning actors—and their effects on the transfer and exploitation of new knowledge, are inconsistent. | 1. There are inconsistencies between suggestions and findings from proximity-oriented research versus "death of distance"-oriented research. 2. It is difficult to conclude about the effects of proximity on knowledge transfers and outcomes, due to the methodological challenges of isolating this variable from other explanatory variables in empirical studies. |

	Cultural Distance	Institutional Distance	Knowledge Characteristics
Unifying theoretical assumption	The degree of similarity/dissimilarity between organizational units' culture and/or nations culture (that is, the common norms, behaviors, beliefs, customs and values shared by a defined group of people) is likely to influence and be the source of variations in knowledge transfer processes across organizational borders.	Similarities and differences between countries' institutional profiles (that is, the typical features of a country's regulative, cognitive, and normative institutions) can be the source of variations in a variety of processes across national borders—including knowledge transfer processes.	Certain properties of the knowledge, especially whether it is ambiguous or not, will influence its transferability across organizational borders. Thus, variations in ambiguity of knowledge are likely to influence and be the source of variations in knowledge transfer processes.
Central independent variable with barring/facilitating effect	Organizational and/or national culture.	Country-specific institutional profiles.	Degree of knowledge ambiguity.
Consistent findings	Increasing national cultural distance between the localization of a source organization and the localization of a recipient organization increases the potential for distortion of messages and problems of knowledge transfers between them.	Studies have found connections between institutional distance and various measures of organizational performance: increasing institutional distance at the country level is associated with increased chances of negative organizational performance.	Increasing tacitness of knowledge to be transferred from a source organization is associated with increasing knowledge transfer difficulties.
Mixed findings/critique	1. Lack of construct clarity (national culture) and flaws in the ways the concept has been applied in knowledge transfer studies. 2. Some recent studies found few effects of national culture distance on outcomes of knowledge transfer processes across national borders.	While institutional distance is a multi-dimensional construct, it is frequently applied as a unidimensional construct in empirical studies. This leads to problems of operationalization and of measuring effects—and feeds into difficulties comparing findings from different studies.	Although it is widely suggested that ambiguous and tacit knowledge is harder to transfer than less ambiguous (explicit and codified) knowledge, surprisingly few empirical studies have documented this suggestion.

barriers are conceptualized as variables, which means that certain scores either hamper or facilitate knowledge transfer and sharing. For example, various designs of formal structure that may decelerate or accelerate transfer, high or low absorptive capacity, central or marginal position in social networks, or high or low distance between source and recipient are all associated with either improved or exacerbated conditions for knowledge flows and exchange.

These theories have made at least two major contributions to our understanding of knowledge transfer across organizational borders. First, during the last three decades, knowledge transfer research has conceptualized the phenomenon and developed a scientific language that makes it possible to communicate much more precisely about knowledge transfer challenges than before. Second, these theoretical constructs and the subsequent empirical research have obviously contributed to our understanding of the puzzles behind variations in knowledge transfer processes and outcomes. We now know that knowledge transfers are influenced by formal organizational structure and that the organizational capacity to absorb and use knowledge is very important and dependent on the ability to discover, acquire, assimilate, adjust, and then exploit the knowledge that has been gained. Further, we know that the characteristics of social networks that connect organizations and actors influence transfers, as do the physical, cultural, and institutional distance between source and recipients. It is also evidenced that characteristics of the transferred knowledge, whether ambiguous or not, influence transfer processes and outcomes.

However, although empirical studies have documented associations between the abovementioned variables and knowledge transfers, most of these effects are modest. In addition, as indicated in this review, results from empirical studies are often mixed, which shows that despite great research efforts, many variations in knowledge transfers remain to be explored and explained. The modest effects revealed in studies reflect, among other things, a methodological bias in knowledge transfer research. A large proportion of this literature, and especially the most influential contributions, are quantitative studies of large samples. Correspondingly, there are few qualitative works. One important implication of this is that the *processes* that connect an independent variable and a registered effect in relation to various knowledge transfer outcomes are mostly assumed and not examined and showed. Another implication stemming from the methodological bias is that we lose sight of the actors—the people—who are involved in knowledge transfers. This book is premised on the suggestion that a path to improved understanding of variations in knowledge transfers

Beyond barrier approaches

The translation theory of knowledge transfer outlined in this book draws on some insights from the review above. One is the conclusion that despite a lot of empirical research inspired by prevailing theories, many variations remain to be explained. In light of this, a promising road ahead that goes beyond traditional barrier approaches is to zoom in more clearly and theorize on the role of processes and involved actors in knowledge transfers. Almost all of the reviewed works from the seven research fields have been carried out without focusing on the roles of actors and processes in knowledge transfers. While most of the reviewed studies indirectly present an image of involved actors as passive carriers of knowledge, a translation approach conceptualizes such actors as mediators who enact the knowledge, and thus influence both knowledge transfer processes and outcomes. Actors involved in knowledge transfers, whether source-based, recipient-based, or others (external consultants, clearinghouses, public authorities, etc.) must regularly face and cope with "stickiness" (Von Hippel, 2004; Szulanski, 1996; Winkless, 2022). Stickiness is a property of knowledge transfers and refers to all barriers and challenges that mediators encounter when trying to transfer knowledge that resides in a certain organizational unit to one or more other units. While mediators' knowledge transfer efforts often fail, they do also regularly manage to cope with stickiness and overcome barriers by processes of knowledge enactment, which can include downplaying and even removing some elements of source versions of knowledge, while amplifying others in order to make knowledge fit into various recipient contexts. Therefore, zooming in on the involved actors and tracing their modes of coping with stickiness is a key to identifying and understanding the antecedents of variations in knowledge transfer processes and outcomes.

Mediators' struggles with stickiness in knowledge transfers unfold over time as more or less connected and coordinated processes, such as those for identifying, interpreting, and encoding knowledge about (desired) source practices, and processes of decoding, implementing, and adapting transferred knowledge in various recipient units. Thus, tracing and theorizing mediators' roles as acts of translation presupposes a process approach to knowledge transfers.

PART II
IN SEARCH OF A NEW THEORY

3
Antecedents of a Translation Theory of Knowledge Transfer

Introduction

This and the following chapters develop the theory of knowledge transfer as translation. The translation theory draws on ideas and perspectives imported from disciplines other than knowledge transfer studies. Therefore, the first section of this chapter is devoted to questions about the development of new theories of organization and management. What characterizes new theories in our field, and how are they made? In particular, what are the challenges, the pros, and the cons of attempts to make theories based on borrowings from other disciplines? This discussion and its insights are related to the challenges of outlining a translation theory of knowledge transfer. The second (and main) part of the chapter addresses the two antecedents of the theory: *translation studies*, a school of thought that originated from linguistics in the early 1970s; and *the French/Scandinavian translation school in organization studies*. Concepts, arguments, images, and models are borrowed from these disciplines, thus providing important elements to the theory-building process.

Sources to new theories of organizations

Theories of organizations can be indigenous, meaning that they have originated within the field of organizations and management research and are explicitly associated with this field. According to Oswick et al. (2011), the three most typical domestic organization theories are stakeholder theory, contingency theory, and sensemaking theory. However, theories of organizations—like the one developed here—can also be based on importations of ideas, images, and models from domains outside the organization and management field. Many attempts to theorize about organizations have been based on borrowed ideas from outside domains (Morgan, 1989;

Chen et al., 2005; Cornelissen, 2005; Floyd, 2009; Suddaby et al., 2011). Oswick et al. (2011) studied which of the top 15 theories about organization and management (OMT) were based on borrowings of ideas from outside, and which were home-grown; that is, generated directly from the OMT field. They concluded that 12 out of the 15 were mainly borrowings—especially from neighboring disciplines, such as sociology, psychology, and economics—but also from more distant domains, such as biology, mathematics, and physics. Whetten et al. (2009) studied the structure of idea-imports to organization theory. They distinguished between vertical borrowings (importing of concepts that were developed at either higher or lower levels of analysis) and horizontal borrowings (importing of concepts used to understand and explain phenomena in different contexts; that is, outside the domain of organizations). They found that one of the most common vertical borrows is attempts to theorize organizations based on ideas imported from psychology and/or from sociology about *individuals'* behavior, such as when identity is ascribed to and constructed as a feature of organizations (Albert and Whetten, 1985).

There is an expanding literature stream on various aspects of horizontal idea-imports to theories of organization and management. Frequently asked questions are (a) What drives scholars to import ideas from foreign domains when developing theories of organizations? (b) What is the content of such borrowings? (c) How are metaphors used in organizational theorizing? (d) How can borrowings from outside be exploited to make high-quality organizational theories?

Borrowings from outer domains

A main driving force behind idea-imports from external sources is the desire to develop novel theories about organizations. Some idea-borrowings provide lenses that can lead to the identification and conceptualization of certain aspects, connections, and patterns that have organizational relevance and were previously not noticed or even known (Lakoff and Johnson, 1980; Inns, 2002; Cornelissen, 2005). The development of new theories is conceived of as the preeminent scholarly effort, since a good theory "gives meaning to data, defines phenomena, explains and interprets findings and fuels discoveries" (Colquitt and Zapata-Phelan, 2007: 1059). However, imported ideas may primarily confirm and strengthen what is already known about organizations. According to Oswick et al. (2002), a borrowed idea (such as one in the form of a metaphor) sometimes "functions as an aid to knowledge dissemination rather than knowledge generation" (p. 298).

The content of imports

The content of the imports from outer domains to organization theory are multifaceted. There are observations of importation of *whole theories*, including both broad paradigmatic theories and propositional theories (Chen et al., 2005; Whetten et al., 2009). Another important group of borrowings is *concepts*, which are most frequently imported to organization theory from neighboring disciplines, such as sociology and psychology (Whetten et al., 2009), but sometimes also from distant domains (Boxenbaum and Rouleau, 2011). However, most of the borrowed elements from outside to the field of organization and management come in the form of metaphors and analogies (Oswick et al., 2011). A metaphor is a figure of thinking, or speech, in which a word or a phrase that belongs to, and literally gives meaning within a certain context, is applied to describe objects, actions, relations, and logics in another and foreign context. Metaphor use presupposes (at least) two contexts, where elements from one context (words and phrases) serve as vehicles for mental border-crossing and comparisons with other contexts (Richards, 1937). This dynamic aspect (border-crossing) is a key feature of metaphors, and clearly echoed in its etymology. The Latin word "metaphora" means *carrying over*. To apply a metaphor means to make an implicit, hidden comparison between two contexts that are unrelated, but share some common characteristics. Thus, a metaphor differs from the rhetorical figure *simile*, which is a description made explicit by the use of "as" or "like" to make a comparison of two contexts (for example, "like a virgin").

The other main type of imports to organization theory is analogies. The definition of an analogy is close to that of a metaphor: a comparison between one phenomenon (x) and another (y) typically in order to clarify, understand, and explain the nature of and variation in y in light of characteristics of x. However, there are some slight differences between metaphors and analogies. Unlike metaphors, analogies are similes. A typical analogy contains both a comparison (between x and y), and an explicit inference that x is "like" or "as" y. Gentner (1982; 1983) highlighted another distinction, pointing at the expressive and heuristic capacity of metaphors to evoke emotions. This contrasts slightly with extended analogies, which are often used for the solely rational purpose of analyzing and explaining variations in y in light of x. Despite these nuances, much more connects metaphors and analogies. The most conspicuous common link is the comparison and crossing of borders between two or more domains—with the potential to explain and gain new knowledge (Tsoukas, 1991; Fauconnier and Turner, 2002). In practice, organization researchers treat metaphors and analogies rather interchangeably (Ketokivi et al., 2017).

Metaphors as means in organizational theorizing: Two approaches

As shown above, imported metaphors are important ingredients in most theories of organizations. However, the ways in which researchers use metaphors and analogies as means to build theories vary considerably. There are two main approaches to the question of how to use metaphors and analogies in theorizing efforts: the theory-confirming approach and the theory-generating approach.

The theory-confirming approach

Since the early 1980s there has been increasing academic interest in understanding how analogies and metaphors work in various human contexts, such as in understanding formal organizations (Morgan, 1980; Alvesson ans Spicer, 2011) and in "everyday life" (Lakoff and Johnson, 1980). The increased interest in clarifying the role of metaphors can also be spawned across a wide and diverse set of academic disciplines, including cognitive psychology (Billow, 1977; Leishman, 1990), philosophy of science (Botha, 1986), anthropology (Poole, 1986), medicine (Geest and Whyte, 1989), linguistics (Shanon, 1992), and teaching (Pickering and Attridge, 1990).

Through his seminal book *Images of Organizations* Gareth Morgan (1980) was among the first to introduce and translate the early 1980s' regenerated interest in metaphors and analogies to organization theory. The many scholarly contributions that followed Morgan's book were characterized by an underlying and unifying notion that the purpose and functioning of imported metaphors to organization theory was to reveal *similarities* between the source domain of the analogies/metaphors and the field of organization to speed up learning and to extend and sharpen our images of organizations (Koch and Deetz, 1981; Oswick et al., 2001; 2002; Inns, 2002). The inherent logic of the similarity approach can be outlined as containing three phases. The first is a *search phase*, in which the borrower looks for an appropriate source domain; that is, an outside domain that may share some features with the target organization and therefore be a candidate from which to import analogies and metaphors. Next is the *comparison* phase. Here, a source domain has been chosen. The borrower, acting in a more or less "systematicity mood" (Lakoff and Johnson, 1980), now zooms in on certain characteristics on the target; that is, the domain of organizations. Through comparisons (cognitive processes of oscillations between source domain and the field of organizations), hidden similarities are revealed and acknowledged. Comparisons can lead to detection of partial resemblances and to discovery of more modest aspects of sameness (Oswick et al., 2002), as well as to the explication of deep structural likenesses between the foreign and the domestic domains (Tsoukas, 1991; 1993). The third and final phase is the *exploitation phase*. Now the metaphor has been established as another organizational image that can be used for broadening and sharpening the understanding of organizations.

This modest ambition of metaphor imports to organization theory—to more clearly see what we already have seen—is a defining feature of many contributions characterized by the similarity—or theory-confirming approach. For example, Morgan (1980) argued that the purpose of his importation of eight metaphors is to make managers and students of organizations more model-rich. Multi-metaphorical actors may have increased capacity to "read" and understand different aspects of organizations, and may also possess an appurtenant broader specter of action alternatives—which increase the possibilities for better fit between organizational problems and solutions. The overall purpose of the theory-confirming approach is to compare the domain of organizations with the domain from which the metaphor is drawn—to look for and highlight eventually likenesses of certain properties. According to Oswick et al. (2002), this approach is an act "of making the familiar more familiar" (p. 295).

The theory-generating approach

Cognitive psychologists have criticized similarity theorists for not being sufficiently concerned with the complex meaning-generating mechanisms involved in metaphor-processing (Camac and Glucksberg, 1984; Fauconnier and Turner, 1998). More specifically, organization researchers have criticized similarity theorists for overlooking the fact that imported metaphors and analogies may be the source of *new* insights and theories of organizations (Cornelissen, 2005; Boxenbaum and Rouleau, 2011). A stream of work within cognitive science has contributed to improved understanding of the creative, heuristic potential of connecting different domains by analogies and metaphors (Tourangeau and Sternberg, 1981; Murphy, 1996; Stamenkovic et al., 2019). When the semantic structure and concepts of different domains are compared by an analogy and/or a metaphor, new insights that were previously inconceivable can emerge. Cornelissen (2005) took these arguments further in his domains-interaction model, in which he identified and conceptualized the complex processes that lie between the import of a metaphor from an outer domain, and the possible development of a new theory of organizations. Cornelissen's model contains the three following phases.

Development of a generic structure. In this initial stage, a comprehender (for example, a theorist) encounters a metaphor and the relevant domains are identified. The structures to be seen as parallel are found, and the correspondence between these structures is mapped. The generic structure is an initial cognitive construct that provides the foundation for further development of the metaphor that goes beyond mere mapping of similarities between the source and the target domain.

Development of blend. Blending is a concept for further juxtaposing elements from the domains and elaboration of meaning, which is made possible within the framework of the generic structure. Throughout the blending process, elements from the two input spaces—the target and the external source domain—are composed and elaborated upon (Grady et al., 1999).

Emergent meaning. In this final phase, new insights can emerge from the blend regarding the target domain and contribute to the shaping of a theory. The blend contains *new* meaning that cannot be traced back either to the target or to the source domain. Cornelissen highlighted the difference between approaches that conceive of metaphors as means to confirm existing organization theories and approaches stressing metaphors' theory-generating potential:

> The basic mechanism involved in the production and comprehension of metaphors is not the selection of pre-existing attributes of the conjoined terms, as the comparison model implies. It is, rather, the generation and creation of new meaning beyond a previously existing similarity. Metaphor involves the conjunction of whole semantic domains in which a correspondence between terms or concepts is constructed, rather than deciphered, and the resulting image and meaning is creative, with the features of importance being emergent.
> (Cornelissen, 2005: 751)

Although the domain-interaction model offers some guidelines to increase the probability of developing new theories of organizations, the creative cognitive process involved when actors encounter metaphors is very difficult to predict and control (Boxenbaum and Rouleau, 2011). It is evidenced knowledge that although metaphors stimulate cognitive creative processes, a fascinating property of such processes is that their outcomes are almost unpredictable.

Metaphors and theory quality beyond novelty

Much of the discussion about the role of imported analogies and metaphors to organization theory has concentrated on their creative potential to generate a supply of *new* theories (Shapehard and Suddaby, 2017). This is the heuristic aspect of an imported analogy or metaphor, which refers to its potential to introduce new concepts and hypothesis that are appropriated to—and conceived of—as promising within the field of organization theory (Davis, 1971; Bacharach 1989). However, novelty is only one of several features of a high-quality theory. Cornelissen and Durand (2014) provided a typology of analogies and metaphors that researchers apply in their efforts to develop theories of organizations. The first is *heuristic analogy*, as mentioned above, which is common and appropriate in the initial phase of theory-building processes. The second is *causal analogy*. Here, the assumption is that the structure of relations between elements in the outer (source) domain can be applied in the target domain. It is asserted that there can be "*a common causal schema*" (Cornelissen and Durand, 2014: 1002) underlying both domains. Reasoning by causal analogy in efforts to develop organization theories could include trying out whether observed causal relationships between elements in the source domain have their representation in the relationships between elements in the domain of organization (such as actors, governing principles, technology, work processes, connections to the environment, etc.). The third is *constitutive analogy*, which refers to the import of "large parts, if not the entirety, of a representation of the source domain, including its key vocabulary, base assumptions, and underlying causal structure" (Cornelissen and Durand, 2014: 1003). One of the few examples of a constitutive analogy in organization theory is the brain (or mind), which has been an underlying and formative model in many works in organization theory (Morgan 1980; Beer, 1981; Walsham, 1991). For example, Morgan (1980) came close to suggesting a full import of the image of the brain to develop a theory of modern organizations: "In the longer term, it is possible to see organizations becoming synonymous with their information systems, since microprocessing facilities create the possibility of organizing without having an organization in physical terms" (Morgan, 1986: 84).

In their analysis of 24 major theoretical breakthroughs in organization and management studies, Cornelissen and Durand (2014) found the use of heuristic analogies in eight theories. They registered usage of causal analogies in only three of the 24 theories and found no usage of constitutive analogy.

Borrowing for a translation theory of knowledge transfer

The translation theory of knowledge transfer is partly based on import of analogies and metaphors from two outer domains. I draw on insights from the above literature about the challenges and possibilities of such imports to organization theory—and especially on the domains-interaction model—to structure and illuminate the efforts to develop a theory of knowledge transfer as translation. Of course, it is to some extent also an ex post interpretation of how my own ideas about a new theory of knowledge transfer have emerged.

The two domains from which the analogies and metaphors are borrowed are *translation studies*, which was originally a pure linguistic research tradition, and the French/Scandinavian translation theory within organization theory, referred to here as *organizational translation*. It is quite common for theories of organizations to be complex constructs that are based on multiple analogies and metaphors from various outer domains (Andriessen and Gubbins, 2009; Oswick et al., 2011). However, in most cases, such borrowings are not made explicit by the authors (Cornelissen and Durand, 2014).

There are two reasons for choosing to use two foreign domains to develop a translation theory of knowledge transfer. First, it provides a richer base for theory development. According to Cornelissen and Kafouros (2008) "Where a single metaphor provides a schematic representation, combining multiple metaphors leads to 'rich' images or scenes that can be extended and elaborated" (p. 972). Together, translation studies, organizational translation, and the stock of existing knowledge transfer literature provide three input spaces for developing such a theory. Second, translation studies and organizational translation have much in common, in the sense that the concept of translation defines the center in both domains. Thus, the concept of translation has the characteristics of a root metaphor, which is "a fundamental image of the world on which one is focusing" (Alvesson, 1993: 116), and which, in this case, connects the two outer domains. However, these domains are also sufficiently different to provide competing as well as complementary inputs to the theory-development process.

Within the literature on metaphor imports to organization theory, a highlighted theme is questions about the semantic distance, or closeness, between the domains from which the metaphor stem and the target domain (Tourangeau and Sternberg 1981; 1982; Chiappe et. al., 2003; Cornelissen and Kafouros, 2008). Cornelissen and Durand (2012) argue for the appropriateness of a fairly large distance between source and target domains, because this increases the chances of gaining completely new and revelatory insights. On the other hand, Whetten et al. (2009) warned against a "lack of context sensitivity" (p. 542) when borrowing metaphors from domains far from the target domain. It can lead borrowers to overlook fundamental differences and/or to situations where the organizational researcher lacks thorough knowledge about the outer domain; such as in cases of borrowing to organization theory from biology (Røvik, 2011).

The two outer domains chosen to borrow from in this study have slightly different distances to the target domain of knowledge transfer between organizational units. The French/Scandinavian camp (Organizational translation) is closest. It has a strong heritage from actor-network theory (ANT), which can be classified as a sociological and philosophical school of thought. However, the early influence of Scandinavian scholars from the mid-1990s has contributed to the definition of this research tradition as a member of the family of organization theories. The domain of translation studies is at a longer distance to the field of knowledge transfer between organizations. Coined in the early 1970s, it was originally a pure linguistic research tradition, which was later transformed to a school of thought increasingly concerned with studies of communication processes at large.

The saliency of domains

The features of the two source domains will be compared with the target domain (knowledge transfer across organizational borders) with reference to Ortony's (1979a; 1979b) seminal works on salience imbalance in metaphors. According to the domains-interaction model, applying a metaphor or analogy initially involves identifying some common features of the source and the target domains. However, the target domain is almost always viewed in terms of the typical—or *salient*—features of the source. Ortony (1979a) conceptualized a salient feature as a strong and dominant characteristic that something has. For example, salient features of viruses include infectiousness, replication, mutation, and immunity (Røvik, 2011). When applying a metaphor, the point of departure is usually the salient features of the source domain. This is a situation of imbalance; the target domain is viewed and interpreted in light of the defining features of a foreign domain. According to Ortony (1979a), salient imbalance is a mechanism that can lead to the creation of novel insights. With salient source features as lenses, one can identify and reinforce features of the target domain that were previously considered nonsalient, or even not noticed, and thus stimulate the development of new concepts and insights about the target (Readence et. al, 1984; Røvik, 2011).

A generic structure for a translation theory

The first step in outlining a theory of knowledge transfer based on importation of metaphors from two outer domains is to establish a generic structure on which theory-building can take place. This work starts here. Initially, it involves comparing the outer two foreign domains (that is, metaphors from translation studies and organizational translation) with the target domain of knowledge transfer across organizational borders—looking for structures to be seen as parallel (Cornelissen, 2005). If/when such parallels are found, they may together constitute a generic structure that provide a basis for further development of meaning and insights that go beyond identifying and mere mapping of similarities between the domains. Some basic parallel structures that unify metaphors from the two foreign domains with the target domain of knowledge transfer come to sight when the involved domains are compared in light of general and simple *models of communication*. Standard presentations of communication models highlights their four main elements, which is source unit, transfer processes, barriers, and recipient unit (Craig, 1999; Lunenburg, 2010). These four elements are all represented and can be observed in the two foreign domains—as well as in the target domain. Thus, they provide a first step in establishing a generic structure for correspondence and comparisons across these domains. From this frame of four corresponding main elements sets of appurtenant features can be derived, thereby constituting even more detailed structures that parallel and connect the foreign and the target domains—and thus, preparing the ground for the theory development process. For example, SOURCE UNITS in various domains where communication takes place, contain and can be compared in relation to appurtenant elements of source-based actors, practices, technologies, images/ideas, meaning-structures, and typical features of the context that surround the source. The second element in the generic structure is THE TRANSFER PROCESS, that is, processes by which a message is conveyed between source and recipient. Common characteristic elements across the involved domains are a) *transferors* (actors involved in transfer processes), b) *encoding* (or decontextualization), that is, processes to make a transferable representation of a source practice/idea, c) *decoding* (or contextualization), that is, efforts to make information out of the coded conveyed message that is meaningful for the recipients, d) *transfer channels*, that is, the medium by which the message is conveyed. The third element is BARRIERS, which refers to factors that have the potential to impede and/or distort the transfer process. The fourth element is the RECIPIENT UNIT, which, in principle, contains the same appurtenant elements as the source units, such as recipient-based actors, practices, technologies, images/ideas, meaning-structures, and typical features of the context that surround the recipient. Figure 3.1 compiles and highlights the elements seen as parallel across the involved domains.

Figure 3.1 Generic model of parallel transfer structures in outer and target domains

1. Source unit
   - Source-based actors, practices, technologies, images/ideas, meaning-structures.
   - Typical features of the context that surround the source.
2. The transfer process
   - Transferors (actors involved in transfer processes)
   - Encoding and decoding processes.
   - Transfer channels
   - Transfers (message being transferred)
3. Barriers
   (Factors that impede and/or distort the flow (information, objects) between source and target units)
4. Recipient unit
   - Recipient-based actors, practices, technologies, images/ideas, meaning-structures, and typical features of the context that surround the recipient.

The generic structure of parallel elements outlined above constitutes a cognitive infrastructure that connects the domains and lays the ground for imaging the target domain of organizational knowledge transfers in light of salient features of the two outer domains.

This simple "skeleton" model of parallel structures provides the basis for the next step, which is further elaboration and detailing of the generic structure. This will take the form of a process of filling in insights, notions, and ideas from the two foreign domains (Translation studies and Organizational translation). In doing so, I first present the two foreign domains. Then the salient features of these domains—which is the seeds to a translation theory of knowledge transfer—will be identified and described throughout the remaining part of this chapter. The theory-developing process then continues in the next three chapters—with the blending and the emergence of meaning—phases.

The domain of translation studies

According to the biblical origin myth of the Tower of Babel (Genesis 11: 1–9), the need for translation across different languages is almost as old as mankind. Initially, the myth says, there was a united humanity speaking one language that everybody understood. However, the people decided to defy God by planning to build a tower so tall that it would reach into heaven. This was a great sin. In response, God confounded their speaking so that they could not understand each other, and scattered them around the world.

Although acts of translation are as old as humanity, the systematic study of translation has a much shorter history. The first known attempt to develop a theory of translation is Cicero's from the first century BC, entitled "*De finibus honorum et malorum*" ("The ends of good and evil")—and "*De optimo Genere Oratorum*" ("On the best kinds of Orators"). Translators reflecting on the challenges of their profession is not a new endeavor. For example, in a work published in 1661, Huet analyzed the principles and practices of great translators of the Antiquity (Lefevere, 1992). Especially Bible translation—which began as early as the Greco-Roman period and has been a huge and challenging (even life-threatening) task for translators—has stimulated much reflection and discussion within the church and among professional translators (Stine, 1990; Woodsworth, 1998). However, translation studies as an academic research field was not established until the late 1970s and early 1980s. James Holmes, a Netherlands-based American scholar, is widely recognized as the founder of the academic discipline. He also coined the generic term "translation studies" in his seminal 1972 article entitled "The Name and Nature of Translation Studies." Holmes defined translation studies as the discipline concerned with the study of translations at large, including literary and nonliterary translations, various forms of oral interpreting, as well as dubbing and subtitling (Baker, 1998: 277). Holmes mapped and defined the terrain of translation studies to consist of a "pure" and an "applied" branch. The pure branch is subdivided into *descriptive* translation studies (concerned with describing various acts of translations as they de facto occur), (Toury, 1995) and translation *theory* (the developing and testing of theories to understand and explain acts of translations) (Malmkjær, 2013). The applied part is concerned with various practical matters, such as translator education and training.

During the last three decades, translation studies has been established as an expanding academic field. It is expressed in several ways, such as in the extensive supply of encyclopedias, handbooks, and readers in translation studies (Kelly and Kelly, 1979; Baker, 1998; Gambier and Van Doorslaer, 2010; Venuti, 2012; Munday, 2013; Millán and Bartrina, 2013; Williams and Chesterman, 2014). A range of international journals have been established to facilitate publishing of scientific works from the field, such as *TextContext* (1986), *Target* (1988), and *The Translator* (1995). The professionalization and institutionalization of the field have also been strengthened by the establishment of international professional networks and associations, such as EST (European Society for Translation Studies), and ATISA (American Translation and Interpretive Studies Association). The scientification of the field also comes to expression in the expansion of university translation-study programs. At least 150 universities in five continents have established such programs, most frequently within language departments (Lambert, 2013).

Six salient features of translation studies

According to Ortony (1979a; 1979b), a generic framework for an analogy or metaphor-based theory of a target domain should be based on an initial mapping of the salient features of the source domain. Based on extensive readings and interviews, six aspects stand out as the most prominent and defining features of the domain of translation studies. These are (1) translation as decontextualization and contextualization, (2) norms of translations, (3) rules of translations, (4) barriers to translations, (5) the role of translators, and (6) translation competence. Inevitably, there are elements of judgment and selections involved when features are chosen for such a list of the most salient features. However, the six selected aspects are undoubtedly central characteristics of the domain of translation studies. For example, they frequently appear as headings (with various labels) and occupy large sections in encyclopedias and readings in translation studies. Together, these features constitute the core of the domain.

Translation as decontextualization and contextualization

In its simplest definition, translation refers to putting what is written or said in one language into another language. Complexity increases if the concept of *meaning*—that translation is *"the conveying of meaning from one language to another"*—is introduced into the definition (Hermans, 2013: 75). The definition becomes even more complex if the notion of different contexts is brought in; that is, translation as the mediation of meaning between a source context and a target context. In linguistic terms, "text" refers to what is literally written or said, while "context" is the surrounding, in which the text is embedded and which provides additional meaning to the text. In analytical terms, a translation contains two highly intertwined processes. One is decontextualization, which refers to the disembedding of the text from the context. The other is contextualization, which refers to bringing the text across to make it comprehensible in the target context language while preserving its source-context meaning.

The text–context relationship is relevant at different levels of analysis. The text can be a single word and the context can be the sentence (clause) or paragraph within which it appears, whether that is a chapter (text) in a book context or a poem (text), and how it relates to the writer's authorship and/or a genre (context). A synonym for "text" is the concept "unit of translation," which refers to the source text that the translator focuses upon and tries to represent as a whole in the target language (Lörscher, 1993: 209; Malmkjær, 1998). In doing so, translators will, to various extents, consider the context in which the chosen unit of translation appears.

During the 1980s, translation studies was transformed through what was later referred to as the cultural turn (Lefevere and Bassnett, 1990; Snell-Hornby, 2006). The most common denominator of this turn was a new awareness among scholars—followed by attempts to understand and theorize—regarding the role of the entire social context involved in translations, such as norms, beliefs, conventions, ideologies, and values (Vermeer, 1978; 1986; Toury, 1980; 1985; Hermans, 1985/2014; Bassnett and Lefevere, 1990). A main expression of this turn was the introduction of new ideas regarding what should be the unit of translation in translation studies. While the common and accepted translation unit is texts (words and/or sentences), cultural turn agents argued for a radical expansion of the translation object "beyond language," which, in principle, included all kinds of cultural/human expressions (Hönig and Kußmaul, 1982; Vermeer, 1986). In Lefevere and Bassnett's (1990) formulation, this means "neither the word, nor the text, but the culture becomes the operational unit of translation" (p. 8). An important implication is that translators should be sensitive to much more than words. They should also be able to make target-context representations of source versions of various social constructs, such as values, beliefs, norms, habits, etc. In this expanded and transformed sense, "translation means cross-cultural understanding" (Rubel and Rosman, 2003: 1). The cultural turn radically expands the role and increases challenges for translators. An important consequence is that it does not suffice for translators to be bilingual—they must also be bicultural in order to master the challenges.

Norms of translation

Another salient feature of translation studies is the persistent discussions among its scholars about the norms of translations, which include questions about the overall purpose of translations and about what should be the yardsticks for evaluating the quality of concrete translations.

The Israeli scholar Gideon Toury coined the concept "norms of translations" and thoroughly researched the subject (Toury, 1978; 1980; 1984). Toury argued that translation norms vary across historical periods and cultural contexts. He conceptualized translators as social actors who operate under the influence of different translation norms in different socio-cultural contexts. Thus, these different norms are likely to be expressed in variations in regularities of translations across various contexts. According to Toury, there are two main and partly competing norms that influence translation practices. One is adherence to the source, and the other is adherence to the target texts and context. In this connection, Toury introduced two appurtenant concepts: a translation's *adequacy* versus its *relevance*. While the norm of adherence to the source increases a translation's adequacy, adherence to the target is likely to increase its relevance for the target context (Baker, 1998: 164).

An antecedent of the norm of translators' adherence to the source is the old tradition of literal translation, also named metaphrase (Robinson 1998a), or simply, word-for-word translation. The text to be translated should be segmented into its single words, and the translator's duty is then to search for the exact target-language word copy of each source-language word. The literal translation ideal was succinctly formulated by Russian-American author and translator Vladimir Nabokov: "The person who decides to turn a literally masterpiece into another language has only one duty to perform, and this is to reproduce with absolute exactitude the whole text and nothing but the text. The term 'literal translation' is tautological, since anything but that is not truly a translation, but an imitation, an adaptation or a parody" (Nabokov, 1955/1992: 134).

The norm of adherence to the source also comes to expression in more recent debates, for example about the concept of equivalence in translations (Nida, 1964; Catford, 1965; Koller, 1989; Snell-Hornby, 2006). Equivalence is usually defined as "the relationship between a source text (ST) and a target text (TT) that allows the TT to be considered a translation of the ST in the first place" (Kenny, 1998: 77). Denotative equivalence is a translation ideal that resembles literal translation, where equivalence increases with the translator's ability to find the exact word-copy in the target language for the actual source language word (Catford, 1965; Koller, 1989). Connotative equivalence is a slightly different ideal, in that the translator's duty is to make a translation in which the chosen target language words and phrases should more or less trigger the same associations by both source and target language users. This ideal has been further elaborated by translator theorist and bible translator Eugene Nida (1964) and conceptualized as "dynamic equivalence." Equivalence, in its various versions, means adherence to the source, in the sense that it is an ideal that limits the translator's degrees of freedom to depart from the source text when rendering it in a target language.

According to Toury, a translation's *relevance* for the target context actors depends on the translator's adherence to the target while translating. Both Horace (65–68 BC) and Cicero (106–143 BC) warned against literal word-for-word translation. They argued for a less slavish rendering of the source text and for more concern among translators about how the translated texts works in the target context. Much more recent and strong voices in favor of target-oriented translations came in the late 1970s and early 1980s in connection with the cultural turn. One of these has been dubbed "the manipulation school," which was a group of researchers with Belgian scholar, Theo Hermans, at the center. In a widely cited book entitled "The manipulation of literature" that Hermans edited (1985/2014), he stated, "All translation implies a certain degree of manipulation of the source text for a certain purpose" (p. 11). Toury, who also was a member of the this group, formulated the essence of the norm of translators' adherence to the target context as follows: "Translators operate first and foremost in the interest of the culture into which they are translating, and not in the interest of the source text, let alone the source culture" (Toury, 1985: 19).

Similar ideas were launched from another group of scholars who almost simultaneously, and centered on the German linguist Hans Vermeer, were concerned with developing the so-called Skopos theory (Vermeer, 1978; Hönig and Kussmaul, 1982; Reiss and Vermeer, 1984). *Skopos* is a Greek word meaning "purpose"; in this context, the purpose of a translation. The basic normative premise of Skopos theory is that it is not the source text as such that should determine the translation process (as opposed to the norm of equivalence).

The *skopos*, or prospective function of a translation, should be determined by the "clients"; that is, the target context actors (Hönig and Kussmaul, 1982).

Skopos scholars (also referred to as "the functionalist school") focus on literary and nonliterary texts. Especially when translating nonliterary texts, such as tourist guides (Schäffner, 1998), scientific papers and instructions (Olohan, 2017), news (Holland, 2017), advertising (Valdés, 2017), children's literature (O'Sullivan, 2017), and sacred texts (Long, 2017), it is important for the translator to be knowledgeable about and to consider the target context in order to make a translation that functions well there.

Rules of translations

Although Cicero conceived of translation as an art and of translators as artists with very special skills, translation is also a highly rule-based professional and academic field. A translation rule can be defined as an established principle that serves as a guideline for translation practice. Although it can be difficult to distinguish between norms and rules, there *are* differences. While discussions of translation norms mostly relate to fundamental questions about the values, ethics, and purpose of translations, the main domain of translation rules is the practical and operational level—rules as helpful devices for problem-solving when the translator must make decisions about how to translate a concrete text (and often smaller parts of it). However, there is a continuum between norms and rules. For example, at the intermediate level on this continuum it is reasonable to place Venuti's (1995; 1998) concept of "translation strategies," which refers to the choice of method for translating an entire text. Venuti outlined two main groups of strategies, which resembles Toury's two norms of adherence, either to the source or to the target. One is domesticating strategies, which means that the translator decides to adjust the text to fit in with the target context. The other is foreignizing, which means striving for high fidelity in relation to the source and preserving linguistic and cultural differences in relation to the target in the translated version.

There is a multitude of translation rules. They are, to various degrees, clearly and consistently conceptualized, shared, known, agreed upon, and used by translators. There has been a relatively rich supply of attempts to classify and to make typologies of translation rules. Vinay and Darbelnet's (1958) typology is among the most cited and acknowledged. They sorted out the following seven main types of translation rules: (a) *borrowing*, which involves using a certain passage in the original source-text untranslated in the target version; (b) *calque*, which means borrowing a word or a phrase from the source text, while translating its components into the target language, but preserving the structure of the source language; (c) *literal translation*, which is the classic word-for-word translation; (d) *transposition*, which is the replacement of a word-class by another word-class without changing the source text meaning in the target-transposed version; (e) *modulation*, which means finding a phrase in the target language that is different from the corresponding source text, but which conveys the same idea; (f) *equivalence*, or reformulation, which involves using very different expressions to transmit the same reality in the target text language as in the source text language; (g) *adaptation*, which is the most radical rule, sometimes called "cultural substitution," and means adjusting the text so that it better fits the target context (Bastin, 2008). Another frequently cited classification is Nida's (1964) typology of three main techniques to adjust a source text to a target context. These are addition, subtraction, and alteration, which resembles Barkhudarov's (1975) adaptation typology of transposition, substitution, addition, and omission.

Translators may deliberately assess a variety of rules and choose the one that is best suited to each concrete case. However, translation rules may also be taken for granted and become translation habits. Such habits can come to expression in specific national translation traditions, such as the French tradition (Salama-Carr, 1998) and the German tradition (Kittel and Poltermann, 1998).

Barriers to translations

A fourth salient feature of translation studies is the strong consciousness and discourse within the domain about translation barriers; that is, factors with the potential to impede and/or distort the translated target version of a source text. Translation barriers are frequently associated with instances of considerable imbalance or differences between source context/text and target context/text. They are often of three main kinds: barriers stemming from considerable language differences, from considerable cultural differences, or from considerable power imbalances.

Differences between the source and target languages are, in themselves, a main translation barrier. When the source and target languages are extremely different (for example, English versus Chinese), it is often challenging for translators to find equivalent expressions of the source text in the target language. Thus, a recurring debate within this domain is about whether some texts are *untranslatable* (Wilss, 1982; Koskinen, 1994; Baer, 2020). *Linguistic untranslatability* refers to the property of a text for which there can hardly be found an equivalent when it is translated into another language. According to Bassnett (2002: 39), linguistic untranslatability means that there is a lack of syntactical or lexical substitute for source language in the target language. *Cultural untranslatability* is likely to occur when it is impossible, or at least very hard, to find relevant features of the contextual meaning from the source text in the target context (Catford, 1965). However, absolute linguistic and/or cultural untranslatability is rare, it is usually more reasonable to talk about *low* translatability (Pym and Turk, 1998). There are also techniques (or rules) that translators can use to cope with low-translatable texts—and even texts considered in the first place to be untranslatable. One such rule is *compensation*, which involves making up for a source text's effect being lost in translation by recreating a similar effect in the target text by means that are specific to the target language and context.

A third type of translation barrier stems from various kinds of *power imbalances* between source and target contexts. Asymmetrical source–target relations are often based on political, economic, ideological, or religious factors. In most cases, the imbalance comes to expression in expectations, or even claims, that the target context will change and adapt a source text so that it fits in with the dominant and accepted ways of thinking and acting within the target context. For example, in the seventeenth and eighteenth centuries (the age of French classicism), translators were instructed to change classic source texts to fit in with French literary fashions, norms, and morality (Berman, 1992). Likewise, in the Soviet-Marxist period, translators were expected to make ideologically "correct" target versions of foreign source texts (Fawcett, 1998; Inggs, 2011).

Sometimes the translation barriers are created by the source context. For example, the Qur'an, the holy book of Islam, is considered to be divine in nature, and therefore untranslatable for humans. Thus, Koran translations are restricted and traditionally conceived of as illegitimate (Mustapha, 1998).

The translator

One of the most salient features of translation studies is its persistent and strong focus on the role of the translator. This reflects that the translator is one of the best-known and institutionalized roles in the history of humankind. Thus, the interest in this role goes far beyond translation studies. Obviously, it reflects that translators have always been the main keys to communication across languages and cultures, and also that they—to varying degrees—put their marks on the translated versions of source texts. Discussions within translation theory about translators' roles are partly premised on normative arguments (that is, arguments about what should be considered as appropriate and acceptable versus inappropriate and not legitimate roles), and partly on empirical observations and descriptions (what translators actually do when they translate). In this overview, four such frequently discussed translator roles are identified.

The first is the translator as a *code-switcher*. This is the ideal of the literal translator who copies word for word and sense for sense—a pure copycat who neither adds nor subtracts anything from the original source text in the target version. Thus, according to this ideal, a high-quality translation should not *look* like a translation. The translator should be invisible, leaving no traces in the translation; his/her duty is limited to switch the language code of a source text to another language. Within this tradition, the copycat ideal is often contrasted to a nondesirable role: the not-faithful translator. This is most clearly expressed in the popular Italian proverb *traduttore, traditore*, which means *translator, you are a betrayer*. This ideal has been held especially high in the translation of sacred texts, sometimes with severe consequences for translators who failed to live up to this ideal. For example, the English scholar William Tynsdale, who was the first to translate the Bible into English from Hebrew texts, was accused of "false translations and heresy" and was executed in 1536.

The second translator role is the ideal one, of a translator as a *creative artist*. Cicero was the first to formulate this ideal in his conceptualization of translation as *exprimere imitando*. In English, the word "imitation" is often associated with copying. However, the meaning of this concept within translation theory is almost quite the opposite: not copying, but doing something very different from the original (Robinson, 1998b). This is also the meaning that Cicero attached to the concept; that is, creating something new under inspiration of something already existing. The literal meaning of the term *exprimere* is "to squeeze out something" (Robinson, 1998b: 112), which indicates that although the translator must relate to the source text, s/he is also allowed and requested to omit elements of it in order to innovate while imitating. This artistic way of translating a source text has been compared to playing a musical composer's composition: "A good translation offers not a reproduction of the work, but an interpretation, a re-representation, just as the performance of a play or a sonata is a representation of the script or the score, one among many possible representations" (Polizzotti, 2018).

The third role conceptualizes the translator as an *intercultural communicator*. The cultural turn in translation studies in the early 1980s brought new ideas and ideals for the role of a translator. It represented a break with the "old" translator ideal as an equivalence-seeking language code-switcher.

Instead, the translator should conceive of the source text as only means to a new text, which should be adopted to and function in the target culture (Vermeer, 1978). German-born Finnish translation researcher Justa Holz-Mänttäri's theory of "translatorial action" (1984) represents an influential and even more radical approach to the role of the translator. She argued for reduced focus on the role of the source text as well as on language if one strives to understand what really goes on in many translation processes. Modern translators, she argued, are involved in communication processes across cultural borders where language is only one of a number of means of communication. Snell-Hornby succinctly illustrated the concrete implications of such a translator role with the following anecdote:

> A Finnish client (such as the head of the marketing department of a firm producing electrical equipment) needs an English (or German or Arabic) version of the instructions for use of a washing machine. His aim is of course to market the washing machine in the countries concerned. As he has no command of their languages himself, he commissions a translator with the job, providing him/her with the instructions for use in Finnish. The task of this translator is to produce a text, which the English/German/Arabic buyers of the washing machine can understand so that they really use the machine. To do this, s/he may need to check internal details with the marketing manager or, particularly in the case of Arabic, to find out further information about the envisaged user (including cultural implications), about possible market restrictions as regards spare parts, or about legal implications concerning the guarantee. In any case, a good deal of cooperation with the firm (and maybe other specialists) is involved, the translator does not operate in isolation. What is not required is an exact reproduction of the sentences or grammatical structures in the Finnish text, as this may not help the English/German/Arabic user to operate the washing machine—and maybe part of the verbal text is in fact better rendered in the form of a diagram or sketch. If the text eventually enables the user to operate the machine, the immediate purpose of the translation has been reached, and the firm's ultimate purpose will be achieved if such texts help to boost their sales. The aim of the translation therefore lies outside the linguistic content of their source text.
>
> (Snell-Hornby, 2006: 58)

The fourth translator role is that of a *decision-maker*. Contrary to simple language code-switching, which can be automatized and sometimes machine-performed, studies of translators' actual behavior indicate that they are, throughout a translation process, often exposed to numerous problems and alternative solutions, and have to make choices under various degrees of uncertainty (Pym, 2015). Texts often contain ambiguous elements that could be interpreted differently and rendered differently in another language. According to Wilss (1998), a translator must make choices about the overall translation strategy for the totality of the text (for example, the appropriate degree of foreignizing and domestication), as well as choices about the microcontext, which refers to the concrete rendering of limited parts of the text (paragraphs, sentences, words, etc.). Most of the problems that translators face are located at this level; for example, challenges of translating complex syntax, semantics vagueness, and metaphors and idioms (Baker, 1992). In such situations there are usually no translation manuals offering exact answers (Fox, 2000). Nevertheless, translators must assess available alternatives and make numerous choices. The observation that different translators often arrive at different solutions when translating the same source text (Granas et al., 2014) indicates the relevance of conceptualizing translators as decision-makers who often make complicated choices in the absence of any manual.

Translation competence

Closely related to translators' roles is the sixth salient feature of the domain of translation studies, which is questions about translation competence. Throughout the history of translations there has been a prevailing discourse about the kind of competence that translators should possess, and how the competence should best be achieved (Toury, 1986; Schäffner and Adab, 2000; Hurtado Albir, 2015). However, unlike many other themes and questions within the domain of translation studies, there has been a relatively high degree of consensus regarding what constitutes a competent translator. The four main elements of translation competence can be summarized as follows.

The first element is *bilingualism*. Obviously, the competent translator must master both the source and target languages. However, there is also widespread agreement on the primacy of excellent mastery of the target language (Presas, 2000; Pym, 2017). Although complete bilingualism is an ideal, most translators are aware that knowledge of the source and target languages is usually asymmetric (Lonsdale, 1998), which tends to influence the direction of translations. In practice, most translators translate from a source language to a target language, which is their own mother tongue.

The second element is translators' *knowledge of translation norms and rules*. To be a professional translator, it is not sufficient to be fluid in the source and target languages. The translator must also be conscious about various norms and values involved in translations and, above all, must possess thorough knowledge about various translation procedures and rules, and be able to choose the appropriate rules in relation to concrete translation challenges (Wilss, 1996; Neubert, 2000).

The third element is *biculturalism*. The translator should be knowledgeable about both the source text's and the target text's contexts, and should be able to deliberately decontextualize the text from the source context, as well as to make a translation that fits into the target context. However, this expanded demand on translators' competence—which is a central element of the cultural turn in the 1980s and 1990s (Witte, 1987; Snell-Hornby, 2006)—is hard to live up to for the practicing translator. Cultures are complex; they contain much more than language and are usually difficult to come into terms with, even for professional anthropologists (Geertz, 1973). In addition to complexity, cultures are often described as being *unique* in character, which anthropologist and linguist Edward Sapir succinctly formulated as follows: "The worlds in which different societies live, are distinct worlds, not merely the same world with different labels attached. Each linguistic community has its own perception of the world, which differs from that of other linguistic communities, and implies the existence of different worlds determined by language" (Sapir, 1929/1949). The uniqueness of cultural contexts increases challenges for the translator, since understanding one or a few contexts does not necessarily qualify a translator to translate between *other* cultural contexts. Another challenge for translators who are supposed to consider cultural contexts and not only language is the vagueness of the frequently used concept of cultural context. For example, there is a tendency within translation studies to equate "contexts" with "cultural context," which is actually reductionism, because the elements of the source and the target that a translator must be sensitive and knowledgeable about when translating contain much more than just "culture." For example, translating into another language often means entering into a new national context and relevant translator knowledge can encompass knowledge about political institutions and traditions, public administration, geography, media, etc.

The fourth and final element is knowledge about *the subject matter*, which refers to the translator's knowledge of the material, or subject, that is being translated. This is a demand on translator's knowledge that goes beyond the traditional demands on bilingualism and biculturalism. It is rather easy to argue for the necessity of subject matter competence. For example, translating a document about cardiology or about advances in green technology requires that the translator is able to find the correct and equivalent technical terms in the associated target language. The volume of specialized translation is increasing rapidly, which brings increasing demands for specialized subject matter–translation competence.

How can translators *in spe* become able to gain and live up to the ideal of the competent translator? Usually, translators have been trained informally outside academic institutions. However, as early as the fifteenth and sixteenth centuries, many states institutionalized translator training, often in order to secure translation competence in nations' foreign affairs. The last 60 years have seen a strong tendency to academize translation education and training. Most of the initial translation training is now carried out by universities and other institutions of higher education and research (Anderman and Rogers, 2000). This development is evidenced by Caminade and Pym (1998), who identified a considerable rise in the number of universities that offer degrees or diplomas in translating and/or interpreting—from 49 in 1960 to 180 in 1980 and at least 250 in 1994.

The domain of organizational translation

While translation studies is the primary external domain to provide an input space for a translation theory of knowledge transfer, the secondary domain is the research field of organizational translation. This field has strong French and Scandinavian origins. An important antecedent is contributions from French scholars working within the traditions referred to as "the sociology of translation" and actor-network theory (ANT), especially Serres (1974/1982), Latour (1983; 1986; 1987), and Callon (1986). Inspired by these works, Czarniawska and colleagues introduced some of their core ideas to organization theory throughout the 1990s (Czarniawska and Joerges, 1996; Czarniawska and Sevón, 1996; 2005; Rottenburg, 1996; Sahlin-Andersson, 1996; Sevón, 1996; Røvik, 1998). This opened a new avenue to study and improve understanding of the circulation (or "travel") of various organizational ideas in time and space. Thus, it has now been recognized and widely accepted as a distinct theoretical approach and school of thought in organization research (Greenwood et al., 2008; Spyridonidis et al., 2014; Wedlin and Sahlin, 2017; Claus et al., 2021.

The translation approach to such phenomena contrasts with the diffusion model, which builds on images of physical laws of energy, speed, motion and inertia, and which, according to Latour (1986), also permeates social sciences in general. Organizational translation researchers offer alternative conceptualizations and models of the spread and circulation of organizational practices and ideas. This alternative translation approach is premised on two interrelated arguments.

The first argument opposes the diffusion-inspired image of how ideas spread between organizations. It is the image of a central powerful broadcasting point (for example, government agencies, large consultancies, or multinational corporations) that provides all the energy to the diffusion process, and an appurtenant image of passive receiving organizations (Sevón, 1996; Powell et al., 2005). In contrast, organizational translation researchers argue that the power behind the travel of ideas between organizations stems not from one powerful central agent, but from the richness of interpretations that the idea triggers in each actor within a given network (Callon, 1986; Latour, 1986). Receivers fuel the spreading process with new energy; thus, actors are active translators, not passive receivers. Put bluntly, the power to the spreading process is the result, not the cause of the circulation of ideas between.

The second core argument from the field of organizational translation concerns the objects that spread between organizations. Here, organizational translation theorists have challenged the physical "thing" and "fixed object"—images of spreading ideas—that is present in various diffusion studies within organization theory (Whittle et al., 2010; Røvik, 2016). In contrast, translation researchers have theorized disseminated constructs as *ideas*, or as "quasi objects" (Czarniawska and Joerges, 1996), that are continually shaped and reshaped as they circulate in, and between, organizations (Andersen and Røvik, 2015). These idea-shaping processes are depicted as processes of translation.

Five salient features of organizational translation

When conceiving of organizational translation as a potential source domain for a translation theory of knowledge transfer between organizations, we must—as in the case of the primary domain of translation studies—first map the salient features of this secondary domain. Based on extensive readings and the author's special knowledge of this field of research (Røvik, 1998; 2007; 2016; 2019), five features stand out as the most domain-defining ones. These are: (1) the translation objects, (2) images of the translator, (3) process orientation, (4) contextualization orientation, and (5) translation as transformation.

Compared with one another, the five salient features also offer a reasonable account of how scholars working within this field have approached the central *what*, *who*, and *how* questions associated with this research tradition, such as: What are the objects of translation? (Feature 1). Who are the translators? (Feature 2), and, How are practices and ideas translated? (Features 3, 4, and 5).

The translation objects

As mentioned above, organizational translation researchers have questioned the inherent physical images of diffusion in many organization theory studies. The alternative image offered from the domain of organizational translation of what "travels" (which is the preferred metaphor instead of diffusion) is *ideas* traveling as quasi-objects, such as concepts, speech, pictures, websites, and manuals (Czarniawska and Joerges, 1996). Although translation researchers have studied very different ideas, the common denominator is that most of them are *organizational* ideas, meaning ideas about the organizing and managing of various organizational activities. The studied ideas often resemble recipes, in the sense that they provide more or less detailed advices about what activities organizations should be involved in, and how they should be appropriately organized and performed. Translation researchers have studied the travel of many such ideas. However, most of these studies have focused on typical macro or master ideas with almost global reach (Røvik and Pettersen, 2014) and how they are translated in local contexts. A list of such translation studies includes Management by Objectives (Stensaker, 2007), Total Quality Management (Giroux and Taylor, 2002; Özen and Berkman, 2007; Ercek and Say, 2008), Workplace democracy (Børve and Kvande, 2022), Balanced Scorecard (Ax and Björnenak, 2005; 2007; Madsen, 2014), Shareholder Value (Meyer and Höllerer, 2010), Business Process Reengineering (Heusinkveld et al., 2013), Reputation Management (Wæraas and Sataøen, 2014), Lean (Morris and Landcaster, 2006; Andersen and Røvik 2015; Larsson, 2019; Hultin et al., 2021), Medical Innovations (Nicolini, 2010), Quality Management Practice (Bausch et al., 2022), auditing (Mennicken, 2008), Strategic Planning (Hwang and Suarez, 2005), Manpower planning (Nilsen and Sandaunet, 2020), Media logics (Pallas et al., 2016), Best Value (Solli et al., 2005), Evidenced-based evaluation (Elvbakken and Hansen, 2019), the Nordic model (Byrkjeflot et al., 2022), Leadership concepts (Nielsen et al., 2020), safety concepts (Berling et al., 2022; Karanikas et al., 2022), organizational ethics (Helin and Sandström,

2010), Quality Improvement (Erlingsdottir and Lindberg, 2005; Mueller and Whittle, 2011), models of leadership; Abrahamsen and Aas, 2016), and accreditation (Hedmo et al., 2005).

The traveling ideas that translation researchers have concentrated on are, to varying degrees, representations of concrete, localized organizational practices. It is often difficult, and sometimes even impossible, to trace the origins of specific circulating macro ideas to a concrete time, place, and practice (Røvik, 2002). These are primarily circulating *ideas*, not carriers of concrete practices. However, there are also a few studies within this domain which deal with the transfer of more practice-carrying ideas. An example is Westney and Piekkari's study (2020) of the movement of Japanese organizational practices (mainly in the car industry) to the United States from the 1970s through the mid-1990s.

Images of the translator

A second salient feature of the domain of organizational translation comes to expression in a persistent focus on the translators; that is, actors involved in the translation of circulating ideas. An important antecedent of the salient status of translators is Bruno Latour's early and precise formulation of a key insight within this domain. "The spread in time and space of anything—claims, orders, artefacts, goods—is in the hands of people; each of these people may act in many different ways, letting the token drop, or modifying it, or deflecting it, or betraying it, or adding to it, or appropriating it" (Latour, 1986: 267). This formulation, which points at the transforming power and potential of every single actor involved in the handling of circulating ideas, has achieved axiomatic status within the domain of organizational translation.

The image of the translator differs in three important respects between the domains of translation studies and organizational translation. First, while the translator in translation studies refers to a fixed, explicit, widely recognized, professionalized, and thus highly institutionalized role, this is *not* the case within the domain of organizational translation. In this tradition, to be a translator is an *aspect* of a role (Barth, 1963), depicting the enactment of circulating ideas, which some actors do while performing other explicit and recognized roles, such as top managers, consultants, etc. To be conceived of as a translator in this sense is also a role that is theoretically *ascribed* to various actors. This means that the actors themselves are not necessarily conscious of or conceptualize what they are doing as translators.

Second, while translation studies often image the translators as actors operating under norms of professional neutralism—seeking some kind equivalence between the source text and the translated target version (Nida, 1964), the translator-image in the domain of organizational translation is frequently of an agent who purse strategies and acts to serve specific interests by creating certain versions of circulating ideas (Kelemen, 2000; Waldorff and Madsen, 2022). For example, Frenkel (2005b) showed how translators at the state level in Israel acted as agents who emulated special versions of two American management models, scientific management and human relations, and adapted them to fit the needs of the political-institutional power structure of the country. In another study, Özen and Berkman (2007) showed how an elite group in Turkey throughout the 1990s translated versions of Total Quality Management (TQM) to fit the interests and needs of a powerful group of Turkish business and industrial organizations.

Third, while the common image of the translator in translation studies is of a single person who performs the whole translation operation of a text from a source to a target context, it is quite different within the domain of organizational translation. An organizational translation process usually involves, many and different types of actors, both external and internal localized actors. According to the Latourian axiom mentioned above, everyone who encounters a circulating idea is, in principle, a translator. In practice, however, some types of actors are undoubtedly more involved than others. Among externals, national governmental agencies frequently act as translators when they transform and regulate macro-ideas into national versions, as observed, for example, within the Norwegian educational sector (Røvik, 2014; Røvik and Pettersen, 2014). The most common external located translators are probably various types of consultants (Crucini and Kipping, 2001; Löfgren, 2005; Sturdy, 2011; Heusinkveld and Visscher, 2012; Czarniawska and Mazza, 2013; Engwall and Kipping, 2013; Kirkpatrick et al., 2013; Madsen and Slåtten, 2022). Among the most frequently studied internal translators are staff in various kinds of research and development units (Lane et al., 2006, Scheuer, 2006; Volberda et al., 2010), HR units (Jiménez-Jiménez and Sanz-Valle, 2005; Slåtten, 2020), quality control units (Scheuer, 2006). However, one of the most important translation positions in modern organizations is held by middle managers (Nehez et al., 2022). This point was also made in Radaelli and Sitton-Kent's (2016) literature review of middle manager research, which is one of very few studies of a specific group of actors as translators to be explicitly framed within organizational translation theory. Middle managers' localization "in the middle" provides the potential for the actors in this position to be important carriers and translators of ideas and information from outside to inside the organizations, as well as from top managers to the frontline level. Radaelli and Sitton-Kent's review reveals that middle managers are, to a large extent, involved in tasks that share core properties of translation, such as idea acquisition, appropriation of translation roles (which means that a middle manager in a given situation may also interpret his/her role as being that of a translator), developing conversations with frontline employees about various aspects of incoming ideas, selling their own version of the idea, and contributing to the implementation and stabilization of the idea.

Process orientation

The third salient feature of this domain is a strong process orientation, which comes to expression in efforts to identify, observe, map and theorize what happens when organizational actors encounter and handle various circulating organizational ideas. Process-oriented translation studies include works such as Yanow (2004), Frenkl (2005a), Erlingsdottir and Lindberg (2005), Powell et al. (2005), Love and Cebon (2008), Jensen, et al. (2009), Demir and Fjellström (2012), Farquharson, et al. (2014), Ciuk and James (2015), Lawrence, (2017), Larsson (2019), and Nielsen et al. (2022). Many such works combine process orientation with a longitudinal approach. For example, for about ten years, Larsson (2019) studied processes of translating the Lean concept to practice in the Swedish healthcare sector. She concluded that "translation is something that is going on everywhere and all the time" (p. 3). Nielsen et al. (2022) drew from a longitudinal 20-year case study to reveal processes of "translation ecologies" when ideas of mobile technology for caregivers spread across the entire Danish homecare field. Wedlin and Sahlin (2017) coined the concept of translation ecology. A strong process orientation is at the forefront of this concept. They argue that organizational ideas are shaped through "continuous translation processes both within and outside the organizational context" (p. 103), and that such processes are nested in complex ways and often involve numerous actors and take place at different arenas—sometimes also within different fields. The concept of translation ecology has been further elaborated by other researchers (Nielsen et al., 2022; Westney et al., 2022).

The strong interest in qualitative process studies obviously reflects this core idea within this domain—the axiomatic notion of complex translation processes where each involved actor who encounters the actual idea enacts and puts his/her mark on it, thus modifying and reshaping it. Therefore, acts of translation are conceived of as a key social mechanism that, through its core logic, continually leads to variations and heterogeneity (Røvik, 2016; Van Grinsven et al., 2016; Claus et al., 2021). However, the complexities involved and the assumed unique character of each translation process make it difficult or impossible to predict the progress and outcomes of such processes. Therefore, although researchers can have a clear, theoretically based understanding of translation processes, this does not necessarily lead to an increased capability to a priori determine concrete translation processes, since it is assumed that such processes are, by their nature, complex and unpredictable. Consequently, if a researcher aims to understand the outcomes of translation processes, the preferred research strategy within this domain is, for the most part, to map each process in detail. This is also why most empirical translation studies within this domain are—according to Ansari et al. (2010)—characterized by "methodological particularism," meaning that each study usually deals with only one or two cases.

By comparison, the process studies paint a picture of organizational translations that run contrary to any notions of straightforward and simple processes. Translation processes are often very time-consuming; they may stretch out over years (Erlingsdottir and Lindberg, 2005; Larsson, 2019). They seldom follow a one-way track from a source version to a target and stabilized version. More often, the movement is circular: back, forward, and then back again (Czarniawska and Joerges, 1996; Jensen et al., 2009). The involved actors are almost never depicted as neutral professional translators, but rather as people with interests and various power bases (Demir and Fjellström, 2012), and the translations often take place in contexts of power plays, conflicts, and bargaining (Morris and Landcaster, 2006; Ciuk and James, 2015).

Contextualization orientation

The final two salient features of this domain are highly interrelated, but should be analytically separated as two features. The first of these, contextualization orientation, refers to an (im)balance within this domain of attention and research efforts in favor of the target context compared to the source context (Røvik, 2016). Although Czarniawska and Joerges' (1996) initially formulated the subject of organizational translation as encompassing both decontextualization (the disembedding of a practice from a source in the form of a representation of the practice) and contextualization (the process of embedding an idea in a target context), the *translation to* and embedding aspect has clearly dominated most subsequent empirical studies (Sahlin and Wedlin, 2008; Van Veen et al., 2011; Kirkpatrick et al., 2013; Scheuer, 2021).

The main research agenda in these works has been to study what happens when circulating ideas are translated into certain national and organizational contexts (Boutaiba and Strandgaard Pedersen, 2003; Saka, 2004; Erlingsdottir and Lindberg, 2005; Bergström, 2007; Glover and Wilkinson, 2007; Frenkel, 2008; Kantola and Seeck, 2011; Mueller and Whittle, 2011; Gond and Boxenbaum, 2013; Ciuk and James, 2015; Nielsen et al., 2020; 2022). Few studies framed within the organizational translation perspective have focused explicitly on the decontextualization phase. Those that have done so include Røvik (2007), Nielsen et al. (2022), and Westney and Pikkari (2020).

Interestingly, the target and contextualization orientation within the domain of organizational translation clearly corresponds to a central feature within the domain of translation studies, and was especially present and conspicuous after the cultural turn of the 1980s. Within translation studies, the corresponding strong adherence to the target context comes to expression in works from the manipulation school and the Skopos theory.

Translation as transformation

The fifth salient feature of organizational translation is expressed in the widely acknowledged axiom among researchers within this domain that to translate is, by definition, to transform. This is a strong carry-over from the sociology of translation and actor network theory. For example, Serre (1974/1982) postulated that translation is not merely linguistics and that it takes many different forms. However, he emphasized, it *always* involves transformation: Each act of translation changes both the translator and what is translated. This axiom is restated in most of the defining works of organizational translation, such as Czarniawska and Joerges (1996), Czarniawska and Sevón (1996; 2005), and Sahlin-Andersson (1996).

There are three main reasons why translation scholars within this domain tend to equate translation with transformation. First, while most physical objects can be exactly copied quite easily, it is much harder (probably impossible) to copy circulating immaterial ideas. Second, unlike physical objects, circulating ideas are often very transformable. Even ideas packed as "evidenced practices" often allow room for alternative interpretations and, thus, for variations and heterogeneity (Røvik, 2019). Third, even if one succeeds in copying a practice and/or an idea from one to another organizational unit, it may lead to transformations, because "the act to set something in a new place is to construct it anew" (Czarniawska and Sevón, 2005: 8).

The axiom that translation of practices and ideas always means transformation of the target organizational context is probably a reason why researchers working within this domain are not, on average, as concerned with the source context and the decontextualization phase as they are with the contextualization phase. This is because the theoretically predicted transformative effects of translations will mainly come to expression, and can therefore be studied in the contextualization phase in the target organization(s).

In a review of 150 central publications framed within the organizational translation theory van Grinsven et al. (2016) focused on how various authors conceive of (1) the source of transformations and why translations lead to variations, and (2) the object of transformation (what is transformed). The review revealed two main answers to the question of why ideas are transformed when they are translated. The first is variations stemming from embeddedness. Ideas are transformed due to the power of contexts, which is expressed among translators in more or less unconscious efforts to interpret and adapt circulating ideas to make them fit into their target local contexts (Kirkpatrick et al., 2013). The second is variation stemming from strategizing. Circulating ideas are sometimes strategically interpreted and translated into specific versions as a means of improving goal achievement (Lervik and Lunnan, 2004; Boxenbaum and Strandgaard Pedersen, 2009). The literature review also revealed two main approaches to questions about the object of variation. The first is representational—or ideational variation. Here, translation means the shaping and reshaping of the language packing and the symbolic meaning of the circulating ideas (Zilber, 2006; Gond and Boxenbaum, 2013). The second approach is structural variation. Studies in this group highlight how translations can lead to transformations, and thus to variations, in structures, procedures, routines, and practices (Ansari et al., 2010).

Summary: A generic structure for a translation theory of knowledge transfer

This chapter has laid the groundwork for the development of a translation theory of knowledge transfer. Building on Cornelissen's (2005) domain-interaction model, a generic structure for the translation theory has been worked out. The content of this structure is summarized as follows:

> Two external domains (translation studies and organizational translations) are chosen to serve as input spaces from which analogies and metaphors can be borrowed as "raw materials" for the theory.

The first step in outlining a generic structure was to work out an abstracted skeleton model, which contains elements that are common to and unify the two external domains and the target domain of knowledge transfer across organizational borders. The four main elements of the skeleton model are features of the source entity, of the transfer process, barriers, and the recipient units.

The generic structure also builds on Ortony's (1979a; 1979b) theory of saliency imbalance in metaphors as a strategy to generate novel theories about a target domain. In light of features that are salient to an external source domain, one can discover aspects of the target domain that were previously unnoticed and can provide the basis for new concepts and theories. In line with Ortony's theory, six salient features of the translation studies—domain and five such features of the domain of organizational translation—have been identified and described. Together, these features and arguments provide the generic structure for a translation theory of knowledge transfer. The next chapter introduces (expressed with a central term from the domain-interaction model) "the blending phase," where insights from the two external domains will be juxtaposed with insights from the target domain of knowledge transfer.

Figure 3.2 Summing up: Salient features of two source domains

The domain of translation studies: Six salient features

1. Decontextualization and contextualization
   Translation contains two intertwined processes: decontextualization, which is disembedding the text from the source context while preserving its meaning; and contextualization, which is bringing across the text and make it comprehensible in the target context while preserving its source context meaning.
2. Norms of translation
   Includes questions about the overall purpose of translations and about the yardsticks for evaluating the quality of concrete translations. There are two main and competing norms. One is adherence to the source text and context (as in literal translation, for example). The other is adherence to the target context (adapting the text to fit into the target context).
3. Rules of translation
   Translation is a rule-based professional activity. Translation rules are established principles that serve as guidelines for translation practices.
4. Barriers to translation
   A translation barrier is a factor that has the potential to impede and/or distort the translated target version of a source text. Barriers may stem from

considerable language differences, from cultural differences, or from power and/or ideological imbalances between source and target contexts.
5. The translator
One of the world's most institutionalized roles. A repertoire of translator roles includes the language code-switcher, the creative artist, the intercultural communicator, and the decision-maker.
6. Translation competence
There are prevailing discourses within the domain about what knowledge and expertise should characterize a competent translator. Four main types of such competence are frequently debated: (a) bilingualism, (b) biculturalism, (c) the consciousness and knowledge of translation norms and rules, and (d) knowledge about subject matter (that is, the translator's knowledge about the material or subject that is being translated). During the last 60 years, translation education and training have been academized and highly institutionalized.

The domain of organizational translation: Five salient features

1. The translation objects
The main objects of translations are various types of organizational ideas traveling as quasi-objects, such as concepts, names, speech, pictures, websites, and manuals.
2. Images of the translator
The image of the translator in organizational translation differs from corresponding images in translation studies in two important respects. First, the translator is not a recognized, explicit and professionalized role, but an *aspect* of a role, depicting the enactment of circulating ideas that some actors do while performing other roles. Second, while language translation is performed by one translator, many and different kinds of actors are involved in translation of organizational ideas.
3. Process orientation
There is a strong and persistent interest within the domain of organizational translation to study translation processes, often in the form of longitudinal one-case studies. This reflects the domain-specific axiom that each translation process is complex and unique in character. Outcomes of translations processes are almost impossible to predict a priori.
4. Contextualization orientation
There is a prevailing imbalance within this domain regarding attention and research efforts in favor of target context and the embedding processes, and, correspondingly, less attention towards the source context and the disembedding processes.

5. Translation as transformation
   A strong axiomatic feature within this domain is the notion that translation always involves transformation of the translation object (for example, a circulating idea), as well as transformation of the target context.

PART III
THE THEORY

4
Reframing Knowledge Transfer as Acts of Translations

Introduction

The core of the translation theory that will be outlined in this and the two subsequent chapters is expressed in three propositions. (1) Knowledge transfer between organizational sources and recipients can be conceptualized and understood as acts of translations. (2) Translation of knowledge (practices and ideas) across organizational borders is a rule-based activity. (3) Translations make a difference; the way translations are performed may explain outcomes of knowledge transfer processes.

This chapter focuses on the first of these propositions and offers a broad reinterpretation of knowledge transfer between organizations in light of the salient features of the two external domains (translation studies and organizational translations). While Chapter 3 represented the first step in the blending process (extracting and describing the external domains' salient features), this chapter takes the blending process further into the next phase, where ideas derived from the salient features are juxtaposed with insights about the target domain of knowledge transfer between organizational units. However, with Cornelissen's (2005) arguments in mind, it is important to note that I do not just decipher any correspondence highlighted throughout the chapter between the salient features of the external domains and the phenomenon of knowledge transfer across organizational borders, but actively construct it. This means that the construct—the theory—emerges from complex cognitive processes of juxtaposing, followed by blending of elements from all three input spaces (the two external domains and the target domain of organizational knowledge transfer). Inherent in such an approach is the potential to gain "revelatory insights" (Corley and Gioia, 2011); that is, insights about organizational knowledge transfer that go beyond ambitions of seeing more clearly what we already know.

This chapter offers a broad interpretation of knowledge transfer between organizational units as acts of translation. The chapter starts with a discussion about the relevance of various salient features of the two external domains to improve understanding of organizational knowledge transfer. This is followed by the main part of the chapter, which conceptualizes and theorizes knowledge transfer between organizations as containing two key processes: de-contextualization and contextualization.

From juxtaposing to blending

So far, features of the two outer domains and the target domain of organizational knowledge transfer have only been juxtaposed; that is, lined up side by side (from the Latin *juxta*, which means place something alongside/nearby). We now enter into the blending phase, where elements are combined in a search for new insights.

The process of conceptualizing knowledge transfer across organizational borders as acts of translations requires mobilization of the entire set of salient features from the two outer domains. However, some features are especially consequential for outlining a translation theory of knowledge transfer. Among these are the image of transferees as translators, and the norms, barriers, and rules of translation, translation competence, and translation as de-contextualization and contextualization.

Transferees as translators. Probably the most consequential reconceptualization stimulated by a salient feature of translation studies is to image mediating actors involved in border-crossing knowledge transfer processes as *translators*. This clearly breaks with the often gently articulated and undertheorized notions of knowledge mediating actors as passive carriers, conveyors, and transporters. The image of knowledge mediators as translators paves the way for reinterpretation of their roles. The role of a "translator" is richer and potentially more important than that of a transporter. For example, in light of insights from the domain of translation studies, a translator can be conceived of as a communicator who actively mediates between various organizational and institutional contexts. In contrast to the passive carrier, the translator role also entails the image of the active decision maker who must make important decisions under varies degrees of uncertainty, such as how to obtain more detailed information about the knowledge and technology base that a desired practice in a source organization is founded on, and how to implement a version of it that is adapted to a target organization, while simultaneously avoiding important aspects of the desired practice being lost in translation. Thus, the image of the knowledge mediator as a translator makes it possible to see the involved actors acting in various roles, spanning from code-switchers, whose ambitions are restricted to copying and reproduction, to creative artists, who do not feel especially committed to the source practice version and are more concerned with inventing something new.

From the domain of organizational translation come two other ideas that advance the reconceptualization of the mediators in knowledge transfers as translators. The first concerns the number of actors involved as translators in such processes. As a rule, only one translator performs translations of texts across languages. However, knowledge transfer processes across organizational borders usually involve many mediators acting as translators. For example, there can be source-based actors who translate practices to representations of practices, and target-based actors who translate images of source practices to target practices. In addition, knowledge transfers often involve externally located translators, such as consultants (Sturdy et al., 2009), national public authorities (Røvik, 2007), and headquarters of multinational corporations (Kern et al., 2019). The second idea from the domain of organizational translation is that individuals performing in ordinary roles, such as leaders, middle managers, consultants, and experts, usually conduct acts of translations in knowledge transfers (Radaelli and Sitton-Kent, 2016). Thus, knowledge translation acts are usually performed as aspects of other roles.

Norms of knowledge translation. The reconceptualization of knowledge mediators as translators is a fundamental and consequential one that helps us clearly see the relevance and necessity of other salient features from the two outer domains to construct a more complete image of knowledge transfer as translation. One such salient feature that becomes relevant is norms of translation, a concept that refers to the purpose(s) of translations and the standards for evaluating the quality of any translation. In light of this salient feature, we zoom in on the overall norms and notions within the field of knowledge transfer about good and acceptable translations versus less good and less acceptable translations across organizational borders. Among the numerous norms in this field, two competing ones largely influence knowledge transfer practices. The first is the norm of adherence to the source organization context. The second is adequacy in relation to the target context; that is, to provide translated target versions of the source practice that are adapted to the needs of the target organization. Thus, the former is a translation norm of adequacy (adherence to the source), while the latter is a norm of relevance (adherence to the target). As will be shown and discussed in the remaining chapters, such norms vary in space and time (Westney, 1987; Westney and Piekkari, 2020). They influence and lead to discernible patterns of knowledge translation processes.

Barriers in organizational knowledge transfers. The notion of translation barriers is a third salient feature from the external domain of translation studies that is highly relevant in reconceptualizing knowledge transfer as acts of translations. The concept of "barriers" includes all factors that complicate knowledge transfer processes. Barriers can delay, halt, and sometimes even terminate translation processes. They can also lead to distortions and sometimes also to destructions; for example, in the sense that the important secrets of a desired source practice are lost in translation. Translation barriers can be of various kinds. Perhaps the best-known hindrance occurs when source organizations act to protect the knowledge base of their successful practices from outsiders' access (Baughn et al., 1997). Barriers also stem from various kinds of differences, distances—or imbalances—between source and target organizational contexts, such as between nations (institutional arrangements, languages, public regulations, etc.), cultures, types of organizations, technologies, etc. Knowledge transfer scholars have identified and thoroughly studied transfer barriers (Szulanski 1996; 2003; Sun and Scott, 2005; Paulin and Suneson, 2015). However, most of these studies have been carried out on samples of knowledge transfers at aggregated levels, and to lesser extent focusing on the *processes* in which involved mediators strive and cope with the challenges of translating knowledge across various transfer barriers. Thus, the focus on how translators relate to and handle knowledge barriers makes it necessary to include insights from the salient feature of *process orientation* from the domain of organizational translation. Knowledge transfer processes often stretch over long periods and may involve many individuals who participate in different phases and at different places throughout the processes. Thus, in order to understand and theorize about the translators and how they de-contextualize desired practices and contextualize representations of practices, it is necessary to zoom in on such translation processes.

Rules of knowledge translation. A central salient feature of the domain of translation studies is rules of translation. There are a multitude of rules regulating linguistic translations. Correspondingly, in light of this salient feature, one can acknowledge and conceptualize that translation of practices and knowledge across organizational borders are rule-based and therefore patterned behavior. Chapter 5 highlights this part of the translation theory of knowledge transfer.

Translation competence in knowledge transfers. The focus on translation rules and on translators' handling of knowledge barriers also makes insights from the salient feature of *translation competence* (from the domain of translation studies) highly relevant in a translation theory. In translation studies, such competence refers to bilingualism, biculturalism, knowledge of translation norms and rules, and knowledge about the subject matter. The reconceptualization of the mediators as active translators—whose actions are keys to understanding the courses and outcomes of knowledge transfer processes—rather than as passive transporters, makes it necessary to look behind the translators' decisions to trace and theorize the competence they are based upon (Chapters 6 and 7 address questions of translators' competence).

The remaining and main part of this chapter is a reinterpretation of organizational knowledge transfer in light of the salient feature of de-contextualization and contextualization.

Two key translation processes: De-contextualization and contextualization

The notion of de-contextualization and contextualization is a preeminent and defining feature of the domain of translation studies. It is a cornerstone in this chapter's attempt to reframing knowledge transfer as acts of translation. In language translation, the concepts of de-contextualization/contextualization points towards texts embedded in contexts. Thus, to translate requires that the translator, when dis-embedding, consciously makes explicit and preserves the often-implicit meaning that the context adds to the text and then makes it comprehensible in the target language and its context. Transfer of knowledge across organizational borders entails challenges that are similar, although not identical. The remainder of this chapter is organized according to these two key processes.

De-contextualization

In the context of knowledge transfers, de-contextualization refers to translating an identified organizational practice in an organization and its appurtenant knowledge base into an abstract representation (images, words, texts, pictures, etc.). The concept of "practice" is often associated with various kinds of *observable actions* (such as workers making movements, using technologies, etc.) rather than with thoughts and ideas. The concept of practice in this book refers to knowledge-based and routinized execution of specific organizational tasks. While the action aspect of a desired practice can often be observed while it is carried out, it is, by definition, much harder to identify and conceptualize the fine-grained knowledge it is based on. The knowledge represented among actors involved in the execution of a practice can be classified according to three main types. The first is *declarative knowledge*, which is also characterized as "knowing *that*," or facts, meaning knowledge of concrete and more or less static phenomenon (Apt et al., 1988). For example, it includes knowledge about the type of technology that is used in the execution of a practice; the types of products and/or services that the organization produces; and types of stakeholders, markets, customers, consumers, competitors, etc. Declarative knowledge is often verbalized and relatively easy to communicate. The second type is *procedural knowledge*, that is, knowledge about how to accomplish a task—insights into what actions are appropriate to take in which sequence to achieve defined goals, etc. (Georgeff and Lansky, 1986). While declarative knowledge is knowledge about concepts and facts, procedural knowledge is skills to perform certain tasks. The third type is *conditional knowledge*, which refers to involved actors' knowledge about the cause-and-effect chains that a desired practice is established on, and how and to what extent such cause-and-effect chains may work or not work under various conditions. Thus, it entails knowledge about why and when; that is, under which conditions the cause-and-effect chains work as desired, planned, and required to achieve goals, as well as knowledge about which conditions are likely to lead to distortions or breaks in the cause-and-effect chains (Antal, 2000).

These three types of knowledge can be summarized as knowing *what* (declarative), knowing *how to* (procedural), and knowing *why* and *when* (conditional). However, although analytically separated, the borders between these knowledge types are blurred. Involved actors usually apply and synthesize all types of knowledge when engaging in the execution of various practices.

Translatability

One of the main challenges when translating a desired practice in a source organization context is ensuring that all of the relevant aspects for how and why the practice works in the source context are identified and expressed in the obtained representations of it (such as images, texts, pictures). This critical phase accounts for many variations in the transfer of knowledge across organizational borders. The challenges of de-contextualization can be conceptualized in terms of the *translatability* of a desired source practice; that is, the extent to which a particular practice in an organizational context can be translated to an abstract representation without excluding the elements required for how it functions in the source context.

Based on synthesized insights from the domain of Translations studies and the target domain of Organizational knowledge transfers, three variables stand out as decisive for the translatability of a practice; the practice's *complexity*, *embeddedness*, and *explicitness*.

Complexity

The translatability of an organizational practice depends partly on its complexity. Two intertwined aspects constitute the antecedent of complexity, the human-technology factor, and the causal ambiguity factor.

The human-technology factor. This factor refers to the number of individuals involved in the accomplishment of a practice, and to the relationship between the involved actors and the technology in use. Based on literature reviews, it is reasonable to outline two general propositions.

The first suggests a connection between the number of individuals involved in the performance of a practice, the degree of required coordination between them, and the translatability of the practice—expressed as follows in propositional form:

> *Proposition 4.1. The higher the number of individuals involved in the accomplishment of a practice, and the more the accomplishment is dependent upon tight mutual coordinated actions among those involved, the more the translatability of the practice decreases.*

The proposed connections can be illustrated with examples from football. A first-class football team competing against another team on a field is the ultimate expression of complex interaction among a group of skilled individuals. What an excited watching audience can observe is the team's structure and the players' moves when defending and attacking the other team. However, what the audience *cannot* observe, and therefore cannot have firm knowledge about, is the continuous flows of decisions that all the players throughout the match are involved in; for example, how to move and act appropriately in relation to how they anticipate that their teammates will move and act, based on experience and intuition. An important part of the players' competence entails knowledge about their teammates and who, among them, have the skills to handle which situations, which is a version of the relational competence referred to as "knowing who knows what" (Argote, 1993; Hollingshead, 1998), or "transactive memory" (Wegner et al., 1991). It is very difficult to model such a complex practice performed by a rather large group of individuals; in other words, it is difficult to translate it to a high-fidelity representation of *what* happened and *why* it happened. Thus, it is hard to recreate such a practice in other contexts. This highlights the general insight that practices that depend on complex interaction among numerous individuals are probably the most difficult to transfer (Argote and Ingram, 2000; Berta and Baker, 2004; Probst and Borzillo, 2008; Tallman and Chacar, 2011).

The second proposition suggests a relationship between the technological base of a practice and its translatability—expressed as follows:

> Proposition 4.2. *The more the accomplishment of a practice is based on a technology with a clear-cut application, and the less it involves human individuals, the more the practice's translatability increases.*

Although such mainly technology-based practices—when transferred to other organizations—often need to be adapted to fit into the new contexts (Leonard-Barton and Deschamps, 1988; Douthwaite et al., 2001; Cascio and Montealegre, 2016), the translatability of such practices is often relatively high, meaning that it is, on average, relatively easy for translators to make high-fidelity representations of technology-driven practices. This reflects the fact that technology is often shaped as physical objects. Thus, although they are often very complex, they can be observed, and their *modus operandi* can be unveiled, understood, and replicated relatively easily. Some studies support these suggestions. Zander and Kogut (1995) found that knowledge that was clearly associated with the operation of certain technologies was more easily codified and transferred more rapidly than knowledge dissociated from technologies. Mansfield (1985) studied the speed at which various kinds of knowledge leaked out from innovating firms to competitor organizations. The study, which encompassed 100 American firms with innovating technology, showed that information about the technologies spread rapidly to rivals—and much faster than knowledge about organizational work processes and routines that were only weakly related to technology. Detailed information about the technology involved in various work processes was in the hands of rivals within a year, on average. Such findings contribute to my main argument about the relatively high translatability of technology, compared, for example, to knowledge about human skills and interpersonal relationships involved in the accomplishment of certain practices.

The causal ambiguity factor. The second antecedent of complexity is causal ambiguity. Attempts to transfer knowledge are often motivated by observations of good or superior results in certain organizations. However, the linkages between the observed results and the underlying factors that have generated the results are often unclear and ambiguous. It can be difficult to identify all the factors that contribute to the results, let alone how these factors intertwine, and thus difficult to define the relative importance of each factor. In their seminal paper, Lippman and Rumelt (1982) coined the concept of causal ambiguity, meaning "a basic, irreducible ambiguity concerning the nature of causal connections between actions and results" (Lippman and Rumelt 1982: 418). The concepts relate to "ambiguity as to how organizational actions and results, inputs and outcomes, or competencies and advantage are linked" (Konlechner and Ambrosini, 2019: 2352). The literature on the subject identifies various degrees of causal ambiguity—and points at possible consequences for knowledge transfer. Total, or basic causal ambiguity, characterizes situations in which the linkage between causes and results are fundamentally ambiguous, meaning that it could not be reduced to certainty even with great effort. According to Lippman and Rumelt (1982), uncertainty about such linkages is basically ambiguous in cases "where the factors responsible for performance differentials will resist precise identification" (p. 418). In such situations, actors in the organization's environment or within the organization do not possess the full knowledge of why a practice works as it does (Barney, 1991; Kaul, 2013).

However, uncertainty about the cause-and-effect linkages that underlie a desired practice is not always of the *total* causal ambiguity type. This means that uncertainty in such cases can be reduced (Mosakowski, 1997; Ambrosini and Bowman, 2005). It also means that superior knowledge of a practice's cause-and-effect relations is often unequally distributed among actors. The most typical asymmetric distribution is instances where actors *within* an organization have superior knowledge of a practice's cause-and-effect linkages, while actors located *outside* the organization may experience causal ambiguity regarding the same linkages. Such asymmetric distribution of knowledge of cause and effects is proclaimed to be a main barrier to imitation by outside located actors (Peteraf, 1993; Kim, 2013) and, consequently, a powerful source of competitive advantage (McEvily and Chakravarthy, 2002; Lawson et al., 2012; Bouncken, 2015). Studies have shown that competitors react to high levels of causal ambiguity in different ways, for example, by either toning down (Strang and Still, 2006) or intensifying their imitation efforts (Ordanini et al., 2008). They may also try to compensate for the causal ambiguity that characterizes the basis for another organization's competitive advantage by competence *substitution*, which means developing new knowledge, and/or new substituting products (Dosi and Marengo, 1993; McEvily et al., 2000).

While causal ambiguity frequently leads to competitive advantage, it also is a main source of distortions to knowledge transfer across organizational borders (Fang et al., 2013; Konlechner and Ambrosini, 2019). Lin (2003) studied learning processes in 86 organizations in Taiwan that transferred technologies from organizations located in foreign countries. He found that causal ambiguity regarding how the technology worked in the donor organizations propagated from the transfer process and left its marks on the subsequent processes of implementing and routinizing the usage of the technologies in the recipient organizations—in the sense that learning problems and implementation failure rates increased with increasing causal ambiguity.

The relationship between causal ambiguity and translatability can be expressed in the following proposition:

Proposition 4.3. Causal ambiguity of a source practice influences the practice's translatability, in that the more ambiguous the linkages between input factors and results, the harder it is to translate the practice to a representation that accounts for all the essentials for how it works in the source organization.

Embeddedness

Embeddedness is the second key variable that determines a practice's translatability. The concept of embeddedness is attributed to the economic historian Karl Polanyi, who developed it in his 1944 book entitled *The Great Transformation* (Polanyi, 1944) to catch what he argued was a typical feature of nonmarket societies. In contrast to modern market-based societies, economic exchanges among actors in nonmarket societies (such as peasant societies) are based on principles of reciprocity and redistribution embedded in social relationships and kinships (Block, 2003). In the 1970s, economic sociologist Mark Granovetter (1973; 1985) revitalized and developed the concept further. He argued against Polanyi's view that the logics of economics in modern market-based societies differed fundamentally from the social relationships-based economic exchanges in nonmarket societies. Granovetter's main argument was that even economic actors and their transactions are severely influenced—although not slavishly determined—by ties embedded in social networks. In addition to complexity, the translatability of a practice also depends on embeddedness; that is, the extent to which the knowledge that constitute a desired practice is anchored in the source organization's intra and/or interorganizational contexts. Two important aspects of the links between translatability and embeddedness need to be clarified. The first is a question about *where*, and the second about *how*.

The *where* question concerns the locus; that is, where and in which contexts are the knowledge embedded? Knowledge is sometimes highly concentrated, such as when almost all the necessary skills and knowledge for performing a desired practice are located within one organization or department (Foss and Pedersen, 2001), or within geographically concentrated clusters (Isaksen, 2009; Langen, 2002). On other occasions, and increasingly commonly, the knowledge is spatially dispersed in various and often loosely connected networks that crisscross organizational and national borders (Powell et al., 1996; Bresman et al., 2010; Fahy et al., 2014).

The degree of concentration or dispersion of a desired practice's knowledge base has consequences for the translatability of the practice, as expressed in the following proposition:

> Proposition 4.4. The more the knowledge base of a practice is spatially concentrated, the easier it is to identify and translate to a high-fidelity representation.

On the other hand, dispersed knowledge bases embedded in loosely connected interorganizational networks deployed at different places present translators with the challenge of how to identify and demarcate the exact knowledge base of a desired practice (Mosakowski, 1997; Hong and Nguyen, 2009; Erkelens et al., 2015). Such a condition has consequences for the translatability of the practice, in propositional form:

> Proposition 4.5. The more the knowledge base of a desired practice is dispersed and embedded in interorganizational networks at different places, the more challenging it is to demarcate and the harder it is to translate to a high-fidelity representation.

The *how* question concerns the type and strength/weakness of the anchoring of the knowledge to the various "beds" in which it is embedded. The concept of "embeddedness" differs from other conceptualizations of how knowledge is deployed in organizations (such as "repositories" and "reservoirs") because it signals that knowledge can be ingrained in, "take root," and be tied to its "beds." A corresponding, almost synonymous concept is "situated knowledge," which is coined and applied within the community of the practice–research tradition (Lave and Wenger, 1991; Brown and Duguid, 2001). According to McGrath and Argote (2001), knowledge can be embedded in four basic elements of organizations: in individuals (both members and nonmembers), in various types of technologies and tools, in tasks, and in various subnetworks that connect the elements.

The translator, whose task here is to make a high-fidelity representation of the embedded knowledge, faces the challenge of *dis-embedding*, which is separating the embedded knowledge from its various "beds." This can sometimes be challenging because the knowledge and the "beds"—such as tools, individuals, tasks, and social networks—are so intertwined that they stand out as almost inseparable, as in cases of intertwining of a certain adapted tool and the human skills needed to operate it. For example, Moreland et al.

(1996) studied an attempt to move a network of member-task relations (called a *transactive memory system* (TMS) network) from the group where it was developed to another group with other members. The researchers explained that because the knowledge of how to make the TMS system work was so embodied in the members of the original group, attempts to replace these members with other individuals caused the failure. Thus, highly embedded knowledge is often nonmigratory in nature. However, knowledge can also be moderately and even loosely embedded, as in cases where the knowledge necessary for operating certain technologies is condensed in written instructions and manuals (Lillrank, 1995).

The above insights can be summarized in propositional form:

Proposition 4.6. The more a desired practice's knowledge base is embedded in organizational elements, such as technologies, tasks, individuals, and social relations, the harder it is to dis-embed and translate to a high-fidelity representation.

Explicitness

Knowledge among the source-based actors about a desired practice can be explicit or tacit (Polanyi, 1958; 1962; 1967). Explicit knowledge is codified, verbalized, well-articulated (Nonaka and Takeuchi, 1995; Li and Gao, 2003) and easily taught, written, and expressed; for example, in formulas and manuals (Bejan and Kraus, 2003; Martin and Salomon 2003). The concept of "proximal"—or tacit knowledge, as theorized by Michael Polanyi (1958), refers to the nonverbalized, noncodified and nonstandardized knowledge that underlies a skillful performance. Tacit knowledge cannot be easily talked about and taught to newcomers, nor transformed to manuals and explicit procedures. There are two main reasons why the whole or parts of the knowledge base of a desired practice can remain tacit. The first is that tacit knowledge is usually developed through practical experience where actors learn skills, not through language lessons, but by observation, imitation, and trial-and-error processes (Nonaka et al. 1994). Such knowledge can be hard to codify and verbalize, both for outsiders and even for the involved practitioners (Howells, 1996). According to Spender (1993), "effortless-ness" is a key feature of tacit knowledge, meaning that practitioners who use it are often unaware of the knowledge being applied. Thus, tacit knowledge is often "incommunicable" (Polanyi, 1962). However, there is also another reason why tacit knowledge is not made explicit. Keeping tacit knowledge tacit and protected from being accessed by outsiders is often part of a strategy to secure competitive advantage (McAuly et al., 1997; Berman et al., 2002). This reflects the fact that tacit knowledge is often conceived of as the most valuable knowledge in an organization (Leonard and Sensiper, 1998; Hadjimichael and Tsoukas, 2019).

The explicit–tacit variable has consequences for the translatability of a desired practice. The more explicit the knowledge, the easier it is to translate into an even more codified and transferable representation. In the translation of tacit knowledge, the source language is somehow missing, which means that the translator must conduct a two-step translation. First, the tacit knowledge must be verbalized in order to be communicable. Then, the verbalized, context-specific knowledge must be translated to a more abstract and transferable representation. This increases the chances of misinterpretation, such that a mismatch may arise between the tacit knowledge and its translated abstract representation. There have been debates within translation studies about how to express explicitly in the translated target text version what is implicit in the source text (Blum-Kulka, 1986). This is referred to as "explicitation," which means making explicit in the target version something that was implied or understood through presupposition in the source version (Øverås, 1998; Abdrashitova et al., 2018). This is a challenging task for the translator, because making the tacit explicit involves increased risks of translation failures, and calls not only for bilingual competence, but also for bicultural competence.

The connections between explicitness/tacitness and translatability can be expressed as follows:

Proposition 4.7. The more explicit (codified and verbalized) a desired source practice is, the higher its translatability. Correspondingly: the less explicit the knowledge base of a desired practice, the lower its translatability—and the higher the chances for loosing of elements that are essential for the functioning of the practice in the source organization.

Source practices as variations of translatability

In principle, all practices can be analyzed as combinations and variations of the three variables that determine translatability. Consider the two following examples:

The case of Airline cabin crews

A passenger aircraft has two crews: the cabin crew and the flight crew (pilots). Here we investigate the translatability of the cabin crew's practices. Such a crew, which handles service and security tasks, usually consists of four to five people on short flights and up to eight people on longer, overseas flights. The two features of complexity are the human-technology factor and the causal ambiguity factor. Regarding the first factor, the service work of cabin crews towards the passengers is carried out with modest use of technology (kitchen heater, credit card machines, etc.). However, an airplane is a coherent technological system with a certain *modus operandi*, which largely defines and determines the roles and tasks of each cabin crew member. For example, the knowledge and drilled skills that cabin crew members possess about on-board security are mostly related to the airplane as a technological system.

One might think that carrying out a practice, which involves up to eight members of a crew team, is complex because it presupposes tight and coordinated actions among the members (cf. proposition 4.1). However, this is not the case here because the roles and tasks of each individual member are described and defined so clearly and in detail that the accomplishment of each individual's tasks is only modestly dependent upon mutual coordinated actions with other crew members.

Due to highly routine- and experience-based work operation, the cabin crew members' practices involve modest levels of causal ambiguity (lack of knowledge about how actions and outcomes are linked). However, the airline industry is an international business, and research has shown that that passengers' expectations of airliners' service types and levels vary significantly between different ethnic groups/nationalities (Gilbert and Wong, 2003. In addition, studies have revealed gaps between the services provided by the cabin crew and passengers' expectations, and further, that such gaps vary with passengers' ethnic and/or national background (Parasuraman et al., 1993; Sultan and Simpson, 2000). This increases the pressure on cabin crew members to reduce standardization, be able to identify various passenger groups' different service expectations, and differentiate the service provided accordingly. It also increases chances for causal ambiguity, meaning that the links between the services provided and passengers' level of satisfaction become more ambiguous.

Cabin crews' practices can also be assessed in light of the explicitness/tacit variable. Although there certainly are elements of tacit knowledge involved when cabin crew members relate to individual passengers (Sigala and Chalkiti, 2007), most of the knowledge that they need to carry out their tasks are highly verbalized and explicit. Each crew member has their own *Cabin Crew Operation Manual* (about 450–500 pages), which describe in detail all kinds of tasks that should be done and situations that may occur during a flight, and how the crew member should handle them. This means that the practice of each cabin member has been de-contextualized and expressed in a detailed representation. Each crew member is also obliged to report explicitly—written and/or orally—all kinds of irregularities they may have observed on a flight. In addition, crew members usually have a tablet on which, before each flight, they are provided with written flight-specific information (weather, number and types of passengers, etc.).

The key variable "embeddedness" concerns questions about where the knowledge to be used is located (concentrated or dispersed), and about how difficult/easy it is to release the knowledge from its "beds." The knowledge that cabin crews use when they practice is only modestly embedded. Most of the knowledge they need is located in the operation manual. This knowledge is also very available in downloaded versions on each crew members' tablet. The members are trained and requested always to have their tablet available and to use it.

Comparatively, the knowledge base of cabin crew members comes out as high on explicitness, low on embeddedness, and rather low on complexity. This indicates that the translatability of this practice is rather high, meaning that the knowledge needed can be quite easily translated to high-fidelity representations without crucial information being lost in translation. For example, the translatability and replicability of this practice come to expression in the high rotation of individuals in cabin teams. It is common for a new crew member to join a cabin crew team almost every day—indicating that the knowledge needed to do the work is not embedded in the relations between particular individuals. A trained cabin crew member can also easily change employer and switch from one airline to another.

The case of stockfish production

The second example is related to the production of stockfish—and especially to the practices of the stockfish quality sorters. Here the translatability is quite different from the cabin crews' practices. Stockfish is made from codfish, a dark-spotted fish that is widespread in the North Atlantic and usually caught at about 25 pounds (11–12 kilos). Each year, in December/early January the cod swim from the Barents Sea, down the coast of Northern Norway and end up in the sea surrounding the Lofoten islands, an archipelago that protrudes into the Norwegian Sea. Here the cods have their spawning ground. The Lofoten cod fishery from late January to the middle of April has taken place for hundreds of years. The total caught varies between approximately 65,000 and 100,000 tons per year. About 18–20,000 tons are used yearly to produce stockfish. The workers hang the cleaned fish on large drying racks. In June, the then-dried fish have turned into stockfish and are collected from the racks and stored in-house. Then, in the autumn, the sorting process starts. Almost all stockfish are exported. In fact, stockfish is the oldest Norwegian export article, with a history starting even before the Viking era (Korneliussen and Panozza, 2005). Roughly half of the yearly stockfish production is exported to various regions in Italy (Korneliussen and Pedersen, 2001). The second largest market is Nigeria, followed by the United States and Croatia. The important point is that the different markets demand different types of stockfish. In Italy, the largest market, there are different quality demands in different regions (Nygård and Ingebrigtsen, 2019).

The different market demands make the knowledge and the work of *the stockfish sorter* (in Norwegian, the *vraker*) very important. The *vraker* must be knowledgeable about the quality of the stockfish and must be able to combine this knowledge with thorough knowledge about the quality demands from each market. Thus, the main challenge for the *vraker* is to inspect each stockfish and to grade and sort it according to 20 different categories, reflecting the demands of the different markets (Borch and Korneliussen, 1995). The competence and skills required to be a *vraker* are scarce, but also very decisive for the fishing company in order to be able to satisfy the various segments of customers, and thus, for the earnings of the fish company. Therefore, the knowledgeable and skilled *vrakers* have been highly esteemed actors in each company and in the fishing villages of the Lofoten islands.

The sorting practices' translatability can be analyzed in terms of its *complexity*. As to the human-technology factor, the sorting practice is done almost without using any machines or other tools. A sorting team usually consists of four or five people: that is, three or four assistants and the *vraker*. The assistants bring the stockfish to the well-lit sorter's table and then use a sharp tool to cut and open up the neck of the fish so that the *vraker* can inspect it, even its insides. The *vraker* assesses and classifies every stockfish. It is a time-consuming work—a skilled *vraker* sorts 200–300 kilos per working hour. The work is carried out as mutually coordinated actions among experienced actors and with minor use of verbal communication. As to *causal ambiguity*, the involved actors in the sorter team usually possess a firm mutual understanding of how knowledge, skills, and each member's task performance are linked to the quality of the outcome; that is, to the level of sustained accuracy of the sorting process in relation to the twenty categories. Thus, the "insiders" usually do not experience causal ambiguity. For outsiders, however (that is, those actors who are not involved in the sorting process and do not share the insiders' knowledge), it is almost impossible to understand and to recreate the stockfish sorting process.

As to the *explicit/tacitness variable*, the practice of stockfish sorting is mainly based on nonverbalized knowledge and skills. Some quality criteria are relatively explicit, such as the length, weight, and thickness of the stockfish. However, numerous other criteria and assessment techniques are much less explicit and hard to express in precise language. Almost all of the sorter's senses—smell, taste, and sight (assessment of the fish' shape and color), in addition to using the fingers to systematically touch and squeeze all parts of the fish, must be applied in order to reach a correct decision. The best way to learn the tacit *vraking* skills is by practicing for a long time in close cooperation with a skilled *vraker*.

Regarding "embeddedness," the crucial knowledge of how to practice stockfish quality assessment is embodied in the *vraker*. However, it is also embedded in a chain of fish-related actors, activities, and competencies at sea and in each local fishing village in the Lofoten islands (Hauan, 2000). Examples include the cod fishermen operating at sea in their vessels, who are aware of and act under the influence of quality standards for how to handle the fish before it is hung; and "the hangmen" who—influenced by the same quality standards—bind two and two raw fishes to each other, hang them appropriately on the enormous racks, and take the dried fish down from the racks about two months later. The practice of stockfish production is also embedded in special natural conditions in the Lofoten area. At the exact time that the steams of cod arrive at the Lofoten Sea (late January) and the spawning process takes place (January–April), the natural conditions for making stockfish in Lofoten are probably the best in the world; the temperature at this time of the year is seldom below the freezing point (which avoids frost damaged fish), and mild but not hot (which prevents hung fish from rotting). Besides, this time of the year usually provides perfect wind conditions for the cod-drying process.

In conclusion, the practice of stockfish production and sorting involves high complexity, low explicitness, and high embeddedness. Taken together, it indicates that this is a practice of low translatability, meaning that it is hard to make high-fidelity representation of, and almost impossible to dis-embed and recreate it at places outside the Lofoten islands.

Translators and de-contextualization processes

De-contextualization processes, which means the translation of identified practices and their knowledge bases into abstract representations, can be scrutinized in light of their *whos* and *hows*. Who are usually "the de-contextualizers" (that is, the translators involved in processes of dis-embedding concrete practices) and how do they do it?

Although various actors are involved in dis-embedding and translating source practices to representations, it is reasonable to distinguish between three main types of such actors—labeled here as outsiders, expatriates, and insiders. They differ, among other things, on key variables, such their localization and proximity in relation to source organizational contexts.

Outsiders as de-contextualizers
Practices can be de-contextualized by outsiders, meaning actors located outside and being nonmembers of the source organization where the desired practice is located. Among the most common external "de-contextualizers" are large and medium-sized consulting companies (Walgenbach and Hegele, 2001; Francis and Holloway, 2007; Gill et al., 2020). They are key actors in what can be termed the modern knowledge transfer industry, a global field of knowledge trading that emerged and has grown since the early 1990s (Røvik, 2007). The core of this industry is built around the concept of "best practices" and on the belief that such practices can be identified in almost all fields of human activities (by systematic surveillance and benchmarking of a large number of organizations), dis-embedded, and thereafter traded and spread. A best practice can be defined as "a set of interrelated work activities repeatedly utilized by individuals or groups" (Tucker et al., 2007) that is accepted as being better than all other known practices because it is supposed to lead to results that are superior to results that are superior to those caused by other known practices.

Within the knowledge transfer industry, benchmarking is the rationalized, scientized, and legitimate method for identifying and comparing almost all kinds of organizational practices—and finding the superior ones among them; that is, those that are held as responsible for the greatest performance and competitive differences between organizations (Bendell et al., 1998). The American consultant company Arthur Andersen was one of the first to systematize the identification, dis-embedding, and transfer of best practices based on a benchmarking strategy. This strategy has been thoroughly described in a book authored by three Arthur Andersen-senior consultants (Hiebeler et al., 1998). The book provides an interesting window into the notions, theories, arguments, and technology that drive what Sanwal (2008: 52) calls the ideology of "best practicism," and also insights into how the search for such practices is organized. Firstly, Arthur Andersen's "Global Best Practice Database" was based on the premise that a common feature of all types of organizations (public services, governmental units, business units, interest groups, etc.) is that they are all formal organizations (Røvik, 2007). Therefore, although they are different, they are variations of the same system. This is an important premise for the notion that they all need and can use more or less the same ideas and practices (Jacobsson, 1994; Brunsson and Sahlin-Andersson, 2000; Røvik, 2012; Bromley and Meyer, 2017). Hiebeler et al.'s (1998) second premise is that all organizations' practices can be subsumed and classified into 260 subprocesses, which are then variations of a set of 13 so-called first-level processes. According to these authors, this process approach makes it possible for consultants to (a) use their classification of processes and practices to identify the corresponding processes and practices in concrete organizations, and (b) to benchmark the practices and results of each process in a concrete organization with information in the database about the corresponding processes and practices. The Arthur Andersen approach is typical of many large and medium-sized consultant companies' best practice and benchmarking strategies (Walgenbach and Hegele, 2001; Kieser, 2002; Castro and Frazzon, 2017; Madsen et al., 2017).

However, consulting companies that have adopted the benchmarking strategy outlined above face many challenges when it comes to identifying organizational best practices and transferring them to high-fidelity representations. One challenge is to ensure that the practices in the consultancies' databases really correspond to the practices identified in concrete organizations. This requires that enormous empirical variations of organizational processes and practices be reduced and subsumed in a far less complex *classification* of such practices. Another challenge is the problem of organizational practices that are embedded in, and thus dependent upon their contexts, which means that it is often hard to overview and know which factors have generated which results (Davies and Kochhar, 2002). Wellstein and Kieser (2011) conducted one of the few empirical studies of how consultant companies cope with these and other challenges related to identifying, translating, and transferring organizational best practices. The study was based on quantitative data from 152 large and medium-sized consultancies consulting on strategy and organizational design in the German market, as well as qualitative data from in-depth interviews with a sample of individual consultants. They found that most of the consulting companies used benchmarking as their main method for identifying and transferring best practices. However, they also found that their definitions and understandings of best practice differed significantly between the consultants, and among consultants belonging to the same company. They also revealed vaguely agreements about how exactly to identify such practices. Wellstein and Kieser showed that consultants tend to conceive of practices as solutions that can easily be identified and transferred within as well as between separate and different organizations. They also focused on the consultants' opinions and experiences concerning "stickiness factors" in identifying best practices and in making high-fidelity representations of them. The quantitative study revealed that consultants conceive of causal ambiguity and the complexities of practices' embeddedness in contexts as a main challenge and threat to realizing the ambition of identifying and representing best practices. Wellstein and Kieser also found a strong inhibiting effect due to the consulting companies' lack of absorptive capacity, meaning that the consultancies themselves have limited capacity to absorb and understand—and thus to describe and communicate to potential customers/target organizations—the causality structures involved in the best practices they have identified in source organizations.

Expatriates as de-contextualizers
Old Norse mythology includes the narrative of Huginn and Muninn, the two ravens of the god Odin, the most powerful and knowledgeable of all the Nordic gods (Sturlusson, 1964). While the Old Norse meaning of Huginn is "thought," the meaning of Muninn is "memory." Every morning, the two ravens fly out from Odin's residence, Valaskjalv, and all over the world ("Midgard") to collect information for Odin. When they return in the evening, they sit down on Odin's shoulders and inform the god about the knowledge they have collected on their journey. This keeps Odin updated and is a main source of his knowledge and his status as the omniscient god.

The tale of Huginn and Muninn has parallels to modern transnational organizations' usage of expatriates—so-called international assignments. An "expatriate" is an employee who is sent abroad to work in a subsidiary unit for periods of varying length, while an "repatriate" is an expatriate who returns to his/her domestic organization, either the headquarter or other units from where they departed (Antal, 2001; McEvoy and Buller, 2013). Such international assignments have increased within transnational organizations (Stahl et al., 2009), partly as a way to spread knowledge from headquarters to subsidiaries, and partly to identify valuable practices and knowledge in subsidiaries abroad and to speed up the transfer of such knowledge to other units.

Here, the focus is upon the potential for expatriates to identify and de-contextualize practices and their appurtenant knowledge bases in subsidiaries. Expatriates' access to such knowledge in subsidiaries differs from that of outsiders (such as external consultants) in two important respects. The first is that expatriates, unlike outsiders, are members of the transnational organization, and therefore belong to a knowledge-sharing community.

The second difference is that they reside—albeit temporarily—in the subsidiary organization, which obviously increases their chances of accessing valuable knowledge. However, an expatriate's access to knowledge will depend on the length of the stay: the longer the stay, the more access. Data from the World Bank on multinational organizations usage of expat works shows that the length of the assignments has fallen. In 2008, 66 percent of the total assignments were long-term (duration of more than one year, typically three years), while only 45 percent of 2014 assignments were long-term (Tung, 1987; Harrison, 2016).

What do expatriates bring with them from subsidiaries? Research shows that they frequently develop networks and social ties with members of the subsidiary organization (Hocking et al., 2007; Burmeister, 2017; Peltokorpi et al., 2022). Such ties facilitate the expatriates' own cultural adjustment (Farh et al., 2010) and are an important source to increased trust (Hansen, 2002; Reiche 2012), and therefore a potential ticket to embedded knowledge (Downes and Thomas, 1999; Burmeister, 2017). Research also shows that the social capital that expatriates develop during their stays abroad can provide access and shorten the route to subsidiary knowledge long after the assignees have repatriated to their home bases (Reiche, 2012).

Few studies have documented what kind of knowledge expatriates are interested in and try to identify, translate, and transfer, and even fewer studies have looked at how they do that. In one of the first studies of repatriates, Antal (2000) distinguished between five types of knowledge that repatriates may bring with them home: know that (declarative), know how (procedures, routines), know when (conditional), know why (axiomatic), and know whom (relational). In a study of expatriates from Austrian commercial banks, Fink and Meierewert (2005) found that expatriates often identify and transfer knowledge of relatively high translatability, such as language, and about technical issues. However, they sometimes also acquire access to less codifiable knowledge, such as job-related management skills, and local experience-based knowledge about problem solving. Oddou et al. (2013) studied knowledge gained by a sample of expatriates who repatriated to their home bases in Germany (15), Japan (17), and the United States (15). Their main finding were that expatriates had gained new networks (*know who*), acquired global mindsets (*know why*), and developed some new competencies (*know how*). They sometimes also identify and try to make representations of valuable knowledge and practices of low translatability (tacit, complex, and embedded). However, neither this nor other studies have specified in detail to what extent or how expatriates are involved in detecting and de-contextualizing practices of low translatability.

Insiders as de-contextualizers

Insiders—that is, actors who are based within the organization where the desired practice to be de-contextualized are performed—can, in addition to outsiders and expatriates, also perform de-contextualization of practices. Insiders are individuals who are members of the source organization where the desired practice is located. Certain insiders can act as de-contextualizers (or "outbringers"), in the sense that they make representations of a practice that they know well, and which they mediate in different ways and on different arenas outside their organization.

Various types of insiders can act as de-contextualizers and outbringers of knowledge about certain organizational practices. There are upper-level as well as lower-level outbringers. Typical upper-level outbringers are top leaders (executives and CEOs) who are clearly associated with successes in their organization. Great successes, especially in large, well-known organizations, are sometimes springboards for their top leaders to be invited to various external arenas to give speeches about "the secrets" of the successes. In addition to speeches, probably the most prominent way for top leaders to bring out their versions of certain organizational successes is to write a book about it and popularize their success formula. Examples of publications in this genre are Iacocca and Novak (1986), who wrote about how Lee Iacocca, CEO of Chrysler throughout the 1980s, changed the automaker company and brought it back from the brink of collapse. Packard et al. (1995) presented "the secrets" of the success of Hewlett & Packard—as told by David Packard—and how he and his colleague managed to found a company "in a one-car garage workshop" that later became the famous science park of Silicon Valley. In his book, Sam Walton, the founder of Wal-Mart, tells the story of how the successful American retail business was created (Walton and Huey, 1993), and Mary Kay Ash, who built one of the world's largest cosmetic retailers, writes about the principles behind her organization's success (Ash, 2008).

While top leaders of large organizations are obviously the most exposed and best-known outbringers, de-contextualization and outbringing by individuals in other, lower positions in the organization are probably even more common. Typical outbringers are middle managers, project managers, team leaders and members, etc. who become associated with a certain practice and are invited to present and talk about the practice in various arenas outside their own organization.

Røvik (2007) studied a sample of such lower-level outbringers. The overarching research purpose was to find out what characterizes the practices that the outbringers bring out, and how they do it. To be included in the sample, the following four criteria had to be fulfilled: (1) What is brought out and presented must be a representation of a certain practice performed in an identified organization; (2) the outbringer must be, or have been, employed in the organization and must have been directly involved in the development and performance of the practice; (3) the outbringer must have presented the practice at least five times in arenas outside her/his own organization; and (4) the sample shall include practices from business organizations as well as public sector and interest organizations.

To identify candidates for inclusion, the author contacted three professional organizations that sell and organize courses and conferences, offering competence on various aspects of working life, such as leadership, budgeting, accounting, human resources, and technology innovations. These are arenas in which insiders associated with certain successful practices are frequently invited to talk about their practice to various audiences. It is worth noting that outbringers performing in such arenas are only taking part in the de-contextualization of a practice. Thus, as a rule, they are not involved in "the other half" of the knowledge transfer process; that is, the contextualization of the representation in a target organization. Fifteen outbringers and their appurtenant practices were initially identified and included. After closer examination, three were excluded, meaning that the study sample contained 12 outbringers.

Three examples of the twelve practices they made representations of are outlined below. The first was a practice termed *wish rotation planning*. This is a practice for how to plan the rotation of personnel within healthcare institutions. The practice emerged within a unit in the healthcare sector in a Norwegian medium-sized municipality. The development of the practice was widely ascribed to and associated with efforts made by the person who later performed at various external arenas and presented the wish rotation planning practice. Instead of applying the most common practice in this field (whereby the leader or the administrator fairly autonomously works out the authoritative rotation plan for the next period), the wish rotation planning practice required that all employees and the leader met every sixth week. In such a meeting, anyone was allowed and encouraged to present and argue for his/her wishes for the next six-week rotation plan. Then there was a negotiation and balancing process. The meeting ended once the new rotation plan had been settled. According to the inventor and outbringer, this rotation planning practice is a procedure that increases employee involvement, enhances legitimacy, prevents conflicts, and reduces sickness absence. Another example is a *professional grief-process practice*. In this case, the outbringer was a hospital priest who had become known and widely respected for his professional methods and practice of approaching people in critical life situations, such as life-threatening illnesses. A third example was the practice of design and operation of a professional *customer service center*. Based on his own experience from working with Hewlett & Packard, this outbringer mediated insights about good practices for how to develop and run a service center for customers in large organizations.

Key questions in this study were, what characterizes the twelve practices that these outbringers present at external arenas, do they have anything in common. One central suggestion concerned the practices' translatability. It was hypothesized that successful practices characterized by a low degree of translatability, more than by outsiders and expatriates, will need to be decontextualized and translated by insiders; that is, by actors who themselves have been involved in performing the practice. Thus, the suggestion was that among the included practices there would be an overrepresentation of practices characterized by low translatability.

To test this suggestion, the twelve practices were analyzed according to operationalized criteria of two of the three determining variables of translatability: complexity and embeddedness. (The practices' degree of "explicitness" were not analyzed, partly because of methodological challenges, and partly because the outbringers themselves had all made explicit versions of their practices). "Degree of complexity" was operationalized as follows: (a) Is the practice mostly performed without (1 point) or with (0 point) the use of technology? (b) Are there many—ten or more (1 point)—or few—fewer than ten (0 points)—individuals involved in the performance of the practice? (c) Does the performance of the practice require involvement of individuals with experience-based special competence? Yes (1 point). No (0 point). The maximum points per practice was three, which indicates high complexity. Zero points indicates low complexity.

"Embeddedness" is operationalized as follows: (a) *Low embeddedness*—all relevant inputs required to perform the practice (such as knowledge, skills, budget, technology, decision-making authority, and workers) are highly spatially concentrated; that is, located within the actual organizational unit (1 point). (b) *Medium embeddedness*—some of the relevant input resources required to perform the practice are located in other units of the organization; that is, outside the unit where the practice is performed (2 points). (c) *High embeddedness*—several of the input resources required to perform the practice are located in networks that connect the organizational unit with different parts of the environment (3 points).

Findings. A high score (maximum 6) indicates low translatability, while a low score indicates high translatability. Eight of the 12 practices were appointed a score of 6 or 5, two practices scored 4 and one practice scored 3.

Thus, data strongly support the suggestion that low translatability is a common feature of practices that the insiders de-contextualize and translate, and are invited to present on external arenas. In other words, most of them are especially hard to translate into high-fidelity representations. In sum, this indicates that insiders as translators have certain advantages compared to outsiders and expatriates to de-contextualize practices of low translatability.

Contextualization

While de-contextualization is the translation from source practice to an abstract representation of the practice, contextualization refers to the translation of such a representation to new practice in the target organization—a process also referred to as "recontextualization" (Bausch, 2022). This means that an attempt has been made to materialize the representation in a foreign organizational context. A target organizational context is never a tabula rasa, a blank slate (Røvik, 2011). When a representation of a source practice enters the target organization where it is supposed to be materialized, it comes into a context of a more-or-less fixed physical structure (buildings, spaces, rooms, walls, furnishings, etc.) and a formal organizational structure, which defines a hierarchy and the division of work. Further, there are various technologies in use, established routines and procedures, informal networks, communication patterns, and organizational cultures and meaning-production systems that provide lenses for interpreting and making sense of the organization's history, as well as its present and future. Finally yet importantly, a target organization includes individuals who act according to reasons, interests, and emotions, using their knowledge and skills to perform existing tasks. Contextualization refers to processes whereby a representation of a source practice both influences and is influenced by the organizational context in which it is introduced. The concept of contextualization encompasses cognitive processes, but also, as highlighted by Reay et al. (2013), concrete materialization processes of transforming the representations into practices and to physical, repeated activities.

Analytically, we can distinguish between three key processes involved in contextualization. These are *conceptualization*, that is, processes whereby the translator gains knowledge about the target context and existing practices, *configuration*, that is, processes of relating the source practice representation to target context features, and *inscribing,* that is, translation processes where meaning, which connects "the new" to the target organizational context, is ascribed to the introduced foreign practice. Although they are presented in the above sequence in the following, these processes are, in reality, highly intertwined. Thus, they may run almost parallel in time and involve various and shifting groups of actors.

Conceptualizing the target organizational context

To conceptualize a representation of a source practice, translators need to gain knowledge about the target organizational context. The outcomes—successes or failures—depend partly on how knowledgeable the translator is about the target organization (Røvik, 2016). Within the domain of translation studies, the care for such knowledge comes to expression in norms for translators to adhere to the target context. According to influential scholars, particularly within Skopos theory (Vermeer, 1978; Hönig and Kußmaul, 1982), and the manipulation school (Hermans, 1985/2014; Toury, 1985), this means being especially sensitive to the logics and the needs of the target context and, subsequently, designing translated versions of the source practice premised on anticipations of whether and how it will fit in and work in the target context. However, for translators it can be challenging to gain knowledge about the target context. *How* challenging it is depends on features of the target context practices—that is, their translatability—and on the location of the translators.

Just as the translatability of the source practice is a key variable with which to understand the challenges of translating such practices to abstract representations, the translatability of existing target organization practices is important in order to get a clearer picture of the challenges that translators face when attempting to gain knowledge about such practices. Here, "translatability" refers to how easy or difficult it is for the translators to obtain accurate knowledge about various existing practices in the target context—practices that may interfere directly or indirectly with the source practice representation determined to be implemented. The translatability of existing target practices can be analyzed in terms of the same three variables as those used to analyze source practices: explicitness, complexity, and embeddedness.

Explicitness of existing target practices
As defined earlier in this chapter, the features of explicitness are codified, verbalized, easily taught and written knowledge, while tacitness refers to nonverbalized, noncodified, and nonstandardized knowledge. The knowledge and skills of actors involved in the performance of existing practices

in target organizations vary according to explicitness/tacitness. The more explicit target practices are, the easier it is for translators to "read," conceptualize and take consideration of them when shaping a target organization version of the source practice to be implemented.

However, the knowledge base of existing target organization practices may also be tacit (uncodified and not verbalized), which can be challenging for the translators, and a potential source of translation failures. An illuminating example is provided by the case of knowledge transfer from the United States to the British coal-mining industry in the early 1930s (Stewart, 1935; Mowat, 1963). What was transferred and implemented was knowledge of new technology, mechanization of production, and scientific management—inspired principles of work organizing. However, the new ideas and practices were introduced in a U.K. context with different existing principles and practices of coal mining. The traditional method of coal mining until the beginning of the 1920s, the so-called *handgot system*, was performed by several groups of three, sometimes two colliers (coal-workers), each group working at different locations on the coalface (the place inside a mine where the coal is cut out of the rock). The coal was obtained by a combination of blasting and the use of a pick, then loaded on tubs and transported by hand power to the pithead. The working unit of three men was largely self-contained. The members performed all the tasks necessary to produce coal—such as blasting, picking, loading the tubs, and transporting the coal. The working groups were also relatively autonomous in relation to the deputy (the local manager). The deputy was the first-line supervisor for 15 up to 20 working units. His function was limited to securing the mine from accidents of explosions and falls, in addition to organizing the transportation of coal out from each team. Thus, the deputy's role in relation to the team was more of a supplier than of a manager. The teams "required neither instruction nor coordination" (Trist and Bamforth, 1951: 215). Each team decided and organized its own work autonomously and was paid each week for the coal volume it produced. The members of the team were independent craftsmen who had learned their skills not from their employers, but from their fathers and relatives (Goldthorpe, 1959). They even used their own tools and "powder" (explosives) in the mines. They were often recruited to the teams through family and kinship ties.

Between the two World Wars, *longwall mining*—a rather new method of coal-getting—was being implemented on a massive scale in British coal mines. This method, which originated in England in the late seventeenth century, and was radically developed in the United States with the use of machinery in the beginning of the twentieth century, is a method for underground coal mining where a long wall, sometimes hundreds of meters long, containing seams of coal, is mined in a single slice (Penn and Simpson, 1986). During the interwar period (1918–1940), the British coal industry was largely mechanized, primarily through the introduction of electric coal-cutting machines and conveyor belts, which automatized the transportation of coal out from the mines. The introduction of new coal-getting methods and new technology were accompanied by scientific management-inspired principles for work organizing. The system of self-contained teams with multi-skilled miners who performed all tasks involved in the coal-mining process was replaced by a strong division of labor into three shifts: one for cutting the coal, another for ripping the coal, and a third shift for fillers (workers who use shovels and load coal on the conveyor belts). Following the logic of the Ford fabric assembly line—organizing, the work process was clearly sequenced (cutting shift, ripping shift, and filling shift) and could not be changed. The multitasking character of work in the self-contained teams was replaced by standardization and specializing at the individual level. Each worker should not perform more than one or two operations. In addition, the role of the deputy changed dramatically. In the new organizing of mining, the deputy was supposed to coordinate and execute tight control over each individual worker's performance of their operations.

In a renowned research program, starting at the Tavistock Institute in London in the late 1940s, Eric Trist and Ken Bamforth studied the consequences of introducing the new technology and the new principles of work organizing in the British coal mines. They concentrated on studying fillers shifts, where most men worked. In their seminal 1951 paper, they showed that the new methods and principles had severe effects on the colliers. The "self-autonomy" from the handgot system was lost and the fillers now experienced "isolated dependence" (pp. 24–25), meaning that each filler now worked alone in his stint, not interacting with or even seeing other colleagues. Absenteeism was high, and a strong norm of low productivity developed among the fillers. These were the behaviors that Trist and Bamforth (1951) used to explain workers' adaptation to the new organizing principles.

The above case from the British mining industry is an example of new technology and practices that were introduced in an organizational context and led to serious tensions in relation to existing ideas and practices of work organizing. Trist and Bamforth's explanation of *why* the transfer and implementation of new technology and work organizing collided with existing practices and caused severe unanticipated consequences is centered on an argument of *low explicitness* of important aspects of the existing practices. They found that the problems of absenteeism, morale hazard, and low productivity largely reflected the workers' psychological and social reactions to the changes in the working conditions. However, Trist and Bamforth revealed that the workers themselves lacked insights into—as well as the language to verbalize and thereby make explicit—the psychological and social consequences of what they had experienced after losing their "responsible autonomy" following the breakup of the self-contained work groups. In addition, the tacitness of the psychological and sociological aspects were also effects of the almost total dominating engineering logic and appurtenant language among the top leaders, middle managers, and local deputies. This engineering logic was an effective hindrance for leaders to conceptualize the psychological and sociological roots of the problems: "That they (the problems of the longwall method) require understanding in social and psychological terms, is something that still remains largely unrecognized. Accounts so far appearing, have presented recent changes almost exclusively in engineering terms" (Trist and Bamforth, 1951: 10).

Complexity of existing target practices

The ability of a translator to conceptualize, comprehend, and consider existing target practices when implementing new practices also depends on the *complexity* of existing practices. The greater the complexity of existing practices—that is, the more such practices are characterized by high numbers of involved actors, crisscrossing relationships and intricate coordinating mechanisms among those involved, ambiguous connections between causes and effects, and modest use of technology—the less the translatability of the practice and, therefore, the more challenging it is for the translator to gain a high-fidelity representation of the practice. The complexity of existing practices makes it hard for the translator to relate and deliberately calibrate "the new" with "the old" and which therefore increases chances for translation failures.

This theoretical argument can be illustrated using an example from the Indo-Norwegian Project (INP), which was the Norwegian government's technical-economic aid project in Kerala (a state on the southwestern coast of India) in the period 1953–1972. The aim of the project was to help modernize the Kerala fish industry, in addition to improving water supply and health conditions for the population in two selected fishing communities. The plan was to achieve these aims by transfer of knowledge, technology, and money from Norway to Kerala. Modernization of the fish industry was the main aim. This part of the project had two pillars. One was to increase the supply of motorized fishing boats with mechanized equipment. By the start of the project in 1953, about 95 percent of the Kerala fishing fleet consisted of nonmotorized canoes. By the end of the project, the motorized fleet had increased dramatically and comprised approximately 4500 boats (Hareide, 1965).

The other main pillar of the INP initiative was rooted in an ambition to increase the efficiency of the marketing, sale, and distribution of fish catches. The most important modernizing means that INP used to realize this ambition was attempts to establish a sales and marketing system based on cooperative business principles; that is, a business organization owned and controlled by the people who use its products, supplies, or services. The principles of cooperative organizing of fish industries were transferred by the project experts from Norway, where they were widely practiced from the late 1940s to the early 1960s (Finstad, 2005). However, the new principles that INP tried to implement soon impinged upon existing and highly complex local practices based on other principles for the marketing, sale, and distribution of caught fish. These were practices that the INP experts had not conceptualized and comprehended when they started to implement the new principles of fishery organizing they had brought with them from Norway.

The existing and very old principles and practices of fish sales and distribution in the southwestern part of India were revealed by Arne Martin Klausen, a Norwegian anthropologist who did his fieldwork in the region from 1960–1962 (Klausen, 1968). What he found was that the traditional fish sales and distribution system involved numerous actors, many types of transactions, complex sets of roles and relationships, and intricate division of labor. The fish catches were landed by the fishing canoes on the beach— which were the location where the first transactions took place: "The beach sale of the fish appears at first sight to be carried out without any plan and practically like a struggle for life" (Klausen, 1968: 140). This phase involved transactions between the different types of fish merchants, agents, and the fishermen, and often resembled planned auctions. The middlemen (that is, the local merchants and agents) played very important roles, not least because they often had some capital, which they lent to the fishermen. In practice, the loan transactions bound the fishermen to this group of actors. However, the sales and distribution of fish (which was either salted or dried) involved many other types of merchants and transactions. One such type was "the bicycle merchants"—mostly Muslims who bought fish from beach middlemen and then biked and sold the fish to their customers at places up to 100 km into the interior part of the county. Then there were groups of "lorry merchants"— truck owners who also bought fish from the beach middlemen and made their incomes from selling fish to customers living at quite a distance from the coast. A third type of merchants was "the basket women"—poor women from the local fishing village who could earn money by carrying the fish in big baskets up to 10–15 km to their customers.

In sum, the traditional sale and distribution systems were characterized by very simple and modest use of technology (such as unmotorized canoes, bicycles, and some old trucks). However, it was a *complex* system that involved many actors who were mutually dependent upon each other and, consequently, upon the system, to make a living. Therefore, the involved actors also had stakes in maintaining and protecting the existing practices of fish sales and distribution. When INP started their efforts to modernize the organization of the sale and distribution system, they did not understand the complexity of the existing system and the fact that the involved actors had stakes in the existing practices, and therefore resisted attempts to change them.

The project leaders' failure to conceptualize the complexity of the existing practices had unforeseen consequences. INP launched two initiatives to modernize the sales and distribution system. One was the building of an ice factory and a cold storage plant with the aim of improving the preservation of fish in iced or frozen form. The other was the establishment of a cooperative organization. This initiative was motivated by INP's ambition to help ensure that the fishermen received fair and stable prizes for their catches. The cooperative organization was also an attempt to remove the middlemen, which INP conceived of "only as moneylenders and ruthless usurers" (Klausen, 1968: 147). However, none of these initiatives were successful. For many years the capacity of the ice fabric and the cold storage plant were poorly exploited, and mostly used to store fish caught by INP's own experiment boats rather than by the local fishermen. It took several years to realize the plan of establishing a cooperative organization, partly due to skepticism, lack of support, and open resistance from actors within the local fishing community. When the cooperative sale and distribution organization was established in October 1961, it led to higher and more stable prices. However, higher prices did not mean that the fishermen stopped selling to the local middlemen. This was due to uncertainty among the fishermen about what could happen when the INP program was terminated. They preferred to maintain the stable and well-known relationship with the middlemen, who provided them with loans and access to the markets. In addition, almost all of the various types of merchants involved in the numerous transactions generated by the fish sales and distribution opposed the INP's cooperative organization, mostly because they feared that it could destroy their own niches in the system.

This Kerala case exemplifies how complexity can mask and lower the translatability of existing practices in an organizational context, and be an important source of failures for translators involved in implementing new ideas in the same context.

Embeddedness of existing target practices

The opportunity for translators to discover and obtain accurate knowledge of existing target context practices will also depend on the practices' degree of embeddedness, such as whether the knowledge base and other prerequisites for how the target practice works is clearly located. Thus, it could be demarcated and concentrated in the target organization in focus or dispersed and floating in social relationships and other networks that connect the target organizational context to the wider society. Another case from the Indo-Norwegian project in Kerala provides example of how high embeddedness of an existing practice can lead to low translatability, and consequently to insufficient transparency for translators concerned with implementing new practices. The main part of the project was attempts to modernize the Kerala fishing fleet with bigger, motorized, and better equipped boats. The aim was to increase catches and stabilize the supply of fish to the markets. However, while implementing the fleet modernizing project, the INP experts noticed that different groups of fishermen reacted very differently to the attempts. To understand the different reactions, it is necessary to note that the chosen geographic area for the project was exceedingly heterogeneous in terms of castes, cultures, and religions. The area contained two distinct fishing communities that lived in two different villages: the Latin Catholics in the southern part, and the Hindu fishing population (the Arayas) in the northern village. While the Catholic fishing population were enthusiastic and rapidly obtained and started to use the modern boats, the Arayas were much more reluctant and often refused to accept the offers of such boats.

Although the INP experts gradually registered the different reactions, they were not able to understand why it happened (Klausen, 1968). The main interpretation among the experts of why some fishermen avoided new, modern boats was that it reflected cases of individuals who were unfitted for modern fishery. However, through anthropological fieldwork, Klausen (1968) revealed that the Araya reluctance to accept modernized boats was that they feared that it would lead to new fishing practices that would collide with suggestions and beliefs deeply embedded in the Hindu society of Araya. For example, the Arayas strongly resisted accepting the most effective type of boat, a 25-foot highly mechanized vessel with a powerful engine (Hareide, 1965). The Arayas were very reluctant to explain why, but Klausen (1968) revealed that the main reason for the avoidance behavior was that accepting the most modern boats would imply that they also had to accept *night fishing*.

This was a taboo: "No Hindu would think of disturbing nature in its naked state of rest" (Klausen, 1968: 137).

Klausen showed that this reason for the Arayas' avoidance—the beliefs embedded in culture and religion—were out of sight for the INP experts:

> The lack of knowledge about Indian local communities and the extreme differences between Norwegian and Indian way of life experienced by the experts made them unable to perceive the differences in the project area. They got a superficial impression of homogeneity among the receivers. Trained as they are in various fields of European technology and economy, the experts are inclined to focus on purely technical and statistical data. I think this is one of the main reasons for lack of interest in the negative reactions of the Arayas. (Klausen, 1968: 138)

To sum up: conceptualization, meaning processes whereby translators gain knowledge about the target context, is one out of three typical contextualization processes. As illustrated above, the ability of translators to gain knowledge about existing practices, and then consider them, will partly depend on the practices' degree of explicitness, complexity, and embeddedness.

Configuring new and existing practices

The second typical feature of contextualization is configuration. It refers to processes where translators relate target and source contexts and practices to each other, and where certain versions of the source practice are arrived at and appropriated to fit into the target organizational context. Configuration processes vary greatly in course and content and in the extent to which they are planned. Sometimes they are planned in detail and attempted to be carried out by translators who are conscious about the challenges involved in extracting practices and knowledge from certain places and move them to other places to try and make them work there (Røvik, 1998). The rational ideal of configuration is a process where a group of translators, who are knowledgeable of both the source and the target organizations, intensively relate the contexts to each other and try to find solutions to the challenges of not losing the essentials of the source practice and knowledge, while simultaneously undertaking deliberate adaptations to make a translated version work in the target context (Graham and Logan, 2004; Bausch et al., 2022). In practice, however, configuration processes are often not in line with this rational ideal. Processes of knowledge transfer between organizations are often poorly planned, and frequently involve translators who do not possess and combine knowledge about the source and the target contexts, as illustrated in the above examples of knowledge transfer to British coal mines and to fishing villages in Kerala.

The challenges of configuring source and target contexts when translating knowledge and practices have a parallel in highly researched challenges within the domain of translation studies of how to overcome various translation barriers when translating a text from one language to another. Such barriers are especially associated with instances of considerable dissimilarities between source and target languages. Configuration challenges in arriving at an acceptable target version of a source text are especially present when a source and a target language are very different (as with Chinese versus English). Correspondingly, in knowledge transfer across organizational contexts, the degree of dissimilarity/similarity on certain variables can be decisive for *how* challenging it is to configure. A lot of research indicates that increasing the distance between source and target organizations—in terms of geography (proximity) (Cooke, 2001, Beissinger et al., 2017), culture (De Long and Fahey, 2000), especially national culture (Kedia and Bhagat, 1988; Kogut and Singh, 1988), and institutional arrangements, such as a country's laws and formal rules (Kostova, 1999; Claus et al., 2021)—increases the potential for distortions in communication, for stickiness, and thus, for misfit when translating knowledge across such borders. Conversely, the more similar the source and target organizational contexts are on critical variables such as those mentioned above, the lower the risk for stickiness and for configuration failures.

Configuring challenges are, not least, about how the representation of source practices to be implemented relates to existing structures, practices, and interests in the target organization. Analytically, one can delineate three main types of relatedness—briefly: *loose coupling*, *weaving*, and *replacement*—each representing different levels of configuring challenges.

"*Loose coupling*" means that the new practice is only loosely related to established practices, and therefore does not directly affect them. For example, an organization may attempt to implement and recreate a structural unit observed in another organization—such as units of research and development, HRM, marketing, and communication. New structural components, like those mentioned above, can sometimes be added to and inserted in the existing formal organizational structure, with only modest consequences for existing structural components and for the practices performed by employees within them (Røvik, 2007). Thus, it is likely that instances of such loose couplings between new and existing practices can simplify the configuration processes.

"*Weaving*" refers to processes whereby the new practice is seen in comparison and interlaced with one or more existing practices. It usually presupposes far more complicated configuring processes than in cases of loose coupling. Reay et al. (2006) provide an example in a study of attempts to incorporate a new role of nurse professionals into an established system of healthcare organizing in Alberta, Canada. They revealed in detail the microprocesses involved in the weaving work of trying to fit the new role of a nurse professional into an institutionalized system where the physician was the central authority. The challenge was to arrive at a fit where the role of the nurse professional differed substantially from the role of ordinary nurses while simultaneously avoiding developing a role that too much resembled and challenged the physicians' domain. The previously presented INP project provides another example. As mentioned, one of the new ideas transferred from Norway to be materialized was to establish a cold storage place to preserve the local fishermen's catches in frozen form. However, after INP's sales organization had been established, the cold plant was hardly used by the local fishing community. The project leaders were very skeptical about cooperating with the local private fish merchants because they thought it would not fit in with the mission and the logic of the state-owned development project. Nor would the fish merchants cooperate with the INP, because they viewed the project as a threat to their commercial interests. However, in the final phase of the Kerala project, a cold storage plant in another part of Southern India broke down. It forced the private fish merchants to come to an agreement with INP about renting their cold storage plant. This triggered many instances where the INP and the private fish merchants' practices were, for the first time, blended and interlaced with each other. For example, four private fish merchant firms established business firms in close cooperation with INP's cooperative sales organization. However, the practical configuration of INP's cooperative-inspired practices with the merchants' practices based on local business traditions turned out to be complicated and time-consuming. Practices had to be seen in comparison and adjusted to each other. While new roles and routines gradually emerged, the process also evoked skepticism and resistance from actors both within INP and among the fish merchants. This illustrates some of the challenges for translators involved in weaving new and existing practices.

"*Replacement*" means that the new practice replaces one or more existing practices in the target organization. The case of introducing new technology and scientific management-inspired principles of work organizing in British coal mines in the 1930s and 1940s (commented on earlier in this chapter) superseded the existing work organization principles and practices of the colliers. At first glance, replacement may seem to be an easier strategy to perform than weaving, since it presumably does not involve complicated processes of trying to interlace new technology and practices with existing ones to make it work. However, of the three outlined strategies, this is probably the one with the highest potential to offend interests and release resistance among actors involved in the performance of the existing practices. The obvious reason is that such actors may expect a loss of value of their knowledge and skills (Jacobsen, 2004; Schmitt et al., 2012) and may even face the risk of losing their jobs. Therefore, replacement strategies often increase the pressure on translators and leaders to handle violated interests and resistance to change (Bateh et al., 2013). Replacement is also a risky strategy, because a sudden replacement of existing practices with new ones can lead to poor performances and decreasing results stemming from a combination of resistance to change and a lack of knowledge and skills to perform the new practices effectively, as demonstrated in Trist and Bamforth's (1951) study of the replacement strategy in U.K. coal mines.

Inscribing the new practice in the target context

A third typical feature of the contextualization phase is processes of inscribing, which means that a new practice—a materialized representation of practices from foreign contexts—is interpreted and ascribed various markers that connect the new practice to the target context and increase the chances of being recognized and accepted among local actors. To "inscribe" involves actively relating and interpreting the imported practice to the target organization's space and time context. Analytically, one can distinguish between *localizing* (ascribing local context markers to the new practice) and *timing* (ascribing local time markers to the practice).

Processes of localizing a foreign practice have a parallel in insights from translation studies, and especially in studies of the translation of dramas from their original to other languages. In dramas, actors, actions and contexts are often strongly interrelated. Therefore, translating a drama to other languages and contexts often presupposes what Brisset (1989) termed "reterritorialization," which means moving the drama into the new language and the surrounding contexts to make it recognizable and comprehensible there. Røvik (1998) studied how two global management concepts (Management by Objectives (MBO) and Total Quality Management (TQM)) stemming from large business firms were translated and inscribed into various Norwegian public sector organizations. The study showed that broad attempts were made to localize the foreign concepts, for example by *renaming*, which means that the two concepts were frequently assigned new local linguistic labels that fitted better with current local contexts' attitudes and challenges.

"Timing" refers to attempts to inscribe the new practice, with its history from a foreign context, into the time frame of the local target organization, meaning its past, present, and future. For example, Røvik's study (1998) revealed cases where local translators tried to reinterpret the logical sequence of problems and solution (problem first, then solution). Modern organizations, and especially their leaders, are sometimes accused of acting as fashion-followers who adopt popular management concepts for symbolic reasons rather than to solve real problems (Piazza and Abrahamson, 2020). In line with this argument, Røvik showed instances where management concepts were adopted before there were clear images of what problems they should solve. However, the study also revealed substantial evidence of ex post reinterpretations of history, which attempted to re-establish that the adoption of the concept was rationally calculated imports of solutions to solve real local problems that had emerged in the organizations at an earlier phase.

Summary—Key concepts and arguments

This chapter has reinterpreted knowledge transfer across organizational borders as acts of translation. Building on salient features from the outer domain of translation studies, knowledge transfers are conceptualized as containing two key processes: de-contextualization and contextualization (Figure 4.1).

De-contextualization refers to the translation of an identified practice in a source organization and its knowledge base into an abstract representation—expressed in images, words, texts, pictures, etc. A main challenge of de-contextualization is conceptualized in terms of the desired source practice's *translatability*, that is, the extent to which a particular practice in an organizational context can be translated to an abstract representation without excluding the elements required for how it functions in the source context. Three variables are theorized as decisive for a source practice's translatability. 1) The practice *complexity*, which is constituted by two intertwined factors. The first is *the human-technology factor* (the ratio between human beings and technology involved in the performance of the practice). The more the accomplishment of a practice is based on coordinated actions among a high number of actors, and the less it is based on technology with a clear-cut application, the more complex it is. The second is *the causal ambiguity factor* (the extent to which observed desired results in a source organization

SOURCE ORGANIZATION (WITH DESIRED PRACTICE)

Translation action : DECONTEXTUALIZATION
(From practice to abstract representation)

Key variable: TRANSLATABILITY
(Extent to which a practice can be translated to an abstract representation without losing the essentials for how it functions in the source).

Depends on the practice
- COMPLEXITY
- EMBEDDEDNESS
- EXPLICITNESS

→ **KNOWLEDGE TRANSFER ACROSS ORGANIZATIONAL BORDERS**

TRANSLATORS AS TRANSFERORS
Types of translators:
- Outsiders
- Expatriates
- Insiders

ORGANIZATIONAL BORDER

→ **RECIPIENT ORGANIZATION**

Translation action : CONTEXTUALIZATION
(From abstract representation to new materialized target practice)

THREE MAIN TRANSLATION PROCESSES:

CONCEPTUALIZATION
(Processes whereby translators try to gain knowledge about the target and about existing target practices)

Challenge: The TRANSLATABILITY of existing target practices
Depends on the practice:
- COMPLEXITY
- EMBEDDEDNESS
- EXPLICITNESS

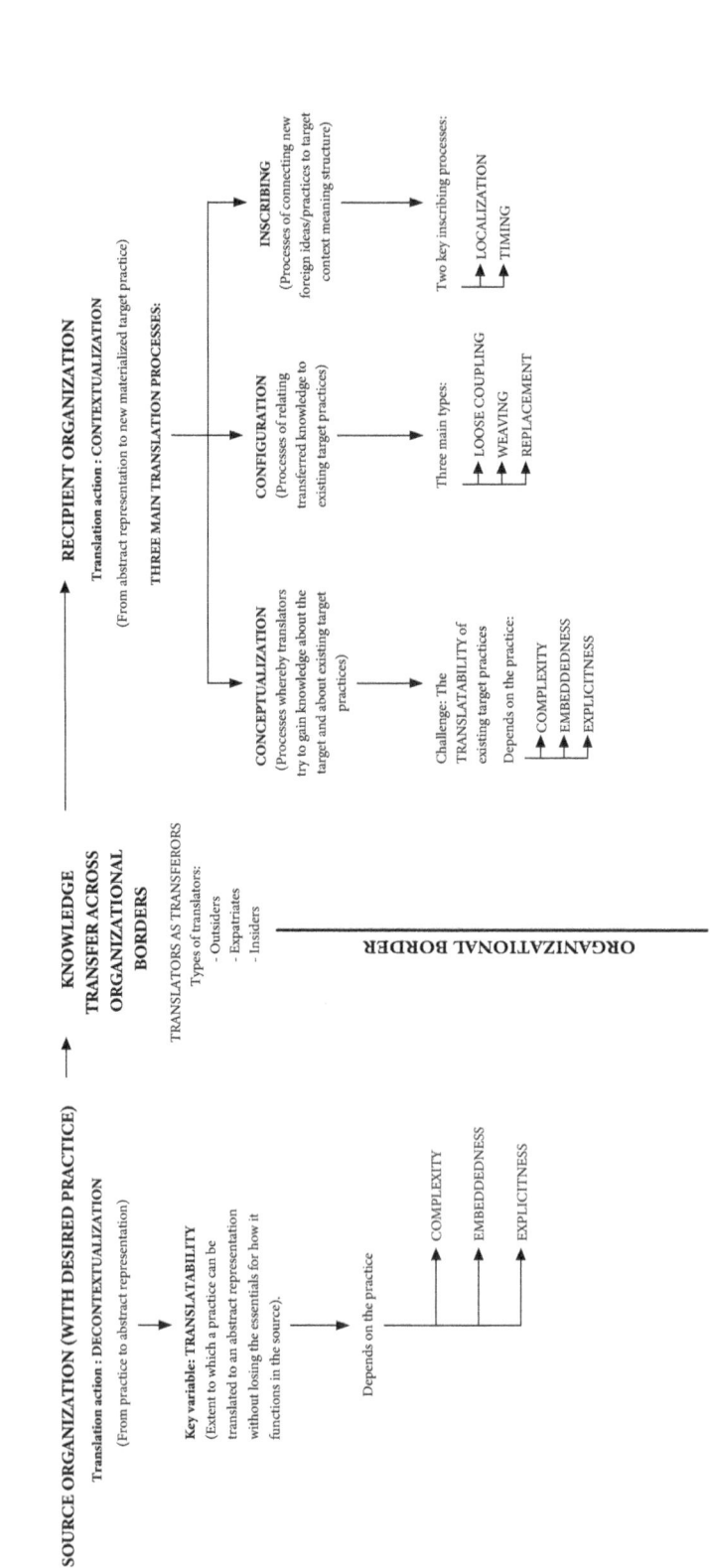

CONFIGURATION
(Processes of relating transferred knowledge to existing target practices)

Three main types:
- LOOSE COUPLING
- WEAVING
- REPLACEMENT

INSCRIBING
(Processes of connecting new foreign ideas/practices to target context meaning structure)

Two key inscribing processes:
- LOCALIZATION
- TIMING

Figure 4.1 Knowledge transfers as acts of translation: Overview

can be determined as caused by one or more identified practice). Increasing complexity is associated with increasing uncertainty about the causal linkages between a practice and observed effects. 2) The practice's *embeddedness*, that is, the extent to which the knowledge that constitute a desired source practice is anchored in—and influenced by the social and cultural environment in which it takes place. 3) The practice's *explicitness*, that is, the degree to which the knowledge base of a desired source practice is codified, verbalized and thereby easily articulated—or nonverbalized, noncodified and tacit. It is argued, that the translatability of a source practice varies with these three factors: The less complex, more explicit and less embedded, the more the translatability of the practice increases (as illustrated above with the cabin crew example), and vice versa (as illustrated with the stockfish production example). De-contextualization, meaning dis-embedding and transforming source practices to representations, are processes accomplished by various groups of actors conceptualized as translators. Translators are not a homogenous group: they differ, among other things, on the formal roles they appear in—and on their localization and proximity in relation to the source organizational context. Three main groups of translators involved in de-contextualization processes are identified. These are outsiders, expatriates, and insiders.

Contextualization encompasses processes of translating a representation of a desired source practice to a new practice in a target organization. Three key- and highly intertwined processes are involved in contextualization efforts. These are conceptualization, configuration, and inscribing. *Conceptualization* refers to processes where the translator gain knowledge about the target organization, such as its history, culture, actors, and existing practices. While the translatability of various source practices is a key for translators striving to translate them to abstract representations, the translatability of existing target organizational practices (that is, how challenging it is for translators to gain knowledge to arrive at representations that account for the essentials of such practices) is a key to understand dynamics of the contextualization phase. The translatability of existing target organizational practices is analyzed in terms of complexity, embeddedness and explicitness—the same variables as used to tap the translatability of desired source practices. The chapter illustrates the importance of the translatability of existing target organization practices for outcomes of knowledge transfer processes by providing two examples: the case of knowledge and technology transfer from the United States to the British coal-mining industry in the mid-war and postwar period, and the case of the Indo-Norwegian modernization project in Kerala in the period 1953–1972. *Configuration* encompasses processes where translators relate to- and try to fit in images of the desired source practice with existing target organization practices. The chapter identifies three main types of configurations between new and existing practices—termed *loose coupling, weaving,* and *replacement. Inscribing* depicts actions to interpret and ascribe various markers to the new and foreign practice that connects it to the meaning structures of the target organizational context. The chapter highlights two central features of inscribing processes: *localization*, which is ascribing local target context markers to the new, foreign practice, and *timing*, which is ascribing local time markers to the practice, thereby associating the foreign practice to target organization's past, present and future.

5
Revealing the Rules of Knowledge Translation

Introduction

A central notion in this book is that translators are important actors who regularly put their marks on the translated and materialized versions of practices and knowledge that are transferred to target organizations from various outer sources. However, questions remain about how such actors de facto perform translation activities. Are there any regularities and grammars of translation actions that can be revealed, described and analyzed? This chapter develops the second key argument on which the translation theory is founded, that is, that translations of practices and knowledge across organizational borders are rule-based activities. The chapter starts with a discussion of the concept of social rule—and the notion of translations as rule-based, and thus, patterned actions. Based on inspirations from the two outer domains (*translation studies* and *organizational translations*) and insights from empirical observations, I then theorize and outline a typology of translation rules—intending to account for variations in practices of translating knowledge across organizational borders. The potential of the typology to map this terrain is illustrated with reference to empirical examples.

Rules

The concepts of rules are among the most eclectic, tricky, and frequently referred to concepts in the social sciences. The centrality of the concept reflects that most human activities are regulated by socially created rules. Rules are guidelines expected to be followed by actors in various positions and situations—and come to expression in routines, procedures, habits, conventions, roles, strategies, codes of conduct, and formal organizational structures. As a pure biological organism, humans are subjects to few constraints on behavior beyond following their instincts. However, a societal regulating order is constituted by socially produced rules, which constrain and enable human actions and interactions (Schutz, 1962; Scott, 1987). Rules are human products, but the societal order they create are explicated and objectified, and then internalized as taken-for-granted facts—succinctly formulated by Berger and Luckmann (1966) as the social construction of reality. Rules can be deliberately constructed, but they can also emerge as unintended byproducts of long-lasting interactions among a group of actors (Christensen et al., 2020)—processes also known from studies of the shaping of organizational cultures (Schein, 2010; Alvesson, 2012).

Rules operate—and can be observed both at macro, meso and micro levels of analysis. Macro-level analysis of rules is often based on insights from new institutionalism as theoretical framework. Seen in comparison, these studies show to what extent and how various rules and rule systems are embedded in different institutions, such as nations (Hofstede, 1984), governmental and political institutions (March and Olsen, 1989; Ostrom, 1990; Olsen, 2010), markets and business institutions (Alchian and Demsetz, 1972; North, 1990), professions (Posner, 1981; Michelotta and Washington, 2013), and media (Pallas et al., 2016). At the meso level, there are studies of the role of specific rule systems in concrete organizations (Selznick, 1949; Clark, 1972)—often framed as studies of the role of corporate cultures (Denison, 1990; Ojo, 2009). At the micro level there are, for example, studies of the extent to which and how formal and informal rules determine individual members' thoughts and behavior (Egeberg, 2007; Egeberg and Trondal, 2018).

Individuals choose and follow rules due to different logics and reasons. Rules can be enforced upon individuals, like upon inmates in prisons (Cressey, 1959), but they can also be deliberately chosen. For example, Harré and Secord (1972) in their theory of man as a rule-following agent emphasize that most social rules that individuals follow are not laws that are forced upon them. There are often many rules available, some are ignored or broken, while others are chosen, based on anticipations of gains and losses. In March and Olsen's (1989) terms, this is the logic of consequentiality—a choice of rules based on individuals' preferences, assessment of various rules, and expectations about their consequences.

However, rather than being deliberately chosen, rules often come to expression as habits or routines that are taken for granted and followed without much reflection. Actors may be socialized into, internalize, and take for granted rules and rule systems embedded in certain contexts, for example nations (Hofstede, 1984), professions (Schein, 1970), and certain organizations (Etzioni, 1961; Van Maanen and Schein, 1978). In contrast to deliberate choice of rules in line with the logic of consequentiality, rules may be chosen and followed according to a logic of appropriateness, meaning to act according to what is socially defined as normal, acceptable, right, or good (March and Olsen, 1995; Christensen and Røvik, 1999).

Rules vary in the extent to which they determine actions. They may be explicit (codified and written) and prescribe expected actions in detail. In such cases, rules' potential to determine actions, are, in general, high (Levitt and March, 1988). Rules may also be uncodified, broad and imprecise, and thus, open to actors' alternative interpretations (Christensen et al., 2020). Consequentially, linkages between such rules and behavior may be loose.

The relationships between rule following and outcomes are tricky. Application of rules are often the antecedents of successful outcomes. Rules are, to various extent, carriers of accumulated knowledge (Olsen, 2010). The challenge for an actor who face a problem, is to analyze the situation and search for å rule that matches the challenges (Bunge, 2004). Thus, a simple stimulus (like an actor who faces a problem and choose a rule) can trigger a rule-based complex response, for example a standard operating procedure founded on experience and learning—and which increases chances for problem-solving (March and Olsen, 1989). As March and Simon (1958) have demonstrated, there can also be rules guiding actors in questions about when and how to switch between rules to handle new or changing situations.

However, rule following can also be an important source to failures. There are, at least, four reasons why undesired outcomes can stem from rule following. First, optimal selection and matching of a rule to handle a situation presupposes that the organization and its members possess thorough knowledge about the situation. Yet, actors' knowledge of the situation can be spare and insufficient—sometimes reflecting that involved actors are only part-time participants (Cohen et al., 1972). This may lead to choices of non-matching and inappropriate rules. Second, rules are often uncodified and only partly verbalized. Thus, actors may try to follow rules that they do not fully comprehend, and thus, which in turn may lead to failures (Cushman and Whiting, 1972). Third, an argument put forward by population ecologists in organization theory (Hannan and Freeman, 1977; Aldrich, 1999) is that organizations and their members may possess a rather meagre and too narrow rule repertoire, which may lead to inflexibility and inertia, and thus, to application of nonmatching rules when conditions change. Fourth, organizations sometimes develop passions about rules and too much confidence in them based on past experience. It may lead to "blind" application of a rule as a standard operating procedure, and correspondingly, to avoidance of learning from *new* experiences under different conditions—a phenomenon Veblen (1914) termed "trained incapacity." Thus, to avoid this phenomenon, organizations should—according to March (1976)—threat "old" experiences as a theory, and memory as an enemy.

Searching for rules of translations

The sociology of rules provides us with many insights that are useful in the search for rules and patterns to better understanding processes of knowledge translation across organizational borders. Do such rules exist; are there any grammar of knowledge translation that can be revealed? A general, but notwithstanding important insight is that most human activities are regulated by rules—some deliberately constructed and chosen, and others socially emerged as byproducts of human interactions. Another appurtenant insight is that rule-influenced actions settle and come to expression in *patterns* of behavior. Correspondingly, it is reasonable to suggest that there are certain rules, too, that influence translations of knowledge across organizational borders—and that these suggested rules will manifest themselves in discernable patterns of behavior and outcomes of translation processes. In searching to identify translation rules this is important, because any observed patterns which come to sight when various translation processes are seen in comparison provide a possible route back to the rules that have contributed to the patterns.

Inspirations from the external domains

The notion of translation rules is also inspired by insights from salient features of the two foreign domains—translation studies, and organizational translation. Within the domain of translation studies and linguistic translation there are, as showed in Chapter 3, a multitude of translation rules. There are also many attempts to overview and make typologies of translation rules (Vinay and Darbelnet, 1958; Nida, 1964; Barkudarov, 1975; Venuti, 2017). Such typologies are primarily classifications of *how* languages and cultures are translated rather than classifications of *what* is being translated.

The translation rules within the domain of translation studies have some typical features in common, which is interesting when searching to identify rules that govern knowledge translation across organizational borders. *First*: The translation typologies are all attempts to map the empirical terrain and make representations of existing translation rules used by different translators—and based on observations of translation practices and patterns. This means that the typologies have clear *empirical* foundations. *Second*: Most translation rules are codified and verbalized, and can be recognized and communicated with defined labels—for example Vinay and Darbelnet's (1958) identified and labeled rules as borrowing, calque, literal translation, transposition, modulation, equivalence, and adaptation. Most professional translators know about these and other translation rules, recognize them, communicate with other translators about them, and use them in their own practice. Obviously, knowledge of translation rules spread among translators within the professional field. However, the spread has also intensified due to the rapid expansion during the last three decades of graduate and Ph.D.—programs in translations studies at universities all over the world (Lambert, 2017). *Third*: Linguistic translators select and apply various translation rules based on rational professional suggestions of what is the best means to render a text in another language (Wilss, 1998). However, use of translation rules can be based on other processes than rational calculations. Studies show that habits and traditions of translations are also important, meaning historically and culturally embedded translation norms and styles. For example, such habits are found in nation-specific translation styles (Duranti, 1998; Kittel and Poltermann, 1998; Salama-Carr, 1998). *Fourth*: Although linguistic translation has many rules and is a rule-based professional field, the rules guide—but do not determine translators' practices (Lörscher, 1991). Most linguistic translation rules presuppose and allow much room for individual translators to interpret and make creative choices within the frames of the rules. It is also stressed that competent linguistic translators should be knowledgeable about a wide repertoire of translation rules, and be able to switch between—and combine various rules to complete a translation task (Krings, 1986).

Within the domain of Organizational translation there are numerous studies reporting about how knowledge and practices are translated and transformed while they are transferred (Sahlin and Wedlin, 2008; Haedicke, 2012; Monstadt and Schramm, 2017; Tracey et al., 2018; Nicolini et al., 2019). However, with some few exceptions, scholars within this tradition have not been concerned with questions of translation rules. One exception is Sahlin-Andersson (1996). She studied the establishment of a research park in Stockholm in the late 1980s, which was modeled on the successes of Silicon Valley, Route 128, and other well-known science parks in the U.K. and in the United States. She found that the local translation in Stockholm of the science parks success stories from abroad followed three types of "editing rules." One was rules concerning contexts. Although the local translators referred to other science park successes, they were distanced and not very knowledgeable about the success-parks that they tried to model. By de-emphasizing and decoupling the Stockholm-version from the details of the source contexts, the translators had many degrees of freedom to make changes in—and adapt the science park concept to the Stockholm context. The second type of rules identified by Sahlin-Andersson concerned the local formulation of the success of the prototypes (the modeled foreign science parks). The local translators dramatized the stories of the successes of the foreign science parks. While it made the local stories more attractive and exiting to tell, it also transformed the realities, leading to more edited and simplified versions of the prototypes. The third type of translation rules concerned the overall rationalistic plot of the local Stockholm stories of the foreign prototypes. The successes of the prototypes were interpreted as resulting from initiatives taken by small groups of actors who had great ideas and who made decisions, planned, implemented and controlled the processes leading up to the successes. In reality, these local plots were ex post rationalizations and simplifications of very complex and not at all straightforward processes.

However, except for Sahlin-Andersson's contribution there are few, if any, attempts within the domain of organizational translation to research and theorize about rules and regularities of translations. It probably reflects two interconnected characteristics of this domain. The first is the axiomatic notion of translations as processes that inevitably lead to transformations of circulating representations of practices, and thus, to generation of new, unique local versions. Translation processes are conceived of as complex and hard to predict. They often involve many actors who interpret and put their signatures on the actual object that is translated. Within this domain, translations are frequently looked upon as a social mechanism which generates heterogeneity (Chandler and Hwang, 2015; Røvik 2016; Claus et al., 2021). To introduce a representation of a foreign practice and/or a circulating idea in a new organizational context is, per definition "to construct it anew" (Czarniawska and Sevón, 2005: 8). Translation is conceived of as a social mechanism that makes it very hard—probably impossible—to reproduce and copy practices and ideas. Thus, the strong notion among many scholars within this domain of translation as a key heterogeneity-producing social mechanism that, in principle, leads to unpredictable numbers and types of new versions—does not correspond easily with a view of translations as rule-based, regulated activities that settle in discernable patterns of actions and outcomes.

The second reason for the absence of interest in translation rules and regulations relates to the dominating research methods within the domain of organizational translation. The strong notion of the complexities of translation processes, and that they generate variance and heterogeneity, have led to a preferred methodological strategy among many scholars within this domain. It is to do qualitative studies of single (or few) cases, where each translation process is mapped in detail and analyzed. However, this methodological approach does not necessarily correspond to an ambition of revealing translation rules and their appurtenant patterned actions and outcomes. Such an ambition is better realized if one can compare and analyze larger samples of translation processes, and especially, if the sample contains processes with different locations in time and space.

A main pattern of translation outcomes

As commented on above, any patterns generated when knowledge is translated and transferred across organizational borders provide a possible route back to the rules, which have generated the patterns. Obviously, such translations have many regularities and patterns. However, a main and most distinct pattern comes to sight when numerous observations of knowledge translations are seen in comparison. The underlying pattern is that translations vary between efforts to *replicate*, meaning to preserve, in principle, all details in the source version in the translated target version—and efforts to *adapt*, meaning to change the source version as much as necessary to make it fit into the target organizational context. There are many studies of knowledge transfers that capture attempts to replicate other organizations' success formulas (Levitt, 1966; Winter and Szulanski, 2001; Winter et al., 2012), as well as studies that show transformation and adaptation of transferred knowledge (Westney, 1987; Sahlin-Andersson 1996). These and other works—when seen in comparison—are indications of the proclaimed overall pattern of knowledge translation.

The replication-adaptation pattern stand out as a generic feature of translations in general. For example, it comes to expression in linguistic translation in two very strong and somehow competing translation ideals. One is foreignizing, meaning metaphrase, or literal, sometimes word-by-word translation—and the other is domestication, meaning adapting the source text to fit the feature and the needs of the target context (Toury, 1978; 1980; Venuti, 2017).

There is no doubt that replication—adaptation is a main translation pattern, and further, that this pattern is generated and continuously regenerated by translators who operate under the influence of some translation rules. That such rules exists—and that there are difficulties and dilemmas involved when they are applied—are reflected in knowledge transfer literature (Røvik, 2007; 2016; Posen and Martignoni, 2018), as well as the translation studies literature (Westney and Piekkari, 2020).

Typologies as means of theorizing

In this chapter, I present a typology of translation rules. A typology is a means to make parsimonious ordering of various phenomena. Within the social sciences, typologies are used to classify and theorize about the occurrence and characteristics of a wide range of entities and activities—based on their key attributes. Among the classic social science typologies are Durkheim's four types of suicide (Moore, 2016), Marx's five basic types of society (Elliott, 1978), and Weber's rationality types (Kalberg, 1980). Typologies have also been widely used in organization theory to generate parsimonious classifications and theories, for instance Etzioni's (1961) typology of reasons for employees to comply with leaders, Miles and Snow's (1978) types of organizational adaptation, and Mintzberg's (1993) typology of organizational structures. There are numerous other typologies, too, such as Burns and Stalker's (1961), Blau and Scott's (1962), Porter's (1980), Foss's (2011), Reinhold et al.'s (2019), and Sandberg and Alvesson's (2021). Typologies offer a framework for ordering of, and theorizing about, complex organizational phenomena, which, subsequently, can be used to explain and predict variance in outcomes of certain dependent variables (Doty and Glick, 1994). The advances of typologies are widely acknowledged, for example as " a key way of organizing complex webs of cause-effect relationships into coherent accounts" (Fiss, 2011: 393), as heuristic tools for researchers and practitioners (Mintzberg, 1993), as means to simplify multiple causal relationships into a few typified and easy-to-remember profiles (McPhee and Scott Poole, 2001), and as "means to reduce information of complex ideal types—or real world things—to those aspects of theoretical significance" (Bailey, 1994: 1).

A main critique against researchers who develop and apply typologies is that they just classify, but do not theorize the organizational phenomenon in focus (Blalock, 1969; Bacharach, 1989; Cornelissen, 2017). Typologists are criticized for overemphasizing the description of the typology and correspondingly for "underemphasizing on developing the underlying theory" (Doty and Glick, 1994: 231). However, Doty and Glick (1994) argue that typologies are, or at least, can be developed, to complex theories, but that they are frequently misinterpreted. An important source to the view of typologies as nontheoretical constructs is the confusing of typologies with taxonomies. A taxonomy is a system of classification of entities into mutually exclusive and exhaustive categories—based on explicated, consistent sorting rules. The process of generating a taxonomy is typical bottom-up (Baden-Fuller and Morgan, 2010), meaning that the classification is often exclusively derived from empirical research and from observations. Typologies, on the other hand, are created top-down, and derived from theorists' sense-making and conceptual work (Hambrick, 1984; Reinhold et al., 2019). While taxonomies are worked out according to predefined sorting rules, typologies are not, but instead they contain sets of interrelated ideal types generated by the typologists' sense-making. This means, that constructs presented as typologies sometimes are primarily taxonomies, not typologies. According to Doty and Glick (1994), for a classification to be a typology, it must fulfill two claims. First, it must contain *ideal types*. In Weber's (1947) definition, ideal types are mental constructs with special characteristics. They are formed by a one-sided accentuation of one or more points of view and by the synthesis of many diffuse and discrete—more or less present—concrete individual phenomena, which are arranged according to those one-sidedly emphasized viewpoints into a unified analytical construct (Shils and Finch, 1997: 90). An ideal type has empirical observations as its raw material, but it does not necessarily correspond to any particular empirical entity and/or activity. Ideal types *might* exist, but they are very rare. Compared to other ideal types, one particular ideal type represents a unique combination of the dimensions that are used to describe the whole set of ideal types in a certain typology.

Doty and Glick's (1994) second claim for a real typology, that is, a typology that is also a theory, is that it should hypothesize relationships between the types and one or more dependent variables. Thus, the typologist should suggest and argue for the similarity of an entity (such as an organization and/or its members' actions) to an ideal type—and scores on a dependent variable. For example, Mintzberg (1979) made many predictions about how certain organizations' level of effectiveness—under various conditions—could depend on the degree to which they resembled (or not) certain of his structural ideal types.

A typology of translation rules

Based on insights about patterns of translation actions and outcomes and on inspirations from salient features of the two foreign domains, a typology is worked out—aiming at mapping and classifying the terrain of rules involved in translation of knowledge across organizational borders. The terrain to be mapped and typologized encompasses all kinds of translation rules applied in knowledge transfers—such as broad, general rules as well as more specific—and procedure-like rules. The typology also includes naturally (or culturally) grown rules, which may come to expression in translation habits as well as rationally constructed and explicitly formulated rules.

The typology conceptualizes translation rules as containing *translation modes* and *operational rules of translation*. The types in this classification are ideal types. It means that the typology is based on empirical observations of translation practices and of various patterns that such translations have generated. Translations leading to replications versus translations leading to adaptations constitute a main translation pattern providing routes back to the generating rules. However, that the translation rules portrayed in the typology are *ideal types* means that certain aspects have been emphasized and cultivated through processes of sense-making. This means that the outlined types are abstract constructs and statements of categories of observations, and that they cannot be "mapped backwards," that is, reduced to specific observations (Priem and Butler, 2001).

The concept "translation mode" is defined as a preferred way of translating across organizational borders, and which comes to expression in a recognized translation style. The typology contains three such ideal-typical modes—the reproducing mode, the modifying mode, and the radical mode. The translation modes are related to the main translation-outcome pattern of replication-adaptation. The pattern represents various degrees of transformation of what is transferred—varying between low degree (replication) and high degree (adaptation). Each translation mode is characterized by actors' inclination to prefer a certain level of transformation on the replication-adaptation scale. Thus, the translation modes differ in the degree to which their application may lead to transformation of what is transferred. Translation modes can be deliberately chosen—resembling a consciously decided transfer/translation strategy. However, translation modes can also reflect habits of translations—resembling what is known from translation studies where linguistic translation modes often co-varies with national borders (Venuti, 1998; Ellis and Oakley-Brown, 2001).

Each translation mode is characterized by some appurtenant operational translation rules. These rules come to expression in practical translation actions. When they are used, they tend to have certain effects, meaning that some lead translation outcomes in the direction of preserving the source version of what is transferred, while others lead—to various degrees—to transform it. The operational rules may be explicitly expressed. However, more often they are informal and implicit (Røvik, 2016). As expressed by Sahlin-Andersson (1996: 85), "they can often be deduced only indirectly," meaning that they come to expression in practice, and can be traced ex post the translation acts, that is, in how actors de facto conduct translations.

In this chapter, the typology of the translation rules is worked out. Chapter 6 focuses on the relationship between the typologized rules and outcomes. In that chapter, I theorize about to what extent and how outcomes of knowledge transfer processes can depend on the match between the applied translation rules—and a defined set of specific conditional variables that characterizes each knowledge transfer process.

The reproducing translation mode

The reproducing translation mode comes to expression in a propensity to identify, preserve, and recreate in the translated target context version all elements and the relationships between them—as they exist in the source context version of an identified practice and its appurtenant knowledge base. The underlying norm is one of recreating a source template with exactitude in the target context. As stated above, the reproducing mode is an ideal type, which means that it rarely occurs in its pure form in certain empirical counterparts. However, although an ideal type, it is possible to identify certain societal entities and fields where the dominating translation style in knowledge transfers resembles—and sometimes come very close—to the reproducing mode. Clear echoes of the reproducing mode can be identified in certain nations, cultures, and social movements.

Reproducing nations

Some nations as much more than others associated with a reproducing translation mode. Undoubtedly, Japan is the prominent example—a nation renowned for its propensity to imitation and copying others. The reproducing mode permeates the Japanese society—its wide reach can be traced in both time and space within this nation. As to the history: Two of the very first reports that depict the Japanese as devoted to mimicry focus both on an incident in 1543 when a Portuguese trading vessel arrived on the Japanese island of Tanegashina. Two independent reports of this early encounter between Western and Asian cultures both describe how the Japanese—after for the first time being exposed to guns, which were brought there by the Portuguese—immediately tried to find out about the technology and then started to make copies (Lidin, 2002). In 1556, 13 years after the initial exposure, there were about 300,000 replica of the Portuguese guns in Japan (Cox, 2007). From the first half of the eighteenth century there was a rapid increase in the number of observations of Japanese mimeticism—often reported in various explorers' travelogues. For example, the German naturalist, Engelbert Kaemper—in his book *History of Japan* (published posthumously in 1727), notes from the city of Kyoto that "There is nothing that a foreigner can bring that some artists or other inhabitants of the city will not undertake to imitate." In the *General History of Travel* (1852) the portrayal of the Japanese is even more stereotyped: "Although the Japanese have invented almost nothing, when they put their hands to something, they make it perfect" (cited in Lucken, 2016: 10). The Western image of the imitative Japan was further strengthened throughout the nineteenth century, not least in the United States and as an effect on the public opinion by the renowned Perry expedition. This was a U.S. government–initiated expedition to Japan. It involved warships, which made two trips from the United States to Japan (1853 and 1854) with the aim of exploring and establishing diplomatic relations and to negotiate trade agreements between the two countries. The official widespread narrative from the Perry expedition portrayed Japan as a nation of inhabitants with "a very characteristic inquisitive and imitative disposition" (Rosenstone, 1980: 72). The notion of "copy-cat Japan" was also put forward and confirmed by prominent nineteenth-century academics. For example, French sociologist, Gabriel Tarde, wrote in his influential work *The Law of Imitation* (1890/1903) that the Japanese proved an important argument in his theory, in the sense that "the inferior" (Japan) usually imitated "the superior" (the West). Although nuanced, the image of Japan as a reproducing nation has been continued and even strengthened throughout the twentieth century (Schwartz, 1996; Morris-Suzuki, 1994).

Shifting the angle from time to space: many observations indicate that a reproducing mode and mimeticism permeate large parts of the Japanese society. There are studies that document how the reproducing mode operates in very different sectors and fields in Japan, such as in missionaries' religious practices (Curvelo, 2007), architecture (Coaldrake, 2007), public administrative reforms (Westney, 1987), models and concepts of democracy (Howland, 2002), car industry (Madeley, 2007), and machine-tool industry (Chokki, 1986). There are also studies revealing strong influence of the reproducing mode in various kinds of Japanese arts, such as poetry (Raud, 2007), painting (Toby, 2007), and theater—and dance performance (Averbuch, 2007).

China is another country renowned for its inclination to reproduce and copy others' knowledge, practices, and products (Pang, 2008; Peng et al., 2017). The pervasiveness of this mode in the Chinese society has—likewise in Japan—a long history and many expressions. One indication is the volume of the counterfeit industry, meaning the manufacturing of fakes or unauthorized replicas of original branded products. About 86 percent of all counterfeit products come from China and account for about 8 percent of China's Gross Domestic Products (GDB). The propensity to reproduce and copy is rooted in China's history and culture, reflecting the old Confucian ideal that promotes individuals to share their ideas and inventions with the society. This ideal is clearly expressed in the Chinese tradition of *Shanzhai*, which refers to low-cost copycat versions of globally branded products, such as electronics, clothing, clocks, etc. (Chubb, 2015). Interestingly, the Shanzhai institution of mass production of low-cost replicas is, largely, not conceived of as morally disgraceful acts. Rather, the production of good reproductions is looked upon as a noble and challenging art. The ability to observe, memorize, and reproduce with accuracy is also highly valued and promoted at all levels in the educational system in China. A prominent expression is the *Gaokao*, which is the old and very difficult Chinese university entrance examination, with much emphasis on students' memorizing and reproducing capacity (Page, 2019).

The typologized reproducing mode is an ideal type—which means that there rarely are any empirical case that perfectly matches. Thus, although both Japan's and China's knowledge transfer practices obviously are strongly influenced by a reproducing translation mode, their practices also deviate in certain respects from this ideal type. For example, China, although a renowned copycat nation, has also fostered several game-changing inventions, among them gunpowder and the compass. Correspondingly, there is a long Western tradition for stereotyping Japan as an aping nation, lacking any inventing capabilities (Schwartz, 1996). However, to understand Japan's enormous postwar industrial and economic success, one has to consider models that account for much more complex relationships between reproducing and invention efforts beyond simple copycat stereotypes (Morris-Suzuki, 1994).

Reproducing cultures

Representations of a reproducing translation mode can also be found within certain cultures. Australian anthropologist R. Bowden studied the Kwoma people, who live in a province of Papua New Guinea (Bowden, 1999). He documented that the Kwoma's rituals (e.g. dances) are continually imitated and ritual objects duplicated. Admiration and high status are ascribed to those who manage to make the most accurate imitations and replicas of the culture's ancestral prototypes. American anthropologist, G. Isaac (2011) reports similar observations from studies of the Zuni, which is a tribe of native Americans living in Western New Mexico. Correspondingly, to Bowden's findings, Isaac shows how a reproducing mode permeates the Zuni people's knowledge system. Unlike Euro-American main tradition, skills and acts of repetition and replication are highly admired: "The duplication or repetition of something is viewed not as an alienating process that separates copies from originals, but as the reproducing of powerful knowledge as a vital part of a cosmology" (Isaac, 2011: 215).

The reproducing evidence movement

An example of a modern, contemporary representation of the reproducing translation mode is the so-called evidence movement (Hansen and Rieper, 2009). The mission and aim of this highly scientized movement is twofold: to promote the production of evidence-based knowledge in various societal fields, and to facilitate the access to and transfer of evidenced best practices to targeted groups of practitioners—and by certain means—to ensure that the evidenced prototypical practices are reproduced with exactitude.

The start of the evidence movement is ascribed to the Scottish medical doctor, Arcibald Cochrane (1909–1988), who in a seminal paper, published in 1972, criticized the medical science and profession for poor scientific quality (Cochrane, 1972). Cochrane advocated much more use of randomized controlled trials (RCT-studies) and comprehensive meta-studies to systematic review and thereby enhance the effectiveness and efficiency of health services. In 1993, his ideas materialized in the establishment of the Cochrane Database for Systematic Reviews and The Campbell and Cochrane Collaboration. The aim was to produce evidenced knowledge about whether and how certain interventions work in practice, and thus, to foster more well-informed decisions among health practitioners. Starting in the early 1990s in the medical field, the efforts to produce evidenced knowledge by doing RCT-studies and meta-studies have spread rapidly to other fields, such as education (Oakley et al., 2005; Røvik and Pettersen, 2014), social welfare (Krejsler, 2013), and criminology (Sherman, 2009).

Within the highly scientized evidence movement, *research-based* evidence is conceived of as the most reliable type, that is, knowledge gained by synthesized reviews of RCT-studies. Evidence can either refer to best practices about implementation, meaning principles—with documented effects—for how to implement and carry out a practice, or to affect evidence, which is documented effects of certain interventions (Hansen, 2014).

Once evidenced knowledge has been gained, the challenge is to spread it to the relevant groups of practitioners—and to secure that is reproduced and practiced according to the recommended, evidenced standards. Thus, the reproducing translation mode is widely recognized and acknowledged within the evidence movement. The value ascribed to this translation mode comes to expression in development and use of various means to secure accurate reproduction, among which the most prominent instrument is fidelity scales. Fidelity refers to the degree to which a practice (e.g. a medical treatment) is implemented and practiced as prescribed. A fidelity scale is a tool to measure the level of implementation of an evidenced best practice. The aim is to preserve the components and the relationships among them that made the original practice effective—based on the view that it will affect the degree to which it works in various recipient contexts. The core argument is that making any changes when transferring, implementing and using an evidenced practice will reduce its effectiveness (Calsyn et al., 1977). Blakely et al. (1987) formulated the rational premise for the preferred reproducing mode in transfer of evidenced practices like this: "Innovations have a number of well-specified program components. Validated innovative programs should be adapted with close correspondence (fidelity) to the original model" (p. 225).

Chosen or taken for granted rules?

How can an "inclination to reproduce" be shaped? Sometimes it can be rather deliberately chosen, and for several reasons. The first is reproduction and copying to enhance chances for increased efficiency. Innovations are often laborious, risky, and costly, in contrast to imitations, which are frequently cheaper and less risky. While innovators, as a rule, bear the development costs, organizations acting in a reproducing mode, may wait to imitate until a more robust prototype has been settled (Henry and Ponce, 2011), saving not only R&D costs, but sometimes also marketing and advertising investments (Shenkar, 2010). Thus, in general, the reproducers—rather than the innovators themselves—are those that reap the initial benefits from innovations.

Secondly, a reproducing mode can be chosen based on knowledge of what can be achieved by using it as a translation rule—more specifically, a calculation that if one succeeds in accurately reproducing another successful organization's means, chances increases for also achieving the same successful outcomes. The hamburger restaurant, McDonalds, is probably the most well-known example of successful application of a replication strategy. The prototype was developed in in the late 1940s when the two McDonald brothers established their first hamburger restaurant in San Bernardino, and developed an initial version of their fast-food concept referred to as Speedy Service System (Schlosser, 2001). The McDonald brothers had established similar hamburger restaurants units in the San Bernardino region. Then, in the early 1950s, the brothers—with the help of Raymond Kroc, later known as the American franchise tycoon, formulated and implemented the replication strategy, which implied that McDonald restaurants—wherever they were located—should be exact replicas of each other (Anderson and Kroc 2018). At the end of 2018, McDonald's restaurants had spread to 120 countries and counted 37,855 units. Together they served about 69 million customers each day (Love and Miller, 1995).

At the core of McDonald's replication strategy—which soon achieved the status as the gold standard for franchise organizing in numerous branches (Schlosser, 2001)—is the idea of developing and exercising very strict control of standardization and replication of all aspects of each McDonald unit, including physical design, technology, work operations, service design, and product types—and quality. Central in this strategy is also the idea of tight surveillance and control with each franchiser unit, who, in principle, have few if any degrees of freedom to make local adaptations and deviations from the "copy exact" strategy.

However, a reproducing mode is not necessarily deliberately chosen. Rather, an inclination to reproduce may reflect specific traditions, cultures and institutional arrangements in certain social entities, such as countries, fields, organizations, etc., which functions as trajectories that lead actors into a reproducing translation mode. For example, in Japan, the propensity to reproduce and copy partly reflects old traditions, such as the kata institution, which strongly influences the learning of skills in various fields (Clarence-Smith, 2007). Kata is a collection of norms for the relationships between the master, who is authorized as especially knowledgeable in a field, and the student/worker (learner) who is supposed to learn from the master. The learner is urged to replicate with exactitude the master's form, for example in various kinds of arts. Only by replicating, can the learner later develop his/her own style and become a master. Therefore, the accurate reproduction is "an accomplishment highly valued in a Japanese view as the most appropriate method of acquiring artistic and other (such as technological) skills" (Hendry, 2000: 179).

Likewise, the copycat nature of China reflects old Chinese institutions, such as the above mentioned Confucian institution of *Shanzhai*, where skills to imitation and reproducing exactly is conceived of as a noble art (Lam, 1995). Another cultural trajectory leading actors into a reproducing mode in China is the Confucian-inspired and strongly politically and ideologically supported notion that knowledge, ideas, and inventions are not individual properties, but something that belongs to the collective, and thus, should be copied and shared (Brander et al., 2017; Peng et al., 2017). There is a divide between Western nations and China in questions of Intellectual Property Rights (IPR), and thus, about the extent to which reproductions of others are legal or not.

In addition to culture and traditions, there are also certain institutional arrangements that channels actors into a reproducing translation mode. An example: during the 1970s and 1980s—the climax period for American firms' fear of Japanese copycats reproducing their inventions—the United States and Japanese patent systems were very differently designed. While the U.S. system honored and gave protection for those "first-to-invent," the Japanese system favored and protected those "first-to-apply" the invention. Further, while U.S. patent applications and appurtenant materials are kept secret to hinder competitors to steal the idea, the Japanese system was open, meaning that the patent applicants' materials were made available to potential challenges and competitors (Melloan, 1988). Thus, the Japanese patent system obviously favored a reproducing translation mode. Fidelity scales are another example of an institutional arrangement that promotes reproduction and copying. Such scales are both a symbol of the importance of accurate, standardized distribution and application of scientifically gained and evidenced knowledge—and simultaneously an instrument for realizing such an ambition.

Operational translation rule: Copying

Within the reproducing mode, *copying* is the main operational translation rule. Copying refers to activities that aim at duplicating, making a similar, or preferably an identical, version of a model conceived of as an original, or a template. While copy exact, meaning the reproduction of an identical version of the original, is challenging and rare, an ambition to copy may, notwithstanding, often lead to *very similar* versions, as expressed in a frequently referred definition: "A copy is which comes so near to the original as to give every person seeing it the idea created by the original" (Justice Bailey, 1822, cited in Clarence-Smith, 2007: 52). In knowledge transfer, copying refers to processes where an organization attempts to achieve a similar successful effect than observed in a certain organization (a model) by replicating and using similar means as the model.

There are many reasons why organizations may try to copy others with as much accuracy as possible. For example, Winter et al. (2012) and their study of a franchising organization documented that those units who most accurately replicated the franchising template, were more successful and had higher survival rates than those who were inaccurate copiers. There are also many examples of high-profiled organizations who pursue copying in their knowledge transfer efforts. Rank Xerox's knowledge transfer policy in relation to their units in various country contexts has been to claim an almost 100 percent accuracy in their implementation of headquarter's decisions, for example about administrative routines and technological improvements (Jensen and Szulanski, 2004). Intel, the world's largest manufacturer of PC microprocessors, is renowned for its Copy EXACT strategy. Especially, it has materialized in routines to transfer new process technology from the original laboratory environment into the ordinary manufacturing phase of high-volume productivity (Iansiti, 1998; McDonald, 1998). The main reason why many organizations cling to copying is the fear that even minor adaptations taken place in processes of translation between source context and recipient context can have severe distorting effects on outcomes (Nelson and Winter, 1982; Szulanski and Winter, 2002).

There is a long history, especially in Western countries, to conceive of copying as a rather simple translation rule to execute and follow. There are several reasons for that. One is the traditional Western image of copying as not only simple, but also as a sign of low morale and of primitiveness. The notion of the simplicity of copying reflects the strong position of the invention/innovation versus imitation–dichotomy in Western thinking. While inventions and innovations are associated with creativity and hard work, imitation is frequently interpreted as acts of relaxed repetition. There are also images of copyists as actors of low moral who steal and take the revenues from the laborious and creative inventors. In Western thinking, primitiveness has also been ascribed to those who copy. For example, the Japanese' copying skills have been compared to the behavior of monkeys and apes (Cox, 2007; Toby, 2007), and referred to as "acts of Japanzees" (Schwartz, 1996: 368).

The image of copying as a simple translation rule has been strengthened in step with technological innovations that facilitates the speedy making of numerous copies of texts, pictures, physical objects and ideas (Clarence-Smith, 2007). The combined effect of progress in digitization technology (such as smartphones with cameras) and computing networking speed up both copying activities as well as the diffusion of copies (Varian, 2005). However, there is a divide between widely held images of copying as simple—and insights from studies of knowledge transfer indicating that it is often extremely difficult. The best indication of the complexities of copying is that the overwhelming majority of attempts to replicate other organizations' successes fail (Szulanski and Winter, 2002). Why such a high failure rate of attempts to copy others' best practices? Ironically, one important reason is the widespread notion of the simplicity of copying *itself*—which may facilitate a too laidback, less than wholehearted approach to the task of copying others. The previously mentioned Japanese institution of Kata illustrates how challenging and laborious copying can be. The student/learner is supposed to copy accurately the masters' acts (e.g. dance, painting, machine design, etc.). First, this requires close observation of the template to be copied, meaning the masters' actions and its outcomes. Then the learner must try to reproduce an exact copy of the template. This is hard work—and may resemble an iterative process where the learner commute in repeated cycles between observing the template—discovering more and more details—and subsequently translating these details into his/her copied versions.

Variations in the type and quality of the template is another challenge for translators aiming at copying. In general, physical objects, like machines and furniture, are easier to copy than work process practices, which often involves complex relationships between many actors. Ideally, a template should be a precise representation of the (best) practice targeted to be copied, and should contain all relevant information that the translator need to make an accurate copy (Winter and Szulanski, 2001). However, templates varies on these points: Sometimes there are elusive links back to the practices to be copied, information is general, while details are missing (Szulanski and Winter, 2002; Baden-Fuller and Winter, 2005).

Translators' access to the template is a third point that may facilitate or hamper copying. The iterative and laborious nature of copying requires good access—such as in the Kata institution where the learner repeatedly can observe all aspects of the master's acts to be copied. However, translators' access to templates are often limited, for example in cases where a potential donor organization take efforts to protect their practice from being copied (Reed and DeFillippi, 1990; Conner, 1995; Amara et al., 2008).

These arguments all run counter to the widely held images of copying as a simple translation rule. In reality, copying is often extremely difficult. According to Popper: "All the repetitions which we experience are approximate repetitions, and by saying that a repetition is approximate, I mean that the repetition B of an event A is not identical with A, or indistinguishable from A, but only more or less similar to A" (Popper, 1959: 420).

The radical translation mode

The second ideal-typical translation mode, the radical mode, is defined as translators' propensity to act relatively unbound by source context versions when creating recipient context versions of them (Røvik, 2016). Thus, under the influence of the radical mode, translated" recipient-organization versions will tend to deviate severely from the source version.

The three translation modes outlined in this chapter are generic features of translation in general. Thus, they are also clearly expressed in the two foreign domains that are antecedents of the translation theory outlined in this book. In translation studies, the radical mode—often referred to as the norm of adherence to—and relevance of a translation for the target context (Toury, 1985)—finds many expressions. For example, according to Cicero, the ideal text translation should resemble "*exprimere imitando*," that is, the artistic creation of something brand new in imitation of something that already exists (Robinson, 1998b). The typical contemporary and influential representations of the radical translation mode within linguistic translations are the Manipulation School (Hermans, 1985/2014), and the Skopos theory school (Hönig and Kußmaul, 1982). In translation studies a radical translation mode is often referred to as *adaptation*, which means a translation that is so radical that the recipient version is sometimes hardly accepted as a translation (Bastin, 2008). In the domain of organizational translation, the radical translation mode comes to expression in the axiom that translations always means transformations of what is transferred (Czarniawska and Sevòn, 1996). The transformation can be severe, since translators in different contexts interpret a source version differently, and thus, create their own context-specific versions, paraphrased as *everything everywhere, yet everywhere different* (Hannerz, 1996).

To better understand organizations and translators' propensity to enter into a radical translation mode in knowledge transfer processes, a set of why, where, and how questions should be answered. There are three main trajectories that may all lead translators to a radical translation mode. These trajectories are constituted by rational calculations, accidents (or imitation failures), and habitual behavior.

Calculated radical translations

A radical translation mode can be based on deliberate calculations and decisions. Such decisions are often premised on two slightly different aims and motives: the radical translation can be executed to (a) achieve effective local problem-solving, and (b) to avoid risks of "foreign imports."

Radical translation to increase local problem-solving capacity. A radical translation can reflect an ambition of effective problem-solving. Major changes to source versions of ideas and practices may be motivated by an aim of developing even more effective and targeted means to handle certain challenges in recipient organizations. Westney (1987) provides an example in her study of the development of the Japanese police system early in the Meiji period 1868–1912. During the Meiji restauration, the police as well as other parts of the Japanese public administration were reformed by systematic attempts to transfer models of institutions and practice from various Western countries to Japan. The search for foreign models was premised on a clear problem definition: the existing police system, which was a heritage from the former Tokugawa regime (1603–1867), was characterized by considerably differentiation of jurisdiction by region and by citizens' status (one law for noble Samurais, and another for commons). Therefore, the Meiji leaders searched for a model that could secure a uniform treatment of citizens, despite their status and localization. Although parts of the model were based on insights from Germany and England, the Meiji leaders choose the French centralized police system as the overall template to emulate.

However, in the early 1880s, it became clear that the centralized police system imported from France had not solved the unreasonable variations in the regional distribution of police services in Japan. Reports from the midst 1980s documented a negligible police presence in the rural districts, and that the French-inspired system of concentrating police posts in the towns restricted the police to play a reactive rather than a preventive role in rural Japan. This recognition sparked a radical transformation of important parts of the adopted centralized French administrative model. Contrary to centralization, decentralization now became the guiding idea for problem solving. As Westney (1987) showed, this was a radically different strategy. Implemented in the second half of the 1880s, it led to severe changes. From 1886 to 1889, the number of police posts in the country made a jump of 270 percent. Police stations were established in each county and a new type of base-level police posts (one-man residential posts) was established under each county station.

Radical translation as risk avoidance. Differences between source and recipient organizational contexts is a critical variable that affects chances for successful knowledge transfer (Kedia and Bhagat, 1988; De Long and Fahey, 2000). Important contextual differences often stem from spatial, cultural, political, and institutional distance between source and recipient. The more the source and the target contexts differs in relation to such variables, the higher the chances that the transferred foreign knowledge contains context-specific elements that do not fit with the recipient context. However, recipient organizations can be aware of the risks involved in such foreign knowledge imports, and may try to avoid or reduce the level of risk by executing radical translations to adapt it to the recipient organization. An example: In the late 1960s, a number of Norwegian organizations had plans to implement versions of American performance-appraisal systems. However, Norwegian leaders as well as representatives of the Norwegian Confederation of Trade Unions (LO) and the Norwegian Confederation of Business and Industry (NHO) early anticipated that the U.S.-performance-appraisal system contained elements from American working-life traditions and institutions, which were very different from the Norwegian working-life context. The overall feature of the U.S. system as a tool for individualized top-down control of workers' performance was anticipated to collide with the Norwegian more collective and bottom-up–oriented tradition. In light of such anticipations, LO and NHO initiated a radical translation of the U.S. performance-appraisal system. The outcome, the so-called Development Dialogue, differed severely from the American system. For example, the dialogue between employer and employee should not focus upon the employee's work performance, results, and payments. Instead, the dialogue was designed as a means to facilitate trusting relationships and to prevent conflicts in the workplace.

Accidental radical translations

As showed above, radical translations can stem from rational calculations. However, it may also be the unintended outcomes of failures, or "accidents," in knowledge transfer processes. Especially, such "accidents" can occur in cases where organizations try to imitate others. The relationship between imitation and innovation is tricky and fascinating. Researchers, such as Alchian (1950) and Levitt (1966) have pointed at how failures to imitate may unintentionally foster the creation of new versions that deviate so severely from the source version that it stands out as something radically new. The main reason why attempts at imitation may lead to radical translations is imperfect knowledge in the imitation organizations about the source template to be imitated. Westney (1987) provides an example from her study of the Meiji regime's attempts to imitate the French police system. In trying to replicate this system exactly, the Japanese designed and implemented a national police force that was considerably more centralized and much more powerful than the French template. According to Westney, this radical deviation was largely caused by poor Japanese knowledge of the French system. In fact, there were only one person in the Meiji administration who possessed firsthand experience of the French model.

Habitual radical translations

Habits and traditions—in addition to deliberate decisions and imperfect imitations—are the third trajectory that can lead organizations and individuals into a radical translation mode. This means that the likelihood to adopt this mode, expressed in the propensity to severely transform transferred source versions, sometimes reflect rule-like taken-for-granted values and assumptions pertinent to certain societal contexts. While a reproducing mode is often especially ascribed to Asian countries and cultures, like Japan and China, the inclination to enter into a radical translation mode is associated with Western countries and ideals. Thus, the radical mode of translation is facilitated by the Western modern project and some of its core ideals: the belief in individualism and rationality, the value of newness and novelty, and the notion of continuous progress toward higher levels of technological development, civilization and welfare. The heroes in this narrative are those organizations and individuals who create inventions, take risks and sparks innovations. The Western admiration for the value of novelty and progress stimulates a radical translation mode—with its characteristic severe changes and, thus, renewal of others' knowledge and practices. The Western celebration of newness, novelty, innovations, and inventors—often contrasted with reproductions and copycats—is expressed in many forms, the most prominent of which are discussed below.

The first is certain patterns in Western interpretations and production of meaning about imitation versus innovation. There is a long Western tradition to speak and write in disparaging terms about nations and organizations renowned for copying. The Australian anthropologist, Michael Taussig (1993), points at a certain "foundational moment" (p. 75) which he argues is an important antecedent of Westerners' patronizing image of organizations and individuals who copy as inferior and primitive. The background for this historic moment was Charles Darwin's voyage as a crewmember on the ship HMS Beagle, which left England for South America in December 1831. In 1832, Beagle arrived at the archipelago of Tierra del Fuego. There, on the beach, Darwin met the native people. In Darwin's extensive notes from this meeting, he described the natives as possessing "the power of mimicking"—resembling apish humans (Darwin et al., 1839). He was especially fascinated by their prowess to mimic himself. In his 1839 publication, Darwin made a very important connection with historical consequences when he described the natives' copying behavior as expressions of a lesser, savage stage of civilization. According to Taussig (1993), this was "the foundational moment in the equation of savagery with mimesis" (p. 75)—which has been very instrumental in shaping the Western image of copying as acts of primitiveness. Simultaneously, when painting the reproducing copycats as the black ones, the inventors and innovators stand out as the white ones.

The second expression is the Western extensive attempts to *incentivize* novelty. Especially, since the early 1970s, numerous Western governmental and regional organizations, as well as business organizations, have invested much money, competence, and efforts in designing and implementing various incentive systems to promote inventions and innovations (Riggs and von Hippel, 1994; Scotchmer, 2004). In addition to incentivizes, novelty and innovation are also promoted by certain institutions (such as governmental patent offices), and by laws and regulations, especially copyright and intellectual property rights.

The chronic shortage of novelty and rich supply of templates to imitate. However, although novelty and inventions are admired and strongly promoted, they are usually extremely hard to achieve. This is indirectly reflected in the definition of novelty as "something that was uncommon before a particular point in time and that, hence, was discovered or created at that point in time" (Witt, 2016: 3). As the definition implies, the concept of *real* novelty is reserved for *universal* novelty, meaning that it must be an idea, or device (invention), that is new at a particular time to *all* domains. Thus, acts of *discovery* can, but usually do not, equate to novelty, since others usually have discovered your "discovery" before. These arguments throw light on why especially Western organizations and individuals experience that the demand for novelty largely exceeds the supply. Organizations will try to overcome the chronic shortage of novelty in various ways. Obviously, they can try even harder to come up with real novelty and inventions. A few will succeed, but real novelty is very scarce, and most organizations will have to live up to the strong expectations of delivering novelty by other approaches. Radical translation is a common approach. Many organizations will try to construct newness and novelty by radically transformations of others' ideas and practices. While there is a chronic shortage of real novelty, there is usually a rich supply of other organizations to imitate in whatever field and subject a translator aims at making a novel contribution to. However, to live up to the very strong Western norms of novelty deliverance, organizations will have to transform what is borrowed so that the heritage from the imitated templates is erased.

Radical translations as habitual acts forced by norms of avoiding copying and producing "something new" can be done in a variety of ways. Renaming others' practices and devices, but keeping the content, is a common means to signal newness (Røvik, 1998), but hardly a *radical* translation. However, there are other more radical types. One is to translate many rather modest changes to a template, which together make the translated version deviate sufficiently from the imitated template to achieve the status of something novel. The domain of popular music provides many examples—a domain with very strict demands for novelty, and yet the very ubiquity of music makes it very difficult for artists to avoid imitation. One example is the story of Elvis Presley's first big hit, "That's All Right," which was recorded in Sun Studios, Memphis, July 5, 1954. This was also the day when Presley for the first time met with two of the musicians who became permanent members of his band, Scotty Moore (electric guitar), and Bill Black (bass). "That's All Right," was the very first song they recorded. The song, and the way Presley performed it, contributed strongly to his image as a very different artist of extreme quality. In 2004, the influential *Rolling Stone* magazine sealed the novelty status of Presley's "That's All Right," by proclaiming that it was "the very first rock-and-roll record" (Cave, et al., 2004). However, while most fans experienced this song as pure novelty, it was in fact a translation, although radical, of the black blues singer Arthur Crudup's song "That's All Right, Mama," which he wrote, recorded, and released in September 1946. In Presley's version, a series of small changes added up to a radical translation. His version was significantly more upbeat than Crudup's original; Elvis changed parts of the lyrics, the bass figure was different, and the blue notes were used differently. Together, this created foreignness and newness compared to Crudup's version. In addition, eight years had passed since Crudup released the original. Thus, to many people in 1954, it was almost forgotten, or conceived of as old-fashioned.

Fashion and radical translation. Habitual radical translation reflects the close connection between the logic of fashion and the Western modern project, with its demand for newness and novelty and the corresponding disparagement of imitation. Fashion is a dynamic social mechanism that can explain how forms of human expression (ideas, practices, objects) can achieve popularity, be massively spread within large populations, and decline and fade (Tarde, 1903; Blumer, 1969; Røvik, 1996; Strang and Macey, 2001; Czarniawska, 2014). Fashion's transient nature is closely interrelated with the modern project's claim for progress and novelty. What drives fashion is the continuous vacillation between two opposing forces: differentiation and imitation. Novelty-seeking actors will try to differentiate from prevailing fashions and attract attention—for example by radical translations. This will trigger processes of imitations and diffusion. When what formerly was novel has been spread and become convention, it has lost its newness and novelty quality—which again triggers differentiation and novelty-seeking processes.

Operational translation rule: Alteration

Within the radical mode, alteration is the operational translation rule. Alteration refers to translation actions that leads to severe transformation of the source version on the road to a target version. As showed above, alteration can be initiated by deliberate decisions, be a byproduct of failures to imitate, or reflect habitual actions. There are many ways that the source template can be severely altered. However, analytically, two main types can be identified: alteration as hybridization and as metamorphosis.

Hybridization. Alteration as hybridization refers to processes where translators select particular elements from various sources and combine them—thereby creating "something new" and different. The elements that are combined may come from different external sources: for example, a certain hybrid can be a combination of elements from two or more external templates. It can also be a combination of elements from one or more external sources with elements from existing practices in the target organization (Røvik 1998; Bausch et al., 2022). A feature of many hybrid translations is that it is often possible to identify the identity of each particular element in the translated version. For example, this was the case in the Meiji regime's chosen police system model. Even after this model was implemented, it was possible to identify the antecedents of each element: The overall formal structure emulated from France, the police education from Germany, and the English-style "patrols, drills, ranks and functions" (Westney, 1987: 38).

Metamorphosis. Alteration as metamorphosis means that the blending and the change of various elements in the translated version is so thorough that it is very hard to identify elements imitated from external sources. The deviation from templates is profound and the transformation almost total. An example is provided by the above-mentioned transformation of the U.S. performance appraisal system to the Scandinavian Development Dialogue. This was a severe radical translation that comes close to metamorphosis.

The modifying translation mode

This mode, rooted in a pragmatic approach, is characterized by translators' awareness of the value and the challenges of balancing competing concerns of replications and adaptations, fidelity versus fit, in knowledge transfers across organizational borders. Thus, the modifying mode comes to expression in translation acts as a propensity to balance concerns regarding inclusion of the essentials of the source practice to be emulated—with concerns about making the translated version work in the recipient context (Røvik, 2016).

While it is rather easy to identify how a modifying mode is used by practitioners involved in concrete knowledge transfers, it is not—unlike the two others—an ideal type with a large distinct body of literature. In this respect, it differs severely from the reproducing and the radical modes. Why? While all the three modes are ideal types, the two latter are also associated with renowned knowledge transfer *ideals*, which is reproduction and copying versus radical translation and innovation. These two modes are often dichotomized and presented as a narrative of two different and competing ideals. It is also a dichotomy that fuels and is itself fueled by a much more overarching narrative: the one about the novelty-seeking innovative Western world against the reproducing copycats of the Orient (the eastern part of Asia). The narratives of these competing ideals for knowledge transfers have been a strong driving force that have generated much attention, research and literature about the reproducing and the radical translation modes. The modifying mode introduced here, is much less conceptualized, discussed, researched and described in the literature than the two others. It probably reflects, that while the reproducing and the radical modes are two opposing forces in the powerful narrative of how the West competes with the Orient, the modifying mode is associated with a pragmatic, less exciting "on the one hand, and on the other"—position. However, in the literature there *are*, in fact, attempts to theorize and describe the modifying mode, and what is more: The modifying mode is probably much more common among practitioners involved in knowledge transfer processes than is reflected in the research literature.

The modifying mode in the research literature

There are works within various research fields that try to define, theorize, and highlight the advantages and challenges of balancing concerns for replication with concerns for adaptations, or fidelity versus fit. For example, such reasoning is found within translation studies and to a large extent in works focusing on equivalence models of translations, and especially in research following the formulation of the so-called *replication dilemma* (Winter and Szulanski, 2001.

In translation studies there are enduring debates about how to ensure that the meaning of source texts is present in the translated target version while it is also sufficiently adapted to be comprehended by target context actors. The translators are the key figures in such balancing acts. Pym (1992) argues that equivalence between source and targets texts is a negotiable entity, and that the translators are those doing the negotiation.

Most of the organizational research and theorizing related to a modifying mode can be traced back to Winter and Szulanski's 2001 conceptualization of the *replication dilemma*. A basic premise for Winter and Szulanski is that there are great advantages of exactly replicating a source practice template. Thus, the norm should be copying. Yet, the dilemma that replicators face is that "they must trade off the advantages of precision against those of learning and adaptation" (p. 737). The 2001 paper by Winter and Szulanski is not in defense of a modifying mode. Rather, exact replication is still the gold standard while the replication dilemma is presented as the mechanism that frequently leads transfer practices to deviate from what is optimal. However, in later works by these authors they are more eager to acknowledge the rationality of a modifying mode and the advantages of balancing competing concerns of replication and adaptation. An example is Baden-Fuller and Winter's (2005) analysis of replicating strategies and their introduction of a distinction between "principles" and "templates." The templates approach, meaning copy exact, is suggested by an order like "Watch me carefully how I do this, then copy it exactly—but don't ask me why" (p. 4). When knowledge transfer is guided by the principles approach, it may, according to Baden-Fuller and Winter, be expressed like this: "Let me explain why this works and the reasons why I do it this way, and then you try to make it work yourself. I will comment on any mistakes I see" (p. 4). Although the authors conceive of both templates and principles as different means to succeed with replications, the principle approach is more in line with a modifying mode, leaving more autonomy to the target organization actors to interpret the template and to adjust based on knowledge about the target context.

Williams (2007) takes a slightly different stand. He argues that organizations can overcome the replication dilemma by replicating some elements in a template, and adapt others to fit into the recipient context. In a study of cross-border knowledge transfer in the telecommunications industry, he shows that elements such as accounting and reporting measures are frequently replicated in transfers, because they are almost noncontext-sensitive practices. However, other elements, such as customer service practices and marketing, are frequently adapted because of "the extent to which they interact with the unique environment of each location" (p. 868). Bauman et al. (1991) studied the debate between "the fidelity camp" (in defense of replication) and "the reinvention camp" (in defense of modification) within the healthcare field of prevention. They concluded—much in line with Williams (2007)—that fidelity should be maintained at the level of each of the prevention programs core causal mechanisms of operation. However, reinvention of parts of a program to better fit into a target context, is permitted, but only when the causal mechanisms is preserved. In a qualitative case study of a multinational electronic organization, D'Adderio (2014) shows that the replication—adaptation dilemma is solved in a way that corresponds to Cyert and March's (1963) theory of sequential attention to—and realization of goals over time. She finds that the organization pays attention to replication at one point in time and then later shifts to attention towards adaptation.

While we know that organizations *do* modify transferred practices, there has been less focus on how the modifications are done and how the modified versions work in recipient organizations. Such shortages are the point of departure in Ringov et al's (2017) study of knowledge transfer in 2.025 units of a large U.S.-based franchise organization. In this project, the researchers move away from a strict either–or conceptualization of replication-adaptation, and studies the effects of replication of an established template compared to the effects of augmentation, meaning versions of the template where some elements have been added that are not part of the template. Their empirical examination shows that both the cases of replication and the cases of augmentation have positive effects on unit performance. They also find that the positive performance effect of accurate replication diminishes over time with unit age, while in contrast, the positive effect of augmentation increases.

The operational translation rules of modifications

Although an intermediate modification mode is not at all as well conceptualized and highlighted in the research literature as the reproducing and the innovation/radical translation modes, there are reasons to believe that modifications are much more common in practice among actors involved in border-crossing knowledge transfers. This suggestion is premised on two main reasons. One is the well-documented insight that "copy exact" is very difficult and that modifications—minor as well as more severe—may occur accidently. Another is a suggestion that modifications of templates often stem from deliberate decisions. Translators who are knowledgeable about both the template and the recipient context may deliberately balance competing concerns for copying and adaptation by translating a modified version. Within the modifying mode, we can analytically distinguish between two main operational translation rules: omission and addition.

Omission

The translation rule "omission" refers to the toning down, or subtraction, of certain elements of the source context template in the translated recipient version. There is a difference in degree of omission between "toning down" and "subtraction." "Toning down" means that the target context narrative about the desired source practice suppresses certain aspects of it or tell them differently. "Subtraction" means that an identifiable element of the desired source-context practice throughout the translation process has been removed and does not appear in the target context version.

What is left out in omissions, and why? There can be several reasons why certain details of a desired source practice have been excluded from—or rewritten in the recipient-context narrative of the "true story." Sometimes certain aspects are toned down because they are *untranslatable*, meaning that hardly any equivalent for the certain source-context aspect can be found in the recipient context. An example is provided by Sahlin-Andersson (1996) in her study of attempts to establish a science park in southern Stockholm in the 1980s—and with the Silicon Valley science park as a main template. Two renowned aspects of Silicon Valley are the stable, very good, sunny weather in this part of California, which attracts competent people from all over the world, and the very special high-competence industrial cluster, which may nurture any firm in Silicon Valley. However, similar conditions are not present in southern Stockholm. Thus, Sahlin-Andersson shows that these two aspects were toned down in the Stockholmian narrative of the Silicon Valley success story. What then happened to these two aspects can be interpreted in light of a concept from translation studies, *implicitation*, meaning the nonverbalization in the target version of aspects that are explicit in the source version (Klaudy, 1998). Although toned down, it is reasonable to think that almost all involved actors in the Stockholm project nevertheless knew about the extreme good weather conditions in California and about the very special industrial and knowledge infrastructure in Silicon Valley. Thus, these aspects became an implicit, not much mentioned part of the Stockholmian narrative of the template. In general, actors with a strong interest in realizing a project by recreating a special template may want to highlight the similarities and suppress the dissimilarities when comparing source and recipient contextual conditions. Thus, while similarities facilitate border-crossing transfers, dissimilarities usually halt such transfers.

Sometimes translators concerned with making a recipient version *subtract* certain elements that are part of the template to be transferred. It can be accidently "lost in translation," but it can also be the outcome of calculated actions. Organizations may leave out an element of a template because it is not considered to be part of the core causal mechanism, and/or because it is anticipated to be too laborious and costly to implement in relation to expected returns. Walgenbach (1997) provides an example in a study of how a group of

German firms reacted to the demands of standardizing authorities to adopt an ISO-9000 quality standard with a number of highly specified elements. Data show that most firms made calculations about what they really needed to control and enhance quality, thus leaving out elements that were conceived of as not necessary. Elements from a source context template are sometimes omitted based on anticipations that it has the potential to release tensions and conflicts in the recipient context. An example: when the U.S.-performance-appraisal system was attempted introduced in Norwegian organizations in the late 1960s, most organizations made radical translation, altered the U.S. concept, and adopted the very different development dialogue. However, some organizations performed less radical modifications of the U.S.-performance-appraisal system. Most of them modified the U.S. template by leaving out the routine of determining parts of individual employee's salary based on evaluation of his/her working performance and results. This subtraction was often based on anticipations of this routine's potential to collide with values and traditions in Norwegian working life (Røvik, 1998).

Addition

The modifying translation rule "addition" refers to adding one or a few elements to the desired source version of a practice—to complete a recipient version of it. The modifiers, meaning the added elements, can, in principle, stem from three different contexts, that is, the source context, the recipient context, and contexts outside the source and recipient contexts.

An added element to the recipient version may come from the source context, in fact, sometimes from the source practice itself. The phenomenon is known in translation studies as *explicitation* (Klaudy, 1998), meaning that an element of the desired practice, which is implicit and taken for granted in the source organizational context, can be made explicit and presented as a necessary element in the translated recipient version of it. The reason may be that what is taken for granted and tacit knowledge in one context, are sometimes not known and as obvious in another context. An example: Røvik (2007) studied how a practice in the health and care sector in a large Norwegian municipality was translated and presented on an external conference arena to other organizations which intended to use the actual practice as a template to emulate themselves. It was a practice containing routines to coordinate efforts across several specialized units within the health and care sector to gain overall and more efficient services to citizens with combined needs for services. In the presentation of the practice, the representatives of the municipality (the source) gave detailed descriptions of how the various units met and coordinated their efforts. They also emphasized the necessity of interdisciplinary identification and close mapping on beforehand of each individual potential candidate to receive the coordinated service. However, this mapping element was hardly mentioned in the internal municipality manual for how to organize and accomplish this practice. It was an obvious and taken for granted element—an implicit, tacit part of the professionals' practices. Yet in the translated version designated for potential adopters and recipients, it was explicated and added as an integral part of the successful practice.

A translated practice can also be modified by adding elements from existing practices in the recipient organization—probably the most common type of addition (Torsteinsen, 2006; Røvik, 2007). It can be an element which is added because it works well, represent a repository of organizational knowledge and experience, and/or is suggested to be rather easily configured with the transferred desired source practice.

Sometimes the added element is brought in from contexts other than the recipient and the main source context. Westney (1987) provides an example in her study of the Meiji regime's design of the Japanese postal system in the early 1870s. The Meiji leaders conceived of the postal system in Great Britain as the world's most modern—and decided to emulate in its entirety in the establishment of the Japanese postal system. However, there were a certain feature of the British postal system that was hard to translate to Japan: the British railroad system, which was the backbone of the U.K. postal system. While Great Britain was largely urbanized around 1870, and had the world's best railroad system, 80 percent of the Japanese population lived in rural areas, and the railroad system was poorly developed. Thus, the Japanese had to compensate and find solutions to postal transportation. One solution was to introduce an old Chinese transportation technology, the man-drawn chart, also known as the rickshaw. The first rickshaws appeared in Japan in 1870, and they were immediately adapted to fit the challenge of post transportation, especially in urban areas. Within a year, there were 25,000 Chinese-inspired rickshaws serving in the mainly Great Britain-inspired Japanese postal system.

Summing up

The aim of this chapter has been to identify, describe, and analyze the rules of translation of practices and knowledge across organizational borders. The chapter has developed a typology of translation rules, which comprises three main translation modes—each with appurtenant operational translation rules. Figure 5.1 sums up the main insights from this work.

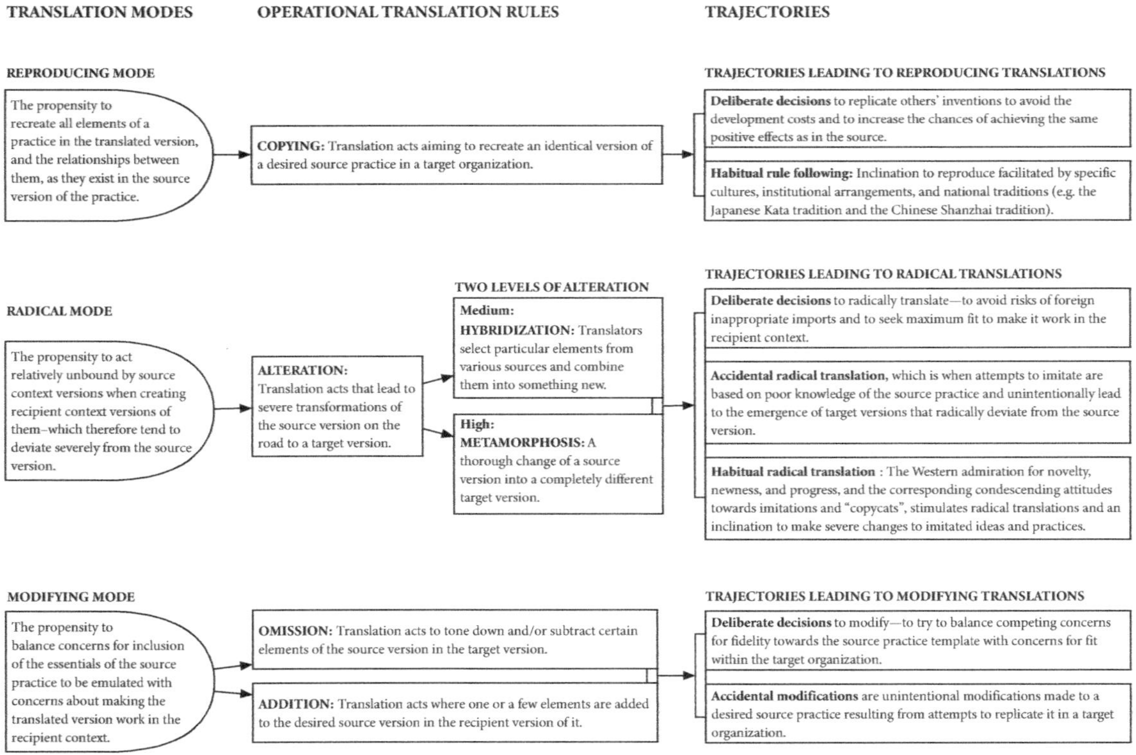

TRANSLATION MODES

REPRODUCING MODE
The propensity to recreate all elements of a practice in the translated version, and the relationships between them, as they exist in the source version of the practice.

RADICAL MODE
The propensity to act relatively unbound by source context versions when creating recipient context versions of them—which therefore tend to deviate severely from the source version.

MODIFYING MODE
The propensity to balance concerns for inclusion of the essentials of the source practice to be emulated with concerns about making the translated version work in the recipient context.

OPERATIONAL TRANSLATION RULES

COPYING: Translation acts aiming to recreate an identical version of a desired source practice in a target organization.

ALTERATION: Translation acts that lead to severe transformations of the source version on the road to a target version.

TWO LEVELS OF ALTERATION

Medium:
HYBRIDIZATION: Translators select particular elements from various sources and combine them into something new.

High:
METAMORPHOSIS: A thorough change of a source version into a completely different target version.

OMISSION: Translation acts to tone down and/or subtract certain elements of the source version in the target version.

ADDITION: Translation acts where one or a few elements are added to the desired source version in the recipient version of it.

TRAJECTORIES

TRAJECTORIES LEADING TO REPRODUCING TRANSLATIONS
Deliberate decisions to replicate others' inventions to avoid the development costs and to increase the chances of achieving the same positive effects as in the source.

Habitual rule following: Inclination to reproduce facilitated by specific cultures, institutional arrangements, and national traditions (e.g. the Japanese Kata tradition and the Chinese Shanzhai tradition).

TRAJECTORIES LEADING TO RADICAL TRANSLATIONS
Deliberate decisions to radically translate—to avoid risks of foreign inappropriate imports and to seek maximum fit to make it work in the recipient context.

Accidental radical translation, which is when attempts to imitate are based on poor knowledge of the source practice and unintentionally lead to the emergence of target versions that radically deviate from the source version.

Habitual radical translation: The Western admiration for novelty, newness, and progress, and the corresponding condescending attitudes towards imitations and "copycats", stimulates radical translations and an inclination to make severe changes to imitated ideas and practices.

TRAJECTORIES LEADING TO MODIFYING TRANSLATIONS
Deliberate decisions to modify—to try to balance competing concerns for fidelity towards the source practice template with concerns for fit within the target organization.

Accidental modifications are unintentional modifications made to a desired source practice resulting from attempts to replicate it in a target organization.

Figure 5.1 A typology of translation rules: Key concepts and how they are related

6
Reimagining That Translators and Translations Make a Difference

Introduction

This chapter returns to the puzzles that sparked this book project: the numerous observations of variations in outcomes following attempts to transfer knowledge across organizational borders. Knowledge transfer successes and failures have many expressions and often have severe consequences, including quality of services and products, financial return, and for organizational competitiveness, growth, decline, reputation, and even survival. How can such variations be interpreted and explained? This is the central question that permeates and connects all parts of the book. Knowledge transfer scholars have gained insights into this question through identifying and studying the effects of various transfer barriers and enablers. Partly in contrast to the barrier approach—but mostly as a supplement to it—this chapter develops the translation approach to understanding and explaining variations in knowledge transfer processes and outcomes. This is done by elaborating the third key argument upon which the translation theory is founded; that is, that translators and their translations make a difference: The ways translations are performed may explain outcomes of knowledge transfer processes.

The barrier approach

The last three decades of knowledge transfer research have materialized in an extensive body of literature on the topic. Although the literature reflects a multitude of perspectives, theories, and findings, it also has much in common. For example, the signal transmission metaphor (Shannon and Weaver 1949; Lin et al., 2005) is an underlying model that most of these studies are framed within. The heritage from this model comes to expression in the positioning of knowledge transfer studies with such key concepts as source (sender), channels, information (message), noise, and recipient. However, despite being influenced by this metaphor, these studies show how the complexities of knowledge transfer processes across organizational borders deviate drastically from simple signal transmission models. Thus, another common characteristic of this literature is the identification and studies of factors—or barriers—that complicate signal transmission images of knowledge transfers. A barrier is a hindrance that makes it difficult or impossible for something to happen. The barrier stops or decelerates the movement of something, thus maintaining separation. A barrier can be concrete, such as a fence that hinders passage between certain geographical areas. Within the field of knowledge transfer studies, a "barrier" is an abstract concept that serves to zoom in on any obstacles that stops or slows down the flow of information between organizations and/or between units within organizations. An often used synonym for barrier is the concept of boundary (Brown and Duguid, 2001; Carlile, 2004). Several knowledge transfer scholars explicitly refer to their research efforts as attempts to identify and measure the effects of certain transfer barriers. One of the first to introduce the barrier concepts was Szulanski, in his seminal 1996 paper, which subsequently appeared as a defining concept in knowledge transfer research and publications (Argote et al., 2000; Sun and Scott, 2005; Minbaeva, 2007; Riege, 2007; Schilling and Kluge, 2009; Paulin and Suneson, 2015).

Von Hippel (1994) introduced the concept of "sticky information," which is closely related to the concept of barriers. It includes all barriers and challenges that mediators may encounter when trying to decontextualize knowledge from a source organization, then transfer and contextualize it in a recipient organization. In subsequent literature, "stickiness" has been used almost as a synonym to barrier (Szulanski, 1996; 2000; Jensen and Szulanski, 2004; Li and Hsieh, 2009; Blackman and Benson, 2012; Karabag and Berggren, 2017).

The factors that knowledge transfer scholars have identified as barriers can also act as windows into understanding what enables knowledge transfer processes. For example, while certain features of social networks that connect source and recipient may decelerate, other network features may accelerate knowledge transfers. Thus, barriers identified in knowledge transfer studies are probably better conceived of as variables, where certain value scores hinder and others promote knowledge transfer across organizational borders. In this way, variations in outcomes of knowledge transfer processes—whether successes or failures—are supposed to stem from different scores on certain barrier variables.

Chapter 2 identifies seven different bodies of literature, each concentrating on theorizing and researching a certain set of factors, or variables, that are supposed to influence upon knowledge transfer across organizational borders. Below is a short version of each of these research traditions' key theoretical assumptions and appurtenant variables that are supposed to have a barring/facilitating effect on knowledge transfer processes and outcomes.

Formal organizational structure. The unifying theoretical assumption is that formal organizational structure is a central independent variable that channels, sometimes determines—and thus, can be the source of variations in border-crossing knowledge transfer processes and outcomes.

Absorptive capacity. The key variable, absorptive capacity, refers to the ability of an organization to recognize the value of new, external information, assimilate it, and exploit it for commercial ends. It is supposed that recipient organizations' level of absorptive capacity is decisive for variations in knowledge transfer processes and outcomes.

Social networks. The unifying theoretical assumption is that social networks within and between organizations—and the actors' position within them—can be decisive for variations in knowledge transfer processes. Thus, the central independent variable with barring/facilitation effect on transfers is features of the social network, such as network position, tie strength, density, and connectedness.

Geographical distance. The unifying theoretical assumption is that physical distance between organizations and individuals can affect and be the source of variations in knowledge transfer processes.

Cultural distance. The central assumption is that the degree of similarity/dissimilarity between organizational units' culture and/or nations' culture (that is, the common norms, behaviors, beliefs, customs and values shared by a defined group of people) is likely to influence—either barring or facilitate—and thus, be the source of variations in border-crossing knowledge transfers processes.

Institutional distance. Similarities and differences between countries' institutional profiles (that is, the typical features of a country's regulative, cognitive, and normative institutions) can be the source of variations in a variety of processes across national borders—including knowledge transfer processes. The central independent variable with barring/facilitating effect is country-specific institutional profiles.

Knowledge characteristics. The central assumption is that certain properties of the knowledge to be transferred, especially whether it is ambiguous or not (tacit and uncodified versus explicit and codified), will influence its transferability across organizational borders.

The translation approach

The seven streams of research and literature that constitute the barrier approach have identified sets of factors that influence knowledge transfers and have documented their effects. This research has greatly advanced the understanding of what causes variations in knowledge flows between organizations. However, the identified barriers only account for limited portions of the actual variations in knowledge transfers processes and outcomes. For more than three decades, knowledge transfer scholars have traced an eventual X factor that can hopefully explain most of the variations. For example, a lot of hope and enthusiasm was attributed to *absorptive capacity*, which long held the status as the potential X factor. However, both the indistinctiveness of the concept (Lane et al., 2006; Duchek, 2013) and results from empirical studies (Szulanski, 1996; van Wijk et al., 2008) have led to reduced optimism regarding the explanatory potential of this variable too. Thus, an X factor has not yet been identified, and a lot of variation remains to be understood and explained regarding knowledge transfer processes and outcomes.

A translation theory approach may be a supplement that pushes understanding of causes of such variations a bit further. However, a translation approach does *not* mean introducing another potential barrier variable to be theorized and empirically tested. Instead, a central element in this approach is methodological advice to zoom in on actors involved in knowledge transfers and trace what they really do throughout such processes. A key concept in this approach is *translation performance*, which means the extent to which and how involved actors—the translators—gain knowledge about source and target contexts, and mobilize such knowledge to choose, use, and eventually combine and shift various translation rules throughout knowledge transfer processes. A central suggestion is that the involved actors' translation performance may be decisive for the processes and outcomes of knowledge transfers between organizations. Thus, studies of translation performance can be a key to improved understanding of the generation of variations in knowledge transfers.

From a barrier approach perspective, the suggestion to study actors' translation performance may be considered unnecessary because it will probably show what we already know from barrier studies. However, as stated above, many variations remain in knowledge transfers that the barrier research has not yet accounted for. The suggestion is that these unexplained variations stem, on one hand, from instances where translators are *not* stopped or hindered by barriers known from the research literature, and, on the other hand, from instances where translators fail to exploit factors identified in the barrier research as enablers—to make successful knowledge transfers. In other words, translators have the potential to successfully overcome stickiness and barriers, as well as to contribute to failures in situations where barriers are modest or absent. This is an important source of variations in knowledge transfer processes and outcomes, and also of variations that—when seen from a barrier approach perspective—are not expected and accounted for.

The theorizing of translation performance as a key to understanding the emergence of and variations in knowledge transfer processes and outcomes has methodological implications. It requires the researchers to zoom in on translation processes—both decontextualization and contextualization processes—and on the involved actors and their translation actions. The dynamics of such processes must be revealed, which means exploring how involved actors choose and use various translation rules and encounter and enact various translation challenges.

The reviewed seven research traditions, all of which study various transfer barriers, have certain limitations as sources to insights about the dynamics of translation processes and actors' translation performances. The limitations stem from the dominant method of identifying transfer barriers and enablers, which is large sample studies and quantitative data. This methodological approach often means less attention to the transfer processes and less focus on the roles of the involved actors. Most of the foundational and most-cited works within each of these traditions are quantitative large-sample studies. These studies are designed primarily to identify the effects of sets of theorized barriers and enablers. However, they are not founded on theorizations of the involved actors as translators and of the importance of their translation performances for outcomes of knowledge transfer processes. Thus, many studies of transfer barriers indirectly create an image of involved actors as carriers or transporters—that is, passive mediators of knowledge—rather than as active translators who themselves make differences in transfer processes and outcomes.

When translators make a difference

A key argument in the translation approach is that the translation rules that the involved actors apply—whether the reproducing, modifying, or radical mode and their appurtenant operational rules—can be decisive for outcomes of knowledge transfer processes. This implies that the translators' usage of rules is important for outcomes. As highlighted in Chapter 5, translation rules are sometimes chosen deliberately based on rational calculations. However, rather than premised on rational calculations, such "choices" sometimes reflect culturally defined norms, values, and habits. Anyway, the appropriateness of a translation rule depends on the extent to which the rule matches in relation to what should be achieved in which contexts and under which conditions. A translation rule applied under different conditions is likely to lead to different results. Thus, a challenge for the translator is to carefully assess the aims of the actual knowledge transfer and its context and conditions—and then apply one or more translation rules that seem to be appropriate. Such challenges that are pertinent to actors' translation performance—and how they are handled—are a main source of variations, meaning the extent to which translations lead to intended and desirable versus unintended and undesirable outcomes. Translators sometimes succeed in assessing the situation and then choose and apply appropriate, matching translation rules, which leads to intended and desirable results. However, sometimes translators fail, and for various reasons. Their assessment and knowledge of the contexts and the actual situation may be superficial and poor, they may choose inappropriate translation rules, and they sometimes can be slow learners who maintain the usage of inappropriate translation rules for too long.

The next three sections present sets of example cases to illustrate how translators and the way they use certain translation rules have consequences for outcomes. The examples show how translation performance may be decisive for successes as well as failures. The six transfer cases take place in different time and spatial contexts: the United States, Norway, Denmark, China, United Kingdom, and India.

Reproducing mode: Successes and failures

The role of involved actors and their translation performance can be decisive for whether organizations succeed or fail in applying a reproducing-copying translation rule. Translators can be instrumental in choosing and using copying in such ways that it leads to desirable outcomes. However, involved actors' translation performance may also be the reason why attempts to copy lead to failures and undesirable outcomes. Critical variables for outcomes are the translators' assessments of the situations that lead to the choice of a reproducing-copying translation rule, and their decisions and actions that follow such a choice. Two examples are provided of the usage of a reproducing-copying translation mode; one with a successful, desirable outcome and another that failed and led to an undesirable outcome. In both cases the processes and outcomes cannot be understood without taking the involved actors' translation performances into account.

The McDonald's copying case

McDonald's is the world's largest fast-food chain and one of the best-known organizational replication successes. The chain's almost identical restaurants are spread all over the world and offer—with some exceptions—the same basic menu with the same taste and quality everywhere. The United States alone has approximately 14,000 outlets. More than half of the U.S. population live within a three-minute drive from a McDonald's restaurant (Tillotson, 2008). About 8 percent of the U.S. population—20 million people—visit a McDonald's restaurant each day, and the chain sells three times as much food as Burger King, the second-largest chain. The first international McDonald's franchise opened in 1967 (British Columbia). Today, there are 30,000 locations of McDonald's restaurants in 118 countries.

However, back in 1954 when McDonald's was established, it was not at all obvious that it would be a success. McDonald's was soon organized according to franchising principles, meaning a continuing relationship between a franchisor and a varying number of franchisees. It is an organizational form where the owner (the franchisor) allows the franchisees to operate under a common brand and to produce and distribute the franchisor's product, service, and method in accordance with more or less detailed specifications set by the franchisor. Franchising was not new in the early 1950s. Several fast-food companies had already tried to make replicas of their core businesses by franchising, but with limited success. So why did McDonald's succeed with *its* replication strategy?

The McDonald's fast-food replication success cannot be understood without zooming in on the translation performance of Ray Kroc, who in the early 1950s was the U.S. national sales manager for Multimix milkshake machines. In 1954, he visited Mac and Dick McDonald's hamburger restaurant in San Bernardino to find out why they had ordered as many as *five* milkshake machines. Kroc was impressed by the brothers' clean, effective, and quick serving of a limited menu of inexpensive and delicious hamburgers. He had realized the demand for high-quality fast food that could be made easily available for the increasing portion of mobile Americans who wanted to eat out. Thus, the McDonald brothers' restaurant in San Bernardino became an important template for Kroc's replicating strategy. While designing his replicas, Kroc also learned from contemporary fast-food franchising failures. One such failure, he thought, was to rapidly sell out franchises, generate money, and grow fast—but simultaneously lose oversight and control with the franchisees. According to Kroc, another typical franchisor failure was to devote too little attention to the key product: the food and the standardization of a high-quality menu (Kroc and Andersson, 1987). Central to Kroc's replication strategy was developing, standardizing, and controlling the distribution of such a menu. He recommended a strict copy exact modus operandi from the franchisees, which included buildings, furniture, uniforms, menu, and food quality. Almost no local adaptations and deviations from the template were allowed.

Kroc's performance in translating the template of the two McDonald brothers' restaurant, as well as the lessons from the failed attempts of contemporary fast-food franchising, into his replicating strategy, can be recognized by three characteristic strategic translation actions.

The first was that he avoided the common practice in the 1950s of selling territorial franchises, which is where the franchisor sells the franchisee the exclusive right to serve a defined territory without competition from other franchisees. Unfortunately, territorial franchises often led to barriers between the franchisor and the territory-ruling franchisee, which came to expression in a loss of control for the franchisor and to local adaptations and deviations from the actual franchising standards (Kunkel and Berry, 1968; Chiou and Droge, 2015). An example stems from McDonald's main competitor, Burger King Corporation (BKC). In 1959, BKC purchased defined rights for many territorial franchises in the United States and grew rapidly (Chiou and Droge, 2015). However, BKC lost control in the territories, which led to lowered and varying food quality and to inconsistency across franchises and territories. BKC had a hard job throughout the 1960s re-establishing standard fidelity among the franchisees. By contrast, even in the early 1950s, Kroc was aware of the potential negative effects of territorial franchises (Kroc and Andersson, 1987). Therefore, he concentrated solely on single-store franchisees, who had to compete with each other without any agreement about exclusive territory control. With reference to the barrier approach, this illustrates how Kroc, through his persistent and proactive translation based on the reproducing mode, managed to overcome the potential barring effect of territorial franchising, which could lead to franchisor's loss of control and increased franchisees' autonomy to make local adaptations to features of their territories.

The second characteristic of Kroc's translation performance refers to how he worked with potential new franchisees and, thus, replicas of McDonald's. Unlike most fast-food competitors, which sold new franchises rapidly, and consequently grew quickly, the entrance process for new McDonald's franchises was thorough and time-consuming. This reflected Kroc's ambition to ensure that each new candidate was knowledgeable about and motivated to fully implement and live up to all McDonald's standardizing requirements.

Thus, the process was effective in terms of recruiting the most able and dedicated franchises. In addition, Kroc wanted to integrate the franchisees as partners. He established a system of economic incentives, where he placed the economic health of each franchisee first. Kroc's efforts to select the most knowledgeable and dedicated applicants and to incentivize them by economic means can be interpreted in light of insights from barrier approach scholars about the importance of absorptive capacity in knowledge transfers. In the actual context, absorptive capacity refers to the franchises' ability to recognize, understand, adopt, and routinely apply McDonald's rigid standards for a uniform fast-food chain. Through proactive translation performance Kroc secured a higher absorptive capacity by only letting in the most knowledgeable and dedicated candidates, and by stimulating increasing absorptive capacity through economic incentives.

The third central feature of Kroc's translation was his continuing efforts to maintain system-wide uniformity and consistency throughout the chain. Kroc opposed the typical Western image of a replication strategy as easy to implement and apply. He stressed the challenges of not only choosing such a strategy, but also adhering to it and maintaining it over time (Kroc and Andersson, 1987; Brunsson and Jacobsson, 2000). He used various means to protect the standards and the replica franchising units from local adaptations and deviations. All day-to-day operations in a McDonald's franchise unit were broken down into single easy-to-learn operations. These operations were codified and described in detail in the McDonalds 700-page operation manual (Tillotson, 2008). As early as the mid-1950s Kroc implemented a system for continuously rigid monitoring and control of franchisees' performances according to McDonalds' standards and procedures.

The McDonald's example above shows how translators can make a difference in knowledge transfers. In order to understand McDonald's success with its fast food-replication strategy, one must zoom in on the knowledge transfer process and trace how a certain translator's performance established very important premises for the success through deliberately choosing and maintaining an appropriate translation rule.

Why Taylorism in the U.K. mines failed

Numerous attempts to use a reproducing-copying translation rule in knowledge transfer fail. Such failures can often be traced back to shortcomings of the involved actors' translation performance. For example, translators may not fully understand the source practice and therefore make inaccurate copies

(Alchian, 1950). Another typical failure is that the translators do not manage to maintain the reproducing-copying strategy and allow contextual adaptations to take place, as was the case with Burger King (mentioned above). Such cases illustrate that copying others' ideas and practices is challenging. However, failures following from the use of a reproducing-copying translation rule sometimes reflect that the chosen rule was inappropriate in the first place, due to a mismatch between the reproduced source practice and the recipient context.

Attempts to implement Taylorism in British coal mines in the interwar period provides an illuminating example. As discussed in Chapter 4, the British coal-mining industry was, until about 1920, characterized by a low degree of mechanization and very labor-intensive coal-getting processes. However, extensive changes took place during the interwar years. The new and much more effective Longwall method for coal getting was introduced simultaneously with new technology, among which the electric coal-cutter machine was especially important. Inspired by templates from American mining industry and from contemporary Fordism and U.S. fabric organizing, the early 1920s was also a period of comprehensive efforts to reproduce scientific management—or Taylorist principles—of management and work organizing in the British coal-mining industry.

An important prerequisite for the Taylorization of U.K. coal mining was mechanization, which took off in the first decades of the twentieth century. The introduction of electric coal-cutting machines and conveyor belts radically transformed colliers' work and paved the way for scientific management principles of work organizing (Tailby, 2011). What was introduced was a rigid job design and detailed organizing of workers' tasks and time. Tasks, which were previously handled flexibly within groups of eight to ten workers, were now split up, standardized, and allocated to single workers who were supposed to specialize and repetitively executing a limited number of tasks. There was also a detailed organizing and prescribing of the timing of the various work operations. The typical cycle of 24-hour operations was first scheduled in three shifts: The night shift undercut the coal by using the machine cutter, the day shift broke down the coal and loaded it on the conveyor belts, while the afternoon shift disassembled the conveyor belts and moved the gear further into the pit. The timing of each operation was further detailed and prescribed in sequences within each shift (Wellisz, 1953). Another central Taylorist-inspired element was the introduction of time studies of the miners' job performances and an incentive wage system with individual payment and bonuses tied strictly to the work actually done (Langrogne, 1919). With Fordism in American fabrics as a template, a new role for supervisors was introduced whose task was to overview and control that the miners performed according to predefined plans and schedules.

By the start of the interwar period, several American organizations, some of them within the mining business, had already implemented Taylorist principles and their experiences were known to many U.K. mine owners and engineers (Stewart, 1935). However, the most important template was Frederick Taylor's own principles, which he had formulated in his publications (e.g. Taylor, 1911). His principles were particularly heralded by his core disciples, which were a group of about 50 American organizations who were early adopters of Taylor's principles (Nelson, 1974). Even more important was the American profession of mechanical engineers (Shenhav, 1999). Taylor's gospel about industrial management as a science was also well known among mining engineers from the early interwar years, both from curriculums in contemporary engineering education and from a new type of publications: engineering periodicals, which were available from around the turn of the century. These publications (such as *Engineering Magazine* and *American Machinist*) were widely distributed and read by members of the engineering profession (Shenhav, 1999).

Even though there were many promotors of the idea of replicating Taylorist work organizing in U.K. coal mines, some actors were much more active than others. A highly influential agent and translator was Samuel Mavor (1863–1943), an electric and mining engineer and partner in Glasgow-based firm Mavor & Coulson. As noted by Tailby (2011), owners of the firms that manufactured coal-getting equipment were among the most eager to promote and prescribe a Taylorist work organization of the mines "to approximate more closely with that in the then modern factory" (Tailby, 2011: 157), and thus to adjust men's work to the logic of the machines. Mavor & Coulson was a major coal technology manufacturer and was the first to manufacture electric coal-cutting machines. By the end of World War I, the continental coal-producing countries bought about 90 percent of their Longwall mining equipment from Mavor & Coulson (Editorial, in *Colliery Guardian*, July 1965). Sam Mavor was very knowledgeable and enthusiastic about Taylorist work organizing. Before the interwar period, he had visited mine owners and mine engineers in Canada and the United States. Some of them had already adopted Taylor's principles. As a major supplier of mining technology, Mavor also personally knew most of the chief engineers and owners of the largest U.K. coal mines. As a promotor of scientific management in the mines, Mavor had two characteristics. Firstly, he was convinced that contemporary Ford fabric organizing was an appropriate template and that the entire Taylor package of principles for work organizing should be transferred and implemented as means of increasing mining efficiency and effectiveness. Mavor especially promoted time studies: "the systematic observation and recording throughout a shift of minute to minute intervals in relation to work done" as a means "to perpetually refining and intensifying the performance of work" (Mavor, 1924). Secondly, Mavor was a very powerful and influential translator. His power base reflected that he combined the authority of being the market-leading manufacturer of mining equipment with deep insight in coal mining from different parts of the world—and strong personal networks to mine owners and engineers.

Throughout the interwar period and into the 1940s and early 1950s there were many indications that the attempts to change the organizing of work in British coal mines by principles of scientific management had largely failed. The mechanization and breakup of the autonomous working group, the introduction of a piece-wage system, and close control-oriented supervision led to much harder worker conditions. Absenteeism increased, and the rigid piece-wage system was a constant source of tension, leading to numerous stoppages and strikes (Phillips, 1976; Church et al., 1990). For example, Wellisz (1953) identified 640 stoppages between 1947 and 1950 due to strikes, just in mines located in the north-western part of the country. Throughout the interwar years, overall productivity in U.K. coal mines was modest (Tailby, 2011), and clearly below the owners' and leaders' ambitions and expectations. In their seminal study of a sample of coal mines in the late 1940s, Trist and Bamforth (1951) revealed that colliers adapted to implemented Taylorist work principles by developing strong norms of low productivity.

How can we understand and explain the many negative consequences that followed from the attempts to replicate fabric and Taylorist organizing in U.K. coal mines in the interwar period? There are three main reasons.

Lack of target context knowledge. Expressed in translation terms, a very important reason for the replication failure was that the main promotors and translators lacked sufficient knowledge of the target context and the existing work practices. The handgot system of coal getting was largely performed by self-contained working units that had internal flexibility and with workers related to strong social ties. These working units were characterized by high internal complexity in task performance and a low degree of explicitness (tacitness), which made them difficult for outsiders to comprehend. The copying of Taylorist principles ripped up the established working units. This led to severe social and psychological reactions and caused absenteeism and stoppages. However, as Trist and Bamforth (1951) revealed, the colliers lacked the precise language to conceptualize and communicate their experiences and emotional reactions towards the supervisors and translators of the Taylorist principles. In addition, the most important translators were engineers by profession. Their training and devotion to physics and the working of machines were often paralleled with a trained incapacity to sense and understand the psychological and sociological reasons for the colliers' reactions to the rigid Taylorist organizing of their work.

The configuring challenges. A challenge for translators is to relate and configure "the new" with "the existing." The more "the new" differs from "the existing," the harder it is to configure, and the more chances increase for translation failure. In Chapter 4, three types of relatedness are outlined: loose coupling, weaving, and replacement. "Replacement" means that the new practice shall replace (not only come in addition to or be weaved together with) existing practices in the target organizational context. This is often the most challenging type of configuration that translators face. In the case of replicating fabric and Taylorist principles in U.K. coal mines, it meant that most colliers had to give up the way they had worked and cooperated before within the relatively autonomous units—and now perform their work with new standardized tasks under close supervision and control. In sum, it meant that the difference between the work organizing in the coal mines that the mechanized Longwall method and the Taylorist principles required—compared to the existing work organizing based on groups for self-regulation and "responsible autonomy" (Trist and Bamforth, 1951: 6), was huge. The challenge for the involved actors on the employer's side—the translators—to try to balance and adapt these two organizing principles was not realized and hardly acknowledged—a conclusion that leads into the third observation.

Slow learning processes. Translators may shift from one initially chosen translation rule to another if they experience that they do not achieve what was expected. As already pointed at, the interwar period was characterized by numerous negative reports and lessons from the British coal-mining industry. Overall, however, this did not lead to changes in the usage of a reproducing translation mode when implementing the templates from fabrics and the Taylorist work organizing principles. The reproducing mode was maintained, and an important reason was the way owners and leaders interpreted the increase in absenteeism, strikes, and persistent low productivity. They were mainly conceived of as expressions of colliers' resistance to change and unwillingness to adapt, but of temporary character (Mitchell, 1933; Wellisz, 1953; Goldthorpe, 1959).

However, there are reasons to suggest that shifts in translation rule from a reproducing mode to a modifying mode could have reduced and somehow also solved the problems. This is indicated by Tavistock researchers' observations and experiments with so-called composite work groups throughout the 1950s (Eijnatten, 1998). These were relatively autonomous groups of eight miners operating within the new mechanical mining system who were given the responsibility for almost a full cycle of mining operations. The composite unit was a modified version of the autonomous work unit from the pre-mechanical handgot period of coal getting. In the years 1955–1958, Trist and associates experimented with the design of working groups in mines of North-West Durham. Operating within a fully mechanized and Taylorist-designed work organization, groups of 40 to 50 miners were selected and included in the experiments. They were allowed to draw up the shift schedules themselves and to deviate from specialized roles by exchanging various tasks, as well as to define a fair and rewarding system among the group members. The results of these modifications of the organizing of work led to 25 percent higher output, a 50 percent cut in absenteeism, and lower production costs (Trist et al., 2013). These results indicate that a main reason for the huge and enduring problems generated after the implementation of the Taylorist work principles in U.K. coal mines was a translation failure to maintain a reproducing translation rule and not enter into a modifying mode. This assessment corresponds to Trist and Bamforth's (1951) overall diagnosis of the source of the problems: "a complicated, rigid and large-scale work system borrowed with too little modification from an engineering culture appropriate to the radically different situation of the factory" (Trist and Bamforth, 1951: 23).

Radical mode: Success and failures

The importance of translation performance and the deliberate choice of translation rules for outcomes of knowledge transfer processes can also be illustrated with examples where translators have applied a radical translation mode. As outlined in Chapter 5, a radical translation mode is defined as translators' inclination to act relatively unbound by the source context version when creating a target context version of it. A radical mode may lead to severe differences between source and target context versions of a certain practice. In the following two cases are presented where involved actors applied a radical translation mode—and with different outcomes.

The making of the Norwegian coworker dialogue

In the late 1960s, there were several attempts to implement various versions of U.S.-based performance appraisal and counselling (PAC) systems in Norwegian organizations. Central features of PAC systems are goal setting, both at the organizational and individual level, surveillance and measuring of individual job performance and goal attainment, and managers' feedback to the employee, including questions of payment in relation to performance (Burke, 1996; Otley, 1999). Among the early adopting organizations in Norway were large multinationals such as Esso, Shell, IBM, and Hydro. However, representations of the Norwegian Confederation of Trade Unions (LO) were rather skeptical. As noted in Chapter 5, implementing U.S.-based PAC systems was seen as a potential attack on the collective wage bargaining institution, a new effective management steering tool, and a threat to the strong values of collectivity and equality in Norwegian working life. Therefore, the very powerful trade unions tried to slow down the further spread of PAC systems in Norway. From the early 1970s, it was evident that the U.S.-based concept could not be adopted by Norwegian organizations without a lot of resistance and conflict (Wollebæk, 1989; Røvik, 2002). On the other hand, both employers' and employees' federations acknowledged the advantages of many other aspects of PAC systems, such as systematized and routinized communication at the individual level between the leaders and the led.

Around the mid-1970s there was a growing mutual awareness among certain actors that the U.S.-based PAC concept needed to be translated to fit into the Norwegian working-life context. Although various actors were involved, three people were especially active translators. The first was Knut Wollebæk, an economist, consultant, and later director in the Confederation of Norwegian Enterprises (NHO). The second was Jan-Erik Stenberg, an engineer who graduated from Michigan Technological University in 1960 and worked with 3M in the United States for five years, especially in transforming the concept of Management by Results to a company-wide practice. He returned to Norway in 1965 and worked with several of the largest Norwegian consultancies. The third was Knut Jorem, an economist and director of IBM in Norway. The three men all knew each other and exchanged ideas about a PAC-concept adapted to the Norwegian context. They also shared some common characteristics. They were leaders in strong and powerful organizations, and they were connected to strong professional networks, which also included international actors. Stenberg, in particular, had strong connections to various American firms and consultancies. They were also authors, who published their ideas on the subject in numerous books. They also had slightly different roles as translators of the PAC concept. Stenberg was inspired by ideas of Management by Results in working out a Norwegian version of PAC. Jorem was primarily concerned about taking care of Norwegian working-life traditions and avoiding developing an "alien" PAC concept for Norwegian organizations. It was also he who, in his 1977 book, coined the concept of coworker dialogue; in Norwegian: "*Medarbeider-samtale*" (Jorem, 1977).

Wollebæk was the more *practitioner*-style translator. His position as a director in the Confederation of Norwegian Enterprises, as well as his various professional networks, added legitimacy and authority to his translation efforts. He early acknowledged that the U.S.-based PAC concept had to be radically transformed if it was to be accepted and adopted widely among Norwegian organizations. His translation performance was characterized by two paths. The first was to decouple a Norwegian version from the strong influence of *Management by Objective* (MBO) ideas in the U.S.-based PAC concept. This was a challenging translation operation because, in the American versions, the MBO ideas and practices were so intertwined with the softer aspects of counselling that it resembled a binary alloy. However, Wollebæk carefully took it apart. For example, the decoupling came to expression in one of the pieces of advice for how to conduct a coworker dialogue: in such a dialogue, the manager and the employee could focus upon the results of the employee's work efforts and could try to interpret the causes behind the results. However, they should try to avoid analyzing results in relation to pre-defined goals (Kummen, 2008). The second path in Wollebæk's translation was his efforts to make the coworker dialogue fit into the Norwegian tradition of the employers' and employees' federations having very strong positions, not least in the institutions of collective bargaining of wages for large groups of employees. To avoid clashing with this tradition, Wollebæk made a radical deviation from the American PAC concept. He advised that any questions about wages and payment should not be a theme in the dialogue. In Norway, there is also a strong and institutionalized tradition that union representatives should participate in meeting and decisions that involve questions about working conditions, wages, hiring, dismissals, major reorganizations, etc. Thus, the idea of a coworker dialogue that only included the manager and the employee was met with skepticism from the unions. Wollebæk was aware of this and paid much attention to translating a role for union representations within the coworker dialogue concept. He advised that they should not participate in the dialogue. However, they were appointed a role in the follow-up of any initiatives that the manager and the employee had eventually agreed upon.

In sum, Wollebæk had made a radical translation of the American PAC concept and transformed it to the Norwegian coworker dialogue. In terms of the barrier approach, this case illustrates how translators can be able to sense and find solutions to national, cultural, and institutional barriers in knowledge transfers between source and target organizational contexts.

In many respects, it was also a successful translation. The coworker dialogue was largely accepted as the authoritative dialogue version. It is widely institutionalized and used in all parts of working life in Norway (Røvik, 2002).

A radical Chinese translation of happiness: Failure or success?

It is not unusual for attempts to apply a radical translation mode in knowledge transfers to fail. One main reason (among several others) is that complex cause-and-effect relationships pertinent to the desired source practice can get lost in radical translations. Thus, it may be hard to recreate the outcomes in the source context in the target contexts. An example of a radical translation that apparently failed is provided in a study of attempts to transfer a Western practice—the routinized measuring of individuals' self-reported happiness (happiness indices)—to Chinese local government (Li, 2015). Happiness indices built on a psychological conceptualization of happiness as each individual's subjective well-being (Veenhoven, 1984) and can be measured with psychometric methods. Happiness indices have attracted a lot of attention, due to research-based insights; an example is the so-called Easterlin paradox, which refers to observations showing that an increase in an individual's income does not necessarily lead to an increase in his/her feeling of happiness and subjective well-being (Easterlin, 1974; Easterlin et al., 2012). Thus, the happiness indices are partly constructed in contrast to traditional indicators and measures of people's level of welfare in terms of classic socio-economic factors. Several Western countries have adopted the happiness indices (among them the United Kingdom, Canada, and France) and incorporated it into their routinized accounting systems.

In 2011, the leadership of the Guangdong province in China decided to adopt and implement the practice of happiness indices. The announced plan was to implement routines to systematically monitor the province inhabitants' happiness and subjective well-being, as had already been done in some Western countries. However, the ideas and practices of happiness indices were very different from the dominant thinking in China about what constitutes peoples' well-being and how it should be measured and accounted. An individualistic, psychological based happiness concept deviates drastically from China's hard-core economically centered systems of performance measurement. China is a highly centralized country, where local officials are held responsible for adding to peoples' welfare almost exclusively by working to achieve predefined economic production goals. In the case of happiness indices, it is hard to concretely identify persons who acted as translators of the practice to the province of Guangdong. However, a study was conducted of certain Chinese print media and the discourses that took place there in connection with the introduction of happiness induces (Li, 2015). Special attention was paid to *Nanfang Daily* because it is the only province-wide newspaper and because it is administered by the local Guangdong branch of the Communist Party. Thus, the opinions of happiness indices that come to expression in this newspaper reflect the official interpretation, and translation, of this practice by the powerful Guangdong Provincial Party Committee, who were the key translators.

The analysis of the print media discourse depicts a radical translation process. Although the translators did not explicitly reject the fundamental source context concept of subjective well-being, they urged that happiness was dependent upon external objective conditions; meaning economic growth. It was acknowledged that happiness reflected each individual's subjective experience, but it was simultaneously argued that the primary determinant was objective socio-economic conditions. Economic growth was defined as an effective means to increase the subjective well-being and feeling of happiness. The radical character of this translation can be depicted like this: While the main insight underlying the Western happiness indices' concept is that subjective well-being is only weakly correlated with objective factors (such as economic growth and income), this was turned around in the Chinese translated version, where such objective factors were interpreted as the main *solution* to increase citizens' happiness.

The radical translation of happiness indices in Guangdong was primarily a radical domestication, meaning that the Western source version was severely adapted to existing thinking and accounting practices in the province. Consequently, this also meant that much of the Western happiness ideas and practices were washed out and lost in translation. This is indicated in a study of the extent to which the Western version of happiness indices materialized in the official Guangdong accounting systems (Li, 2015). Data shows that although some happiness indicators were included, they were assigned limited weighting, in contrast to the dominant weightings assigned to the traditional objective indicators, where economic growth was the most prominent indicator.

From one angle, this transfer process can look like a translation failure, caused by usage of an inappropriate translation rule. Thus, the translation process can be interpreted through the lens of the barrier approach and as an example of a knowledge transfer that fails because of the presence of certain barring factors. In this perspective, the effect of barriers overrules the efforts of translators: It is supposed that the translators were not able to find solutions to and overcome the challenges of barriers constituted by severe institutional and cultural distance between source and target contexts.

However, viewed from a different angle the transfer of the Happiness indices—practice to Guangdong can be conceived more of as a translation success. In this interpretation, which is the most likely one, the radical domestication of Happiness indices is the result of deliberate translation work performed by involved actors and thus, which cannot be understood and explained without considering the role of the translators. In fact, the outcome of this transfer reflects the role of very powerful translators who made deliberate choices and who also managed to balance competing concerns. First: Far from the ancient ideal of the translator as a neutral mediator who conscientiously recreates a target version of a source text, the involved actors in the transfer of happiness indices to Guangdong were very powerful actors with strong interests in certain outcomes. The powerful and thus most important translations that occurred in *Nanfang Daily* were largely the voice of the Communist Party—the Guangdong Provincial Party Committee. The Party obviously had strong interests and was dedicated to preserving the official Chinese policy on economic growth—and the underlying strongly institutionalized belief that this is the main route to a happier Chinese people. In this respect, this case is another reminder that translators and their translations make a difference. Second: Translation failures in knowledge transfers often stem from translators who are not sufficiently knowledgeable about either the source version or the target context. However, this was not the case in the transfer for happiness indices to Guangdong. The Chinese translators were aware of and knowledgeable about the Western happiness indices and its foundation upon subjective well-being and explicit dissociation from the notion that happiness is a reflection of an individual, a group, or a nations' objective socio-economic conditions. Obviously, the Chinese translators were also even more knowledgeable about their own target context—the province of Guangdong. Thus, they were able to make deliberate decisions—and so they did—about how to transform the Western version to make it fit into the Guangdong context. Although they radically domesticated the Western happiness indices version, also some elements of the source version were taken care of and came to expression in the Guangdong target version as a minor set of indicators reflecting a more subjective Western-inspired happiness indices concept. By the translation work they performed, they also balanced two different concerns. On the one hand, the translators created a Guangdong version that was severely adapted to institutionalized Chinese notions of what makes a happy population. On the other hand, the inclusion of some elements from the highly legitimized subjective well-being concept of happiness indices in the Guangdong version is also suitable to signal that China, too, lives up to expectations from broad institutionalized environments of what it means to be a modern nation.

Thus, this case is another example of the importance of considering translators and how they work when encountering traditional transfer barriers—to improve understanding of outcomes of knowledge transfer processes.

Modifying mode: Successes and failures

Translators also frequently operate in a modifying mode in knowledge transfers. This mode is associated with attempts to balance concerns for replicating a source context practice with concerns for adapting the practice sufficiently to make it fit in with and work in the target context. Such balancing acts are challenging. While modification can be a route to success in knowledge transfers, it may also lead to failures. Outcomes will often depend on the translators' knowledge of the source and target contexts and on how they perform the translation.

Modifying co-production in Denmark

An example of successful modification is provided by an attempt to transfer the practice of co-production to the municipality of Aalborg in Denmark. The concept of co-production refers to direct participation by citizens in the delivery of various public sector services (Parks et al., 1981; Van Eijk and Gascó, 2018). The concept and practices of co-production have spread rapidly since the turn of the millennium, especially in Western countries (Pestoff, 2012), but now also to non-Western parts of the world (Cepiku and Giordano, 2014). An important driver is the widespread acknowledgement that governments are no longer able to be the only provider of public services. The civil society, citizens, and various stakeholders must be involved as co-producers (Osborne, 2010). As in other European countries, co-production has also become very popular among Danish municipalities (Torfing and Triantafillou, 2016; Brix et al., 2020). However, although a popular concept, less is known about what happens when municipalities learn from each other and attempt to translate representations of practices to co-production practices in their own organization. Nanna Møller Mortensen (2020) has studied an attempt to transfer and implement co-production in the department for elderly and disabled people in the municipality of Aalborg. The two main goals were (a) to secure more active input (co-production) from the service users themselves to the service production and delivery, and (b) to secure power-sharing, meaning that not only the professional but also the service user should have a say in questions about the design and quality of the provided service.

The external template that guided the implementation in the municipality was made up of a mix of other municipalities' experiences with co-production, in addition to what were conceived of as the core ideas from the literature about what co-production practices should consist of and the outcomes to which it probably would lead. There were five such "outcome logics" in the template: (1) *Innovation potential*; that is, increasing collaboration with service users and incorporating actors in their networks and the civil society in co-production. (2) *Individual well-being and empowerment*, meaning that service users should actively participate in the service production and delivery process, and also be empowered and co-deciders. (3) *Effectiveness and efficiency*, which means producing and delivering public services at high quality and with lower costs. (4) *Mobilization of resources*; that is, producing new public services and retaining old ones with increased use of nongovernmental resources. (5) *Democracy*, which means enabling and encouraging service users to participate in debates about the type, design, and quality of public services, and, in general, decentralize power down to the service users.

Mortensen (2020) analyzed the translation processes, which took place at three hierarchical levels in the organization, starting at the first (top) level (department level), via the second level (the Center for Vitality), and then continuing at the third level (three frontline units). This means that several actors were involved as translators in a hierarchical translation chain. Mortensen's study reveals a pattern in the translation processes over the three organizational layers that is characteristic for a modifying translation mode. On each level, as the idea of co-production finds its way through the translation chain, involved actors carefully either add some elements or make explicit elements implicit, or they subtract some elements or make explicit elements implicit, or toned down, in *their* translated versions. For example, at the top (first) level, the translators added an element (improving the work environment for the employees) that was not present in the template, while they omitted the element of "democracy." Further, the concern for power sharing between service users and professionals in the template was toned down at the first level translation. However, at the third level, in the frontline units, this element was made explicit and re-emphasized.

At the final stage, when the concept of co-production was about to be implemented in the three frontline units, several groups of translators had contributed with their modifications. Is it possible to identify an overarching pattern that makes the magnitude of modifications more intelligible? A central feature of a modifying mode is efforts to balance concerns about preserving the core cause-effect mechanisms of the template with concerns about adapting sufficiently to conditions of the target context. When the numerous single modifications of co-operation in Aalborg are seen in comparison, a main pattern of balancing efforts is revealed. What is totally left out, however, is the element of "increasing democracy" and "increasing effectiveness and efficiency." In fact, a clear indication of the elimination of the economic element was that co-production efforts were initiated alongside economic cutbacks. In addition, the element "innovation" was toned down. What was especially taken care of from the template and emphasized in the version to be implemented in the frontline units were the elements of involving the service users in the production and distribution of the services, and the idea of power sharing between the service users and the professionals. These elements were emphasized, enlarged, and concretized with detailed methods for how to cooperate and coproduce in practice.

The transfer and translation of co-production to Aalborg municipality is largely conceived of as successful, in the sense that the idea was materialized and, so far, has led to enduring improved practices of cooperation and co-production. There is a clear connection between the performance of the translators and the successful outcomes. What the translators managed through a series of deliberate modifications was to identify, preserve, and recreate in the target version the core co-production cause–effect mechanisms in the template, while they also eliminated some elements and toned down others that did not fit in or were conceived of as unnecessary and potentially claims on limited resources. Thus, the translators' modifying mode was undoubtedly decisive for the successful outcome of the knowledge transfer process. An interesting question is whether the translation mode was deliberately chosen or not. The modifying mode was not chosen explicitly, but more indirectly. Mortensen (2020) showed that the strategic level provided the second and especially the third level—the frontline units—with relatively high degrees of autonomy to translate co-production into practice. Such autonomy encouraged the translators to modify and adapt the concept. However, the autonomy provided to the second and third level was based on a mutual understanding among the involved actors at all hierarchical levels about what the core ideas of co-production was (more involvement of the service users and stakeholders in the production of service, combined with more empowerment of the service users), and, simultaneously, a mutual understanding that the general concept of co-production had to be sufficiently shaped into a concrete and effective local version.

When modifying fails

The key feature of the modifying mode is acts of balancing. Thus, the main reason for modifying failures is translators failing in their efforts to balance between concerns for preserving source versions and concerns for making it work in the target context. An appropriate balancing point can be lost for two reasons: either because of too much domestication, meaning too much adaptation of the transferred representation to the target context; or too much foreignizing, which means too little adaptation of the source version to fit in with the target context and host environment.

An example of the effects of too much domestication is provided in Szulanski and Jensen's (2008) study of transfer of franchising knowledge from the headquarter of a large U.S.-based multinational corporation (MailBoxes Etc.) to 23 of its foreign subsidiaries. The researchers collected data from the processes between 1989 and 2003. The headquarters had made detailed manuals and blueprints for how the Master Licenses (MLs—individuals who own the right to build a ML-network in a country or region) should work to make their network grow and prosper. Data showed positive correlations between outcomes and the degree to which the subsidiaries followed the blueprints. The more the subsidiaries made local adaptations, the less their own networks grew and prospered. Thus, local adaptations were not balanced against the concern of preserving complex sets of interdependent activities inherent in the headquarters' franchising blueprint.

However, there are also numerous examples of transfer failures that can be traced back to translators who miss the balancing point because they do not sufficiently manage to modify and domesticate the template. One such example stems from the Indo Norwegian Project (INF) 1953–1972, which is broadly presented in Chapter 4. Part of this project was attempts to modernize the Indian state of Kerala's fish industry and fishing fleet with bigger, mechanized boats of about 25 feet. This project was founded on knowledge and practices from Norwegian coastline fishery, but also adjusted to local conditions in India. As outlined in Chapter 4, the southern and northern fishing villages reacted differently towards the modernizing project. While the project was widely acknowledged and accepted in the Latin Catholic south, the Hindu fishing population in the north, the Arayas, were much more reluctant and dismissive. Arne Martin Klausen (1968), an anthropologist, revealed that the Arayas's avoidance of the project was deeply rooted in their culture and their religious beliefs. For example, they resisted the modernization of the fleet with 25-foot fully mechanized and motorized fishing vessels because such boats would force them to even do night fishing, which collided with the strong Hindu belief of not disturbing "sleeping nature."

It is reasonable to interpret the Arayas's avoidance of the modernizing project as caused by a translation failure. The knowledge and practices that were transferred from Norway had not been sufficiently modified to fit into the complex cultural and institutional context of the Hindu fishing society of Araya. One important reason for the insufficient modification was that the INF translators lacked knowledge about the Arayas and their culture. Another appurtenant reason was the translators' beliefs. They were convinced that the 25-food highly mechanized and motorized vessels were the appropriate means for the Keralan fishers, as they had proved to be as cornerstones in Norwegian coastline small-scale fishery. Thus, there are reasons to believe that the INP translators neither possessed nor searched for modified versions in response to the Arayas's reluctance to the project. However, the modernization project *could* have been further modified based on a premise of more adaptation to the Araya context. For example, motorizing the unmotorized canoes (which were the common fishing boats in the area) without offering the fishers the 25-foot modern vessels could have been an appropriate solution, closer to the balancing point between concerns for both source and target contexts.

Discussion

A key feature of the six knowledge transfer cases presented above is the variation in outcomes. Four of the cases can be interpreted as successes and two as less successful, or even as failures. How can these variations be understood and explained? The six cases represent considerable variation in terms of the organizational types involved (public organizations, business firms, and interest organizations), their localization in space (United States, England, China, Norway, Denmark, and India) as well as localization in time (varying between 1920 and 2020). However, it is hard to imagine how the revealed variations in successes could be traced back to these variables (time, space, and organizational type). Many knowledge transfer scholars would try to interpret the variations in light of insights from the barrier approach. Therefore, it is likely that such explanation attempts will be made with reference to variations in terms of absorptive capacity, formal organizational structure, social networks, cultural, geographic and/or institutional distance, and characteristics of the transferred knowledge. In one of the described cases (the transfer of modern fishing technology to Kerala), the outcome can be interpreted as reflecting certain barriers that have negatively influenced the transfer processes (commented on below). Although some of the typical barriers are also present in the remaining cases, their effects on the transfer processes were more indirect and modest.

To what extent can the observed variations in success between the cases be explained with reference to the translators' knowledge of context and their use of translation rules? There is no doubt that the translation rules and the ways they are used set out important premises for the outcomes in the six cases. However, there is no "one rule that fits all." As illustrated, while different rules may all lead to successes, the same rule applied in different situations may lead to different outcomes. What is decisive is the involved actors' translation performance: how and to what extent they possess knowledge about the relevant contexts, and how they choose, use, and eventually shift translation rules.

A comparative analysis of the six cases reveals some interesting patterns that may contribute to improved understanding of factors that generate the variations in outcomes. Translation barriers and other challenges are involved in all six cases. However, there are certain variations in the way they are dealt with in the four successful cases (the McDonald's case, the case of the Norwegian coworker dialogue, the case of co-production in Aalborg, and the case of happiness indices in China) compared to the two others with less favorable outcomes.

The McDonald's case is an example of successful application of a reproducing-copying translation mode. Ray Kroc, the key actor and translator, faced two challenging barriers in his attempts to create a franchised chain of numerous fast food replica units. One was the potential barring effects of territorial franchising, which was the common principle of franchise organizing in the early 1950s. The other was the potentially low degree of absorptive capacity among the franchisees to pick up, understand, implement, and follow the franchisor's detailed recipes for the replicas without any deviations. The way in which Kroc acted and managed to deal with these two potential threats to his replication strategy is described above. Another central feature of Kroc's translation performance was his *continuous* translation activities, which means his efforts to maintain the replication strategy for years; for example, by implementing and using a system for continuously rigid monitoring of the franchisees' performances.

The case of making a Norwegian coworker dialogue had a successful outcome, too. However, compared to the MacDonald replication case, it involved the use of the "opposite" rule of radical translation. The attempt to transfer the American Performance Appraisal and Counselling (PAC) systems to Norway was challenging for the translators. The cultural and institutional differences between American and Norwegian working life amounted to a serious transfer barrier. However, as shown above, the translators handled the barrier by radically transforming the American PAC system to what is known as the Norwegian coworker dialogue. An important feature of the group of translators was that they combined insights into American working life and the PAC system (the source context) with thorough knowledge of the Norwegian society and working life. The usage of a radical translation mode was based on deliberate decisions (information provided to the author in interview with Stenberg and Wollebæk, July 2020). Early in the transfer process, the group of three core translators discussed and knew that neither a copy nor a slightly modified version of the American PAC system would be possible in Norway.

The translation of co-production in Aalborg is a case where the modifying translation rule was successfully chosen and applied. A potential transfer barrier was formal organizational structure. The concept was adopted at the top strategic level and was implemented from the top down across three hierarchical levels. Transfer across such vertical formal structures represents risks of both distorting what is transferred and decelerating and even stopping the process. However, such effects were avoided by choosing a modifying translation mode, combined with high degrees of autonomy provided from the strategic level to the two lower hierarchical levels. This translation and implementation strategy, which was obviously built on trustful networks and relationships across the hierarchical levels, was an important reason why the involved actors managed to balance concerns for preserving the core cause–effect mechanisms inherent in the concept of co-production with concerns for making it work in the frontline units. Thus, the social networks among the involved actors modified the potential barring effect of the formal vertical structure and facilitated the successful outcome. Another reason for the successful translation was the organizing of the translation process across the three hierarchical layers. At each level, new sets of actors got involved as translators. However, a selection of these translators from each level met at various arenas organized for information exchange and discussions about the co-production project. This organizing principle increased translators' knowledge of the translations that took place at the different hierarchical levels, and also increased coordination and calibration of the translations across the layers.

From one perspective, the outcome of the transfer of happiness indices to Guangdong can be interpreted as a translation failure stemming from the usage of an inappropriate radical translation mode. The alteration following from the radical mode was so severe that the Western original core idea of a psychological-individualistic conceptualization of happiness was almost totally washed out. In this perspective, the institutional, cultural, and political differences between the Western happiness indices and the Chinese target context was an insurmountable barrier for the translators. However, there are many indications that the outcome of this transfer should better be conceived of as a partial success. Undoubtedly, there were high barriers to overcome for the translators. The difference is huge between the Western-inspired individualistic-psychological happiness concept of subjective well-being and the dominant Chinese thinking of degree of happiness in a population as a reflection of the socio-economic conditions of the nation. Nevertheless, the translators managed to enact the barriers by balancing competing concerns for a radical domestication of the concept to the Chinese context, while simultaneously including a few elements from the source version in the Chinese version—thereby also signaling adherence to norms of modernity circulating in broad institutional environments. The outcome and partial success of this transfer process can be traced back to three key features of the translation performance. First, the involved actors were highly knowledgeable about both the Western happiness indices (source) and the Chinese target context. Second, radical translation was an appropriate translation rule to apply, and probably the only possible one. Third, the translators were very powerful. They made authoritative decisions throughout the process and ensured that their translated version materialized in Guangdong practices.

The two remaining cases had unsuccessful or less successful outcomes. Did they have something in common that can shed light on why they did not succeed?

The case of attempts to replicate Ford fabric and Tayloristic work organizing in U.K. mines between 1920 and 1955 had severe long-lasting negative consequences for the working environment and led to strikes and low productivity. There are three main reasons for this transfer failure. First, the replication strategy was founded on poor knowledge about the existing collier work organizing, which were characterized by strong social ties among the workers and much autonomy for each working unit. Second, the replication of Taylorism in the mines ripped up the existing collier work organizing with its social ties and replaced it with a very different organizing. Third, in addition to poor knowledge about the existing collier work organizing, the replication strategy was founded on engineers' strong belief in Taylorism. This amounted to a trained incapacity to adjust the principles to better fit in with the target context of U.K. coal mines. The trained incapacity came to expression in slow learning processes despite severe and enduring negative consequences following the Taylorization of the mines. However, with better translation work this barrier could and should have been overcome, for two main reasons. First, the negative consequences of the attempts to Taylorize the U.K. mines were severe and lasted for decades. Normally, such enduring negative effects would trigger intense learning efforts to find out what causes the problems (Argyris, 1976). However, in this case, the learning efforts were few and the learning processes were very slow. Second, despite the strong belief in scientific management principles of work organizing among engineers, many of them possessed firm experience-based knowledge about the traditional way of work organizing in U.K. mines: the autonomous work group with strong social ties and high internal flexibility. For example, Samuel Mavor, the highly influential agent of Taylorism, obviously possessed such knowledge.

Thus, an important reason for this transfer failure was that the involved actors maintained the reproducing mode long after it should have been changed to a modifying mode. The Tavistock researchers' results from experiments with alternative models for coal mine work organizing clearly indicated that a shift to modifying translation rules would probably have led to fewer problems.

The failures to transfer knowledge and modern fishing technology from Norway to Araya in Kerala in the 1950s can also be traced back to aspects of the involved translators' performances. Although the translators had initially applied a modifying mode and tried to balance between the Norwegian source context practices and the Kerala context, the cultural barriers between these contexts were severe and difficult to conceptualize and enact. Thus, the Norwegian translators lacked insights into the Arayas's cultural and religious beliefs. The cultural barrier was the main reason why the translators were not able to understand the Arayas's avoidance of the modernization efforts and, consequently, why they did not manage to further modify to make the modernizing initiatives fit into the Araya context. This illustrates a point made in Chapter 4 about the importance of the translatability of existing practices in the target organization. In this case, the translatability of the desired source practice (the Norwegian modern fishing technology) was high among the

Norwegian-based translators, while they did not understand how existing Araya fishing practices were deeply tied to cultural norms.

Translation performance versus transfer barriers

This chapter has focused upon the role of translators' performance; that is, how they de facto act in knowledge transfer processes. The cases presented above indicate the importance of involved actors' translation performance to understand why transfer outcomes vary. The translation approach has been contrasted with a barrier approach to understand variations in transfer outcomes. However, there is a complex interplay between the barriers known from knowledge transfer studies and translators' performances (Carlile, 2004). Obviously, outcomes of knowledge transfer processes can sometimes be traced back to the presence of certain transfer barriers, which translators do not manage to overcome (as illustrated in the case of the transfer of modern fishing technology to the Arayas in India). However, involved actors' translation performance often have a clear independent effect on the transfer barriers, which may cause both transfer failures and successes. For example, transfer barriers are sometimes modest or almost absent, but poor translation work still leads to undesirable outcomes. The case of transfer of Tayloristic working organizing principles to the U.K. coal mines provides an illuminating example. Especially from the late 1950s and until the early 1970s, the involved leaders and mining engineers were poor translators; they were slow learners and should have shifted from a reproducing translation mode to a modifying mode.

Yet, most clearly, the independent effects of translation performance frequently come to expression in processes where translators face barriers, overcome them, and contribute to successful outcomes. Such successful barrier-handling translation performances are demonstrated in the McDonald's case, the making of the Norwegian coworking dialogue, the case of co-production in Aalborg, and partly also in the case of transfer of happiness indices to Guangdong. Bluntly, in these cases the explanation for outcomes of knowledge transfer processes is *not* transfer barriers, but the translators' performances. They manage to enact and overcome the barriers based on knowledge of source and target contexts and by choices of appropriate translation rules. In the successful cases highlighted above, the translators managed to handle various potential transfer barriers, such as formal organizational structure, lack of absorptive capacity, and geographical, national, cultural, and institutional distance between source and target organizational contexts. A common denominator in these cases is that the translators—based on knowledge of the source context, the desired source practice, and the target context—chose and used appropriate translation rules.

In addition to knowledge of contexts and usage of appropriate translation rules, there were some characteristic details pertinent to the translation performance in each of the four cases that contributed to the outcomes. For example, in the McDonald's case, the central translator Ray Kroc's strong efforts to *maintain* the replication strategy for years, not allowing local adaptations, was clearly important for the company's worldwide franchising success. An interesting feature in the case of translating the American PAC concept to the Norwegian Development dialogue was the knowledge and power base of the core group of three translators. Together they possessed and combined considerable knowledge about the American and the Norwegian contexts, while they were simultaneously powerful, well-known, and widely respected actors based in various very powerful Norwegian organizations. This background increased the chances of having their translated versions accepted, for example by the strong Confederation of Norwegian Enterprises (NHO) and the strong (and skeptical) Norwegian Confederation of Trade Unions (LO). Powerful translators are also a central feature in the Guangdong-case and an important factor to consider in order to understand how the translators managed to handle national, cultural, and institutional barriers. In the case of translating co-production in Aalborg, a specific translation performance element contributed to the positive outcome. The translators handled the potential barring effect of the formal organizational structure that separated hierarchical (vertical) levels in the municipality by organizing arenas where a selection of involved actors from each hierarchical level met and coordinated translated versions across the vertical layers.

Although transfer barriers are important, empirical studies of such barriers, when seen in comparison, account for a limited portion of the variations in outcomes of knowledge transfer processes. This indicates that the relative impact of how involved translators de facto perform the translations is high, and is therefore important to consider in order to understand and explain variations in transfer outcomes. In fact, involved translators make significant differences in knowledge transfer processes, far beyond what barrier approaches so far have accounted for. Table 6.1 sum ups the main insights from this chapter.

Table 6.1 Summary: Six cases illustrating the role of translators in knowledge transfers

Variables/Cases	1 The McDonald's franchising case, United States	2 Coworking dialogue, Norway	3 Co-production, Denmark	4 Happiness indices, China	5 Taylorism in mines, United Kingdom	6 Modern fishing technology, Araya, India
Outcome of the transfer	Mainly successful	Mainly successful	Mainly successful	Partly successful	Failure	Failure
Barriers involved	- Geographical distance - Absorptive capacity	Cultural, institutional, and national barriers	Formal organizational structure (vertical)	Cultural, institutional/political, and national distance barriers	Trained incapacity, mainly among mining engineers	Cultural distance—barrier
Main translation rule applied	Reproducing mode (Copying)	Radical mode (Alteration)	Modifying mode (Addition and omission)	Radical mode (Alteration)	Reproducing mode (Copying)	Modifying mode (Addition and omission)
Actors involved as translators	One key translator: Ray Kroc	A core group of three translators: Knut Jorem, Jan-Erik Stenberg, and Knut Wollebæk	Three groups of employees at three hierarchical levels in the municipality of Aalborg acting as translators	Hard to identify the concrete individual translators. The translation unit was the local Guangdong branch of the Chinese Communist Party	Many translators and especially U.K.-based mining engineers. A powerful and influential translator was Glasgow-based engineer and business-owner Samuel Mavor	A group of Norwegian experts on technological and economic modernization and members of the Indo-Norwegian project 1953–1972

Translators' knowledge of source and target contexts	Kroc combined firm knowledge about the source (McDonald's brothers' restaurant) and the various target potential franchisees	Norwegian-based translators who possessed and combined extensive knowledge about the source and target contexts	Translators based in the municipality of Aalborg who combined together possessed and combined extensive knowledge of source and target contexts	Guangdong-based translators who were highly knowledgeable about the target context and moderately knowledgeable about the Western happiness indices concept	U.K.-based translators who were highly knowledgeable about scientific management and Ford fabric principles of work organizing and Ford, and moderately knowledgeable about the target U.K. mining context	Translators were extensively knowledgeable about the source context and the desired source practice (fishing technology), but they lacked insight into the cultural context of Araya
Additional features of the translators and/or their performance—with consequences for outcomes	Kroc's efforts (a) to stimulate franchisees' absorptive capacity through economic incentives, and (b) to maintain the replication strategy for years, thereby denying deviation by local franchisees from the template	The very strong knowledge base and power base of the three-person core group of translators	The handling of the potential barring effect of formal organizational structure by a special routine to coordinate and calibrate three unit-specific translations across the units	Important premise for outcome: the very strong political power base of the translators—the local branch of the Chinese Communist Party	Strong adherence to Taylorism/scientific management as template amounted to trained incapacity among translators, expressed in slow learning processes—and maintenance of inappropriate translation rules	Due to lack of knowledge of the target (Araya) context, the translators were unable to understand the Arayas's avoidance of the modernity efforts

PART IV
IMPLICATIONS FOR KNOWLEDGE TRANSFER PRACTICES

7
Translation Competence
Implications for Knowledge Transfer Practices

Introduction

This final chapter zooms in on the consequences of the translation theory for knowledge transfer practices. I argue that the theory has the potential to influence involved actors' translation performance, increasing the chances of achieving desirable outcomes. The chapter coins and develops the key concept of *translation competence*, which refers to translators' knowledge about how to translate practices and ideas to achieve desired ends in knowledge transfers across organizational units.

Translation competence

The *implication-for-practice* theme, introduced earlier, immediately connects to the enduring rigor-relevance debate within the field of organization and management research (meaning the scientific quality of a contribution) and its relevance for practices and practitioners. There is a strong notion within the research community that there is a gap between rigor and relevance that needs to be closed (Gulati, 2007; Nicolai and Seidl, 2010; Bartunek and Rynes, 2014; Joullié and Gould, 2022). The literature on this theme is comprehensive. In a literature review, Carton and Mouricou (2017) identified 253 articles published in 11 top-tier journals between 1994 and 2013 that mainly focused on the rigor-relevance theme. It is also a fast-growing body of literature (Kieser, 2011) that offers various answers to the questions of why the gap has arisen and whether and how it can be closed. Top-tier journals are often the most prominent gatekeepers of the orthodoxy of rigor. From this angle, the main reason for the rigor-relevance gap is the lack of attention and the indifference of media and practitioners to organization and management research (Rousseau and McCarthy, 2007; Guest, 2007; Clark et al., 2013). There are numerous observations indicating that executives/practitioners rarely consider findings from management research when making their decisions (Rynes et al., 2001; Bailey, 2016; Božič et al., 2022). However, viewed from an orthodoxy position, it is not acceptable to try to close the rigor-relevance gap by negotiating and reducing the claim on scientific rigor (Hambrick, 1994; Cummings, 2007).

From other less orthodox and more practice-oriented positions come another main type of explanation: the gap has arisen because most of the published management research lacks usefulness and thus, relevance for practitioners. This may reflect the fact that researchers too seldom turn to practitioners to get inspiration for new research projects (Sackett and Larson 1990). However, some analysts interpret the lack of relevance as an expression of a fundamental divide between the domains of organization and management research—and practice. These two activities (research and practice) have been described as two specialized autonomous systems operating according to different logics and in a high degree of isolation from each other (Kieser and Leiner, 2009; Patterson and Harms, 2019; Cooren and Seidl, 2020). The main reward system in management research, which is most clearly spelled out in the "author guidelines" in the top journals, encourages researchers to concentrate on publishing theory and not worry about the practical relevance of their work (Podolny, 2009; Tourish, 2020), beyond writing the two symbolic "implications for practice" paragraphs at the end of the article (Bartunek and Rynes, 2010). According to Kieser and Leiner (2009), the logics of organization and management research and the logics of practices are so different that the gap is unbridgeable. However, many contributions to this literature have taken a more pragmatic stand and discussed various means of increasing the practical relevance of organization and management research (Starkey and Madan, 2001; Lillis and Mundy, 2005; Reay et al., 2009; Sharma and Bansal, 2020; Wickert et al., 2021).

I too contribute to the pragmatic approach by attempting to narrow the rigor-relevance gap by extracting practical consequences of the translation theory of knowledge transfer across organizational borders. The main argument is that translation theory has the potential to not only improve analysis and understanding of knowledge transfer processes, but also to guide deliberate interventions in such processes. This argument rests on a premise outlined and empirically illustrated over the three previous chapters—that *translation performance* (which refers to how actors involved in knowledge transfers gain and use knowledge about source and target contexts—and chose and use various translation rules throughout knowledge transfer processes) are often decisive for the outcomes of such transfer processes. As demonstrated in Chapter 6, involved actors' translation performance may explain variations in outcomes: It sometimes leads to successes and sometimes to failures. It is also reasonable to suggest that involved actors' translation performance is influenced by their translation knowledge and skills. Thus, a key concept to understand variations in actors' translation performances is *translation competence*, which refers to the sum of knowledge and skills that an involved actor mobilizes and applies in acts of transferring knowledge across organizational borders.

In addition to insights from the three foregoing chapters, the development of this concept is also influenced by the corresponding defining salient feature of translation competence within the source domain of translation studies (see Chapter 3). Within that domain, four elements together shape a translator's competence. The first is bilingualism, which means that the translator ultimately must master both the source and the target language. The second is the translator's knowledge of translation norms and rules, which means possessing thorough knowledge about various translation rules and being able to choose the rules that are the most appropriate in relation to concrete translation challenges. The third is biculturalism, meaning that the translator's knowledge of source and target should reach beyond knowledge of the involved languages and include thorough knowledge of the source and target contexts' cultures. The fourth element is knowledge about the subject matter, which means that a competent translator should be knowledgeable about the substance of what is being translated. For example, if you translate a text about modern electronic equipment, green technology, or cross-country skiing, the quality of your translation is likely to gain increase if you are knowledgeable about these certain subjects.

Building on these ideas and on insights from the three previous chapters, it is reasonable to conceive of the translation competence of actors involved in knowledge transfers as constituted by two features. The first is the translator's knowledge of contexts, which includes knowledge of practices to be transferred (the subject matter), as well as knowledge of relevant aspects of source and target organizational contexts. The second is knowledge about translation rules and about how to select and use appropriate rules under various conditions.

The rest of this chapter is organized into three sections. The first section contains a discussion of translators' knowledge of contexts, and the second discusses their knowledge of—and the conditions for more deliberate use of translation rules. The third and final section sums up the insights gained and highlights the relationship between translators' knowledge of contexts and their knowledge and usage of translation rules.

Translators' knowledge of contexts

Translators obviously need deep insights into the contexts between which they mediate. The quality of such context knowledge has a determining effect on the quality of a translation. Thus, outcomes of knowledge transfer processes—successes and failures—can often be traced back to variations in the involved translators' knowledge of contexts. Chapter 6 provides several illustrations of the close linkages between context knowledge and transfer outcomes. One of the common features of the three most successful transfer processes highlighted there—the McDonalds' replication case, the coworker dialogue case, and the co-production case—was that the involved translators were highly knowledgeable about the respective contexts. On the contrary, in two of the three cases where the transfer processes failed (the transfer of Taylorism to U.K. coal mines, and the transfer of modern fishing technology to Kerala), the translators lacked thorough knowledge about the target contexts.

The need for translators to be knowledgeable about source and target contexts may seem so obvious that it hardly needs mentioning. However, there are still several *whats*, *hows*, and *whys* to be answered in connection with the translators' knowledge of contexts. When assessing conditions for developing translation competence, the *why* question should be answered by stressing that thorough knowledge of contexts is a prerequisite for involved actors to make (more) deliberate choices of translation rules to apply. For example, a striking common feature of the three successful knowledge transfer cases mentioned above was that the choices of appropriate translation rules were premised on the involved translators' thorough knowledge of contexts. Correspondingly, in the transfer failure cases, the choices and application of inappropriate translation rules followed translators' poor knowledge of contexts.

The quality of translators' knowledge of contexts—what and how much they need to know—can be conceptualized in terms of the viscosity and the velocity of the knowledge (Davenport and Prusak, 1998). These are metaphors that have been imported from physics and applied to knowledge management. Viscosity is a quantitative measure of a fluid's resistance to flow, and velocity is an expression of the speed at which a fluid flows. In analysis of knowledge transfers, viscosity refers to the richness (or thickness) of the knowledge to be transferred, while velocity refers to the speed at which knowledge moves across and through organizations. For example, highly viscous knowledge can be tacit, but highly critical knowledge about how to perform a certain successful practice—and deeply embedded in the source context (Dhanaraj et al., 2004; Bacon et al., 2019). Such knowledge is often characterized by low velocity, meaning it is hard to move at all, let alone fast. Bluntly, the challenge for knowledge translators is sometimes "to fight against physical laws," meaning to try to overview and gain source-based knowledge of high viscosity, make representations of it, and make sudden swifts between source and target contexts to arrive at the most appropriate target context version of it.

Translators face two challenges related to the viscosity and the velocity of the knowledge in the contexts. These are the challenges of gaining knowledge of various viscosity, and of securing velocity through bilingualism and biculturalism.

Gaining knowledge of contexts

A key part of involved actors' translation competence is the competence to decontextualize, or dis-embed; that is, to identify and make a representation of the desired source practice that accounts for the way it works in the source organizational context. Another is the competence to contextualize; that is, to re-embed the representation of the desired source practice in a version that works in the target organizational context. A prerequisite for building such competence is that the translator is able to gain knowledge about the source and the target contexts. How challenging it is for a translator to gain knowledge about a practice to be transferred and its context depends on certain features of the practice/context—and on features of the translator.

The central feature of the desired source practice is its degree of translatability (the extent to which a certain practice can be translated to an abstract representation without excluding the elements required for how it functions in the source organizational context). As outlined in Chapter 4, three variables are decisive for the translatability of a practice. The first is complexity, which consists of two intertwined aspects. One is the human-technology aspect. As proposed in Chapter 4 (proposition 4.1), "The higher the number of individuals involved in the accomplishment of a practice, and the more the accomplishment is dependent upon tight mutual coordinated actions among those involved, the more the translatability of the practice decreases."

The other aspect with implications for translatability is the technological base of a practice. It is proposed (proposition 4.2.) that the more the accomplishment of a practice is based on a technology with a clear-cut application, and the less it involves human individuals, the more the practice's translatability increases. The second aspect that defines a practice' complexity is the degree of *causal ambiguity*. It has been proposed (proposition 4.3) that the causal ambiguity of a source practice influences the practice's translatability, in that the more ambiguous the linkages between input factors and results, the harder it is to translate the practice to a representation that accounts for all the essentials for how it works.

The second variable that defines the translatability of a practice is embeddedness, which refers to the extent to which the knowledge and capabilities that constitute a desired source practice are anchored in its intra- and/or interorganizational contexts. It is proposed (proposition 4.5) that the more the knowledge base of a desired practice is dispersed and embedded in interorganizational networks at different places, the more challenging it is to demarcate and the harder it is to translate to a high-fidelity representation. Further, the more a desired practice's knowledge base is embedded in organizational elements, such as technologies, tasks, individuals and social relations, the harder it is to dis-embed and translate to a high-fidelity representation. The third variable to define translatability is *explicitness*; that is, the degree to which knowledge of a desired practice is codified, verbalized, and well articulated. It is proposed (proposition 4.7) that the more explicit (codified and verbalized) a desired source practice is, the higher its translatability. Correspondingly, the less explicit the knowledge base of a desired practice, the lower its translatability—and the higher the chances of losing elements that are essential for the functioning of the practice in the translation process.

The central argument of translatability can be summed up as follows: the more complex, more embedded, and tacit a desired practice is, the lower its translatability and the higher its viscosity.

Translators also face challenges of gaining knowledge about target contexts. Translatability of the target context refers to how easy or difficult it is for the translator to gain accurate knowledge about the target context. It is especially important for translators to gain knowledge about existing target practices that may be affected by and/or may affect a source practice representation that is determined to be implemented and contextualized. Such knowledge is necessary in order for the translator to arrive at a version of the source practice that fits in with and works in the target organization. As outlined in Chapter 4, the translatability of the existing target practices is—like the translatability of the source practice—determined by their degree of complexity, embeddedness, and explicitness.

Two features of the translator seem to be important for their chances of gaining insights into desired source practices: their localization and their relationships to the source organization.

Outside-located translators. Translators are sometimes located outside and are nonmembers of the source organizations. For example, they may be consulting companies engaged in identifying, selling, and spreading best practices in various fields. However, an outside and distant localization normally limits translators' possibilities of gaining knowledge about source contexts, and especially about practices of low translatability (Wellstein and Kieser, (2011). Research indicates that access to source context knowledge depends on trustful relationships (Levin and Cross, 2004), and that translators who represent potential competitors will have limited access—especially to knowledge of high viscosity and value for competitiveness (Norman, 2002; Hackney et al., 2005; Rouyre and Fernandez, 2019). Likewise, translators acting in the role of expatriates (employees who come from a parent organization and work for a while in a subsidiary unit) have higher chances of identifying and gaining knowledge about eventually successful practices in the subsidiary.

Inside-located translators. Translators can be insiders; that is, actors who are based within the source organization. They normally have good access to the knowledge base of source practices and especially to practices in which they are directly involved. Thus, insiders possess thicker and more viscous knowledge about source practices than outsiders. However, the challenge is to combine viscosity with velocity; that is, to move the insiders' rich knowledge across organizational borders to target units. Efforts to do so frequently fail (Foos et al., 2006; Seidler-de Alwis and Hartmann, 2008). Davenport and Prusak (1998) provided an illuminating example from the Mobil Oil Company. The company's engineers had developed an innovative method to determine exactly the volume of steam required for drilling under various conditions. This was a very valuable method because the company could save steam, buy less, and thereby make huge returns. Thus, this knowledge had the potential to greatly increase Mobil's competitiveness in the drilling market. However, the technology was sophisticated and the use of it required thorough knowledge and training of the drilling operators. The leaders of Mobil Oil were eager to quickly transfer the new technology to the various drilling units and have the steam-saving method implemented. To speed up the transfer (increase velocity), the headquarters sent a memo to all units, describing the procedures to be followed and their benefits—and asked for an immediate change of practice. However, the implementation rate was very slow; in fact, nothing happened. The company's evaluation concluded that the reason for the transfer failure was that chosen memo form was too simple to mediate the highly viscous knowledge of the new drilling technology.

An alternative way to increase the chances of transferring viscous knowledge across organizational borders is to involve insiders from the source context directly in the transfer process. Westney and Piekkari (2020) showed how such an approach has been widely used to move knowledge of various production practices from Japanese firms to the United States. The early 1970s was the start of a period with massive setup of Japanese subsidiaries in the United States—most of them production units staffed with Japanese managers and engineers and American workers. The way the Japanese moved the production knowledge from the Japanese parent companies to their American factories was mainly through what Westney and Piekkari (2020) called "direct translation." The translators were Japanese insiders; that is, Japanese expatriates both managers and factory-floor operatives. The knowledge was transferred directly, mainly on the production unit floors from the Japanese to the American workers—often by "showing," which means demonstrating how certain work operations should be performed rather than by "telling," due to the problems that the involved actors had communicating across the Japanese–American language barrier. Thus, the concept of "direct translation" means translation from practice in the source organization to practice in the recipient organization. By this approach, complex and viscous knowledge could be transferred relatively quickly to and implemented by the target organization.

Combining knowledge of source and recipient contexts

Bilingualism and biculturalism

Within translation studies, a key feature of translation competence is bilingualism, which means that the translator is knowledgeable about both the source and the target language and can understand and express her/himself with ease in both languages (Macnamara, 1967; Shreve, 2012). In addition to being bilingual, a competent translator should also be bicultural, which means being knowledgeable about the societal source context from which the text stems—and about the societal target context (Witte, 1987; Vermeer, 1998; Ringberg, et al., 2010; Lörscher, 2012). Although arguments of the need for bilingualism/biculturalism are most clearly spelled out and associated with linguistics (Grosjean, 1982; 2010), its scope reaches far beyond linguistics and includes communication and mediation of messages across various borders in general, as well as knowledge transfers between organizations.

It requires that the mediator/translator relates to—and therefore has some knowledge of—both source and recipient contexts. The translation theorist James Holmes described bilingualism/biculturalism as the translator's consciousness of two maps:

> I have suggested that actually the translation process is a multi-level process; while we are translating sentences, we have a map of the original text in our minds and at the same time, a map of the kind of text we want to produce in the target language. Even as we translate serially, we have this structural concept so that each sentence in our translation is determined not only by the sentence in the original but by the two maps of the original text and the translated text which we are carrying along as we translate. (Holmes, 1972/1988: 96)

The research literature differs and exposes disagreements when it comes to defining the phenomenon of bilingualism. One position reserves bilingualism to instances where an individual has perfect mastery of two languages and their contexts. The knowledge and mastery should be so thorough that the bilingual is considered a native in both languages/contexts (Halliday et al., 1964). At the opposite extreme of perfect bilingualism are definitions that tend to include in this concept almost all abilities to express a complete utterance in a language other than one's mother tongue (Haugen, 1956; Lörscher, 2012).

Cognitive processes and translation competence

Why is bilingualism/biculturalism—the combination of knowledge of both source and target contexts—a required component in translation competence? The common-sense answer is that an actor who wants to translate obviously needs at least two parts to mediate between—and also needs a minimum of knowledge of both to be able to understand the source version and to render it and make it understandable in the target context. A much more complex approach (1) takes into account the highly intertwined cognitive processes involved in translations; further (2) reveals the links between some especially "productive" cognitive processes and bilingualism/biculturalism; and then (3) highlights the connection between degree of bilingualism/biculturalism involved in a translation—and the *quality* of the actual translation.

Numerous cognitive processes are involved in a translation process performed by bilingual actors. However, such processes are hard to research and make clear representations of, partly due to the extreme complexity of the ways in which they are interwoven, and partly because they are not amenable to direct observations (Seleskovitch 1978a; Dechert and Sandrock, 1986; Paradis, 2004; Rothe-Neves, 2007; Albir and Alvarez, 2009). This means that there still are many white spots on the map. For example, researchers still lack thorough knowledge about processes involved in translators' storing and retrieving of knowledge of source and target contexts when translating between them (Pearson and Fernández, 1994). While some scholars have postulated a two-store model, meaning that knowledge of the two contexts are stored in "maps" at two different places in the brain (Fabbro, 2001), proponents of one-store models argue that knowledge of both contexts is stored in the same cortex area (Price et al., 1999).

However, there seems to be general agreement among researchers that the cognitive processes involved in acts of translations can be subsumed under three main and interrelated phases (Seleskovitch, 1978b; Lederer, 1994/2003; Alvez and Albir, 2017). The first is to *understand* the source contexts and the message to be translated, activating an array of complex cognitive processes to make sense of the message and its contexts. The processes triggered in sensemaking also mobilize and interfere with processes of cognitive memory ("have I (the translator) seen or heard this before?")—both short- and long-term memory (Kroll and Stewart, 1994). The second phase is *de-verbalization*. At this intermediate stage between understanding and re-expression, various cognitive processes are activated to extract the pure *meaning* of the source message (Gile, 1990). The third phase is *re-expression*, which is expressing the source version in another language. This phase activates numerous cognitive processes (such as attention, perception, memorizing, selecting, and deciding) to arrive at an acceptable target version of the source version (Alvez and Albir, 2017).

In the listing of cognitive processes involved in translation processes one may get the impression that these are sequenced, linear processes that unfold within the translation period. However, the cognitive translation processes are not constrained by a sequential logic. Instead, they are non-linear and highly interconnected processes that run simultaneously—and at an extremely high speed. More than being one-directional and sequenced, cognitions involved in translations are alternating processes where the translator mentally oscillates, at high speed, between the source and the target context—a logic of iteration that successively may lead to an even more appropriate and high-quality translated version. Thus, the individual bilingual/bicultural translator has the capacity to cognitively move large amounts of information instantly (or with high velocity (Davenport and Prusak, 1998))—between her/his mental maps of source and target contexts. Such high-velocity alternations are a premise for key translation processes of relating, confronting, blending, and balancing the bodies of knowledge from the source and target contexts (Pym, 2004), and thus for arriving at an appropriate target version of a desired source text/practice. However, in addition to high-velocity mental commuting processes, the quality of the translation also depends on viscosity; that is, the thoroughness and quality of the knowledge that the bilingual/bicultural translator possesses and *combines* of both the source and the target—including knowledge of the desired source practice to be transferred and translated. Thus, the following proposition:

> *Proposition 7.1. The more the translator possesses and combines high-viscosity knowledge about the source contexts, the desired source practice, and the recipient context, the more likely it is that the translated version will account for the essentials of the desired source practice and be appropriately adjusted to the recipient context.*

Bilingualism as a variable in knowledge transfers

What makes bilingualism/biculturalism a possible unique and necessary ingredient of translation competence—both in linguistic translations and in the transfer of knowledge across organizational borders—is the potential to combine high-viscosity knowledge of both contexts—with high velocity iterative moves across the translator's mental maps (or "lexicons") of the contexts. It is important to recall that the capacity of making extremely high-velocity mental oscillations between source and target contexts is embodied in—and is therefore a key feature of the *individual* translator. In linguistic translations, the common and institutionalized practice is the individual translator who alone performs the entire translation. However, in knowledge transfers between organizations bilingualism is better conceived of as a scarce resource and a variable. Thus, there are high—as well as medium and low levels of bilingualism. Obviously, there are examples of single actors possessing high levels of bilingual/bicultural translation competence who operate as translators in knowledge transfers across organizational borders. One of the six knowledge transfer cases discussed in Chapter 6 involved a typical bilingual/bicultural translator. That was Ray Kroc, who in the early 1950s replicated a certain hamburger restaurant and made the world's largest fast-food franchising organization. Kroc had firsthand and detailed knowledge about the source, which was the McDonald brothers' hamburger restaurant in San Bernardino, California. Kroc combined that knowledge with his thorough knowledge of trends in the fast-food market in the United States. He also invested much energy in trying to get to know personally each relevant candidate who wished to become a MacDonald's franchisee. Kroc's extensive knowledge of both source and target contexts was undoubtedly an important reason behind the success of his replication strategy.

However, even in language translation of texts most translators do not manage to live up to the ideal of full bilingualism with total mastery of both the source and the target language. Historically, most language translators and interpreters are medium bilingual. Often they are more knowledgeable about the target language and culture than about the source, because they belong to—and have their mother tongue from the target context (Baker, 1998: 13–14). High level of bilingualism is even more infrequent in knowledge transfer between organizations than in linguistic translations. Few actors possess the knowledge needed to master thoroughly more than either the source or the recipient context (Levina and Vaast, 2005)—especially in knowledge transfers between separate and independent organizations. One example of *medium* bilingualism is the making of the Norwegian coworker dialogue as a translation of U.S.-based performance and counseling systems (see Chapter 6). Although a successful transfer, the Norwegian translators possessed significantly more viscous knowledge about the Norwegian than about the American organizational contexts.

Sometimes bilingualism is low, almost absent—such as in cases where external actors mediate between source and target contexts without possessing firsthand high-viscous knowledge of none of them. For example, large consulting houses are described as "knowledge systems" (Werr and Stjerberg, 2003) that regularly span and transfer knowledge between different organizational contexts (Suddaby and Greenwood, 2001). However, observers have questioned external consultants' knowledge of the contexts they mediate between (O'Shea and Madigan, 1997; Armbrüster, 2006; Røvik, 2007).

There is a striking difference between translation of language/texts and translation of knowledge across organizational borders. While text translations are mostly conducted by one single translator, knowledge mediation across organizations often resembles complex ecologies of several, diverse, shifting, and variously interconnected and coordinated groups of actors—such as authors of popular management books (Furusten, 1999), external consultants (Clark and Fincham, 2002), internal consultants (Sturdy and Wright, 2011), HRM staff (Iles et al., 2004), R&D staff (van Gils et al., 2009), shop-floor workers (Letmathe et al., 2012), and managers at various levels (Radaelli and Sitton-Kent, 2016), both in the source and the recipient organization. This implies that individual translators are often part-time participants who are involved in limited sequences of the transfer process. It also means that actors involved in contextualization processes in the target organization sometimes are others than those involved in processes of decontextualization in the source organization. Thus, under such conditions the potential quality of bilingualism in knowledge transfers—that is, the capability of combining high viscosity (thick knowledge of source organization, desired practice and recipient organization), with high velocity (speed of iterative moves between translator's mental maps of source and target contexts)—may suffer and even get lost. Real bilingualism in knowledge transfers is scarce and hard to obtain (Lazarova and Tarique, 2005; Burmeister and Deller, 2016; Waardenburg et al., 2022). However, organizations can take efforts to avoid maximum loss of bilingual capability by organizing for *pseudo-bilingualism* in knowledge transfers. A route to such bilingualism is to establish a team consisting of actors from both the recipient and the source context (Peal and Lambert, 1962) who together possess knowledge of high viscosity about both contexts and the desired source practice.

Deliberate usage of translation rules

The second pillar of translation competence—in addition to translators' knowledge of source and recipient contexts—is their knowledge and usage of translation rules. There *are* translation rules, which were described and typologized in Chapter 5. Translation rules can be deliberately selected to achieve certain effects, or they can be taken for granted and just followed. Regardless of the level of rationality upon which the choice of particular translation rules is premised, the use of a rule will have consequences for outcomes of knowledge transfer processes. For example, the effects of choosing and using various translation rules are clearly demonstrated in the six knowledge transfer cases presented in Chapter 6. A key question concerning this pillar of translation competence is how and to what extent it is possible to increase the chances for translators to more deliberately chose translation rules.

Scope conditions of translation rules

The above arguments point to the need to specify the translation rules' "scope conditions"—a concept that stems from the philosophy of science (Toulmin 1953/1967; Popper, 1959), which means making statements that serve to define and constrain the circumstances in which a theory is applicable (Cohen, 1989: 83). While it sometimes might be possible to formulate almost universal applicable theories within physical science, it is impossible to outline such theories within the human sciences, including the science of organizations. Those who eventually claim that they have discovered universal applicable social scientific laws will immediately be met with test results that contradict them (Walker and Cohen, 1985; Harris, 1997). Suddaby (2010) has concentrated especially on the scope conditions, or boundary limits, of "theoretical constructs" within organization theory. The typology of translation rules contains a set of such theoretical constructs. In contrast to physical science, organizational constructs lack universality. Thus, "it is very important for theorists to spell out the contextual conditions under which a proposed construct will or will not adhere" (Suddaby, 2010: 349). Suddaby warned against overgeneralization and claims of universality of theoretical constructs. The way to avoid this is by placing scope conditions on the constructs, which means carefully outlining their boundary limits.

Specifying the translation rules' scope conditions, or their range of application, means theorizing the conditions under which it will be reasonable, or unreasonable, to apply which rules. If we are able to define some of the scope conditions for the outlined translation rules, it can be useful knowledge with the potential to guide the choices of translators' (in other words, practitioners) who are involved in knowledge transfer processes across organizational borders. Being aware of the complex ecologies of such processes (Wedlin and Sahlin, 2017; Westney and Piekkari, 2020), which makes it hard to identify and outline more than just parts of each translation rule's scope condition, I have deliberately written "*some*" (scope conditions). Thus, efforts to outline the translation rules' range of applicability start here, while keeping in mind Whetten's (1989) argument that the "*who*, the *where*, and the *when*" of a theory are usually discovered and refined through subsequent empirical research, which means that defining theoretical constructs' scope conditions is an enduring task.

At the most general level, the scope conditions of a construct should be defined in relation to its applicability in space and time. However, these are very broad categories. Thus, this chapter zooms in at a more operationalized level of analysis. Attempts to trace translation rules' scope conditions are based on close readings of the vast literature on knowledge transfer studies, and especially on observations of the usage of translation rules in transfers that respectively lead to appropriate and inappropriate outcomes. These observations center around two key elements of knowledge transfer processes, which is (a) the source, as well as (b) the recipient and its relation to the source. Numerous studies and observations indicate that specific features of these two elements represent important conditions for translators involved in knowledge transfers in various organizational contexts and who search for the most appropriate translation rules. The key features of each of the two elements are defined below, followed by an outline of the scope conditions for each translation rule in relation to these features.

Features of the source

The source context—that is, where a desired practice is located and the ways it varies—constitute an important condition that influences the appropriateness of each translation rule. The key variable of source contexts is *translatability*, which is the extent to which a desired practice can be translated into an abstract representation that includes the essential elements for how it functions in the source context. More specifically, translatability is defined as a source practice's degree of explicitness (tacit and noncodified versus verbalized and codified), complexity (the technological vs the human component, in addition to the degree of causal ambiguity), and embeddedness (whether the knowledge base is dispersed and ingrained in intra- and/or interorganizational networks, or concentrated and thus, easier to demarcate). The translatability of a source practice varies between *high*, in cases with high explicitness, low complexity, and low embeddedness, and *low*, in cases where the desired practice is tacit, complex, and embedded.

Features of the relation between recipient and source.

Certain aspects of the recipient and its relation to the source may be decisive for the appropriateness of the various translation rules. The key variable is *similarity*, which is the extent to which the recipient and the source context differ or resemble each other in certain respects. Studies of language translation have verified that the greater the difference between recipient and source language contexts, the harder it is to arrive at proper translations (House, 2006; Dohan and Levintova, 2007). Recipient and source contexts can be similar or different in many ways, which can influence the transferability of knowledge between them. An important condition with impacts on the transferability is whether both the source and the recipient units belong to the same large organization. Within the resource-based view of the firm (Barney 1991; Kogut and Zander, 1993) a central insight is that intra-organizational knowledge transfer is, on average, easier than transfer across separate organizations (Tsang, 2002). Thus, a main driving force behind the establishment of multinational corporations is that it reduces friction and eases cross-unit knowledge transfers. Much research has focused upon and found effects of knowledge transfers of source and recipient units being located in similar/different cultures (Strang and Meyer, 1993; Javidan et al., 2005; Kayes et al., 2005; Lucas, 2006). Other researchers have focused specifically on the degree of similarity/difference of *national* cultures—and their effect on source–recipient knowledge transfers (Kedia and Bhagat, 1988; Kogut and Singh, 1988). One of the main findings of such studies is that the effectiveness of knowledge transfers decreases with increased national cultural differences between sources and recipients, while simultaneously increasing with increased national culture similarity. Another stream of studies has focused on the effects on knowledge transfers of similarity/differences between nation's *institutional* arrangements (Kostova, 1999; Dikova and Van Witteloostuijn, 2007). For example, Kostova (1999) argued that the likelihood of having transferred practices implemented depends on the extent to which the institutional arrangements, such as public regulations, laws, and formal rules, is similar or different in the source and recipient country contexts.

One insight from the above-mentioned studies that corresponds to the insights from translation studies is that the greater the difference between the recipient and source organizational contexts, the more challenging the knowledge transfer processes. Conversely, the more similar source and recipients contexts are in terms of the variables mentioned above, the easier the knowledge transfer process will be.

In what follows, the scope conditions of each of the main translation rules (the reproducing mode, the modifying mode, and the radical mode) are discussed and clarified in relation to the two key variables: translatability and similarity.

Scope conditions: The reproducing mode

Translatability and copying

Reproduction or copying as a translation rule refers to acts of replicating with great exactitude an identified desired source practice in one or more recipient organizations. The dominating motivation behind copying is to achieve successful outcomes by recreating and repeating in the recipient the elements that constitute the desired source practice (Nelson and Winter, 1982; Winter et al., 2012). However, successful copying is associated with certain scope conditions. These are conditions that are considerably influenced by the translatability of the desired source practice. Specifically, there are two required conditions of copying that vary with the degree of translatability. One is the need for the translator to know what to copy. In other words, copying requires a relatively clear and stable template. Thus, under conditions where a desired source practice is characterized by low translatability (such as tacit, nonverbalized practice, complex relationships among a high number of involved actors who together carry out the practice and, perhaps, which result in unclear cause–effect chains), it is hard for the translator to arrive at a clear image of a template to copy. The other condition that influences the appropriateness of copying is translators' access to additional information about the desired practice. As noted in Chapter 5, it is widely believed—especially in the Western world—that copying is rather simple and that it is usually quickly done—such as imaging an object by using a cell phone to take a picture of it. However, numerous observations and studies indicate that copying is a complex and enduring task. In contrast to the simplicity of taking a cell phone photo, good copying often requires a time-consuming process of learning. Thus, in the renowned Japanese culture of copying, the linguistic term for copying, *manebu*, has almost the same meaning as "learning" and is referred to as *manabu* (Clarence-Smith, 2007: 56).

Acknowledging that copying is hard and enduring work, a translator who attempts to copy needs good access to information about the desired source practice. At its best, an act of copying proceeds as an iterative process where the translator commutes between confronting and learning about the template, on one hand, and, on the other hand, engaging in filling out his/her copied version of it, and gradually arriving at a more refined high-fidelity copy of the desired source practice. Thus, access to the template is a very important condition for the translator. In fact, such access can sometimes compensate for low translatability in the first place (Inkpen, 2000). However, even in situations where the translatability of a desired source practice is low, and access to additional information is restricted, external located organizations/actors will sometimes take the risk of trying to copy the practice. Such risk-taking copying can be based on insights and reasoning that the value of tacit and uncodified knowledge is often higher and has more potential to gain competitive advantage than what is the case with practices based on codified, explicit, and more accessible knowledge. In such cases, the risk of copying failures increases. Thus, I offer the following proposition:

> *Proposition 7.2. The lower the translatability of a desired source practice and the more that access to additional information about the practice is restricted for outside-located organizations and potential adopters, the less appropriate copying will be as a translation rule.*

The above arguments indicate that the appropriateness of copying as a translation rule depends on the translatability of the template and on the translators' access to information about it. Thus, instances of high translatability of desired source practices and of good translator-access to additional information about it provide good conditions for copying. An example, outlined more in detail in Chapter 6, is the translation acts by Ray Kroc, who successfully used the McDonald brothers' hamburger restaurant as template from which he made a large number of replicas. A key premise for Kroc's replication success was that he had a clear and stable template, and almost no restrictions on repeatedly confronting it and gaining additional information throughout the long period of establishing and refining the replica hamburger restaurants. This leads to the next proposition.

> *Proposition 7.3. High translatability of a desired source practice—in combination with few restrictions on translator's access to additional information about the practice—increase the appropriateness of copying as a translation rule.*

As noted above, it is important that translators have opportunities to gain additional information about the desired source practice—and it can even compensate for a situation in which the translatability of the desired source practice is low. This can often be the case, for example, in attempts to transfer knowledge between units within large multinational corporations. Although an identified good practice in a certain unit may have low translatability in the first place, translators in other units have almost unrestricted access to gain additional information about it—and thus, to thereby increase its translatability and the appropriateness of copying.

> *Proposition 7.4. Low translatability of a desired source practice in the first place can be compensated by few restrictions on translators' access to gain additional information about the practice, and subsequently increase the appropriateness of applying copying as a translation rule.*

Similarity and copying

In addition to the translatability of the desired source practice, the degree of similarity between the source and the recipient contexts represents another important condition that may be decisive for the appropriateness of applying copying as translation rule. The basic argument is that the more dissimilar the source and the recipient contexts, the more risky it becomes to copy, because the way a practice is performed and the outcomes it leads to often reflect context-specific factors. Thus, the more the source and the recipient contexts differ, the more likely it is that the context-specific, noncodified and necessary features of the source are not present in the recipient context. It can be challenging for translators in potential adopting/recipient organizations to know how and to what extent a desired practice performed in a source in a rather dissimilar organizational context—is dependent upon noncodified context-specific factors. Therefore, a translator who aims to translate a desired practice from such a context may make inferences about the importance of the relative similarity between source and recipient contexts, without knowing exactly how and to what extent the functioning of the concrete source practice depends on its local context (Røvik, 2016: 301), and avoid copying in such cases.

Obviously, a source and a recipient organization can be similar/dissimilar in numerous ways. However, some features, or variables of similarity, are more important than others in defining the scope conditions of the reproducing mode and copying. In searching for such critical variables, it is reasonable to consider the entirety of knowledge transfer studies and concentrate on insights from various studies of knowledge transfer barriers. From such studies three variables seem to be of especial relevance to define scope condition of copying: corporate culture distance, national culture distance, and institutional distance.

Corporate culture distance. Hofstede et al. (2010) defined the concept of culture as "the collective programming of the mind that distinguishes the members of one group or category of people from others" (p. 6). There are many possible "categories" of culture. Among the most frequently referred to categories are organizational or corporate culture, and national culture. These are very different, but also highly interesting, categories when defining the scope conditions of translation rules.

Corporate culture includes implied but not expressed beliefs, assumptions, and customs that affect how members make sense of phenomena and how they act (Schein, 1985; De Long and Fahey, 2000). Research indicates that increased cultural dissimilarity may hamper knowledge transfers between source and recipient organizations (Shenkar et. al., 2008; Beugdelsdijk et al., 2018). Hardly discernable cultural elements can be involved in the ways a desired source practice is performed (Wenger and Snyder, 2000; De Long and Fahey, 2000). Therefore, with increasing corporate cultural distance, the risk of failing increases if the translator aims to copy the desired source practice.

> *Proposition 7.5. The more dissimilar source and recipient corporate cultures, the more likely that any cultural-specific elements inherent in the desired source practice will not "fit" in the recipient organizations, and the less appropriate copying will be as a translation rule.*

The proposed connection between high corporate culture distance and reduced appropriateness of copying as translation rule can be modified in cases of increased access for recipient-based translators to gain additional information about the desired source practice. Conversely:

> Proposition 7.6. The more similar source and recipient corporate cultures are, the more likely it is that any cultural-specific elements inherent in the desired source practice will fit with the recipient organizations, and the more appropriate copying will be as a translation rule.

National culture distance. In addition to organizations, nations are the other main entity that fall into Hofstede et al.'s (2010) definition of culture as the collective programming of the mind that distinguishes the members of one group or category from others. In speaking of national culture, the category is "nation," which refers to the norms, beliefs, behaviors, customs, and values shared by the population in a sovereign nation. Certain features distinguish organizational cultures from national cultures. While membership of an organization (and, thus, its culture) is usually limited in time and space, membership of a nation is usually established at birth and is often permanent. In two large research projects, Hofstede (1980) and Hofstede et al. (1990) described and compared national cultures in nearly 100 countries in relation to the following six value dimensions: (1) power distance, related to solutions to the basic problems of human inequality; (2) uncertainty avoidance, related to level of stress in a society on the face of an unknown future; (3) individualism versus collectivism; (4) masculinity versus femininity; (5) long-term versus short-term orientation, related to the choice of focus of people's efforts: the future or the present and past; and further (6) indulgence versus restraint, related to the extent of gratification of human desires for enjoying life.

By comparing nations according to their scores on these dimensions, a complex pattern emerges of similar and dissimilar national cultures. For example, there are very high scores for high power distance for Latin America, Asian countries, and Africa. The United States is in the middle, while Sweden and Denmark are characterized by low power distance. The value of individualism is very high in the United States, in Australia, and in Great Britain, while collectivism is high in nations such as Sweden, Serbia, and Portugal.

Research shows that differences in national cultures influence knowledge transfer processes, and especially dissimilarities related to individualism/collectivism and degrees of power distance (Lucas, 2006; Chen et al., 2010). Translators should be cautious about trying to copy a desired source practice in cases where the source and recipient are located in very different national cultures. The risk of including culturally biased elements in the copy that do not fit with the recipient increases with increasing differences in national cultures.

> Proposition 7.7. The more dissimilar the national cultures of source and recipient organizations, the more likely it is that the desired source practice contains national culture-biased elements that do not fit in with the recipient—and the less appropriate copying will be as a translation rule.

Conversely:

> Proposition 7.8. The more similar the national cultures of source and recipient organizations, the more likely it is that national culture-biased elements inherent in the desired source practice will eventually fit in with the recipient—and the more appropriate copying will be as a translation rule.

Institutional distance. The concept of "institutional distance" was coined and developed by Kostova in the late 1990s (Kostova, 1997; 1999), and refers to the differences/similarities between two countries according to their regulatory, cognitive, and normative institutions. The regulatory pillar encompasses a country's laws, formal rules, and regulations, and includes typical activities such as rule setting, monitoring, and sanctioning. The regulatory aspect of a country may come to expression in various ways, such as in typical features of the formal structure, procedures, and routines of the country's public administration.

Institutional distance is an important variable when theorizing the scope condition of knowledge translation rules, including the reproducing mode and the rule of copying. Especially interesting is the regulatory pillar, partly because it is the most researched of the three pillars (Kostova et al., 2020: 474), but mainly because the two others—the cognitive and the normative pillars—overlap to some extent with definitions and insights already taken care of within the literature of corporate and national cultural distance (Kostova, 1999: 314). Somewhat surprisingly, there are relatively few studies of the effects of regulatory distance, and even fewer of how regulatory distance affects knowledge transfers (For example, in their studies of the effects of institutional distance on knowledge transfer, both Kostova (1999) and Jensen and Szulanski (2004) left out regulatory distance). However, it is reasonable to suggest that regulatory distance is an important variable in knowledge transfers. Countries differ greatly on the regulatory variable. Thus, more specifically, it is reasonable to suggest that the functioning of a desired source practice may depend partly on laws, rules, and institutions that regulate political, social, and economic conditions within a host country. Such dependencies can be challenging for recipient-based translators as they are often hard to discover and may not fit with regulatory conditions in the host country of the recipient. Therefore, it can be risky to apply copying as a translation rule since the desired source practice may require certain regulative conditions that are not present in the home country of the recipient. Thus, the following proposition:

Proposition 7.9. The more dissimilar the regulatory condition of the host country of the source organization and the recipient organization, the more likely it is that any dependencies of country-specific regulations for the functioning of the desired source practice will not fit with the regulative conditions in the recipient country—and the less appropriate copying will be as a translation rule.

Summing up. Some scope conditions of a reproducing translation mode (copying) have been defined above according to certain features of the relation between source and recipient contexts. It is argued that the more dissimilar a source and a recipient are on three variables (corporate culture-distance, national culture-distance, and regulatory distance), the more limited the scope condition of copying. Conversely, increasing similarity between source and recipient contexts on these variables tends to increase the appropriateness of copying as a translation rule.

It has been suggested that the proposed connections between each of the three types of dissimilarity and increasing limitation in the scope conditions of copying can be modified and compensated by (a) the extent to which recipient actors have access to gain additional information about the desired source practice and its context, and (b) the extent to which recipient actors de facto exploit such access to gain additional information.

As mentioned earlier, the examination of the three "distance" variables identifies *some*—but obviously not all—actual scope conditions of the reproducing mode. Thus, "organizational type" is another promising variable to further define the scope conditions of the reproducing mode construct. For example, copying in cases of transfer of a desired source practice across different industries can be challenging (Tell et al., 2017), as can transferring from private sector to public sector organizations (Diefenbach, 2009).

Scope conditions: The radical mode

As outlined in Chapter 5, the radical translation mode is featured by a propensity of translators to act relatively unbounded by a source context version when translating a recipient version of it. There are two main reasons why recipient-based translators can be inclined to alter and thus make versions that deviate severely from source practice versions. The first is the notion that all knowledge transfers should be clearly related to the needs of the recipient organization. Thus, the driving force of knowledge transfers should be to solve problems in the recipient organization. Any transferred practice should be domesticated according to this premise; that is, adapted to be effective means of meeting defined, concrete challenges in the recipient. Viewed from this perspective, the way in which such adopted and adapted practices de facto *work* as problem-solving means in the recipient is the key criteria to assess the outcome of the knowledge transfer. These arguments correspond to similar arguments by Skopos theorists (Hönig and Kußmaul, 1982; Schäffner, 1998) and manipulation school theorists (Hermans, 1985/2014) within translation theory. Instead of adherence to the source and living up to the ideal of searching for equivalence between the recipient and the source version, they argued that the source text should *not* determine the translation process. The function of a translation should be determined by target context actors and their needs (Holz-Mänttäri, 1984).

The other main reason why organizations can enter into a radical translation mode can be traced back to certain habits and traditions frequently associated with Western values and ideals. The enduring Western world project of progress towards higher levels of technological development, welfare, and civilization is deeply rooted in the values of individualism, novelty, inventions, and innovations (Meyer et al., 1997). The admiration for and celebration of novelty and innovations go hand in hand with a corresponding deep skepticism towards copycat culture and reproductions. However, as outlined in Chapter 5, while there is a chronic shortage of real novelty and simultaneously a rich supply of templates that could be imitated, organizations are tempted to radically transform imitations so that they stand out as innovations.

It is important to keep these (and others) social mechanisms in mind when defining scope conditions of the radical translation mode.

Translatability and radical translation

The translatability of a desired source practice constitutes important scope conditions for radical translations and the rule of alteration. However, the relationship between alteration and its scope conditions set by the desired practice's translatability is complex. In cases with a desired source practice of low translatability and with restricted access to gain additional information, translators face a dilemma. Acknowledging that superior results and competitive advantages often stem from knowledge that is tacit, complex, and embedded in networks and cultures may encourage organizations to take the chance of copying—even if the translatability is low and the template blurry. This may lead to misinterpretations and copying failures, and thus, to *unintentional alteration* and emergent of recipient versions that do not work (Babson, 1998). For example, most attempts to copy the success of Silicon Valley Science Park have failed (DesForges, 1986). However, in cases of low translatability, alteration and radical translation can also be a deliberately chosen translation rule. The less translatable a desired source practice is (for example, one characterized with irreducible causal ambiguity), the more sense it might make to conceptualize the available and limited information about such practices as rough templates and sources of inspiration that can be altered and radically mixed and transformed (Røvik, 2016), thereby creating something new under the inspiration of something that already exists (Alchian, 1950; Erlingsdottir and Lindberg, 2005). In propositional form:

> *Proposition 7.10. The lower the translatability of a desired source practice (that is, the more tacit, complex and embedded it is), the more a radical translation will become an appropriate translation rule.*

Conversely, it is suggested that increasing the translatability of the desired source practice makes alteration less necessary and, thus, less appropriate.

> *Proposition 7.11. The higher the translatability of a desired source practice, the more that copying—and the less alteration—will become an appropriate translation rule.*

However, under such conditions, organizations' acts of knowledge translations can also be modified by the influence of strong societal values and norms of demonstrating novelty, newness, and innovations, and therefore, avoiding copying. As outlined in Chapter 5, such values and norms are defining features of the Western world's ideals and ideology. Under such societal conditions—and with a chronic shortage of real novelty and newness and a corresponding rich supply of well-known practices and templates to imitate—organizations may try to make changes to known templates to live up to norms of novelty and newness. The changes translated to the source practice may be modest and/or radical. In propositional form:

Proposition 7.12. The stronger the influence of the societal norms and values of novelty, newness, inventions, and innovations, the more likely it is that organizations in such a context will avoid copying a desired source practice and will instead prefer modification and/or alteration as appropriate translation rules.

Similarity and radical translation

Like the reproducing mode, the degree of similarity between the source and recipient organizational context may also define the scope conditions of a radical translation mode. Some of these conditions can be defined in relation to the three key variables for characterizing the degree of similarity/dissimilarity introduced above: corporate culture, national culture, and regulatory conditions (institutional distance). Source and recipient contexts can differ on some variables (for example, in relation to corporate culture) while being more similar on the others. However, there can also be instances where the contexts co-varies in such a way that they are clearly different on all three variables: different corporate cultures, different national cultures, and different national regulatory conditions. Under such conditions, it is likely that the desired practice contains various source context-specific elements that differ severely from and do not fit in with the recipient context. Thus, it can be risky for translators to try to copy, and even to modify, the desired practice—and, correspondingly, it can be wise to act relatively unbounded by such a practice, conceive of it as a source of inspiration, and be willing to radically transform it and make a domesticated version.

Proposition 7.13. The more dissimilar the source and the recipient contexts (in terms of corporate culture, national culture, and national regulatory conditions), the more likely it is that the source practice contains context-specific elements that do not fit with the recipient context, and the more appropriate alteration will be as a translation rule.

A translation process may involve shifts in translation rules, which means usage of different rules in different phases of the process. Such shifts often reflect processes of learning and adaptation related to efforts to make a transferred practice work in the recipient organization. A typical trajectory in such cases starts with attempts to copy a desired source practice and then sequences into a more radical translation. An example is attempts in the late 1960s to transfer the U.S.-based performance and appraisal system (PAC) to Norwegian organizations. Most of the early adopters among Norwegian organizations tried to copy the U.S.-based practices, including tight top-down surveillance of the individual employees and with individualized payment systems based on performance and results. By the early 1970s, many employers and employees had experienced that replicas of the U.S.-based PAC practice did not work in the Norwegian working-life context. Acknowledging the severe dissimilarities between American and Norwegian working life with reference to national cultures as well as regulatory conditions, the PAC practice was radically transformed and adapted to fit the Norwegian context. In propositional form:

> Proposition 7.14. Under conditions where a copied and/or slightly adapted practice from a dissimilar source context does not work in the recipient organization according to local needs and expectation, the appropriateness of alteration as a translation rule increases.

Scope conditions: The modifying mode

As outlined in Chapter 5, the modifying translation mode reflects acknowledgments of the value of balancing concerns for replication (that is, to avoid the essentials of the source practice being lost in translation), with concern for adaptation (meaning to translate a version of the source practice that is sufficiently adapted to and therefore works in the recipient organization). Although not a knowledge transfer ideal like the reproducing and the radical modes, and also less researched than those two mentioned, there are reasons to believe that, in practice, knowledge transfer processes often proceed as modifying processes with translators aiming to balance concerns for replication and adaptation. Like the reproducing and radical modes, some important scope conditions of the modifying mode can be defined in relation to the two key variables of translatability and similarity.

Translatability and modifying

Desired source practices to be translated and transferred sometimes consist of interconnected elements with different levels of translatability. For example, a desired source practice may include technological components (machinery, tools, equipment, etc.) that translators relatively easily can make representations of and copy. However, the practice may be carried out by a number of involved actors who use the technology and who cooperate and works on more or less tacit and implicit knowledge (as illustrated in Chapter 4 in the practicing of the handgot method of coal-getting in U.K. coal-mining industry until the 1920s). In such cases, with medium translatability, translators may combine attempts to reproduce the high-translatable elements with attempts to modify the less translatable elements. An appropriate translation rule can be explication, a version of addition, meaning that translators may try to make the implicit and tacit elements verbalized and explicit in the recipient version. In propositional form:

> Proposition 7.15. Under conditions of medium translatability where a desired source practice contains some nonexplicit (tacit) elements that are important for the way it works, it is appropriate to use explication as translation rule to balance concerns for replication and adaptation.

However, to make explicit what is implicit in a source practice may be a challenging translation rule, which involves identifying tacit and assumed knowledge behind a desired practice and then verbalizing and expressing it in ways that make sense and make it work in the recipient context (Nonaka and Takeuchi, 1995; Collins, 2010).

To define scope conditions also means indicating the conditions under which a certain construct does *not* apply. While it is generally difficult to define the limitations of a modifying mode, it is especially challenging to specify the borderline between conditions that facilitate a modifying mode versus conditions that facilitate a reproducing mode (Szulanski and Winter, 2002; Baden-Fuller and Winther, 2005).

What characterizes knowledge transfer situations where modifying and adaption should be avoided in favor of copying? To some extent, the translatability of a desired source practice can guide decisions to choose between these two rules. As outlined in proposition 7.2, high translatability of a desired source practice, expressed in a clear and stable template—and with good access for recipient actors to achieve additional information about the practice—increases the appropriateness of copying as translation rule. However, a clear and stable template of a desired practice can also be modified, due to attempts to balance concerns for replication with concerns for sufficiently adaptations to make it work in the recipient context.

Limited or low translatability is also a challenging condition that has implications for choosing between copying and modification. Instances characterized by a good working desired practice of limited translatability can be tempting for translators to apply copying as a translation rule. For example, this could be cases where there is a source practice that leads to desired results, but where the translators lack insights into the inherent cause–effect mechanisms. The main argument for copying in such cases is that if a practice works, but the translators do not know why, they should be especially cautious and avoid changing *anything* that could influence the critical components and the relationships among them that makes the desired source practice effective (Calsyn, et al., 1977; Blakely et. al., 1987). However, the inherent dilemma here is that if the translator lacks knowledge into the cause effect—relationships of a desired source practice, and especially where there are restrictions on gaining such knowledge—translators will also lack a clear template to copy, and run the risk of accidentally making changes to it that may also change the way it works. In such cases, it can be wiser to modify and domesticate to increase the chances that it will work in the recipient context.

An important factor to guide choices about whether to copy or modify is whether or not it is evidenced that replicas of an actual source practice have led to desired results in other organizations. The more such evidence is available, the more the appropriateness of copying increases, and the more cautious should translators be to avoid introducing modifications.

The various concerns discussed above (translatability, access to additional information, and evidenced effects) are seen in comparison and indicate important borderlines between a reproducing mode and a modifying translation mode. In propositional form:

> Proposition 7.16. The higher the translatability of a desired source practice, the better the recipient-based translators' access to additional information about it, and the more the practice's desired effects are evidenced from other organizations, the less appropriate a modifying mode will be and, conversely, the more appropriate a reproducing mode will be as a translation rule.

Similarity and a modifying mode

The degree of similarity/dissimilarity between the source and recipient organizational contexts may help define some scope conditions of the modifying mode. While a high degree of dissimilarity facilitates a radical mode, and a high degree of context similarity facilitates a reproducing mode, it is proposed that the appropriateness of a modifying mode probably increases under conditions of medium similarity/dissimilarity. The concept of medium similarity/dissimilarity can be clarified in relation to national cultural distance and institutional distance (regulatory conditions). Hofstede (1980) and Hofstede, Hofstede and Minkov (2010) described and analyzed types and degree of cultural similarities between nations. For example, Sweden and Denmark are rather similar when compared on the dimensions of *power distance, individualism/collectivism, masculinity, uncertainty avoidance, long-term orientation,* and *indulgence/restraint*. According to the same dimensions, these two nations differ greatly from many other nations, such as

Brazil, China, and Japan. However, according to Hofstede's (1980) research, Sweden and Denmark are relatively (medium) similar/dissimilar compared to some other nations, including Finland, the United States, and Canada. Nations also vary according to regulatory conditions, which refer to a country's laws, formal rules and regulations (Kostova, 1999; Kostova et al., 2020). For example, while the Nordic countries are rather similar on many variables in terms of public administrative regulatory conditions (Kuhlmann and Wollmann, 2019), some studies show that the Nordic countries are quite dissimilar to some Mediterranean countries (Greve et al., 2020). However, research also indicates that European states that are members of the European Union (E.U.)—although different on a number of variables—have developed increasingly similar public administrative structures, laws, regulations, and practices as effects of the European integration process (Knill et al., 2001; Olsen, 2002; Kuhlmann and Wollman, 2019), to such an extent that they appear as moderately similar/dissimilar.

Under such conditions of medium similarity/dissimilarity between the source and the recipient organizational contexts, translators may be reluctant to apply copying as a translation rule, due to the differences between the contexts, and also reluctant to radically transform the desired source practice, due to acknowledging the relative similarity between the contexts and therefore, a fair chance of being able to recreate the source practice desired effects in the recipient organization. A situation characterized by medium similarity/dissimilarity between the source and the recipient contexts is likely to be a condition that facilitates use of a modifying translation rule where translators try to balance concerns about not losing the essentials of the desired practice with concerns about making the practice work in the recipient context.

One such balancing act can be to apply the modifying translation rule of "omission," which refers to the toning down and/or the subtraction of an element present in the source version in the translated recipient version. An example (highlighted in Chapter 5) was the attempts to recreate the success of the Silicon Valley science park in California—in Stockholm, Sweden. The source and the recipient contexts were relatively similar on a number of variables, and different on others. For example, the pleasant weather conditions in California were not the same in Stockholm, so this aspect was toned down in the Stockholm narrative of the Silicon Valley success (Sahlin-Andersson, 1996). Conditions of medium similarity/dissimilarity between source and recipient contexts may also facilitate the use of the modifying mode and the translation rule of addition. For example, translators can carefully try to familiarize a desired source practice by adding elements from existing good-functioning practices in the recipient organization—as illustrated by Møller Mortensen (2020) in her study of the case of transferring and translating co-production in the Danish municipality of Aalborg. In practice, under conditions of medium similarity, translators may combine the rules of omission and addition.

Proposition 7.17. Under conditions of medium similarity/dissimilarity between source and recipient contexts, the appropriateness increases for applying a modifying translation mode, and inter alia, omission and addition as translation rules—to balance concerns for replication and adaptation.

Translation competence: Key concepts and arguments

A central suggestion in this book is that translation theory has the potential to guide translators' deliberate actions in knowledge transfer processes. This chapter has focused on *how* insights derived from the translation theory can be useful for practitioners. The point of departure in this chapter is the concept of *translation performance*, which refers to how actors involved in knowledge transfers gain and use knowledge about source context, the desired source practice and the recipient context—and how they choose, use, and eventually combine and shift various translation rules throughout the knowledge transfer process. A main argument is that actors' translation performance may explain outcomes of knowledge transfers. Therefore, studies of translators' performances can be a route to reveal reasons for variations in transfer outcomes that have not previously been fully understood and explained. The chapter argues that variations in translators' performances reflect their *translation competence*. This concept refers to the sum of knowledge and skills that an involved actor mobilizes and applies in acts of transferring knowledge across organizational borders. The two pillars of translation competence are translators' knowledge of source and target contexts—and their knowledge about translation rules and about how to select the appropriate rules under various conditions.

Modelling knowledge of contexts

Translators' knowledge of contexts encompasses their knowledge about the source and target contexts and about the desired source practice to be transferred. This chapter has proposed connections between the quality of translators' knowledge of contexts and outcomes of knowledge transfer processes, in terms of the degree to which the translated version accounts for the essentials of the desired source practice and is appropriately adjusted to and

Translation Competence: Implications for Knowledge Transfer

Translator's knowledge of contexts → 1 Degree of viscosity → 2 Degree of bilingualism → 3 Level of velocity → Outcome of knowledge transfer processes

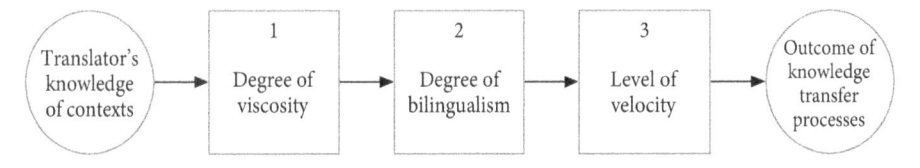

Figure 7.1 Links between translators' knowledge of contexts and outcomes of knowledge transfers

works in the recipient context. However, translators' knowledge of contexts does not necessarily lead to a desired transfer outcome. This chapter proposes that it depends, among other things, on the scores of three sequenced intermediate variables. As indicated in Figure 7.1, this sequence of variables is degree of viscosity, degree of bilingualism, and level of velocity.

A central feature of the quality of translators' knowledge of contexts is the *viscosity* of the knowledge (1), which refers to the degree of thickness, or thoroughness of translators' knowledge about the source context, the desired source practice, and the recipient context. The degree of viscosity of translators' knowledge depends (a) on features of the translator's localization (for example, inside or outside the source/target organizations), length of experience, etc.; and (b) on three features of the practice to be transferred and existing practices in the recipient organization, which is their explicitness, complexity, and embeddedness. The less explicit, more complex and more embedded, the harder it is for translators to gain high viscous knowledge, and vice versa. The degree of viscosity of translators' knowledge of contexts sets out important premises for the outcome of transfer processes.

The second intermediate variable is *degree of bilingualism* (2); that is, the degree to which individual translators *combine* high viscous knowledge about source and target contexts. The degree of bilingualism varies between high (individual translators combining high viscous knowledge of both source and recipient context), and low (absence of viscous knowledge of both source and recipient context among involved translators). Most common in knowledge transfers is versions of medium bilingualism. Bilingualism is a premise for the third intermediate variable: level of velocity (3), that is, the speed at which the translator can alternate between her/his mental maps containing representations of source context, source desired practice, and recipient context. Bilingual translators' high-velocity iterative moves are an important premise for arriving at high-quality translations. To some extent, albeit not fully, the lack of individual bilingual translators in knowledge transfers can be compensated by establishing pseudo-bilingual translation teams.

By comparison, the above arguments highlight the logic upon which proposition 7.1 is formulated: "The more the translator possesses and combines high-viscosity knowledge about the source contexts, the desired source practice, and the recipient context, the more likely it is that the translated version will account for the essentials of the desired source practice and be appropriately adjusted to—and work the recipient context." However, for certain other scores on the intermediate variables, outcomes of knowledge transfer processes can be less desirable. For example, translators may lack viscous knowledge about one or both contexts. Further, in cases where viscous knowledge *is* present among translators, conditions for optimal outcomes can still be missing due to a lack of bilingual translators—which reduces the chances of high levels of velocity in translation processes.

Deliberate usage of translation rules
The second pillar of translation competence is premised on insights about translation rules. There *are* translations rules, which are used in all acts of knowledge transfer across organizational borders and are decisive for outcomes of transfer processes. Translation rules are sometimes deliberately chosen and sometimes taken for granted and just followed. It is argued that a key component in translation competence is consciousness and knowledge about how to make more deliberate choices of translation rules. Therefore, this chapter has concentrated on specifying some important *scope conditions* for usage of the various rules. The first is features of the source context and the desired source practice. The key variable is *translatability*; that is, the extent to which the desired source practice can be translated to a representation without losing the essential elements that account for how it works in the source context. The second is features of the relationship between recipient and source organization. The key variable is *similarity*, which is the degree to which source and recipient differ/resemble each other on variables such as nationality and cultural, institutional, and geographical distance/proximity. The chapter has then argued and developed a set of 17 specific proposals (see Table 7.1) about which translation rules are appropriate/inappropriate under certain degrees of translatability of source context/source desired practice—and degrees of similarity between source and recipient contexts.

The attempts to specify the range of application of the various translation rules have certain limitations. The efforts are put forward in terms of a set of proposals, which are not empirically evidenced facts. However, while the proposals represent the ceiling in this chapter, it should obviously be the floor for other researchers who set out to test and refine them.

Table 7.1 Appropriate translation rules under various scope conditions

Translation rules' scope conditions	Reproducing mode Copying	Radical mode Alteration	Modifying mode Addition & Omission
FEATURES OF THE SOURCE Key variable: Translatability of source context/desired source practice	*Proposition 7.2. The lower the translatability of a desired source practice and the more that access to additional information about the practice is restricted for outside-located organizations and potential adopters, the less appropriate copying will be as a translation rule.* *Proposition 7.3. High translatability of a desired source practice—in combination with few restrictions on translator's access to additional information about the practice—increase the appropriateness of copying as a translation rule.* *Proposition 7.4. Low translatability of a desired source practice in the first place can be compensated by few restrictions on translators' access to gain additional information about the practice, and subsequently increase the appropriateness of applying copying as a translation rule.*	*Proposition 7.10. The lower the translatability of a desired source practice (that is, the more tacit, complex and embedded it is), the more a radical translation will become an appropriate translation rule.* *Proposition 7.11. The higher the translatability of a desired source practice, the more that copying—and the less alteration—will become an appropriate translation rule.* *Proposition 7.12. The stronger the influence of the societal norms and values of novelty, newness, inventions, and innovations, the more likely it is that organizations in such a context will avoid copying a desired source practice and will instead prefer modification and/or alteration as appropriate translation rules.*	*Proposition 7.15. Under conditions of medium translatability where a desired source practice contains some nonexplicit (tacit) elements that are important for the way it works, it is more appropriate to use explication as translation rule to balance concerns for replication and adaptation.* *Proposition 7.16. The higher the translatability of a desired source practice, the better the recipient-based translators' access to additional information about it, and the more the practice's desired effects are evidenced from other organizations, the less appropriate a modifying mode will be and, conversely, the more appropriate a reproducing mode will be as a translation rule.*

Continued

Table 7.1 Continued

Translation rules'	Reproducing mode	Radical mode	Modifying mode
FEATURES OF THE RELATION BETWEEN RECIPIENT AND SOURCE Key variable: Similarity	*Proposition 7.5. The more dissimilar source and recipient corporate cultures, the more likely that any cultural-specific elements inherent in the desired source practice will not "fit" in the recipient organizations, and the less appropriate copying will be as a translation rule.* *Proposition 7.6. The more similar source and recipient corporate cultures are, the more likely it is that any cultural-specific elements inherent in the desired source practice will fit with the recipient organizations, and the more appropriate copying will be as a translation rule.* *Proposition 7.7. The more dissimilar the national cultures of source and recipient organizations, the more likely it is that the desired source practice contains national culture-biased elements that do not fit in with the recipient—and the less appropriate copying will be as a translation rule.*	*Proposition 7.13. The more dissimilar the source and the recipient contexts (in terms of corporate culture, national culture, and national regulatory conditions), the more likely it is that the source practice contains context-specific elements that do not fit with the recipient context, and the more appropriate alteration will be as a translation rule.* *Proposition 7.14. Under conditions where a copied and/or slightly adapted practice from a dissimilar source context does not work in the recipient organization according to local needs and expectation, the appropriateness of alteration as a translation rule increases.*	*Proposition 7.17. Under conditions of medium similarity/dissimilarity between source and recipient contexts, the appropriateness increases for applying a modifying translation mode, and inter alia, omission and addition as translation rules—to balance concerns for replication and adaptation.*

Proposition 7.8. The more similar the national cultures of source and recipient organizations, the more likely it is that national culture-biased elements inherent in the desired source practice will eventually fit in with the recipient—and the more appropriate copying will be as a translation rule.

Proposition 7.9. The more dissimilar the regulatory condition of the host country of the source organization and the recipient organization, the more likely it is that any dependencies of country-specific regulations for the functioning of the desired source practice will not fit with the regulative conditions in the recipient country—and the less appropriate copying will be as a translation rule.

The relationship between knowledge of contexts and deliberate usage of translation rules

This chapter has identified and theorized two intertwined pillars of translation competence: knowledge of contexts and knowledge and deliberate usage of translation rules. High viscous knowledge of contexts among involved actors is important for outcomes of knowledge transfer processes. However, although firm knowledge of contexts is a necessary element of translation competence, it is not sufficient because it does not necessarily lead to deliberate usage of translation rules. Actors involved in knowledge transfers should avoid habitual (non)choices of translation rules and should be aware of and knowledgeable about the *repertoire* of translation rules available. Based on knowledge of contexts, scope conditions pertinent to each transfer process should be scrutinized and the insights gained should premise deliberate choices of translation rules.

Knowledge transfer processes frequently call upon translators' skills to *combine* various translation rules and/or to *shift* rules throughout the transfer process. Regarding the need for combination of rules: When scrutinizing a desired source practice, involved translators may conclude that some elements represent the core cause–effect mechanism of the practice and should therefore be copied, while other elements require modifications and sometimes perhaps radical transformations as adaptions to the target context. An example is provided in Mortensen's (2020) study of the transfer of the practice of co-production to the municipality of Aalborg, Denmark (cf. Chapter 6). She showed that while what was conceived of as the core of the practice was largely copied (involving the service receivers in the production of the service), other elements were subtracted or toned down and some new elements were added.

It can also be appropriate and necessary to shift from some translation rules to some other ones due to characteristics of how certain transfer processes proceed. Knowledge transfer processes often resemble processes of experiential learning, where translators gradually learn about the desired source practice, as well as about how the translated version works in the recipient context. Such learning processes may come to expression in some typical trajectories of changes in translation rules throughout the transfer. One example is trajectories where translators initially modify a desired source practice and, after a while, change to copying. In such cases, a modifying mode may have been chosen deliberately, but it may also be "accidental modifications" because the translators initially lacked thorough knowledge of the desired source practice that they wanted to recreate. For example, such processes are common in knowledge transfers of training methods and technologies within various sports (Erhardt et al., 2014). Depending on the availability of additional knowledge about the desired source practice, athletes may gradually learn more about the template and, after a while, be able to reproduce fully. Another typical translation trajectory runs in reverse order; that is, from an initial usage of copying and to modifications, and sometimes ending as a radical translation. Such a trajectory may reflect experiential learning, where an initial copying strategy turns out not to work in the recipient context, and is therefore followed by shifts in translation rules to modifying and/or to alteration. The capacity of translators to sense changes in scope conditions and to shift to more appropriate rules accordingly can be decisive for outcomes. An example of the lack of such capacity is provided in the analysis of the enduring attempts over three decades to replicate Ford fabric and Tayloristic organizing principles from the United States in British coal mines. Although this led to numerous negative effects (such as decreased quality of working environment, stoppages, and lowered efficiency), the reproducing mode was maintained long after it should have been changed to a modifying mode.

References

Abdrashitova, L., Sadykova, G., and Anthony, N. (2018) Explicitation in translation studies: Defining theoretical framework, *National Academy of Managerial Staff of Culture and Arts Herald*. https://doi.org/10.32461/2226-3209.3.2018.171173

Abrahamsen, H. and Aas, M. (2016) School leadership for the future: Heroic or distributed? Translating international discourses in Norwegian policy documents, *Journal of Educational Administration and History*, 48(1): 68–88.

Acemoglu, D., Johnson, S., Querubin, P., and Robinson, J.A. (2008) When does policy reform work? The case of central bank independence, *Working Paper 14033*, National Bureau of Economic Research, Cambridge, MA.

Adler, P. (1999) Hybridization, human resource management at two Toyota plants, in J.K. Liker, M.W. Fruin, and P. Adler (eds.), *Remade in America, Transplanting and Transforming Japanese Management Systems*, New York: Oxford University Press: 75–116.

Adler, P.S. (2001) Market, hierarchy, and trust: The knowledge economy and the future of capitalism, *Organization Science*, 12(2): 215–34.

Adler, P.S. and Kwon, S.W. (2002) Social capital: Prospects for a new concept, *Academy of Management Review*, 27(1): 17–40.

Agarwal, R., Echambadi, R., Franco, A.M., and Sarkar, M.B. (2004) Knowledge transfer through inheritance: Spin-out generation, development, and survival, *Academy of Management Journal*, 47(4): 501–22.

Aghion, P., Howitt, P., Brant-Collett, M., and García-Peñalosa, C. (1998) *Endogenous Growth Theory*, Cambridge, MA: MIT Press.

Aguilera, R. V., and Grøgaard, B. (2019) The dubious role of institutions in international business: A road forward, *Journal of International Business Studies*, 50(1): 20–35.

Ahmad, A., Bosua, R., and Scheepers, R. (2014) Protecting organizational competitive advantage: A knowledge leakage perspective, *Computers & Security*, 42: 27–39.

Ahuja, G. (2000) Collaboration networks, structural holes, and innovation: A longitudinal study, *Administrative Science Quarterly*, 45(3): 425–55.

Alavi, M. and Leidner, D. (1999) Knowledge management systems: Issues, challenges, and benefits, *Communications of the Association for Information systems*, 1(1): 1–28.

Alavi, M., and Leidner, D.E. (2001) Knowledge management and knowledge management systems: Conceptual foundations and research issues, *MIS Quarterly*, 25 (1): 107–36.

Albert, S. and Whetten, D.A. (1985) Organizational identity, in L.L. Cummings and M. Staw (eds.), *Research in Organizational Behavior*, Greenwich, CT: JAI: 263–95.

Albir, A.H. and Alves, F. (2009) Translation as a cognitive activity, in J. Munday (ed.), *The Routledge Companion to Translation Studies*, London: Routledge: 54–73.

Alchian, A.A. (1950) Uncertainty, evolution, and economic theory, *Journal of Political Economy*, 58(3): 211–21.

Alchian, A.A. and Demsetz, H. (1972) Production, information costs, and economic organization, *The American Economic Review*, 62(5): 777–95.

Aldrich, H. (1999) *Organizations Evolving*, Thousand Oaks, CA: SAGE.

Alexander, A.T. and Childe, S.J. (2013) Innovation: A knowledge transfer perspective, *Production Planning & Control*, 24(2–3): 208–25.

Alves, F. and Albir, A.H. (2017) Evolution, challenges, and perspectives for research on cognitive aspects of translation, in J.W. Schwieter and A. Ferreira (eds.), *The Handbook of Translation and Cognition*, West Sussex: Wiley Blackwell: 537–54.

Alvesson, M. (1993) The play of metaphors, in J. Hassard. and M. Parker (eds.), *Postmodernism and Organizations*, London: Sage: 114–131.

Alvesson, M. (2012) *Understanding Organizational Culture*, London: Sage.

Alvesson, M. and Spicer, A. (2011) Introduction, in M. Alvesson and A. Spicer (eds.), *Metaphors We Lead By*, London and New York: Routledge: 1–7.

Amara, N., Landry, R., and Traoré, N. (2008) Managing the protection of innovations in knowledge-intensive business services, *Research Policy*, 37(9): 1530–47.

Ambos, T.C. and Ambos, B. (2009) The impact of distance on knowledge transfer effectiveness in multinational corporations, *Journal of International Management*, 48: 24–41.

Ambrosini, V. and Bowman, C. (2005) Reducing causal ambiguity to facilitate strategic learning, *Management Learning*, 36(4): 493–512.

Amin, A. and Cohendet, P. (2004) *Architectures of Knowledge: Firms, Capabilities, and Communities*, Oxford: Oxford University Press.

Ancona, D.G. and Caldwell, D.F. (1992) Bridging the boundary: External activity and performance in organizational teams, *Administrative Science Quarterly*, 3(3): 634–65.

Anderman, G. and Rogers, M. (2000) Translator training between academia and profession: A European perspective, in C. Schäffner and B. Adab (eds.), *Developing Translation Competence*, Amsterdam/ Philadelphia: John Benjamins: 63–73.

Andersen, H. and Røvik, K.A. (2015) Lost in translation: A case-study of the travel of lean thinking in a hospital, *BMC Health Services Research*, 15(1): 1–9.

Andersen, H., Røvik, K.A., and Ingebrigtsen, T. (2014) Lean thinking in hospitals: Is there a cure for the absence of evidence? A systematic review of reviews, *BMJ Open*, 4(1). https://doi.org/10.1136/bmjopen-2013-003873

Anderson, R. and Kroc, R. (2018) *Grinding It Out: The Making of McDonald's*, Old Saybrook, Connecticut: Tantor Media.

Andriessen, D. and Gubbins, C. (2009) Metaphor analysis as an approach for exploring theoretical concepts: The case of social capital, *Organization Studies*, 30(8): 845–63.

Ansari, S.M., Fiss, P.C., and Zajac, E.J. (2010) Made to fit: How practices vary as they diffuse, *Academy of Management Review*, 35(1): 67–92.

Antal, A.B. (2000) Types of knowledge gained by expatriate managers, *Journal of General Management*, 26(2): 32–51.

Antal, A.B. (2001) Expatriates' contributions to organizational learning, *Journal of General Management*, 26(4): 62–84.

Apriliyanti, I. D., and Alon, I. (2017) Bibliometric analysis of absorptive capacity, *International Business Review*, 26(5): 896–907.

Apt, K.R., Blair, H.A., and Walker, A. (1988) Towards a theory of declarative knowledge, in J. Minker (ed.), *Foundations of Deductive Databases and Logic Programming*, Morgan Kaufmann: 89–148.

Ardichvili, A. and Cardozo, R.N. (2000) A model of the entrepreneurial opportunity recognition process, *Journal of Enterprising Culture*, 8(2): 103–19.

Argote, L. (1993) Group and organizational learning curves: Individual, system and environmental components, *British Journal of Social Psychology*, 32(1): 31–51.

Argote, L. (1999) *Organizational learning: Creating, Retaining and Transferring Knowledge*, Boston, MA: Kluwer Academic Publishers.

Argote, L. (2015) Knowledge transfer and organizational learning, in K. Kraiger, J. Passmore, N.R. dos Santos, and S. Malvezzi, *The Wiley Blackwell Handbook of the Psychology of Training, Development, and Performance Improvement*, New York: Wiley: 154–70.

Argote, L. and Ingram, P. (2000) Knowledge transfer: A basis for competitive advantage in firms, *Organizational Behavior and Human Decision Processes*, 82(1): 150–69.

Argote, L., Ingram, P., Levine, J.M., and Moreland, R.L. (2000) Knowledge transfer in organizations: Learning from the experience of others, *Organizational Behavior and Human Decision Processes*, 82(1): 1–8.

Argyris, C. (1976) Single-loop and double-loop models in research on decision making. *Administrative Science Quarterly*, 21(3): 363–75.

Armbrüster, T. (2006) *The Economics and Sociology of Management Consulting*, Cambridge: Cambridge University Press.

Arundel, A. and Geuna, A. (2001) Does proximity matter for knowledge transfer from public institutes and universities to firms? *SPRU-Science Policy Research Unit, University of Sussex Business School, SPRU Electronic Working Paper Series*, no. 73.

Ash, M.K. (2008) *The Mary Kay way: Timeless Principles from America's Greatest Woman Entrepreneur*, New York: John Wiley & Sons.

Askim, J., Christensen, T., Fimreite, A.L., and Lægreid, P. (2008) Reorganizing the Norwegian Welfare Administration, *The Stein Rokkan Centre for Social Studies*, Working Paper No. 10.

Averbuch, I. (2007) Body-to-body transmission: the copying tradition of Kagura, in R. Cox (ed.), *The Culture of Copying in Japan*, New York: Routledge: 33–51.

Ax, C., and Bjørnenak, T. (2005) Bundling and diffusion of management accounting innovations: the case of the balanced scorecard in Sweden, *Management Accounting Research*: 16(1): 1–20.

Ax, C. and T. Bjørnenak (2007) Management accounting innovations: origins and diffusion, in Hopper, T., Northcott, D and Scapens, R.W (Eds.), Issues in Management Accounting, 3. edition, 357–376, Hertfordshire: Prentice-Hall.

Axelsson, B. and Johanson, J. (1992) Foreign market entry—the textbook vs. the network view. In B. Axelsson and G. Easton (eds.), *Industrial Networks: A New View of Reality*, London: Routledge: 218–34.

Babson, S. (1998) Mazda and Ford at flat rock: Transfer and hybridization of the Japanese model, in E. Boyer, E. Charron, U. Jürgens, and S. Tolliday (eds.), *Between Imitation and Innovation: the Transfer and Hybridization of Productive Models in the International Automobile Industry*, Oxford: Oxford University Press: 161–88.

Bacharach, S.B. (1989) Organizational theories: Some criteria for evaluation, *Academy of Management Review*, 14(4): 496–515.

Bacon, E., Williams, M.D., and Davies, G.H. (2019) Recipes for success: Conditions for knowledge transfer across open innovation ecosystems, *International Journal of Information Management*, 49: 377–87.

Baden-Fuller, C. and Morgan, M.S. (2010) Business models as models, *Long Range Planning*, 43(2–3): 156–71.

Baden-Fuller, C. and Winter, S.G. (2005) Replicating organizational knowledge: principles or templates? Available at SSRN: https://ssrn.com/abstract=1118013 or http://dx.doi.org/10.2139/ssrn.1118013

Baer, B. J. (2020) From cultural translation to untranslatability, *Alif: Journal of Comparative Poetics*, (40): 139–163.

Bailey, C. (2016) Employee engagement: do practitioners care what academics have to say–And should they? *Human Resource Management Review*. doi:10.1016/j.hrmr.2016.12.014

Bailey, K.D. (1994) *Typologies and Taxonomies: An Introduction to Classification Techniques*, Thousand Oaks: Sage.

Baker, M. (1992) *In other words: A Coursebook On Translation*, London, New York: Routledge.

Baker, M. (1998) Introduction, in M. Baker (ed.), *Routledge Encyclopedia of Translation Studies*, London: Routledge, 1–6.

References

Barkhudarov, L-A. (1975) *Yasik I Perevod (Language and Translation)*, Moscow: Mezhdunarodye Otnoshenyiya.

Barnes, J.A. (1954) Class and committees in a Norwegian island parish, *Human Relations*, 7(1): 39–58.

Barney, J. (1991) Firm resources and sustained competitive advantage, *Journal of Management*, 17(1): 99–120.

Barros, M. and Rüling, C. C. (2019) Business media, in A. Sturdy, S. Heusinkveld, T. Reay, and D. Strang (eds.), *The Oxford Handbook of Management Ideas*, Oxford: Oxford University Press: 195–215.

Barth, F. (1963) *The Role of the Entrepreneur in Social Change in Northern Norway*, Oslo: The University Press.

Bartunek, J.M. and Rynes, S.L. (2010) The construction and contributions of implications for practice: What's in them and what might they offer? *The Academy of Management Learning and Education*, 9(1): 100–17.

Bartunek, J.M. and Rynes, S. L. (2014) Academics and practitioners are alike and unlike: The paradoxes of academic–practitioner relationships, *Journal of Management*, 40(5): 1181–201.

Bassnett, S. (2002) *Translation Studies*, London: Routledge.

Bassnett, S. and Lefevere, A. (1990) *Translation, History, and Culture*, London: Burns & Oates.

Bassnett, S. and Lefevere, A. (1998) *Constructing cultures: Essays on literary translation*, Clevedon: Multilingual Matters.

Bastin, G.L. (2008) Adaptation, in M. Baker (ed.), *The Routledge Encyclopedia of Translation Studies*, London and New York: Routledge: 3–6.

Bateh, J., Castaneda, M.E., and Farah, J.E. (2013) Employee resistance to organizational change, *International Journal of Management & Information Systems (IJMIS)*, 17(2): 113–16.

Baughn, C. C., Denekamp, J. G., Stevens, J. H., and Osborn, R. N. (1997) Protecting intellectual capital in international alliances, *Journal of World Business*, 32(2), 103–117.

Baum, J. A., Calabrese, T., and Silverman, B. S. (2000) Don't go it alone: Alliance network composition and startups' performance in Canadian biotechnology, *Strategic Management Journal*, 21(3): 267–94.

Bauman, L.J., Stein, R.E., and Ireys, H.T. (1991) Reinventing fidelity: The transfer of social technology among settings, *American Journal of Community Psychology*, 19(4): 619–39.

Bausch, M. (2022) *Intercultural Transfer of Management Practices of German MNC to Brazil: The Interplay of Translation and Recontextualization*, Wiesbaden: Springer Nature.

Bausch, M., Barmeyer, C., and Mayrhofer, U. (2022) Facilitating factors in the cross-cultural transfer of management practices: The case of a German multinational in Brazil. *International Business Review*, 31(2): 101921.

Becerra, M., Lunnan, R., and Huemer, L. (2008) Trustworthiness, risk, and the transfer of tacit and explicit knowledge between alliance partner, *Journal of Management Studies*, 45(4): 691–713.

Becker, M.C. (2004) Organizational routines: a review of the literature, *Industrial and Corporate Change*, 13(4): 643–78.

Beer, S. (1981) *Brain of the Firm*, London: Chichester Wiley.

Beissinger, S.R., Ackerly, D.D., Doremus, H., and Machlis, G.E. (2017) *Science, Conservation, and National Parks*, Chicago, IL: University of Chicago Press.

Bejan, A. and Kraus, A.D. (2003) *Heat Transfer Handbook*, New York: John Wiley & Sons.

Bendell, T., Boulter, L., and Kelly, J. (1998) *Benchmarking for Competitive Advantage*, London: Pitman Publishing.

Berger, P. and Luckman, T. (1966) *The Social Construction of Reality—A Treatise in the Sociology of Knowledge*, Harmondsworth, Middlesex: Penguin.

Bergström, O. (2007) Translating socially responsible workforce reduction—A longitudinal study of workforce reduction in a Swedish company, *Scandinavian Journal of Management*, 23(4): 384–405.

Berling, T.V., Gad, U.P., Petersen, K.L., and Wæver, O. (2022) *Translations of security: A framework for the study of unwanted futures*, London: Taylor & Francis.

Berman, A. (1992) *The Experience of the Foreign: Culture and Translation in Romantic Germany*, Albany: SUNY Press.

Berman, S.L., Down, J., and Hill, C.W. (2002) Tacit knowledge as a source of competitive advantage in the National Basketball Association, *Academy of Management Journal*, 45(1): 13–31.

Berta, W.B. and Baker, R. (2004) Factors that impact the transfer and retention of best practices for reducing error in hospitals, *Health Care Management Review*, 29(2): 90–7.

Beugelsdijk, S., Ambos, B., and Phillip C.N. (2018) Conceptualizing and measuring distance in international business research: Recurring questions and best practice guidelines *Journal of International Business Studies*, 49(9): 1113–37.

Beugelsdijk, S., Kostova, T., Kunst, V.E., Spadafora, E., and Van Essen, M. (2018) Cultural distance and firm internationalization: A meta-analytical review and theoretical implications, *Journal of Management*, 44(1): 89–130.

Beugelsdijk, S., Kostova, T., and Roth, K. (2017) An overview of Hofstede-inspired country-level culture research in international business since 2006, *Journal of International Business Studies*, 48(1): 30–47.

Bierly III P.E., Damanpour, F., and Santoro, M.D. (2009) The application of external knowledge: organizational conditions for exploration and exploitation, *Journal of Management Studies*, 46(3): 481–509.

Bignami, F., Mattsson, P., and Hoekman, J. (2020) The importance of geographical distance to different types of R&D collaboration in the pharmaceutical industry, *Industry and Innovation*, 27(5): 513–37.

Billow, R. M. (1977) Metaphor: A review of the psychological literature. *Psychological Bulletin*, 84(1) 81–92.

Björkman, I., Barner-Rasmussen, W., and Li, L. (2004) Managing knowledge transfer in MNCs: The impact of headquarters control mechanisms, *Journal of International Business Studies*, 35(5): 443–55.

Blackman, D. and Benson, A.M. (2012) Overcoming knowledge stickiness in scientific knowledge transfer, *Public Understanding of Science*, 21(5): 573–89.

Blakely, C.H., Mayer, J.P., Gottschalk, R.G., Schmitt, N., Davidson, W.S., Roitman, D.B., and Emshoff, J.G. (1987) The fidelity-adaptation debate: Implications for the implementation of public sector social programs, *American Journal of Community Psychology*, 15(3): 253–68.

Blalock, H.M. (1969) *Theory Construction: From verbal to mathematical formulations*, Englewood Cliffs, NJ: Prentice-Hall.

Blau, P.M. and Scott, W.R. (1962) *Formal Organizations: A Comparative Approach*, San Francisco: Chandler.

Blau, P.M. and Scott, W.R. (1963) *Formal organizations: A Comparative Approach*. London: Routledge & Kegan Paul.

Block, F. (2003) Karl Polanyi and the writing of the Great Transformation, *Theory and Society*, 32(3): 275–306.

Blumer, H. (1969) Fashion: From class differentiation to collective selection, *The Sociological Quarterly*, 10(3): 275–91.

Blum-Kulka, S. (1986) Shifts of cohesion and coherence in translation, in J. House and S. Blum-Kulka (eds.) *Interlingual and Intercultural Communication: Discourse and Cognition in Translation and Second Language Acquisition Studies*, 17–36, Tübingen: Narr.

Bodin, Ø. and Crona, B. I. (2009) The role of social networks in natural resource governance: What relational patterns make a difference? *Global Environmental Change*, 19(3): 366–74.

Boh, W.F., Nguyen, T.T., and Xu, Y. (2013) Knowledge transfer across dissimilar cultures. *Journal of Knowledge Management*, 17 (1): 29–46.

Borch, O.J. and Korneliussen, T. (1995) Norsk tørrfisknæring: Markedstilpasning og eksportorganisering ("The Norwegian stockfish industry: Adjustments to markets and export organizing"), Bodø: *NF-rapport*, 2: 36–7.

Borges, R., Bernardi, M., and Petrin, R. (2019) Cross-country findings on tacit knowledge sharing: evidence from the Brazilian and Indonesian IT workers, *Journal of Knowledge Management*, 23(4): 742–62.

Børve, H. E. and Kvande, E. (2022) The translation of Nordic workplace democracy to the United States, *Nordic Journal of Working Life Studies*, 12(3). https://doi.org/10.18291/njwls.131535

Botha, M.E. (1986) Metaphorical models and scientific realism, *South African Journal of Philosophy*, 5: 83–7.

Bouncken, R.B. (2015) Ambiguity and knowledge transfer in innovation alliances, *International Journal of Entrepreneurial Venturing*, 7(4): 309–23.

Bouncken, R.B. and Kraus, S. (2013) Innovation in knowledge-intensive industries: The double-edged sword of coopetition, *Journal of Business Research*, 66(10): 2060–70.

Boutaiba, S. and Strandgaard Pedersen, J. (2003) Creating MBA identity—Between field and organization, in R.P. Amdam, R. Kvålshaugen, and E. Larsen (eds.), *Inside the Business School: The Contents of European Business Education*, Oslo, Norway/Stockholm/Copenhagen, Denmark: Abstrakt, Lieber, and CBS Press: 197–218.

Bowden, R. (1999) What is wrong with an art forgery? An anthropological perspective, *The Journal of Aesthetics and Art Criticism*, 57(3): 333–43.

Bower, G. H. and Hilgard, E.R. (1981) *Theories of Learning*, Englewood Cliffs, NJ: Prentice-Hall

Boxenbaum, E and Jonsson, S. (2017) Isomorphism, diffusion and decoupling: Concept evolution and theoretical challenges, in R. Greenwood, C. Oliver, T. B. Lawrence, and R. E. Meyer (eds.), *The SAGE Handbook of Organizational Institutionalism* (2nd ed.), London: SAGE Publications: 77–101.

Boxenbaum, E. and Rouleau, L. (2011) New knowledge products as bricolage: Metaphors and scripts in organizational theory, *Academy of Management Review*, 36(2): 272–96.

Boxenbaum, E. and Strandgaard Pedersen, J. (2009) Scandinavian institutionalism: A case of institutional work, in T.B. Lawrence, R. Suddaby, and B. Leca (eds.), *Institutional Work: Actors and Agency in Institutional Studies of Organizations*, Cambridge: Cambridge University Press: 178–204.

Božič, K., Bachkirov, A. A., and Černe, M. (2022) Towards better understanding and narrowing of the science–practice gap: A practitioner-centered approach to management knowledge creation, *European Management Journal*, 40(4): 632–44.

Brander, J.A., Cui, V., and Vertinsky, I. (2017) China and intellectual property rights: A challenge to the rule of law, *Journal of International Business Studies*, 48(7): 908–21.

Breschi, S. and Malerba, F. (2001) The geography of innovation and economic clustering: some introductory notes, *Industrial and Corporate Change*, 10(4): 817–33.

Bresman, H., Birkinshaw, J., and Nobel, R. (1999) Knowledge transfer in international acquisitions, *Journal of International Business Studies*, 30(3): 439–62.

Bresman, H., Birkinshaw, J., and Nobel, R. (2010) Knowledge transfer in international acquisitions, *Journal of International Business Studies*, 41(1): 5–20.

Brisset, A. (1989) In Search of a Target Language: The Politics of Theatre Translation in Quebec, *Target—International Journal of Translation Studies*, 1(1): 9–27.

References

Brix, J., Krogstrup, H.K., and Mortensen, N.M. (2020) Evaluating the outcomes of co-production in local government, *Local Government Studies*, 46(2): 169–85.

Bromley, P. and Meyer, J.W. (2017) "They are all organizations": The cultural roots of blurring between the nonprofit, business, and government sectors, *Administration & Society*, 49(7): 939–66.

Bromley, P. and Powell, W.W. (2012) From smoke and mirrors to walking the talk: Decoupling in the contemporary world, *Academy of Management Annals*, 6(1): 483–530.

Brown, J.S. and Duguid, P. (1991) Organizational learning and communities-of-practice: Toward a unified view of working, learning, and innovation, *Organization Science*, 2(1): 40–57.

Brown, J.S. and Duguid, P. (2001) Knowledge and organization: A social-practice perspective, *Organization science*, 12(2): 198–213.

Brunsson, N. (1989) *The Organization of Hypocrisy: Talk, Decisions and Actions in Organizations*, New York: John Wiley & Sons.

Brunsson, N. and Jacobsson, B., (2000) Following standards, in N. Brunsson and B. Jacobsson (eds.) A world of standards, 125–37, Oxford: Oxford University Press

Brunsson, N. and Sahlin-Andersson, K. (2000) Constructing organizations: The example of public sector reform, *Organization studies*, 21(4): 721–46.

Bunge, S.A. (2004) How we use rules to select actions: a review of evidence from cognitive neuroscience, *Cognitive, Affective, & Behavioral Neuroscience*, 4(4): 564–79.

Bunnell, T. and Coe, N. (2001) Spaces and Scales of Innovation, *Progress in Human Geography*, 25(4): 569–89.

Burke, R.J. (1996) Performance evaluation and counselling in a professional services firm, *Leadership & Organization Development Journal*, 17: 21–7.

Burmeister, A. (2017) Repatriate knowledge transfer: a systematic review of the literature, in B. Bader, T. Schuster, and A.K. Bader (eds.), *Expatriate Management*, London: Palgrave Macmillan: 225–64.

Burmeister, A. and Deller, J. (2016) A practical perspective on repatriate knowledge transfer, *Journal of Global Mobility: The Home of Expatriate Management Research*, 4: 68–87.

Burns T. and Stalker, G.M. (1961) *The Management of Innovation*, New York: Barnes & Noble.

Burt, R. S. (1992) *Structural holes*, Harvard University Press.

Burt, R. S. (2004) Structural holes and good ideas, *American Journal of Sociology*, 110(2): 349–99.

Byrkjeflot, H., Mjøset, L., Mordhorst, M., and Petersen, K. (2022) *The Making and Circulation of Nordic Models, Ideas and Images*, London: Taylor & Francis.

Caimo, A. and Lomi, A. (2015), Knowledge sharing in organizations: A Bayesian analysis of the role of reciprocity and formal structure, *Journal of Management*, 41(2): 665–91.

Cairncross, F. and Cairncross, F. (1997) *The Death of Distance: How the Communications Revolution will Change our Lives*, Boston, MA: Harvard Business School Press.

Callon, M. (1986) Some elements of a sociology of translation: Domestication of the scallops and the fishermen of St Brieu's Bay, in J. Law (ed.), *Power, Action and Belief. A New Sociology of Knowledge?* London: Routledge & Keegan Paul: 196–229.

Calsyn, R., Tornatzky, L.G., and Dittmar, S. (1977) Incomplete adoption of an innovation: The case of goal attainment scaling, *Evaluation*, 4: 127–30.

Camac, M.K. and Glucksberg, S. (1984) Metaphors do not use associations between concepts, they are used to create them, *Journal of Psycholinguistic Research*, 13(6): 443–55.

Caminade, M. and Pym, A. (1998) Translator-training institutions, in M. Baker (ed.), *Routledge Encyclopedia of Translation Studies*, London: Routledge: 280–5.

Camisón, C. and Forés, B. (2010) Knowledge absorptive capacity: New insights for its conceptualization and measurement, *Journal of Business Research*, 63(7): 707–15.

Carayannis, E.G., Pirzadeh, A., and Popescu, D. (2011) *Institutional Learning and Knowledge Transfer Across Epistemic Communities: New Tools of Global Governance*, New York: Springer Science & Business Media.
Cardinal, L.B. (2001) Technological innovation in the pharmaceutical industry: The use of organizational control in managing research and development. *Organization Science*, 12(1): 19–36.
Carlile, P. R. (2004) Transferring, translating, and transforming: An integrative framework for managing knowledge across boundaries, *Organization science*, 15(5): 555–68.
Carpenter, M. A., Li, M., and Jiang, H. (2012) Social network research in organizational contexts: A systematic review of methodological issues and choices, *Journal of Management*, 38(4): 1328–61.
Carrillo, F.J., Rivera-Vazquez, J.C., Ortiz-Fournier, L.V., and Flores, F.R. (2009) Overcoming cultural barriers for innovation and knowledge sharing, *Journal of Knowledge Management*, 13(5): 257–70.
Carton, G. and Mouricou, P. (2017) Is management research relevant? A systematic analysis of the rigor-relevance debate in top-tier journals (1994–2013), *M@n@gement*, 20(2): 166–203.
Cascio, W.F. and Montealegre, R. (2016) How technology is changing work and organizations, *Annual Review of Organizational Psychology and Organizational Behavior*, 3: 349–75.
Castells, M. (2014) *Technopoles of the world: The Making of 21st Century Industrial Complexes*, London: Routledge.
Castro, V.F.D. and Frazzon, E.M. (2017) Benchmarking of best practices: an overview of the academic literature, *Benchmarking: An International Journal*, 24(3): 750–74.
Catford, J.C. (1965) *A Linguistic Theory of Translation: An Essay in Applied Linguistics*, Oxford, UK: Oxford University Press.
Cave, D., Diehl, M., and Edwards, G. (2004) Truck Driver Invents Rock, *Rolling Stone* (951): 84–5.
Centola, D. (2018) *How Behavior Spreads*, Princeton, NJ: Princeton University Press.
Cepiku, D. and Giordano, F. (2014) Co-Production in Developing Countries: Insights from the community health workers experience, *Public Management Review*, 16(3): 317–40.
Chalmers, D.M. and Balan-Vnuk, E. (2013) Innovating not-for-profit social ventures: Exploring the microfoundations of internal and external absorptive capacity routines, *International Small Business Journal*, 31(7): 785–810.
Chandler, D. and Hwang, H. (2015) Learning from learning theory: A model of organizational adoption strategies at the microfoundations of institutional theory, *Journal of Management*, 41(5): 1446–76.
Chao, M.C.H. and Kumar, V. (2010) The impact of institutional distance on the international diversity–performance relationship, *Journal of World Business*, 45(1): 93–103.
Chassin, M.R. (1998) Is health care ready for Six Sigma quality? *The Milbank Quarterly*, 76(4): 565–91.
Chatterjee, S., Lubatkin, M.H., Schweiger, D.M., and Weber, Y. (1992) Cultural differences and shareholder value in related mergers: Linking equity and human capital, *Strategic Management Journal*, 13(5): 319–34.
Chen, C.J. and Huang, J.W. (2007) How organizational climate and structure affect knowledge management—The social interaction perspective, *International Journal of Information Management*, 27(2): 104–18.
Chen, C.J., Huang, J.W., and Hsiao, Y.C. (2010) Knowledge management and innovativeness, *International Journal of Manpower*, 31(8): 848–70.

Chen, G., Bliese, P.D., and Mathieu, J.E. (2005) Conceptual framework and statistical procedures for delineating and testing multilevel theories of homology, *Organizational Research Methods*, 8(4): 375–409.

Chen, J., Sun, P.Y., and McQueen, R.J. (2010) The impact of national cultures on structured knowledge transfer, *Journal of Knowledge Management*, 14 (2): 228–42.

Chen, S.T. and Chang, B.G. (2012) The effects of absorptive capacity and decision speed on organizational innovation: a study of organizational structure as an antecedent variable, *Contemporary Management Research*, 8(1): 27–50.

Chiappe, D.L., Kennedy, J.M., and Smykowski, T. (2003) Reversibility, Aptness, and the Conventionality of Metaphors and Similes, *Metaphor and Symbol*, 18(2): 85–105.

Chiou, J.S. and Droge, C. (2015) The effects of standardization and trust on franchisee's performance and satisfaction: A study on franchise systems in the growth stage, *Journal of Small Business Management*, 53(1): 129–44.

Chokki, T. (1986) A History of the Machine Tool Industry in Japan, in M. Fransman (ed.), *Machinery and Economic Development*, London: Macmillan Press, 124–52

Christensen, T., Danielsen, O.A., Lægreid, P., and Rykkja, L. (2016) Comparing coordination structures for crisis management in six countries, *Public Administration*, 94(2): 316–32.

Christensen, T. and Lægreid, P. (2008) The challenge of coordination in central government organizations: the Norwegian case, *Public Organization Review*, 8(2): 97–116.

Christensen, T., Lægreid, P., and Røvik, K.A. (2020) *Organization Theory and the Public sector, Instrument, Culture, and Myth*, London: Routledge.

Christensen, T. and Røvik, K.A. (1999) The ambiguity of appropriateness, in M. Egeberg and P. Lægreid (eds.), *Organizing Political Institutions: Essays for Johan P. Olsen*, Oslo: Universitetsforlaget, 159–80.

Chubb, A. (2015) China's Shanzhai culture: "Grabism" and the politics of hybridity, *Journal of Contemporary China*, 24(92): 260–79.

Church, R., Outram, Q., and Smith, D.N. (1990) British coal mining strikes 1893–1940: Dimensions, distribution and persistence, *British Journal of Industrial Relations*, 28(3): 329–49.

Ciabuschi, F., Dellestrand, H., and Kappen, P. (2011) Exploring the effects of vertical and lateral mechanisms in international knowledge transfer projects, *Management International Review*, 51(2): 129–55.

Ciuk, S. and James, P. (2015) Interlingual translation and the transfer of value-infused practices: an in-depth qualitative exploration, *Management Learning*, 46(5): 565–81.

Clarence-Smith, K. (2007) Copying in Japanese magazines: unashamed copiers, in R. Cox (ed.), *The Culture of Copying in Japan*, New York: Routledge: 63–80.

Clark, B.R. (1972) The organizational saga in higher education, *Administrative Science Quarterly*, 17(2): 178–84.

Clark, T., Floyd, S.W., and Wright, M. (2013) In search of the impactful and the interesting: Swings of the pendulum? *Journal of Management Studies*, 50(8): 1358–73.

Clark, T.A. and Fincham, R. (2002) *Critical Consulting: New Perspectives on the Management Advice Industry*, Oxford: Blackwell.

Claus, L., Greenwood, R., and Mgoo, J. (2021) Institutional translation gone wrong: The case of villages for Africa in rural Tanzania, *Academy of Management Journal*, 64(5): 1497–526. https://doi.org/10.5465/amj.2017.1089

Claver-Cortés E., Marco-Lajara, B., Manresa-Marhuenda, E., Garcia-Lillo, F., and Seva-Larossa, P. (2017) Location decisions and agglomeration economies: Domestic and foreign companies, *Journal of Regional Research*, 39: 99–135.

Coaldrake, W.H. (2007) Beyond mimesis: Japanese architectural models at the Vienna exhibition and 1910 Japan British exhibition, in R. Cox (ed.), *The Culture of Copying in Japan*, New York: Routledge: 211–24.
Cobb, M. (2015) *Life's Greatest Secret. The Race to Crack the Genetic Code*, London: Profile Books LTD.
Cochrane, A.L. (1972) *Effectiveness and Efficiency: Random Reflections on Health Services*, London: Nuffield Provincial Hospitals Trust.
Coff, R.W., Coff, D.C., and Eastvold, R. (2006) The knowledge-leveraging paradox: How to achieve scale without making knowledge imitable, *Academy of Management Review*, 31(2): 452–65.
Cohen, B.P. (1989) *Developing sociological knowledge: Theory and method* (2nd ed.), Chicago, IL: Nelson-Hall.
Cohen, M.D., March, J.G., and Olsen, J.P. (1972) A garbage can model of organizational choice, *Administrative Science Quarterly*, 17(1): 1–25.
Cohen, W.M. and Levinthal, D.A. (1989) Innovation and learning: the two faces of R & D., *The Economic Journal*, 99(397): 569–96.
Cohen, W.M. and Levinthal, D.A. (1990) Absorptive capacity: A new perspective on learning and innovation, *Administrative Science Quarterly*, 35 (1): 128–52.
Cohen, W.M. and Levinthal, D.A. (1994) Fortune favors the prepared firm, *Management Science*, 40(2): 227–51.
Cole, C. (1993) Shannon revisited: Information in terms of uncertainty, *Journal of the American Society for Information Science*, 44(4): 204–11.
Collins, D. (2019) Management's gurus, in A. Sturdy, S. Heusinkveld, T. Reay, and D. Strang (eds.), *The Oxford Handbook of Management Ideas*, Oxford: Oxford University Press: 216–31.
Collins, H. (2010) *Tacit and Explicit Knowledge*, London: University of Chicago Press.
Colquitt, J.A. and Zapata-Phelan, C.P. (2007) Trends in theory building and theory testing: A five-decade study of the Academy of Management Journal, *Academy of Management Journal*, 50(6): 1281–303.
Conner, K.R. (1995) Obtaining strategic advantage from being imitated: When can encouraging "clones" pay? *Management Science*, 41(2): 209–25.
Contractor, N.S. and Monge, P.R. (2002) Managing knowledge networks, *Management Communication Quarterly*, 16(2): 249–58.
Cooke, P. (2001) Regional innovation systems, clusters, and the knowledge economy, *Industrial and Corporate Change*, 10(4): 945–74.
Cooke, P., Uranga, M.G., and Etxebarria, G. (1997) Regional innovation systems: Institutional and organisational dimensions, *Research Policy*, 26(4–5): 475–91.
Cooren, F. and Seidl, D. (2020) Niklas Luhmann's radical communication approach and its implications for research on organizational communication, *Academy of Management Review*, 45(2): 479–97.
Cordón-Pozo, E., García-Morales, V.J, and Aragón-Correa, J.A. (2006) Inter-departmental collaboration and new product development success: a study on the collaboration between marketing and R&D in Spanish high-technology firms, *International Journal of Technology Management*, 35(1/2/3/4): 52–79.
Corley, K.G. and Gioia, D.A. (2011) Building theory about theory building: what constitutes a theoretical contribution? *Academy of Management Review*, 36(1): 12–32.
Cornelissen, J. (2017) Editor's comments: Developing propositions, a process model, or a typology? Addressing the challenges of writing theory without a boilerplate, *Academy of Management Review*, 42 (1): 1–9.

Cornelissen, J., and Durand, R. (2012) More than just novelty: Conceptual blending and causality, *Academy of Management Review*, 37(1): 152–54.

Cornelissen, J., Höllerer, M. A., and Seidl, D. (2021) What theory is and can be: Forms of theorizing in organizational scholarship, *Organization Theory*, 2(3): 26317877211020328.

Cornelissen, J.P. (2005) Beyond compare: Metaphor in organization theory, *Academy of Management Review*, 30(4): 751–64.

Cornelissen, J.P., and Durand, R. (2014) Moving forward: Developing theoretical contributions in management studies, *Journal of Management Studies*, 51(6): 995–1022.

Cornelissen, J.P. and Kafouros, M. (2008) The emergent organization: Primary and complex metaphors in theorizing about organizations, *Organization Studies* 29(7): 957–78.

Costumato, L. (2021) Collaboration among public organizations: A systematic literature review on determinants of institutional performance, *International Journal of Public Sector Management*, 34(3): 247–73. https://doi.org/10.1108/IJPSM-03-2020-0069

Cowan, R. and Jonard, N. (2004) Network structure and the diffusion of knowledge, *Journal of Economic Dynamics and Control*, 28(8): 1557–75.

Cox, R. (2007) Introduction, in R. Cox (ed.) *The Culture of Copying in Japan: Critical and Historical Perspectives*, New York: Routledge: 1–17.

Craig, R.T. (1999) Communication theory as a field, *Communication theory*, 9(2): 119–61.

Cressey, D.R. (1959) Contradictory directives in complex organizations: The case of the prison, *Administrative Science Quarterly*, 4(1): 1–19.

Cross, R., Parker, A., Prusak, L., and Borgatti, S.P. (2001) Knowing what we know: Supporting knowledge creation and sharing in social networks, *Organizational Dynamics*, 30(2): 100–20.

Crossan, M.M. and Inkpen, A.C. (1995) The subtle art of learning through alliances, *Business Quarterly*, 60(2): 68–78.

Crucini, C. and Kipping, M. (2001) Management consultants as global change agents? Evidence from Italy, *Journal of Organizational Change Management*, 14: 570–89.

Cummings, J.L. and Teng, B.S. (2003) Transferring R&D knowledge: The key factors affecting knowledge transfer success, *Journal of Engineering and Technology Management*, 20(1–2): 39–68.

Cummings, T.G. (2007) Quest for an engaged Academy, *Academy of Management Review*, 32(2): 355–60.

Curvelo, A. (2007) Copy to convert: Jesuits' missionary practice in Japan, in R. Cox (ed.), *The Culture of Copying in Japan: Critical and Historical Perspectives*, New York: Routledge: 111–27.

Cushman, D. and Whiting, G.C. (1972) An approach to communication theory: Toward consensus on rules, *Journal of Communication*, 22(3): 217–38.

Cyert, R.M. and March, J.G. (1963) *A Behavioral Theory of the Firm*, New Jersey: Englewood Cliffs.

Czarniawska, B. (2014) *A theory of organizing*, Cheltenham, UK: Edward Elgar Publishing.

Czarniawska, B. and Joerges, B. (1996) Travels of Ideas, in Czarniawska, B. and Sevón, G. (eds.), *Translating Organizational Change*, Berlin: Walter de Gruyter: 13–48.

Czarniawska, B. and Mazza, C. (2013) Consulting university: A reflection from inside, *Financial Accountability & Management*, 29(2): 124–39.

Czarniawska, B. and Sevón, G. (1996) Introduction, in B. Czarniawska and G. Sevón (eds.), *Translating Organizational Change*, Berlin: Walter de Gruyter: 1–12.

Czarniawska, B. and Sevón, G. (2005) Translation is a vehicle, imitation its motor, and fashion sits at the wheel, in B. Czarniawska and G. Sevón (eds.), *Global ideas: How Ideas, Objects and Practices Travel in the Global Economy*, Malmø: Liber & Copenhagen Business School Press: 7–14.

D'Adderio, L. (2014) The replication dilemma unravelled: How organizations enact multiple goals in routine transfer, *Organization Science*, 25(5): 1325–50

Darwin, C., Fitzroy, R., and King, P.P. (1839) *Narrative of the Surveying Voyages of His Majesty's Ships Adventure and Beagle, Between the Years 1826 and 1836: Describing Their Examination of the Southern Shores of South America, and the Beagle's Circumnavigation of the Globe*, London: Henry Colburn.

Davenport, T.H., De Long, D.W., and Beers, M.C. (1998) Successful knowledge management projects, *Sloan Management Review*, 39(2): 43–57.

Davenport, T.H. and Prusak, L. (1998) *Working Knowledge: How Organizations Manage What They Know*, Boston, MA: Harvard Business School Press.

Davidson, W.H. (1980) The location of foreign direct investment activity: country characteristics and the theory of the firm, *Journal of International Business Studies*, 12 (Fall): 9–22.

Davies, A.J. and Kochhar, A.K. (2002) Manufacturing best practice and performance studies: a critique, *International Journal of Operations & Production Management*, 22(3): 289–305.

Davis, M.S. (1971) That's interesting! Towards a phenomenology of sociology and a sociology of phenomenology, *Philosophy of the Social Sciences*, 1(2): 309–44.

De Clercq, D., Dimov, D., and Thongpapanl, N. (2013) Organizational social capital, formalization, and internal knowledge sharing in entrepreneurial orientation formation, *Entrepreneurship Theory and Practice*, 37(3): 505–37.

De Long, D.W. and Fahey, L. (2000) Diagnosing cultural barriers to knowledge management. *Academy of Management Perspectives*, 14(4): 113–27.

Delios, A. and Beamish, P.W. (1999) Geographic scope, product diversification, and the corporate performance of Japanese firms. *Strategic Management Journal*, 20(8): 711–27.

Demir, R. and Fjellström, D. (2012) Translation of relational practices in an MNC subsidiary: Symmetrical, asymmetrical and substitutive strategies, *Asian Business & Management*, 11(4): 369–93.

Denison, D.R. (1990) *Corporate Culture and Organizational Effectiveness*, New York: John Wiley & Sons.

DesForges, C.D. (1986) US and UK experience in technology transfer. A comparative analysis, *International Journal of Technology Management*, 1(3–4): 457–75.

Dhanaraj, C., Lyles, M.A., Steensma, H.K., and Tihanyi, L. (2004) Managing tacit and explicit knowledge transfer in IJVs: the role of relational embeddedness and the impact on performance, *Journal of International Business Studies*, 35(5): 428–42.

Diefenbach, T. (2009) New public management in public sector organizations: the dark sides of managerialistic "enlightenment," *Public Administration*, 87(4): 892–909.

Dikova, D. and Van Witteloostuijn, A. (2007) Foreign direct investment mode choice: entry and establishment modes in transition economies, *Journal of International Business Studies*, 38(6): 1013–33.

Dima, A. M., and Vasilache, S. (2015). Social network analysis for tacit knowledge management in universities, *Journal of the Knowledge Economy*, 6(4): 856–64.

Dixon, N.M. (2000) *Common knowledge: How Companies Thrive by Sharing What They Know*, Boston, MA: Harvard Business School Press.

Dohan, D. and Levintova, M. (2007) Barriers beyond words: cancer, culture, and translation in a community of Russian speakers, *Journal of General Internal Medicine*, 22(2): 300–5.

Dosi, G. and Marengo, L. (1993) Some elements of an evolutionary theory of organizational com- potencies, in R. W. England (ed.), *Evolutionary Concepts in Contemporary Economics*, Ann Arbor: University of Michigan Press: 234–74.

Doty, D.H. and Glick, W.H. (1994) Typologies as a unique form of theory building: Toward improved understanding and modeling, *Academy of Management Review*, 19(2): 230–51.

Dougherty, D. and Corse, S.M. (1995) When it comes to product innovation, what is so bad about bureaucracy? *The Journal of High Technology Management Research*, 6(1): 55–76.

Douthwaite, B., Keatinge, J.D.H., and Park, J.R. (2001) Why promising technologies fail: the neglected role of user innovation during adoption, *Research Policy*, 30(5): 819–36.

Downes, M. and Thomas, A.S. (1999) Managing Overseas Assignments to Build Organizational Knowledge, *Human Resource Planning*, 22(4): 33–48.

Downs, A. (1995) *Corporate Executions*, New York: AMACOM.

Drago, R. (1988) Quality circle survival: An exploratory analysis, *Industrial Relations: A Journal of Economy and Society*, 27(3): 336–51.

Drucker, P.F. (1971) What we can learn from Japanese management, *Harvard Business Review*, March–April: 110–22.

Drucker, P.F. (1988) The coming of the new organization, *Harvard Business Review*, 66(1): 45–53.

Duchek, S. (2013) Capturing absorptive capacity: A critical review and future prospects, *Schmalenbach Business Review*, 65(3): 312–29.

Duranti, R. (1998) Italian tradition, in M. Baker (ed.), *The Routledge Encyclopedia of Translation Studies*, London and New York: Routledge: 459–68.

Dyer, J. H., and Nobeoka, K. (2000) Creating and managing a high-performance knowledge-sharing network: the Toyota case, *Strategic Management Journal*, 21(3): 345–67.

Easterby-Smith, M., Graca, M., Antonacopoulou, E., and Ferdinand, J. (2008) Absorptive capacity: A process perspective, *Management learning*, 39(5): 483–501.

Easterlin, R.A. (1974) Does economic growth improve the human lot? Some empirical evidence, in P.A. David and M.W. Reder (eds.), *Nations and Households in Economic Growth*, New York, Academic Press: 89–125.

Easterlin, R.A., Morgan, R., Switek, M., and Wang, F. (2012) China's life satisfaction, 1990–2010, *Proceedings of the National Academy of Sciences*, 109(25): 9775–80.

Editorial, (23 July 1965) On Mavor and Coulson, Ltd., *Colliery Guardian*.

Edquist, C. (1997) *Systems of Innovation: Technologies, Institutions, and Organizations*, London: Routledge.

Egeberg, M. (2007) How bureaucratic structure matters: An organizational perspective, in G. Peters and J. Pierre (eds.), *The Handbook of Public Administration*, Thousand Oaks, CA: SAGE Publications: 77–87.

Egeberg, M. and Trondal, J. (2018) *An Organizational Approach to Public Governance: Understanding and Design*, Oxford: Oxford University Press.

Eijnatten, F.V. (1998) Developments in socio-technical systems design, *Handbook of Work and Organizational Psychology*, 4, Hove: Psychology Press: 61–88.

Elliott, J.E. (1978) Marx's socialism in the context of his typology of economic systems, *Journal of Comparative Economics*, 2(1): 25–41.

Ellis, R. and Oakley-Brown, L. (2001) *Translation and Nation: Towards a Cultural Politics of Englishness*, New York: Tonawanda.

Elmore, R.F. (1979) Backward mapping: Implementation research and policy decisions, *Political Science Quarterly*, 94(4): 601–16.

Elvbakken, K.T. and Hansen, H.F. (2019) Evidence producing organizations: Organizational translation of travelling evaluation ideas, *Evaluation*, 25(3): 261–76.

Empson, L. (2001) Fear of exploitation and fear of contamination: Impediments to knowledge transfer in mergers between professional service firms, *Human Relations*, 54(7): 839–62.

Engwall, L., and Kipping, M. (2013) Management consulting: dynamics, debates, and directions, *International Journal of Strategic Communication*, 7(2): 84–98.

Enkel, E., Groemminger, A., and Heil, S. (2018) Managing technological distance in internal and external collaborations: absorptive capacity routines and social integration for innovation, *The Journal of Technology Transfer*, 43(5): 1257–90.

Ensign, P.C., Lin, C.D., Chreim, S., and Persaud, A. (2014) Proximity, knowledge transfer, and innovation in technology-based mergers and acquisitions, *International Journal of Technology Management*, 66(1): 1–31.

Ercek, M. and Say, A.I. (2008) Discursive ambiguity, professional networks, and peripheral contexts: the translation of total quality management in Turkey, 1991–2002, *International Studies of Management and Organization*, 38(4): 78–99.

Erhardt, N., Martin-Rios, C., and Harkins, J. (2014) Knowledge flow from the top: the importance of teamwork structure in team sports, *European Sport Management Quarterly*, 14(4): 375–96.

Erkelens, R., van den Hooff, B., Huysman, M., and Vlaar, P. (2015) Learning from locally embedded knowledge: Facilitating organizational learning in geographically dispersed settings, *Global Strategy Journal*, 5(2): 177–97.

Erlingsdottir, G. and Lindberg, K. (2005) Isomorphism, isopraxism, and isonymism: complementary or competing processes? in Czarniawska, B. and Sevón G. (eds.), *Global Ideas. How Ideas, Objects and Practices Travel in the Global Economy*, Malmø: Liber & Copenhagen Business School Press: 47–70.

Escribano, A., Fosfuri, A., and Tribó, J.A. (2009) Managing external knowledge flows: The moderating role of absorptive capacity, *Research Policy*, 38(1): 96–105.

Estes, W.K. (1970) *Learning theory and mental development*, New York: Academic Press.

Etzioni, A. (1961) *A comparative Analysis of Complex Organizations: On Power, Involvement, and their Correlates*, New York: The Free Press of Glencoe.

Fabbro, F. (2001) The bilingual brain: Cerebral representation of languages, *Brain and Language*, 79(2): 211–22.

Fabrizio, K.R. (2009) Absorptive capacity and the search for innovation, *Research Policy*, 38(2): 255–67.

Faems, D., Bos, B., Noseleit, F., and Leten, B. (2020) Multistep Knowledge Transfer in Multinational Corporation Networks: When do Subsidiaries Benefit from Unconnected Sister Alliances? *Journal of Management*, 46(3): 414–42.

Fahy, K.M., Easterby-Smith, M., and Lervik, J.E. (2014) The power of spatial and temporal orderings in organizational learning, *Management Learning*, 45(2): 123–44.

Fang, S.C., Yang, C.W., and Hsu, W.Y. (2013) Inter-organizational knowledge transfer: the perspective of knowledge governance, *Journal of Knowledge Management*, 17(6): 943–57.

Farh, C.I., Bartol, K.M., Shapiro, D.L., and Shin, J. (2010) Networking abroad: A process model of how expatriates form support ties to facilitate adjustment, *Academy of Management Review*, 35(3): 434–54.

Farquharson, M., Örtenblad, A., and Hsu, S.W. (2014) Trusting local translation: Experiences from transplanting a "Made in Britain" entrepreneurship course in China, *Management Learning*, 45(2): 182–99.

Farrell, C.C., Coburn, C.E., and Chong, S. (2019) Under what conditions do school districts learn from external partners? The role of absorptive capacity, *American Educational Research Journal*, 56(3): 955–94.

Fauconnier, G., and Turner, M. (2002) *Conceptual blending and the mind's hidden complexities*, New York: Basic Books.

Fauconnier, G. and Turner, M. (1998) Conceptual integration networks, *Cognitive Science*, 22(2): 133–87.

Fawcett, P. (1998) Ideology and translation, in M. Baker (ed.), *Routledge Encyclopedia of Translation Studies*, London: Routledge, 106–10.

Feldman, M., and Pentland, B. (2003) Reconceptualizing organizational routines as a source of flexibility and change, *Administrative Science Quarterly*, 48(1): 94–118.

Ferlie, E., Fitzgerald, L., Wood, M., and Hawkins, C. (2005) The nonspread of innovations: the mediating role of professionals, *Academy of Management Journal*, 48(1): 117–34.

Fink, G. and Meierewert, S. (2005) The use of repatriate knowledge in organizations, *Human Resource Planning*, 28(4): 30–7.

Finstad, B. P. (2005) Finotro: statseid fiskeindustri i Finnmark og Nord-Troms: fra plan til avvikling (Translation: Finotro: State-owned fish industry in Finnmark and Northern-Troms: from plan to termination), *Ph.D. thesis*, Tromsø: University of Tromsø.

Fiss, P.C. (2011) Building better causal theories: A fuzzy set approach to typologies in organization research, *Academy of Management Journal*, 54(2): 393–420.

Fleming, L. (2001) Recombinant uncertainty in technological search, *Management Science*, 47(1): 117–32.

Flor, M.L., Cooper, S.Y., and Oltra, M.J. (2018) External knowledge search, absorptive capacity and radical innovation in high-technology firms, *European Management Journal*, 36(2): 183–94.

Florida, R. and Kenney, M. (1991) Transplanted organizations: The transfer of Japanese industrial organization to the US, *American Sociological Review*, 56: 381–98.

Floyd, S.W. (2009) Borrowing theory. What does this Mean and When does it Make Sense in Management Scholarship? *Journal of Management Studies*, 46(6): 1057–58.

Foos, T., Schum, G., and Rothenberg, S. (2006) Tacit knowledge transfer and the knowledge disconnect, *Journal of Knowledge Management*, 10(1): 6–18.

Forgatch, M.S. and DeGarmo, D.S. (2011) Sustaining fidelity following the nationwide PMTO™ implementation in Norway, *Prevention Science*, 12(3): 235–46.

Forrester, R. H. (2000) Capturing learning and applying knowledge: an investigation of the use of innovation teams in Japanese and American automotive firms, *Journal of Business Research*, 47(1), 35–45.

Fortwengel, J. (2017) Understanding when MNCs can overcome institutional distance: A research agenda, *Management International Review*, 57(6): 793–814.

Foss, N.J. (2011) Why micro-foundations for resource-based theory are needed and what they may look like, *Journal of Management*, 37(5): 1413–28.

Foss, N., and Pedersen, T. (2001, September), Building a MNC knowledge structure: the role of knowledge sources, complementarities and organizational context, In LINK Conference, Copenhagen, Denmark.

Fox, O. (2000) The use of translation diaries in a process-oriented translation teaching methodology, *Benjamins Translation Library*, 38: 115–30.

Francis, G. and Holloway, J. (2007) What have we learned? Themes from the literature on best-practice benchmarking, *International Journal of Management Reviews*, 9(3): 171–89.

Fredrickson J.W. (1986) The strategic decision process and organizational structure, *Academy of Management Review*, 11(2): 280–97.

Freeman, L. C. (1977) A set of measures of centrality based on betweenness, *Sociometry*, 40: 35–41.

Frenkel, M. (2005a) Something new, something old, something borrowed: the cross-national translation of the "family friendly" organization in Israel, in B. Czarniawska and G. Sevón (eds.), *Global Ideas. How Ideas, Objects and Practices Travel in the Global economy*. Malmø: Liber & Copenhagen Business School Press: 147–66.

Frenkel, M. (2005b) The politics of translation: how state-level political relations affect the cross-national travel of management ideas, *Organization*, 12(2): 275–301.

Frenkel, M. (2008) The Americanization of the antimanagerialist alternative in Israel, *International Studies of Management and Organization*, 38: 17–37.

Fritsch, M. and Kauffeld-Monz, M. (2010) The impact of network structure on knowledge transfer: An application of social network analysis in the context of regional innovation networks. *The Annals of Regional Science*, 44(1): 21–38.

Frost, T.S., Birkinshaw, J.M. and Ensign, P.C. (2002) Centers of excellence in multinational corporations, *Strategic Management Journal*, 23: 997–1018

Fruin, W.M., Liker, J.K., Adler, P.S., and Adler, P.S (1999) *Remade in America: Transplanting and Transforming Japanese Management Systems*, Oxford, UK: Oxford University Press.

Fu, X., Fu, X. M., Ghauri, P., and Hou, J. (2022), International collaboration and innovation: Evidence from a leading Chinese multinational enterprise, *Journal of World Business*, 57(4): 101329.

Furusten, S. (1999) *Popular Management Books*, London: Routledge.

Galbraith, J.R. (1973) *Designing Complex Organizations*, Boston, MA: Addison-Wesley.

Galbreath, J. (2019) Drivers of green innovations: The impact of export intensity, women leaders, and absorptive capacity, *Journal of Business Ethics*, 158(1): 47–61.

Gambier, Y. and Van Doorslaer, L. (2010) *Handbook of Translation Studies*, Amsterdam: John Benjamins Publishing.

Ganguly, A., Talukdar, A., and Chatterjee, D. (2019) Evaluating the role of social capital, tacit knowledge sharing, knowledge quality and reciprocity in determining innovation capability of an organization, *Journal of Knowledge Management*, 23(6): 1105–35.

Gargiulo, M. and Benassi, M. (2000) Trapped in your own net? Network cohesion, structural holes, and the adaptation of social capital, *Organization Science*, 11(2): 183–96.

Gebauer, H., Worch, H., and Truffer, B. (2012) Absorptive capacity, learning processes and combinative capabilities as determinants of strategic innovation, *European Management Journal*, 30(1): 57–73.

Geertz, C. (1973) *The interpretation of cultures*, New York: Basic Books.

Geest, S.V.D. and Whyte, S.R. (1989) The charm of medicines: metaphors and metonyms, *Medical Anthropology Quarterly*, 3(4): 345–67.

Gentner, D. (1982) Are scientific analogies metaphors? in D. Miall (ed.), *Metaphor: Problems and Perspectives*, Brighton: Harvester: 106–32.

Gentner, D. (1983) Structure-mapping: A theoretical framework for analogy, *Cognitive Science*, 7: 155–70.

Georgeff, M.P. and Lansky, A.L. (1986) Procedural knowledge, *Proceedings of the IEEE*, 74(10): 1383–98.

Gertler, M.S. (2003) Tacit knowledge and the economic geography of context, or the undefinable tacitness of being (there) *Journal of Economic Geography*, 3(1): 75–99.

Ghoshal, S. and Bartlett, C.A. (1990) The multinational corporation as an interorganizational network. *Academy of Management Review*, 15(4): 603–26.

Ghoshal, S. and Gratton, L. (2002) Integrating the Enterprise, *MIT Sloan Management Review*, 44(1): 31–8.

Ghoshal, S., Korine, H., and Szulanski, G. (1994) Interunit communication in multinational corporations. *Management Science*, 40(1): 96–110.

Gilbert, D. and Wong, R.K. (2003) Passenger expectations and airline services: a Hong Kong based study, *Tourism Management*, 24(5): 519–32.

Gile, D. (1990) Scientific Research vs. Personal Theories in the Investigation of Interpretation, in L. Gran and C. Taylor (eds.), *Aspects of Experimental Research on Conference Interpretation*, Udine: Campanotto: 28–41.

Gill, M.J., McGivern, G., Sturdy, A., Pereira, S., Gill, D.J., and Dopson, S. (2020) Negotiating Imitation: Examining the interactions of consultants and clients to understand institutionalization as translation, *British Journal of Management*, 31: 470–86.

Gillath, O., Karantzas, G.C., and Selcuk, E. (2017) A net of friends: Investigating friendship by integrating attachment theory and social network analysis, *Personality and Social Psychology Bulletin*, 43(11): 1546–65.

Giroux, H. and Taylor, J.R. (2002) The justification of knowledge: tracking the translation of quality, *Management Learning*, 33(4): 497–517.

Glover, L. and Wilkinson, A. (2007) Worlds colliding: The translation of modern management practices within a UK based subsidiary of a Korean-owned MNC, *The International Journal of Human Resource Management*, 18(8): 1437–55.

Goldthorpe, J.H. (1959) Technical organization as a factor in supervisor-worker conflict: Some preliminary observations on a study made in the mining industry, *The British Journal of Sociology*, 10(3): 213–30.

Gölgeci, I. and Kuivalainen, O. (2020) Does social capital matter for supply chain resilience? The role of absorptive capacity and marketing-supply chain management alignment, *Industrial Marketing Management*, 84: 63–74.

Gond, J.P. and Boxenbaum, E. (2013) The glocalization of responsible investment: Contextualization work in France and Quebec, *Journal of Business Ethics*, 115(4): 707–21.

Grady, J., Oakley, T., and Coulson, S. (1999) Blending and metaphor, *Amsterdam Studies in the Theory and History of Linguistic Science Series*, 4: 101–24.

Graham, I.D. and Logan, J. (2004) Translating research-innovations in knowledge transfer and continuity of care, *Canadian Journal of Nursing Research Archive*, 36(2): 89–104.

Granas, A.G., Nørgaard, L.S., and Sporrong, S.K. (2014) Lost in translation? Comparing three Scandinavian translations of the Beliefs about Medicines Questionnaire, *Patient Education and Counseling*, 96(2): 216–21.

Grandi, A. and Grimaldi, R. (2005) Academics' organizational characteristics and the generation of successful business ideas, *Journal of Business Venturing*, 20(6): 821–45.

Granovetter, M. (1985) Economic action and social structure: The problem of embeddedness, *American Journal of Sociology*, 91(3): 481–510.

Granovetter, M.S. (1973) The strength of weak ties, *American Journal of Sociology*, 78(6): 1360–80.

Granovetter, M. (1992) Economic institutions as social constructions: a framework for analysis, *Acta Sociologica*, 35(1): 3–11.

Granstrand, O. (2000) *The Economics and Management of Intellectual Property*, London: Edward Elgar.

Grant, R. M. (1996) Toward a knowledge-based theory of the firm, *Strategic Management Journal*, 17(S2), 109–22.

Greenwood R., Oliver, C., Sahlin, K., and Suddaby, R. (2008) Introduction, in R. Greenwood, C. Oliver, K. Sahlin, and R. Suddaby (eds.), *The Sage Handbook of Organizational Institutionalism*, London: SAGE Publications: 1–46.

Greve, C., Ejersbo, N., Lægreid, P., and Rykkja, L.H. (2020) Unpacking Nordic administrative reforms: Agile and adaptive governments, *International Journal of Public Administration*, 43(8): 697–710.

Griffith, D.A., Kiessling, T.S., and Dabic, M. (2005) An exploratory examination into the challenges to technology transfer in the transitional economy of Croatia, *Thunderbird International Business Review*, 47(2): 163–81.

Grol, R. (2001) Successes and failures in the implementation of evidence-based guidelines for clinical practice, *Medical Care*, 39(8): II46–54.

Grol, R. and Grimshaw, J. (2003) From best evidence to best practice: effective implementation of change in patients' care, *The Lancet*, 362(9391): 1225–30.

Grosjean, F. (1982) *Life with Two Languages: An Introduction to Bilingualism*, Cambridge MA: Harvard University Press.

References 267

Grosjean, F. (2010) *Bilingual*, Cambridge, MA: Harvard University Press.

Guest, D.E. (2007) Don't shoot the messenger: A wake-up call for academic, *Academy of Management Journal*, 50(5): 1020–26.

Gulati, R. (2007) Tent poles, tribalism, and boundary spanning: The rigor-relevance debate in management research, *Academy of Management Journal*, 50(4): 775–82.

Gulick, L. (1937) Notes on the theory of organization, in L. Gulick, and L.F. Urwick (eds.), *Papers on the Science of Administration*, Institute of Public Administration, New York, NY.

Gunther, R., Diamandouros, P.N., and Puhle, H.J. (1995) *The Politics of Democratic Consolidation: Southern Europe in Comparative Perspective*, Baltimore and London: John Hopkins University Press.

Gupta, A.K. and Govindarajan, V. (1994) Organizing for knowledge flows within MNCs, *International Business Review*, 3(4): 443–57.

Gupta, A.K. and Govindarajan, V. (2000) Knowledge flows within multinational corporations. *Strategic Management Journal*, 21(4): 473–96.

Hackney, R., Desouza, K., and Loebbecke, C. (2005) Cooperation or competition: knowledge sharing processes in inter-organizational networks, in S. Hawamdeh (ed.), *Knowledge Management: Nurturing Culture, Innovation and Technology*, Singapore: World Scientific Press: 79–99.

Hadjimichael, D. and Tsoukas, H. (2019) Toward a Better Understanding of Tacit Knowledge in Organizations: Taking Stock and Moving Forward, *Academy of Management Annals*, 13(2): 672–703.

Haedicke, M.A. (2012) Keeping our mission, changing our system: translation and organizational change in natural foods co-ops, *The Sociological Quarterly*, 53(1): 44–67.

Hage, J. (1965) An axiomatic theory of organizations, *Administrative Science Quarterly*, 10(3): 289–320.

Hage, J. (1975) *Occupations and the Social Structure*, New Jersey: Englewood Cliffs, Prentice Hall.

Hage, J. (1980) *Theories of Organizations: Form, Process, and Transformation*, John Wiley & Sons.

Hage, J. and Aiken, M. (1967) Relationship of centralization to other structural properties, *Administrative Science Quarterly*, 12(1): 72–92.

Hagopian, F. and Mainwaring, S.P. (2005) *The Third Wave of Democratization in Latin America: Advances and Setbacks*, Cambridge: Cambridge University Press.

Håkanson, L. (2005) Epistemic communities and cluster dynamics: On the role of knowledge in industrial districts, *Industry and Innovation*, 12(4): 433–63.

Hall, R. (1987) *Organizations. Structures, Processes & Outcomes*, New Jersey: Prentice Hall, Englewood Cliffs.

Halldin-Herrgård, T. (2000) Difficulties in diffusion of tacit knowledge in organizations, *The Journal of Intellectual Capital*, 1(4): 357–65.

Halliday, M.A.K., McIntosh, A., and Strevens, P. (1964) *The Linguistic Sciences and Language Teaching*, London: Longman.

Hambrick, D.C. (1984) Taxonomic approaches to studying strategy: Some conceptual and methodological issues, *Journal of Management*, 10(1): 27–41.

Hambrick, D.C. (1994) What if the academy actually mattered? *Academy of Management Review*, 19(1): 11–6.

Hanafizadeh, P. and Ghamkhari, F. (2019) Elicitation of tacit knowledge using soft systems methodology, *Systemic Practice and Action Research*, 32(5): 521–55.

Hannerz, U. (1996) *Transnational connections: Culture, people, places*, New York: Routledge.

Hansen, H.F. (2014) Organization of evidence-based knowledge production: Evidence hierarchies and evidence typologies, *Scandinavian Journal of Public Health*, 42: 11–7.

Hansen, H.F. and Rieper, O. (2009) The evidence movement: the development and consequences of methodologies in review practices, *Evaluation*, 15(2): 141–63.

Hansen, M.T. (1999) The search-transfer problem: The role of weak ties in sharing knowledge across organization subunits, *Administrative Science Quarterly*, 44(1): 82–111.

Hansen, M.T. (2002) Knowledge networks: Explaining effective knowledge sharing in multiunit companies, *Organization Science*, 13(3): 232–48.

Hareide, J.H. (1965) Sidelengs i Sanden: Førti Måneder med det Norske Prosjektet i Kerala (*Sideways in the Sand: Forty Months with the Norwegian Project in Kerala*), Oslo: Det Norske Samlaget.

Harré, R. and Secord, P.F. (1972) *The Explanation of Social Behavior*, Oxford, UK: Blackwell.

Harris, W.A. (1997) On scope conditions in sociological theories, *Social and Economic Studies*, 46(4): 123–27.

Harrison, M. (2016) *The decline of the traditional expat*? (https://www.eca-international.com/insights/articles/may-2016/the-decline-of-the-traditional-expat).

Harrison, T. (2000) Urban policy: addressing wicked problems, in H.T.O. Davies, S.M. Nutley, and P.C. Smith (eds.), *What Works? Evidence-based Policy and Practice in Public Services*, Bristol: Policy Press: 207–28.

Hauan, A. (2000) Kunnskap i Kontekst. Betydningen av kunnskap i kontekst for samhandling i økonomiske verdikjeder (Knowledge in context: The importance of knowledge in context for cooperation in economic value chains), Bodø, Nord University: *Working paper 8/2000*.

Haugen, E.I. (1956) *Bilingualism in the Americas: A Bibliography and Research Guide*, Alabama: University of Alabama Press.

Heckathorn, D.D. and Cameron, C.J. (2017) Network sampling: From snowball and multiplicity to respondent-driven sampling, *Annual Review of Sociology*, 43: 101–19.

Hedlund, G. and Zander, U. (1993) Architectonic and List-like Knowledge Structuring: Critique of Modern Concepts of Knowledge Management. *Research Paper 1993/2*. Institute of International Business, Stockholm School of Economics.

Hedmo, T., Sahlin-Andersson, K., and Wedlin, L. (2005) Fields of imitation: The global expansion of management education, in B. Czarniawska and G. Sevón (eds.), *Global Ideas: How Ideas, Objects and Practices Travel in the Global Economy*, Malmö: Liber & Copenhagen Business School Press: 190–212.

Heeley, M. (1997) Appropriating rents from external knowledge: the impact of absorptive capacity on firm sales growth and research productivity, *Frontiers of Entrepreneurship Research*, 17: 390–404

Helfat, C.E., Finkelstein, S., Mitchell, W., Peteraf, M., Singh, H., Teece, D. and Winter, S. (2007) *Dynamic Capabilities: Understanding Strategic Change in Organizations*, London: Blackwell.

Helfat, C.E. and Peteraf, M.A. (2003) The dynamic resource-based view: Capability lifecycles, *Strategic Management Journal*, 24(10): 997–1010.

Helin, S. and Sandström, J. (2010) Resisting a corporate code of ethics and the reinforcement of management control, *Organization Studies*, 31(5): 583–604.

Helper, S., MacDuffie, J.P., Pil, F., Sako, M., Takeishi, A., and Warburton, M. (1999) Modularization and Outsourcing: Implications for the future of automotive assembly, *Paper presented at the IMVP Annual Forum*, MIT, Boston, 6–7 October.

Hendry, J. (2000) *The Orient Strikes Back: A global view of cultural display*, London: Routledge.

Henry, E. and Ponce, C.J. (2011) Waiting to imitate: on the dynamic pricing of knowledge, *Journal of Political Economy*, 119(5): 959–81.

Hermans, T. (1985/2014) *The Manipulation of Literature* (Routledge Revivals) Studies in Literary Translation. London: Routledge.

Hermans, T. (2013) What is (not) translation? In M. Baker (ed.), *The Routledge Handbook of Translation Studies*, London: Routledge: 93–105.

Hernes, T. (2014) *A Process Theory of Organization*, Oxford: Oxford University Press.
Hersey, P. and Blanchard, K. H. (1969) *Management of Organizational Behavior—Utilizing Human Resources*, New Jersey:Prentice Hall.
Heusinkveld, S., Benders, J., and Hilleband, B. (2013) Stretching concepts: the role of competing pressures and decoupling in the evolution of organizational concepts, *Organization Studies*, 34(1): 7–32.
Heusinkveld, S. and Visscher, K. (2012) Practice what you preach: how consultants frame management concepts as enacted practice, *Scandinavian Journal of Management*, 28(4): 285–97.
Hiebeler, R., Kelly, T.B., and Ketteman, C. (1998) *Best Practices: Building your Business with Arthur Andersen's Global Best Practices*, New York: Simon & Schuster.
Hislop, D., Bosua, R., and Helms, R. (2018) *Knowledge Management in Organizations: A Critical Introduction*, Oxford: Oxford University Press.
Ho, M.H.W., Ghauri, P.N., and Larimo, J.A. (2018) Institutional distance and knowledge acquisition in international buyer-supplier relationships: The moderating role of trust, *Asia Pacific Journal of Management*, 35(2): 427–47.
Hocking, J.B., Brown, M., and Harzing, A.W. (2007) Balancing global and local strategic contexts: Expatriate knowledge transfer, applications, and learning within a transnational organization, *Human Resource Management*, 46(4): 513–33.
Hofstede, G. (1980) Culture and organizations, *International Studies of Management & Organization*, 10(4): 15–41.
Hofstede, G. (1984) *Culture's consequences: International Differences in Work-Related Values*, London: Sage.
Hofstede, G. (2001) *Culture's Consequences: Comparing Values, Behaviors, Institutions and Organizations Across Nations*, Thousand Oaks, CA: SAGE publications.
Hofstede, G., Hofstede, G.J., and Minkov, M. (2010) *Cultures and Organizations: Software of the Mind*, New York: McGraw-Hill.
Hofstede, G., Neuijen, B., Ohayv, D.D., and Sanders, G. (1990) Measuring organizational cultures: A qualitative and quantitative study across twenty cases, *Administrative Science Quarterly*, 35(2): 286–316.
Holland, R. (2017) News translation, in C. Millán and F. Bartrina (eds.), *The Routledge Handbook of Translation Studies*, Abingdon, Oxon: Routledge, 332–46.
Hollingshead, A.B. (1998) Communication, learning, and retrieval in transactive memory systems, *Journal of Experimental Social Psychology*, 34(5): 423–42.
Holmes, J.M. (1972/1988) The name and nature of translation studies, in J.M. Holmes (ed.), *Translated! Papers on Literary Translations and Translation Studies*, Amsterdam: Rodopi, 67–80.
Holz-Mänttäri, J. (1984) *Translatorisches Handeln. Theorie und Methode*.[2] Annales Academiae Scientarum Fennicae, Helsinki: Suomalainen Tiedeakatemia.
Hong, J.F. and Nguyen, T.V. (2009) Knowledge embeddedness and the transfer mechanisms in multinational corporations, *Journal of World Business*, 44(4): 347–56.
Hönig, H.G. and Kußmaul, P. (1982) *Strategie der Übersetzung: Ein Lehr-und Arbeitsbuch*, Tübingen: Günter Narr Verlag.
Horvat, D., Dreher, C., and Som, O. (2019) How firms absorb external knowledge—Modelling and managing the absorptive capacity process, *International Journal of Innovation Management*, 23(1): 1950041.
House, J. (2006) Text and context in translation, *Journal of Pragmatics*, 38(3): 338–58.
Howells, J. (1996) Tacit knowledge, *Technology Analysis and Strategic Management*, 8(2): 91–106.

Howland, D. (2002) *Translating the West: Language and Political Reason in Nineteenth-Century Japan*, Honolulu: University of Hawaii Press.

Hsu, M.H., Ju, T.L., Yen, C.H., and Chang, C.M. (2007) Knowledge sharing behavior in virtual communities: The relationship between trust, self-efficacy, and outcome expectations, *International Journal of Human-Computer Studies*, 65(2): 153–69.

Hu, Y.S. (1995) The international transferability of the firm's advantages, *California Management Review*, 37(4): 73–88.

Huergo, E. and Jaumandreu, J. (2004) How does probability of innovation change with firm age? *Small Business Economics*, 22(3): 193–207.

Huggins, R., Johnston, A., and Thompson, P. (2012) Network capital, social capital and knowledge flow: how the nature of inter-organizational networks impacts on innovation. *Industry and Innovation*, 19(3): 203–32.

Hultin, L., Introna, L.D., and Mähring, M. (2021) The decentered translation of management ideas: Attending to the conditioning flow of everyday work practices, *Human Relations*, 74(4): 587–620.

Hunt, W. and Downing, S. (1990) Mergers, acquisitions and human resource *Journal of Human Resource Management*, 1(2): 195–210.

Hurtado Albir, A. (2015) The acquisition of translation competence. Competences, tasks, and assessment in translator training, *Meta: Journal des Traducteurs/Translators' Journal*, 60(2): 256–80.

Hutzschenreuter, T., Kleindienst, I., and Lange, S. (2016) The concept of distance in international business research: A review and research agenda. *International Journal of Management Reviews*, 18(2): 160–79.

Hwang H., and Suárez D. F. (2005) Lost and found in the translation of strategic plans and websites, in B. Czarniawska and G. Sevón, (Eds.), *Global ideas: How ideas, objects, and practices travel in a global economy*: 71–93. Malmö, Sweden: Liber & Copenhagen Business School Press.

Iansiti, M. (1998) *Technology Integration*, Boston, MA: Harvard University Press.

Iles, P., Wong, A.R., and Yolles, M. (2004) HRM and knowledge migration across cultures issues, limitations and Mauritian specificities, *Employee Relations*, 26(6): 643–62.

Inggs, J.A. (2011) Censorship and translated children's literature in the Soviet Union: The example of the Wizards Oz and Goodwin, *Target. International Journal of Translation Studies*, 23(1): 77–91.

Ingram, P. and Baum, J. A. (1997) Chain affiliation and the failure of Manhattan hotels, 1898-1980, *Administrative Science Quarterly*, 42(1): 68–102.

Inkpen, A.C. (2000) Learning through joint ventures: a framework of knowledge acquisition, *Journal of Management Studies*, 37(7): 1019–44.

Inkpen, A.C. and Tsang, E.W. (2005) Social capital, networks, and knowledge transfer, *Academy of Management Review*, 30(1): 146–65.

Inns, D. (2002) Metaphor in the literature of organizational analysis: A preliminary taxonomy and a glimpse at a humanities-based perspective, *Organization*, 9(2): 305–30.

Isaac, G. (2011) Whose idea was this? Museums, replicas, and the reproduction of knowledge, *Current Anthropology*, 52(2): 211–33.

Isaacson, W. (2011) *Steve Jobs*, New York: Simon & Schuster.

Isaksen, A. (2009) Innovation dynamics of global competitive regional clusters: The case of the Norwegian centres of expertise, *Regional Studies*, 43(9): 1155–66.

Jackson, G., and Deeg, R. (2019) Comparing capitalisms and taking institutional context seriously, *Journal of International Business Studies*, 50(1): 4–19.

Jacobsen, D. I. (2004) *Organisasjonsendringer og endringsledelse* (*Organizational change and change management*), Bergen: Fagbokforlaget.

Jacobsson, B. (1994) Reformer och organisatorisk identitet (Reforms and organizational identity), in B. Jacobsson (ed.), *Organisationsexperiment i kommuner och landsting (Organizational experiments in municipalities and counties)*, Stockholm: Nerenius & Santerus: 38–61.
Jansen, J.J., Van den Bosch, F.A., and Volberda, H.W. (2005) Exploratory innovation, exploitative innovation, and ambidexterity: The impact of environmental and organizational antecedents, *Schmalenbach Business Review*, 57(4): 351–63.
Jasimuddin, S. M. and Zhang, Z. (2011), Transferring stored knowledge and storing transferred knowledge, *Information Systems Management*, 28(1): 84–94.
Javidan, M., Stahl, G.K., Brodbeck, F., and Wilderom, C.P. (2005) Cross-border transfer of knowledge: Cultural lessons from Project GLOBE, *Academy of Management Perspectives*, 19(2): 59–76.
Jensen, R. and Szulanski, G. (2004) Stickiness and the adaptation of organizational practices in cross-border knowledge transfers, *Journal of International Business Studies*, 35(6): 508–23.
Jensen, T., Sandström, J., and Helin, S. (2009) Corporate codes of ethics and the bending of moral space, *Organization*, 16(4): 529–45.
Jiménez-Jiménez, D., and Sanz-Valle, R. (2005) Innovation and human resource management fit: an empirical study, *International Journal of Manpower*, 26(4): 364–81.
Jorem, K. (1977) *Menneskeverdig Personalpolitikk* (A Human Personnel Policy), Oslo: Tanum.
Joullié, J. E., and Gould, A. M. (2022) Having nothing to say but saying it anyway: Language and practical relevance in management research, *Academy of Management Learning & Education*, 21(2): 282–302.
Kaemper, E. (1727/2001) *History of Japan/Heutiges Japan*, München: Ludicium.
Kalberg, S. (1980) Max Weber's types of rationality: Cornerstones for the analysis of rationalization processes in history, *American Journal of Sociology*, 85(5): 1145–79.
Kantola, A. and Seeck, H. (2011) Dissemination of management into politics: Michael Porter and the political uses of management consulting, *Management Learning*, 42(1): 25–47.
Karabag, S. F. and Berggren, C. (2017) Struggling with knowledge boundaries and Stickiness; Case studies of innovationg firms in an emerging economy, in F. Tell, C. Berggren, S. Brusoni, and A. Van De Ven (eds.), *Managing Knowledge Integreation Across Boundaries*, 139–154, Oxford: Oxford University Press.
Karanikas, N., Khan, S.R., Baker, P.R., and Pilbeam, C. (2022) Designing safety interventions for specific contexts: results from a literature review, *Safety Science*, 156. https://doi.org/10.1016/j.ssci.2022.105906
Kasper, H., Mühlbacher, J., and Müller, B. (2008) Intra-organizational knowledge sharing in MNCs depending on the degree of decentralization and communities of practice, *Journal of Global Business & Technology*, 4(1): 59–67.
Katz, D. and Kahn, R.L. (1978) *The Social Psychology of Organizations*, New York: Wiley.
Kaul, A. (2013) Entrepreneurial action, unique assets, and appropriation risk: Firms as a means of appropriating profit from capability creation, *Organization Science*, 24(6): 1765–81.
Kayes, A.B., Kayes, D.C., and Yamazaki, Y. (2005) Transferring knowledge across cultures: A learning competencies approach, *Performance Improvement Quarterly*, 18(4): 87–100.
Kedia, B.L. and Bhagat, R.S. (1988) Cultural constraints on transfer of technology across nations: Implications for research in international and comparative management, *Academy of Management Review*, 13(4): 559–71.
Kelemen, M. (2000) Too much or too little ambiguity: the language of total quality management, *Journal of Management Studies*, 37: 483–98.
Keller, W. (1996) Absorptive capacity: On the creation and acquisition of technology in development, *Journal of Development Economics*, 49(1): 199–227.

Kelly, L.G. (1979) *The True Interpreter: A History of Translation Theory and Practice in the West*, Oxford: Basil Blackwell.

Kenny, D. (1998) Equivalence. *Routledge encyclopedia of translation studies*, in M. Baker (ed.), *Routledge Encyclopedia of Translation Studies*, London: Routledge: 77–80.

Kern, A. (2006) Exploring the relation between creativity and rules: the case of the performing arts, *International Studies of Management & Organization*, 36(1): 63–80.

Kern, P., Almond, P., Edwards, T., and Tregaskis, O. (2019) Multinational and Transnational Organisations: The Role of Globalizing Actors, in A. Sturdy, S. Heusinkveld, T. Reay, and D. Strang (eds.), *The Oxford Handbook of Management Ideas*, Oxford: Oxford University Press: 177–94.

Ketokivi, M., Mantere, S., and Cornelissen, J. (2017) Reasoning by analogy and the progress of theory, *Academy of Management Review*, 42(4): 637–58.

Kettley, P. (1995) *Is Flatter Better? Delayering the Management Hierarchy*, Brighton, UK: Institute for Employment Studies.

Keuning, D. and Opheij, W. (1994) *Delayering Organizations: How to Beat Bureaucracy and Create a Flexible and Responsive Organization*, London: Financial Times/Pitman.

Khalil, O. and Marouf, L. (2017) A cultural interpretation of nations' readiness for knowledge economy, *Journal of the Knowledge Economy*, 8(1): 97–126.

Kieser, A. (2002) On communication barriers between management science, consultancies and business companies, in T. Clark and R. Fincham (eds.), *Critical Consulting: New Perspectives on the Management Advice Industry*, Oxford: Blackwell: 206–27.

Kieser, A. (2011) Between rigour and relevance: Co-existing institutional logics in the field of management science, *Society and Economy*, 33(2): 237–47.

Kieser, A. and Leiner, L. (2009) Why the rigour–relevance gap in management research is unbridgeable, *Journal of Management Studies*, 46(3): 516–33.

Kieser, A., Nicolai, A., and Seidl, D. (2015) The practical relevance of management research: Turning the debate on relevance into a rigorous scientific research program, *The Academy of Management Annals*, 9: 143–233.

Kikoski, C.K. and Kikoski, J.F. (2004) *The inquiring organization: Tacit knowledge, conversation, and knowledge creation: Skills for 21st-century organizations*, Westport, CT: Greenwood Publishing Group.

Kilduff, M. and Brass, D.J. (2010) Organizational social network research: Core ideas and key debates, *Academy of Management Annals*, 4(1): 317–57.

Kilduff, M., and Tsai, W. (2003) *Social Networks and Organizations*, London: Sage Press.

Kim, M. (2013) Many roads lead to Rome: Implications of geographic scope as a source of isolating mechanisms, *Journal of International Business Studies*, 44(9): 898–921.

Kim, S. and Anand, J. (2018) Knowledge complexity and the performance of inter-unit knowledge replication structures, *Strategic Management Journal*, 39(7): 1959–89.

Kirkpatrick, I., Bullinger, B. Lega, F. and Dent, M. (2013) The translation of hospital management models in European health systems: a framework for comparison, *British Journal of Management*, 24: S48–61.

Kittel, H. and Poltermann, A. (1998) German tradition, in M. Baker (ed.), *Routledge Encyclopedia of Translation Studies*, London: Routledge: 418–26.

Klaudy, K. (1998) Explicitation, in M. Baker (ed.), *The Routledge Encyclopedia of Translation Studies*, London and New York: Routledge: 80–4.

Klausen, A.M. (1968) *Kerala Fishermen and the Indo-Norwegian Pilot Project*, Oslo: Universitetsforlaget.

Knill, C., Christoph, K., and Føllésdal, A. (2001) *The Europeanisation of National Administrations: Patterns of Institutional Change and Persistence*, Cambridge: Cambridge University Press.

Know, K. W. W. (2001) Supporting knowledge creation and sharing in social networks, *Organizational Dynamics*, 30(2): 100–20.

Koch, S. and Deetz, S. (1981) Metaphor analysis of social reality in organizations, *Journal of Applied Communication Research*, 9(1): 1–15.

Kogut, B. and Singh, H. (1988) The effect of national culture on the choice of entry mode, *Journal of International Business Studies*, 19(3): 411–32.

Kogut, B. and Zander, U. (1992) Knowledge of the firm, combinative capabilities, and the replication of technology, *Organization Science*, 3(3): 383–97.

Kogut, B. and Zander, U. (1993) Knowledge of the firm and the evolutionary theory of the multinational corporation, *Journal of International Business Studies*, 24(4): 625–45.

Kohtamäki, M., Heimonen, J., and Parida, V. (2019) The nonlinear relationship between entrepreneurial orientation and sales growth: The moderating effects of slack resources and absorptive capacity, *Journal of Business Research*, 100: 100–10.

Koller, W. (1989) Equivalence in translation theory, in A. Chesterman (ed.), *Readings in Translation Theory*, Helsinki: Oy Finn Lectura: 99–104.

Konlechner, S., and Ambrosini, V. (2019) Issues and Trends in Causal Ambiguity Research: A Review and Assessment, *Journal of Management*, 45(6): 2352–86.

Korneliussen, T. and Pedersen, P.A. (2001) Quality assessment in international industrial markets: The case of Norwegian stockfish, *paper presented at the 17th Annual Industrial Marketing and Purchasing Conference*, Oslo, 9th–11th September 2001.

Korneliussen, T and Panozzo, F. (2005) From "nature" to "economy" and "culture": How stockfish travels and constructs an action net. In B. Czarniawska and G. Sevón (Eds.) *Global ideas. How ideas, objects and practices travel in the global economy*, Liber and Copenhagen Business School Press, Malmö, 106–125

Koskinen, K. (1994) Translating the Untranslatable: The Impact of Deconstruction and Poststructuralism on Translation Theory, *Translators' Journal*, 39(3): 446–52.

Kostopoulos, K., Papalexandris, A., Papachroni, M., and Ioannou, G. (2011) Absorptive capacity, innovation, and financial performance, *Journal of Business Research*, 64(12): 1335–43.

Kostova, T. (1997) Country institutional profiles: Concept and measurement, *Academy of Management Best Paper Proceedings*, 24: 64–81.

Kostova, T. (1999) Transnational transfer of strategic organizational practices: A contextual perspective, *Academy of Management Review*, 24(2): 308–24.

Kostova, T., Beugelsdijk, S., Scott, W.R., Kunst, V.E., Chua, C.H., and van Essen, M. (2020) The construct of institutional distance through the lens of different institutional perspectives: Review, analysis, and recommendations, *Journal of International Business Studies*, 51(4): 467–97.

Kostova, T. and Roth, K. (2002) Adoption of an organizational practice by subsidiaries of multinational corporations: Institutional and relational effects, *Academy of Management Journal*, 45(1): 215–33.

Krejsler, J.B. (2013) What works in education and social welfare? A mapping of the evidence discourse and reflections upon consequences for professionals, *Scandinavian Journal of Educational Research*, 57(1): 16–32.

Krings, H. (1986) Translation problems and translation strategies of advanced German learners of French, in J. House and S. Blum-Kulka (eds.), *Interlingual and Intercultural Communication: Discourse and Cognition in Translation and Second Language Acquisition studies*, Tubingen, G. Narr: 263–76.

Kroc, R. and Anderson, R. (1987) *Grinding It Out: The Making of McDonald's*, New York: Macmillan.

Kroll, J.F. and Stewart, E. (1994) Category interference in translation and picture naming: Evidence for asymmetric connections between bilingual memory representations, *Journal of Memory and Language*, 33(2): 149–74.

Kuhlmann, S. (2001) Future governance of innovation policy in Europe—three scenarios, *Research Policy*, 30(6): 953–76.

Kuhlmann, S. and Wollmann, H. (2019) *Introduction to comparative public administration: Administrative systems and reforms in Europe*, Cheltenham: Edward Elgar Publishing.

Kuhn, T.S. (1970) *The Structure of Scientific Revolutions*, Chicago: University of Chicago Press.

Kumar, J.A. and Ganesh, L.S. (2009) Research on knowledge transfer in organizations: a morphology, *Journal of Knowledge Management*, 13(4): 161–74.

Kummen, A. (2008) *Hva mener medarbeidere og ledere om medarbeidersamtaler? En SWOT-analyse* (Employees' and leaders' opinions about Development Dialogue. A SWOT analysis), Master's thesis, April 2008, Department of Psychology, The University of Oslo.

Kunkel, J.H. and Berry, L.L. (1968) A behavioral conception of retail image, *Journal of Marketing*, 32(4): 21–27.

Kwon, S.W., Rondi, E., Levin, D.Z., De Massis, A., and Brass, D.J. (2020) Network brokerage: An integrative review and future research agenda, *Journal of Management*, 46(6): 1092–120.

Lado, A.A. and Zhang, M.J. (1998) Expert systems, knowledge development and utilization, and sustained competitive advantage: A resource-based model. *Journal of Management*, 24(4): 489–509.

Lægreid, P. and Rykkja, L. H. (2015) Hybrid Collaborative Arrangements: The welfare administration in Norway–between hierarchy and network, *Public Management Review*, 17(7): 960–80.

Lægreid, P. and Rykkja, L.H. (2022) Accountability and inter-organizational collaboration within the state, *Public Management Review*, 24(5):683–703.

Lakoff, G. and Johnson, M. (1980) The metaphorical structure of the human conceptual system, *Cognitive Science*, 4(2): 195–208.

Lam, A. (2000) Tacit knowledge, organizational learning and societal institutions: An integrated framework. *Organization Studies*, 21(3): 487–513.

Lam, P. (1995) Copyright protection of foreign computer software in the People's Republic of China: significant progress in two years, *Loyola of Los Angeles International and Comparative Law Journal*, 17(4): 861–90.

Lambert, J. (2017) Prelude: The institutionalization of the Discipline, in C. Millán and F. Bartina (eds.), *The Routledge Handbook of Translation Studies*, Abingdon, Oxon: Routledge: 7–28.

Lambert, W.G. (2013) *Babylonian Creation Myths*, Winona Lake: Eisenbrauns.

Lane, P.J., Koka, B.R., and Pathak, S. (2006) The reification of absorptive capacity: A critical review and rejuvenation of the construct, *Academy of Management Review*, 31(4): 833–63.

Lane, P.J. and Lubatkin, M. (1998) Relative absorptive capacity and interorganizational learning, *Strategic Management Journal*, 19(5): 461–77.

Lane, P.J., Salk, J.E., and Lyles, M.A. (2001) Absorptive capacity, learning, and performance in international joint ventures, *Strategic Management Journal*, 22(12): 1139–61.

Langen, P.D. (2002) Clustering and performance: the case of maritime clustering in The Netherlands, *Maritime Policy & Management*, 29(3): 209–21.

Langrogne, M. (1919) Taylorism in the Mine: Efficiency Methods below Ground, *Colliery Guardian*, 28 November, pp. 429–30, 12 December, p. 1574, and 24 December, p. 1714.

Larsson, I. (2019) *Att översätta Lean till praktik i hälso-och sjukvården* (trans: To translate Lean into practice in the health-care sector), Doctoral dissertation, Uppsala University: Företagsekonomiska institutionen, ISBN: 978-91-506-2776-3.

Latour, B. (1983), Give me a laboratory and I will raise the world, in M. Knorr Cetina and M. Mulkay (Eds.), *Science Observed,* Sage Publications, London, 141–70

Latour, B. (1986) The powers of associations, in J. Law (ed.), *Power, Action and Belief: A New Sociology of Knowledge?* London: Routledge and Kegan Paul: 261–77.

Latour, B. (1987) *Science in Action: How to Follow Scientists and Engineers Through Society*, Cambridge, MA: Harvard University Press.

Lave, J. and Wenger, E. (1991) *Situated Learning: Legitimate Peripheral Participation*, Cambridge: Cambridge University Press.

Lawrence, P.R. and Lorsch, J.W. (1967) Differentiation and integration in complex organizations, *Administrative Science Quarterly* 12: 1–47.

Lawrence, T. B. (2017) High-stakes institutional translation: Establishing North America's first government-sanctioned supervised injection site, *Academy of Management Journal*, 60(5): 1771–800.

Lawson, B., Samson, D., and Roden, S. (2012) Appropriating the value from innovation: inimitability and the effectiveness of isolating mechanisms, *R&D Management*, 42(5): 420–34.

Lazarova, M. and Tarique, I. (2005) Knowledge transfer upon repatriation, *Journal of World Business*, 40(4): 361–73.

Lederer, M. (1994/2003) *La traduction aujourd'hui: Le modèle interprétatif* (N. Larché as Translation: The interpretive model), Paris: Hachette, Manchester: St Jerome.

Lee, C., Lee, K., and Pennings, J.M. (2001) Internal capabilities, external networks, and performance: a study on technology-based ventures, *Strategic Management Journal*, 22(6–7): 615–40.

Lee, H. and Choi, B. (2003) Knowledge management enablers, processes, and organizational performance: An integrative view and empirical examination, *Journal of Management Information Systems*, 20(1): 179–228.

Lefevere, A. (1992) *Translating literature: Practice and Theory in a Comparative Literature Context*, New York: Modern Language Association of America.

Lefevere, A. and Bassnett, S. (1990) Introduction: Proust's Grandmother and the Thousand and One nights: The Cultural Turn in Translation Studies, in S. Bassnett and A. Lefevere (eds.), *Translation, History and Culture*, London: Pinter: 1–13.

Leishman, D. (1990) An annotated bibliography of works on analogy, *International Journal of Intelligent Systems*, 5(1): 43–82.

Leonard, D. and Sensiper, S. (1998) The role of tacit knowledge in group innovation, *California Management Review*, 40(3): 112–32.

Leonard-Barton, D. and Deschamps, I. (1988) Managerial influence in the implementation of new technology, *Management Science*, 34(10): 1252–65.

Lervik, J.E. and Lunnan, R. (2004) Contrasting perspectives on the diffusion of management knowledge: Performance management in a Norwegian multinational, *Management Learning*, 35(3): 287–302.

Letmathe, P., Schweitzer, M., and Zielinski, M. (2012) How to learn new tasks: Shop floor performance effects of knowledge transfer and performance feedback *Journal of Operations Management*, 30(3): 221–36.

Levin, D.Z. and Cross, R. (2004) The strength of weak ties you can trust: The mediating role of trust in effective knowledge transfer. *Management Science*, 50(11): 1477–90.

Levina, N. and Vaast, E. (2005) The emergence of boundary spanning competence in practice: implications for implementation and use of information systems, *MIS Quarterly*, 29(2): 335–63.

Levitt, B. and March, J.G. (1988) Organizational learning, *Annual Review of Sociology*, 14(1): 319–38.

Levitt, T. (1966) Innovative imitation, *Harvard Business Review*, 44(5): 63–70.
Lewin, A. Y., Massini, S., and Peeters, C. (2011) Microfoundations of internal and external absorptive capacity routines, *Organization Science*, 22(1): 81–98.
Leydesdorff, L. (2021) *The Evolutionary Dynamics of Discursive Knowledge: Communication-Theoretical Perspectives on an Empirical Philosophy of Science*, Amsterdam: Springer Nature: 247.
Li, C.Y. and Hsieh, C.T. (2009) The impact of knowledge stickiness on knowledge transfer implementation, internalization, and satisfaction for multinational corporations, *International Journal of Information Management*, 29(6): 425–35.
Li, J. (2015) Towards a Happier Society? Subjective Well-being and the Happiness Index of Guangdong, China, Doctoral thesis, University of Birmingham, UK.
Li, M. and Gao, F. (2003) Why Nonaka highlights tacit knowledge: a critical review, *Journal of Knowledge Management*, 7(4): 6–14.
Liao, J., Welsch, H., and Stoica, M. (2003) Organizational absorptive capacity and responsiveness: An empirical investigation of growth–oriented SMEs, *Entrepreneurship Theory and practice*, 28(1): 63–86.
Lichtenthaler, U. (2009) Absorptive capacity, environmental turbulence, and the complementarity of organizational learning processes, *Academy of Management Journal*, 52(4): 822–46.
Lidin, O.G. (2002) *Tanegashima: The Arrival of Europe in Japan*, Copenhagen: NIAS Press.
Lillis, A.M. and Mundy, J. (2005) Cross-sectional field studies in management accounting research—closing the gaps between surveys and case studies, *Journal of Management Accounting Research*, 17(1): 119–41.
Lillrank, P. (1995) The transfer of management innovations from Japan, *Organization Studies*, 16(6) 971–89.
Lin, B.W. (2003) Technology transfer as technological learning: a source of competitive advantage for firms with limited R&D resources, *R&D Management*, 33(3): 327–41.
Lippman, S.A., and Rumelt, R.P. (1982) Uncertain imitability: An analysis of interfirm differences in efficiency under competition, *The Bell Journal of Economics*, 13(2): 418–38.
Littler, C.R., Wiesner, R., and Dunford, R. (2003) The dynamics of delayering: Changing management structures in three countries, *Journal of Management Studies*, 40(2): 225–56.
Löfgren, O. (2005) Cultural alchemy: Translating the experience economy into Scandinavian, in B. Czarniawska and G. Sevón (eds.), *Global Ideas. How Ideas, Objects and Practices Travel in the Global economy*, Malmö: Liber & Copenhagen Business School Press: 15–29.
Long, L. (2017) The translation of sacred texts, in C. Millán and F. Bartrina (eds.), *The Routledge Handbook of Translation Studies*, Abingdon, Oxon: Routledge: 464–74.
Lonsdale, A.B. (1998) Direction of translation, in M. Baker (ed.), *Routledge Encyclopedia of Translation Studies*, London: Routledge: 63–67.
Lörscher, W. (1991) *Translation Performance, Translation Process, and Translation Strategies: A Psycholinguistic Investigation*, Tübingen, Gunter Narr.
Lörscher, W. (1993) Translation process analysis, in Y. Gambier and J. Tommola (eds.), *Translation and Knowledge*, Finland: University of Turku: 195–212.
Lörscher, W. (2012) Bilingualism and translation competence, *SYNAPS—A Journal of Professional Communication*, 27: 3–15.
Love, E.G. and Cebon, P. (2008) Meanings on multiple levels: the influence of field-level and organization-level meaning systems on diffusion, *Journal of Management Studies*, 45: 239–67
Love, J.F. and Miller, A.W. (1995) *McDonald's: Behind the Arches*, New York: Bantam Books.
Lucas, L.M. (2006) The role of culture on knowledge transfer: the case of the multinational corporation, *The Learning Organization*, 13(3): 257–75.

Lucken, M. (2016) *Imitation and Creativity in Japanese Arts: From Kishida Ryusei to Miyazaki Hayao*, New York: Columbia University Press.

Lundvall, B.A. (1988) Innovation as an interactive process: from user-producer interaction to national systems of innovation, in G. Dosi, C. Freeman, R. R. Nelson, G. Silverberg, and L. Soete (eds.), *Technical change and economic theory*, London: Pinter Publisher: 349–69

Lundvall, B.A. and Borrás, S. (2005) Science, technology and innovation policy, in J. Fagerberg, D.C. Mowery, and R. Nelson (eds.), *The Oxford Handbook of Innovation*, Oxford: Oxford University Press: 599–631.

Lunenburg, F.C. (2010) Communication: The process, barriers, and improving effectiveness, *Schooling*, 1(1) 1–11.

Macdonald, G. (2000) Social care: rhetoric and reality, in H.T.O. Davies, S.M. Nutley, and P.C. Smith (eds.), *What Works? Evidence-based Policy and Practice in Public Services*, Bristol: Policy Press: 117–40.

Macnamara, J. (1967) The bilingual's linguistic performance—a psychological overview, *Journal of Social Issues*, 23(2): 58–77.

Madeley, C. (2007) Copying cars: forgotten licensing agreements, in R. Cox (ed.), *The Culture of Copying in Japan, Critical and Historical Perspectives*, New York: Routledge: 251–68.

Madsen, D.Ø. (2014) Interpretation and use of the Balanced Scorecard in Denmark: Evidence from suppliers and users of the concept, *Danish Journal of Management & Business*, 78(3/4): 13–25.

Madsen, D. Ø. and Slåtten, K. (2022) The Diffusion of Human Resource Transformation in Scandinavia: A Supply-Side Perspective, *Societies*, 12(3): 2–18.

Madsen, D.Ø., Slåtten, K., and Johanson, D. (2017) The emergence and evolution of benchmarking: A management fashion perspective, *Benchmarking: An International Journal*, 24(3): 775–805.

Majchrzak, A., More, P.H., and Faraj, S. (2012) Transcending knowledge differences in cross-functional teams, *Organization Science*, 23(4): 951–70.

Maleszka, M. (2019) Application of collective knowledge diffusion in a social network environment, *Enterprise Information Systems*, 13(7-8): 1120–42.

Malik, T.H. (2013) National institutional differences and cross-border university–industry knowledge transfer, *Research Policy*, 42(3): 776–87.

Malmkjær, K. (2013). Where are we? (From Holmes' map until now). In C. Millán and F. Bartrina (Eds.), *The Routledge Handbook of Translation Studies*, London: Routledge : 31–44.

Malmkjær, K. (ed.) (1998) *Translation and Language Teaching, Language Teaching and Translation*, Manchester: St Jerome Publications.

Mansfield, E. (1985) How rapidly does new industrial technology leak out? *The Journal of Industrial Economics*: 34(2): 217–23.

Mansfield, E., and Romeo, A. (1980) Technology transfer to overseas subsidiaries by US-based firms, *The Quarterly Journal of Economics*, 95(4): 737–50.

March, J.G. (1976) The technology of foolishness, in J.G. March and J.P. Olsen (eds.), *Ambiguity and Choice in Organizations*, Oslo: Universitetsforlaget: 69–81.

March, J.G. and Olsen, J.P. (1989) *Rediscovering Institutions—The Organizational Basis of Politics*, New York: The Free Press.

March, J.G. and Olsen, J.P. (1995) *Democratic Governance*, New York: Free Press.

March, J.G. and Simon H.A. (1958) *Organizations*, New York: Wiley.

Marchiori, D. and Franco, M. (2020) Knowledge transfer in the context of inter-organizational networks: Foundations and intellectual structures, *Journal of Innovation & Knowledge*, 5(2): 130–39.

Martin, X. and Salomon, R. (2003) Knowledge transfer capacity and its implications for the theory of the multinational corporation, *Journal of International Business Studies*, 34(4): 356–73.

Martinkenaite, I. and Breunig, K.J. (2016) The emergence of absorptive capacity through micro–macro level interactions, *Journal of Business Research*, 69(2): 700–08.

Maseland, R., Dow, D., and Steel, P. (2018). The Kogut and Singh national cultural distance index: Time to start using it as a springboard rather than a crutch, *Journal of International Business Studies*, 49(9): 1154–66.

Massey, D. and Wield, D. (2003) *High-tech Fantasies: Science Parks in Society, Science and Space*, London: Routledge.

Mavor, S. (1924) Problems of Mechanical Coal Mining, *Collier Guardian*, 20 June, 1924.

McAuly, L., Russell, G., and Sims, J. (1997) Tacit knowledge for competitive advantage, *Management Accounting*, 75(11): 36–37.

McDermott, R., and O'Dell, C. (2001) Overcoming cultural barriers to sharing knowledge, *Journal of Knowledge Management*, 5(1): 76–85.

McDonald, C.J. (1998) The evolution of Intel's Copy EXACTLY!—technology transfer method, *Intel Technology Journal*, 4(1): 1–6.

McDonough III, E.F. (2000) Investigation of factors contributing to the success of cross-functional teams. *Journal of Product Innovation Management: An International Publication of the Product Development & Management Association*, 17(3): 221–35.

McEvily, B., Soda, G., and Tortoriello, M. (2014) More formally: Rediscovering the missing link between formal organization and informal social structure, *Academy of Management Annals*, 8(1): 299–345.

McEvily, S.K. and Chakravarthy, B. (2002) The persistence of knowledge-based advantage: an empirical test for product performance and technological knowledge, *Strategic Management Journal*, 23(4): 285–305.

McEvily, S.K., Das, S., and McCabe, K. (2000) Avoiding competence substitution through knowledge sharing, *Academy of Management Review*, 25(2): 294–311.

McEvoy, G.M. and Buller, P.F. (2013) Research for practice: The management of expatriates, *Thunderbird International Business Review*, 55(2): 213–26.

McGrath, J.E. and Argote, L. (2001) Group processes in organizational contexts, in M.A.

McPhee, R.D. and Poole, M.S. (2001) Organizational structures and configurations, in F.M. Jablin and L.L. Putnam (eds.), *The New Handbook of Organizational Communication: Advances in Theory, Research, and Methods*, Thousand Oaks, CA: Sage: 503–43

Melloan, G. (1988) An American views Japan's copycat culture, *The Wall Street Journal*, July 12: pp. 29.

Mennicken, A. (2008) Connecting worlds: the translation of international auditing standards into post-Soviet audit practices, *Accounting Organizations & Society*, 33(4–5): 384–414.

Meschi, P.X. and Métais, E. (2015) Too big to learn: The effects of major acquisition failures on subsequent acquisition divestment, *British Journal of Management*, 26(3): 408–23.

Meyer, J.W., Boli, J., Thomas, G.M., and Ramirez, F.O. (1997) World Society and the Nation State, *American Journal of Sociology*, 103: 144–81.

Meyer, J.W and Rowan, B. (1977) Institutionalized organizations: Formal structure as myth and ceremony, *American Journal of Sociology*, 83 (2): 340–63.

Meyer, R.E. and Höllerer, M.A. (2010) Meaning structures in a contested issue field: a topographic map of shareholder value in Austria, *Academy of Management Journal*, 53(6): 1241–62.

Michelotta, E.R. and Washington, M. (2013) Institutions and maintenance: the repair work of Italian professions, *Organization Studies*, 34(8): 1137–70.

Miles, R.E., and Snow, C.C. (1978) *Organization Strategy, Structure, and Process*, New York: McGraw-Hill.
Millán, C. and Bartrina, F. (2013) Introduction, in C. Millán and F. Bartrina (eds.), *The Routledge Handbook of Translation Studies*, London: Routledge: 1–6.
Milton, N. (2007) *Knowledge Acquisition in Practice: A Step-by-Step Guide*, London: Springer-Verlag.
Minbaeva, D., Pedersen, T., Björkman, I., Fey, C.F., and Park, H.J. (2014) MNC knowledge transfer, subsidiary absorptive capacity and HRM, *Journal of International Business Studies*, 45(1): 38–51.
Minbaeva, D.B. (2007) Knowledge transfer in multinational corporations, *Management International Review*, 47(4): 567–93.
Mintzberg, H. (1979) *The Structuring of Organizations*, Englewood Cliffs: Prentice-Hall.
Mintzberg, H. (1993) *Structure in fives: Designing Effective Organizations*, New Jersey: Prentice-Hall, Inc.
Mishra, A.K. and Mishra, K.E. (2013) The research on trust in leadership: The need for context. *Journal of Trust Research*, 3(1): 59–69.
Mitchell, J.H. (1933) The Worker's Point of View. XIII. The Mechanization of the Miner, *Human Factor*, 7: 139–50.
Mohamed, M., Stankosky, M., and Murray, A. (2004) Applying knowledge management principles to enhance cross-functional team performance, *Journal of Knowledge Management*, 8(3): 127–42.
Monstadt, J. and Schramm, S. (2017) Toward the networked city? Translating technological ideals and planning models in water and sanitation systems in Dar es Salaam, *International Journal of Urban and Regional Research*, 41(1): 104–25.
Moore, M.D. (2016) Durkheim's types of suicide and social capital: a cross-national comparison of 53 countries, *International Social Science Journal*, 66(219–220): 151–61.
Moreland, R.L., Argote, L., and Krishnan, R. (1996) Socially shared cognition at work: Transactive memory and group performance, in J. L. Nye and A. M. Brower (eds.), *What's So Social About Social Cognition? Social Cognition Research in Small Groups*, Thousand Oaks, CA: Sage: 57–84.
Morgan, G. (1980) Paradigms, metaphors, and puzzle solving in organization theory, *Administrative Science Quarterly*, 25(4): 605–22.
Morgan, G. (1986) *Images of Organization*, Beverly Hills, CA: SAGE Publications.
Morgan, G. (1989) *Creative Organization Theory: A Resourcebook*, Newbury Park, London: Sage.
Morris, T. and Lancaster, Z. (2006) Translating management ideas, *Organization Studies*, 27(2): 207–33.
Morris-Suzuki, T. (1994) *The Technological Transformation of Japan: From the Seventeenth to the Twenty-first Century*, Cambridge: Cambridge University Press.
Mortensen, N.M. (2020) The challenges of translating and implementing co-production in care services—A Danish case study, *Unpublished Ph.D. thesis*, Aalborg University.
Mosakowski, E. (1997) Strategy making under causal ambiguity: Conceptual issues and empirical evidence, *Organization Science*, 8(4): 414–42.
Mowat, C.L. (1963) *Britain Between the Wars: 1918–1940*, Abingdon, Oxon: Taylor & Francis.
Mowery, D.C., Oxley, J.E., and Silverman, B.S. (1996) Strategic alliances and interfirm knowledge transfer, *Strategic Management Journal*, 17(S2): 77–91.
Mueller, F. and Whittle, A. (2011) Translating management ideas: a discursive devices analysis, *Organization Studies*, 32(2): 187–210.
Mukhtarov, F. (2014) Rethinking the travel of ideas: policy translation in the water sector, *Policy & Politics*, 42(1): 71–88.

Munday, J. (2013) *Introducing Translation Studies: Theories and Applications*, London: Routledge.
Muniz Jr, J., Wintersberger, D., and Hong, J. L. (2022) Worker and manager judgments about factors that facilitate knowledge-sharing: Insights from a Brazilian automotive assembly line, *Knowledge and Process Management*, 29(2): 132–146.
Murphy, G.L. (1996) On metaphoric representation, *Cognition*, 60(2): 173–204.
Mustapha, H. (1998) Qur'an (Koran) translation, in M. Baker (ed.), *Routledge Encyclopedia of Translation Studies*, London: Routledge: 200–4.
Nabokov, V. (1955/1992) *Lolita*, London: Everyman's Library.
Nahapiet, J. and Ghoshal, S. (1998) Social capital, intellectual capital, and the organizational advantage. *Academy of Management Review*, 23(2): 242–66.
Naqshbandi, M. M., and Kamel, Y. (2017) Intervening role of realized absorptive capacity in organizational culture–open innovation relationship: Evidence from an emerging market, *Journal of General Management*, 42(3): 5–20.
Neef, D. (1997) *The Knowledge Economy*, Boston, MA: Butterworth-Heinemann.
Nehez, J., Blossing, U., Gyllander Torkildsen, L., Lander, R., and Olin, A. (2022) Middle leaders translating knowledge about improvement: Making change in the school and preschool organisation, *Journal of Educational Change*, 23(3): 315–41.
Nelson, D. (1974) Scientific management, systematic management, and labor, 1880–1915, *The Business History Review*, 48(4): 479–500.
Nelson, R., and Winter, S. (1982) *An Evolutionary Theory of Economic Change*, Cambridge, MA: Belknap Press.
Neubert, A. (2000) Competence in language, in languages, and in translation, *Benjamins Translation Library*, in C. Schäffner and B. Adab (eds.), *Developing Translation Competence*, Amsterdam: John Benjamins: 3–18.
Nicolai, A. and Seidl, D. (2010) That's relevant! Different forms of practical relevance in management science, *Organization Studies*, 31(9–10): 1257–85.
Nicolini, D. (2010) Medical innovation as a process of translation: A case from the field of telemedicine, *British Journal of Management*, 21(4): 1011–26.
Nicolini, D., Lippi, A., and Monteiro, P. (2019) Systematic Heterogeneity in the Adaptation Process of Management Innovations, in T. Reay, A. Langley, and H. Tsoukas (eds.), *Institutions and Organizations: A Process View*, Oxford: Oxford University Press: 194–226.
Nida, E. A. (1964) *Toward a Science of Translating: With Special Reference to Principles and Procedures Involved in Bible Translating*, Leiden: E.J. Brill Archive.
Nielsen, J. A., Mathiassen, L., and Newell, S. (2022) Multidirectional idea travelling across an organizational field, *Organization Studies*, 43(6): 931–52.
Nielsen, J.A., Wæraas, A., and Dahl, K. (2020) When management concepts enter the public sector: a dual-level translation perspective, *Public Management Review*, 22(2): 234–54.
Nieves, J. and Osorio, J. (2013) The role of social networks in knowledge creation, *Knowledge Management Research & Practice*, 11(1): 62–77.
Nilsen, E. A. and Sandaunet, A. G. (2020) Implementing new practice: The roles of translation, progression and reflection, *Journal of Change Management*, 21(3): 307–32.
Nohria, N., Eccles, R.G., and Press, H.B. (1992) *Networks and Organizations: Structure, Form, and Action*, Boston, MA: Harvard Business School Press.
Nonaka, I., Byosiere, P., Borucki, C.C., and Konno, N. (1994) Organizational knowledge creation theory: a first comprehensive test, *International Business Review*, 3(4): 337–51.
Nonaka, I. and Reinmoeller, P. (2002) Knowledge Creation and Utilization: Promoting Dynamic Systems of Creative Routines, in M.A. Hitt, R. Amit, C.E. Lucier, and R.D. Nixon (eds.), *Creating Value: Winners in the New Business Environment*, Oxford: Blackwell, 104–27.

Nonaka, I. and Takeuchi, H. (1995) *The Knowledge-Creating Company: How Japanese Companies Create the Dynamics of Innovation*, Oxford UK: Oxford University Press.

Nonaka, I., Von Krogh, G., and Voelpel, S. (2006) Organizational knowledge creation theory: Evolutionary paths and future advances, *Organization Studies*, 27(8): 1179–208.

Norman, P.M. (2002) Protecting knowledge in strategic alliances: Resource and relational characteristics, *The Journal of High Technology Management Research*, 13(2): 177–202.

North, D.C. (1990) *Institutions, Institutional Change and Economic Performance*, Cambridge: Cambridge University Press.

Novak, J.D. and Gowin, D.B. (1984) *Learning How to Learn*, New York: Cambridge University Press.

Novak, W.L. (1986) *Iacocca: An Autobiography*, New York: Bantam Books.

Nygård, E.R. and Ingebrigtsen, K.S. (2019) *Tørrfiskmarkedet i Italia–et tradisjonelt marked i endring. En studie av tørrfiskhandelen mellom Norge og Italia: relasjoner, verdi og posisjonering* (The Italian stockfish market—a traditional market in change. A study of the stockfish trade between Norway and Italy: relationships, values and positioning), Bodø: Master's thesis, Nord Universitet.

O'Dell, C. and Grayson, C. J. (1998) If only we knew what we know: Identification and transfer of internal best practices, *California Management Review*, 40(3): 154–74.

O'Loughlin, J., Ward, M.D., Lofdahl, C.L., Cohen, J.S., Brown, D.S., Reilly, D., and Shin, M. (1998) The diffusion of democracy, 1946-1994, *Annals of the Association of American Geographers*, 88(4): 545–74.

O'Shea, J.E. and Madigan, C. (1997) *Dangerous Company: The Consulting Powerhouses and the Businesses They Save and Ruin*, New York: Times Business.

O'Sullivan, E. (2017) Children's literature and translation studies, in C. Millán and F. Bartrina (eds.), *The Routledge Handbook of Translation Studies*, Abingdon, Oxon: Routledge: 451–62.

Oakley, A., Gough, D., Oliver, S., and Thomas, J. (2005) The politics of evidence and methodology: lessons from the EPPI-Centre, *Evidence & Policy: A Journal of Research, Debate and Practice*, 1(1): 5–32.

Ober, J. (2008) *Democracy and knowledge: Innovation and Learning in Classical Athens*, Princeton, NJ: Princeton University Press.

Oddou, G., Szkudlarek, B., Osland, J.S., Deller, J., Blakeney, R., and Furuya, N. (2013) Repatriates as a Source of Competitive Advantage: How to manage knowledge transfer, *Organizational Dynamics*, 42(4): 257–66.

Ojo, O. (2009) Impact assessment of corporate culture on employee job performance, *Business Intelligence Journal*, 2(2): 388–97.

Okafor, E. and Osuagwu, C.H. (2006) The Underlying Issues in Knowledge Elicitation, *Journal of Information, Knowledge, and Management*, 1: 96–108.

Olie, R. (1994) Shades of culture and institutions-in international mergers, *Organization Studies*, 15(3): 381–405.

Olivera, F. (2000) Memory systems in organizations: an empirical investigation of mechanisms for knowledge collection, storage and access, *Journal of Management Studies*, 37(6): 811–32.

Olohan, M. (2017) Scientific and technical translation, in C. Millán and F. Bartrina (eds.), *The Routledge Handbook of Translation Studies*, Abingdon, Oxon: Routledge, 425–37.

Olsen, J.P. (2002) The many faces of Europeanization, *JCMS: Journal of Common Market Studies*, 40(5): 921–52.

Olsen, J.P. (2010) *Governing through institution building: institutional theory and recent European experiments in democratic organization*, Oxford: Oxford University Press.

Ordanini, A., Rubera, G., and DeFillippi, R. (2008) The many moods of inter-organizational imitation: A critical review, *International Journal of Management Reviews*, 10(4): 375–98.

Ortiz, B., Donate, M.J., and Guadamillas, F. (2021) Intra-organizational social capital and product innovation: the mediating role of realized absorptive capacity, *Frontiers in Psychology*, 11: 38–59.

Ortony, A. (1979a) Beyond literal similarity, *Psychological Review*, 86(3): 161–80.

Ortony, A. (1979b) The role of similarity in similes and metaphors, in A. Ortony (ed.), *Metaphor and Thought*, Cambridge: Cambridge University Press: 186–201.

Osborne, S. (2010) The (new) public governance: A suitable case for treatment? in S. Osborne (ed.), *The New Public Governance*, Abingdon, Oxon: Routledge: 1–16.

Ostroff, F. (1999) *The horizontal organization: What the organization of the future actually looks like and how it delivers value to customers*, New York: Oxford University Press.

Ostrom, E. (1990) *Governing the Commons: The Evolution of Institutions for Collective Action*, Cambridge: Cambridge University Press.

Oswick, C., Fleming, P., and Hanlon, G. (2011) From borrowing to blending: Rethinking the processes of organizational theory building, *Academy of Management Review*, 36(2): 318–37.

Oswick, C., Keenoy, T., and Grant, D. (2001) Dramatizing and organizing: Acting and being, *Journal of Organizational Change Management*, 14(3): 218–24.

Oswick, C., Keenoy, T., and Grant, D. (2002) Note: Metaphor and analogical reasoning in organization theory: Beyond orthodoxy, *Academy of Management Review*, 27(2): 294–303.

Otley, D. (1999) Performance management: a framework for management control systems research, *Management Accounting Research*, 10(4): 363–82.

Ouchi, W.G. (1981) *Theory Z: How American Management Can Meet the Japanese Challenge*, New York: Addison-Wesley.

Ouchi, W. G. (2006) Power to the principals: Decentralization in three large school districts, *Organization Science*, 17(2): 298–307.

Øverås, L. (1998) In search of the third code: An investigation of norms in literary translation. *Journal des Traducteurs/Meta: Translators' Journal*, 43(4): 557–70.

Owen-Smith, J., and Powell, W. W. (2004) Knowledge networks as channels and conduits: The effects of spillovers in the Boston biotechnology community, *Organization science*, 15(1): 5–21.

Oyemomi, O., Liu, S., Neaga, I., and Alkhuraiji, A. (2016) How knowledge sharing and business process contribute to organizational performance: Using the fsQCA approach, *Journal of Business Research*, 69(11): 5222–27.

Özen, Ş. and Berkman, Ü. (2007) Cross-national reconstruction of managerial practices: TQM in Turkey, *Organization Studies*, 28(6): 825–51.

Packard, D., Kirby, D., and Lewis, K.R. (1995) *The HP way: How Bill Hewlett and I built our Company*, New York: Harper Business.

Page, L. (2019) Goodbye, shanzhai: Intellectual property rights and the end of copycat China, *University of Western Australia Law Review*, 45(1): 185–95.

Pallas, J., Fredriksson, M., and Wedlin, L. (2016) Translating institutional logics: When the media logic meets professions, *Organization Studies*, 37(11): 1661–84.

Pang, L. (2008) China Who Makes and Fakes: A Semiotics of the Counterfeit, *Theory, Culture & Society*, 25(6): 117–40.

Paradis, M. (2004) *A Neurolinguistic Theory of Bilingualism*, Amsterdam: John Benjamins Publishing.

Parasuraman, A., Berry, L.L., and Zeithaml, V.A. (1993) More on improving service quality measurement, *Journal of Retailing*, 69(1): 140–8.

Parks, R.B., Baker, P.C., Kiser, L., Oakerson, R., Ostrom, E., Ostrom, V. and Wilson, R. (1981) Consumers as coproducers of public services: Some economic and institutional considerations, *Policy Studies Journal*, 9(7): 1001–11.

References

Parsons, T. (1951) *The Social System*, New York: The Free press.

Pascale, R.T. and Athos, A.G. (1981) The art of Japanese management, *Business Horizons*, 24(6): 83–5.

Patel, P.C., Kohtamäki, M., Parida, V., and Wincent, J. (2015) Entrepreneurial orientation-as-experimentation and firm performance: The enabling role of absorptive capacity. *Strategic Management Journal*, 36(11): 1739–49.

Patterson, T. and Harms, P. (2019) "That's Interesting! Or is it? On the Incommensurability of Academic and Practitioner Interests, *Academy of Management Proceedings* 1: Published online https://journals.aom.org/doi/abs/10.5465/AMBPP.2019.276

Paulin, D. and Suneson, K. (2015) Knowledge transfer, knowledge sharing and knowledge barriers—three blurry terms in KM, *Leading Issues in Knowledge Management* 2(2): 78–92.

Pavlou, P.A., and El Sawy, O.A. (2006) From IT leveraging competence to competitive advantage in turbulent environments: The case of new product development, *Information Systems Research*, 17(3): 198–227.

Peal, E. and Lambert, W.E. (1962) The relation of bilingualism to intelligence, *Psychological Monographs: General and Applied*, 76(27): 1–23.

Pearson, B.Z., and Fernández, S.C. (1994) Patterns of interaction in the lexical growth in two languages of bilingual infants and toddlers, *Language Learning*, 44(4): 617–53.

Peltokorpi, V., Froese, F.J., Reiche, B.S., and Klar, S. (2022) Reverse knowledge flows: How and when do preparation and reintegration facilitate repatriate knowledge transfer?, *Journal of Management Studies*. doi:10.1111/joms.12802

Peng, M.W., Ahlstrom, D., Carraher, S.M., and Shi, W.S. (2017) History and the debate over intellectual property, *Management and Organization Review*, 13(1): 15–38.

Penn, R. and Simpson, R. (1986) The development of skilled work in the British coal mining industry, 1870–1985, *Industrial Relations Journal*, 17(4): 339–49.

Perry-Smith, J. and Mannucci, P.V. (2015) 12 social networks, creativity, and entrepreneurship, in C.E. Shalley, M. Hitt, and J. Zhou (eds.), *The Oxford Handbook of Creativity, Innovation, and Entrepreneurship*, Oxford: Oxford University Press: 205–24.

Pertusa-Ortega, E.M., Zaragoza-Sáez, P., and Claver-Cortés, E. (2010) Can formalization, complexity, and centralization influence knowledge performance?, *Journal of Business Research*, 63(3): 310–20.

Pertusa-Ortega, E. M., Molina-Azorín, J. F., and Claver-Cortés, E. (2009) Competitive strategies and firm performance: A comparative analysis of pure, hybrid and 'stuck-in-the-middle'strategies in Spanish firms, *British Journal of Management*, 20(4): 508–23.

Pescosolido, B.A. and Levy, J. (2002) The role of social networks in health, illness, disease and healing: The accepting present, the forgotten past, and the dangerous potential for a complacent future, in J.A. Levy and B.A. Pescosolido (eds.) *Social Networks and Health*. New York: JAI: 3–28.

Pestoff, V. (2012) Co-production and third sector social services in Europe: Some concepts and evidence, *Voluntas: International Journal of Voluntary and Nonprofit Organizations*, 23(4): 1102–18.

Peteraf, M.A. (1993) The cornerstones of competitive advantage: a resource-based view. *Strategic Management Journal*, 14(3): 179–91.

Phelps, C., Heidl, R., and Wadhwa, A. (2012) Knowledge, networks, and knowledge networks: A review and research agenda. *Journal of Management*, 38(4): 1115–66.

Phillips, G.A. (1976) *The General Strike: The Politics of Industrial Conflict*, London: Weidenfeld and Nicolson.

Piazza, A. and Abrahamson, E. (2020) Fads and fashions in management practices: Taking stock and looking forward, *International Journal of Management Reviews*, 22(3): 264–86.

Pickering, J. and Attridge, S. (1990) Viewpoints: Metaphor and Monsters: Children's Storytelling, *Research in the Teaching of English*, 24(4): 415–40.
Pierce, J.R. (2012) *An Introduction to Information Theory: Symbols, Signals and Noise*, New York: Dover Publications.
Pil, F.K. and MacDuffie, J.P. (1999) Transferring competitive advantage across borders: a study of Japanese auto transplants in North America, in J.K. Liker, W.M. Fruin, and P.S. Adler (eds.), *Remade in America: Transplanting and Transforming Japanese Management Systems*. Oxford, UK: Oxford University Press: 39–74.
Pinch, S., Henry, N., Jenkins, M., and Tallman, S. (2003) From "industrial districts" to "knowledge clusters": a model of knowledge dissemination and competitive advantage in industrial agglomerations, *Journal of Economic Geography*, 3(4): 373–88.
Podolny, J.M. (2009) The buck stops (and starts) at business school, *Harvard Business Review*, 87(6): 62–7.
Podolny, J.M. and Page, K.L. (1998) Network forms of organization, *Annual Review of Sociology*, 24(1): 57–76.
Polanyi, K. (1944) *The Great Transformation*, Boston, MA: Beacon Press.
Polanyi, M. (1958) *Personal Knowledge. Towards a Post Critical Philosophy*, London: Routledge.
Polanyi, M. (1962) Tacit knowing: Its bearing on some problems of philosophy, *Reviews of Modern Physics*, 34(4): 601–16.
Polanyi, M. (1967) *The Tacit Dimension*, New York: Anchor Books.
Polizzotti, M. (2018) *Sympathy for the Traitor: A Translation Manifesto*, Cambridge, MA: MIT Press.
Poole, F.J.P. (1986) Metaphors and maps: Towards comparison in the anthropology of religion, *Journal of the American Academy of Religion*, 54(3): 411–57.
Popper, K.R. (1959) *The Logic of Scientific Discovery*, New York: Science.
Porter, M.E. (1980) *Competitive Strategy: Techniques for Analyzing Industries and Competitors*, New York: The Free Press.
Porter, M.E. (1990) *The Competitive Advantage of Nation*, New York: Free Press.
Posen, H.E. and Martignoni, D. (2018) Revisiting the imitation assumption: Why imitation may increase, rather than decrease performance heterogeneity, *Strategic Management Journal*, 39(5): 1350–69.
Posner, R.A. (1981) The economics of privacy, *The American Economic Review*, 71(2): 405–9.
Postrel, S. (2002) Islands of shared knowledge: Specialization and mutual understanding in problem-solving teams, *Organization Science*, 13(3): 303–20.
Powell, W.W. (1998) Learning from collaboration: Knowledge and networks in the biotechnology and pharmaceutical industries. *California Management Review*, 40(3): 228–40.
Powell, W.W. and Brantley, P. (1992) Competitive cooperation in biotechnology: Learning through networks? in N. Nohria and R. Eccles (eds.), *Networks and Organizations*, Boston, MA: Harvard Business School Press: 366–94.
Powell, W.W., Gammal, D.L., and Simard, C. (2005) Close encounters: The circulation of reception of managerial practices in the San Francisco bay area nonprofit community, in B. Czarniawska and G. Sevón (eds.), *Global Ideas. How Ideas, Objects and Practices Travel in the Global Economy*, Malmö: Liber & Copenhagen Business School Press, 233–58.
Powell, W.W., Koput, K.W., and Smith-Doerr, L. (1996) Interorganizational collaboration and the locus of innovation: Networks of learning in biotechnology, *Administrative Science Quarterly*, 41(1): 116–45.
Powell, W.W. and Snellman, K. (2004) The knowledge economy, *Annual Review Sociology*, 30(1): 199–220.

Presas, M. (2000) Bilingual competence and translation competence, in C. Schäffner and B. Adab (eds.), *Developing Translation Competence*, Amsterdam: John Benjamins: 19–31.

Pressman, J.L. and Wildavsky, A. (1973) *Implementation: How Great Expectations in Washington are Dashed in Oakland; Or, Why It's Amazing That Federal Programs Work at All*, Berkeley, CA: University of California Press.

Price, C.J., Green, D.W., and Von Studnitz, R. (1999) A functional imaging study of translation and language switching, *Brain*, 122(12): 2221–35.

Priem, R.L. and Butler, J.E. (2001) Tautology in the resource-based view and the implications of externally determined resource value: Further comments, *Academy of Management Review*, 26(1): 57–66.

Probst, G. and Borzillo, S. (2008) Why communities of practice succeed and why they fail, *European Management Journal*, 26(5): 335–47.

Provan, K.G., Fish, A., and Sydow, J. (2007) Interorganizational networks at the network level: A review of the empirical literature on whole networks, *Journal of Management*, 33(3): 479–516.

Prusak, L. (1997) *Knowledge in Organizations*, Boston, MA: Butterworth-Heineman.

Pugh, D.S., Hickson, D.J., Hinings, C.R., and Turner, C. (1968) Dimensions of organization structure, *Administrative Science Quarterly*, 13(1): 65–105.

Puhakka, V. (2006) Effects of social capital on the opportunity recognition process, *Journal of Enterprising Culture*, 14(02): 105–24.

Putnam, R.D. (1993) *Making democracy work:Civic traditions in modern Italy*, Princeton: Princeton University Press.

Pym, A. (1992) The relations between translation and material transfer, *Target*, 4(2): 171–89.

Pym, A. (2004) *The Moving Text: Localization, Translation, and Distribution*, Amsterdam: John Benjamins Publishing.

Pym, A. (2015) Translating as risk management, *Journal of Pragmatics*, 85: 67–80.

Pym, A. (2017) *Exploring Translation Theories*, London: Routledge.

Pym, A. and Turk, H. (1998) Translatability, in M. Baker (ed.), *Routledge Encyclopedia of Translation Studies*, London: Routledge: 273–76.

Pyun, H.O. and Lallemand, A.S. (2014) To reform the public administration, is it an impossible mission? Case study of French public administration reforms since 1980s, *Gestion et Management Public*, 3(3): 75–88.

Radaelli, G. and Sitton-Kent, L. (2016) Middle managers and the translation of new ideas in organizations: A review of micro-practices and contingencies, *International Journal of Management Reviews*, 18(3): 311–32.

Ranson, S., Hinings, B., and Greenwood, R. (1980) The structuring of organizational structures, *Administrative Science Quarterly*, 25(1): 1–17.

Rao, H. and Drazin, R. (2002) Overcoming resource constraints on product innovation by recruiting talent from rivals: A study of the mutual fund industry, 1986–1994, *Academy of management Journal*, 45(3): 491–507.

Rashman, L., Withers, E., and Hartley, J. (2009) Organizational learning and knowledge in public service organizations: A systematic review of the literature, *International Journal of Management Reviews*, 11(4): 463–94.

Raud, R. (2007) An investigation of the conditions of literary borrowings in late Heian and early Kamakura Japan, in R. Cox (ed.), *The Culture of Copying in Japan—Critical and Historical Perspectives*, New York: Routledge: 155–67.

Readence, J.E., Baldwin, R.S., Martin, M.A., and O'Brien, D.G. (1984) Metaphorical interpretation: An investigation of the salience imbalance hypothesis, *Journal of Educational Psychology*, 76(4): 659–67.

Reagans, R. and McEvily, B. (2003) Network structure and knowledge transfer: The effects of cohesion and range, *Administrative Science Quarterly*, 48(2): 240–67.

Reay, T., Berta, W., and Kohn, M. K. (2009) What's the evidence on evidence-based management?, *Academy of Management Perspectives*, 23(4): 5–18.

Reay, T., Chreim, S., Golden-Biddle, K., Goodrick, E., Williams, B. E., Casebeer, A., and Hinings, C. R. (2013) Transforming new ideas into practice: An activity based perspective on the institutionalization of practices, *Journal of Management Studies*, 50(6): 963–90.

Reay, T., Golden-Biddle, K., and Germann, K. (2006) Legitimizing a new role: Small wins and microprocesses of change, *Academy of Management Journal*, 49(5): 977–98.

Reed, R. and DeFillippi, R.J. (1990) Causal ambiguity, barriers to imitation, and sustainable competitive advantage, *Academy of Management Review*, 15(1): 88–102.

Reiche, B.S. (2012) Knowledge benefits of social capital upon repatriation: A longitudinal study of international assignees, *Journal of Management Studies*, 49(6): 1052–77.

Reinhold, S., Beritelli, P., and Grünig, R. (2019) A business model typology for destination management organizations, *Tourism Review*, 74(6): 1135–52.

Reiss, K. and Vermeer, H.J. (1984) *Grundlegung einer allgemeinen Translationstheorie*, Tübingen: Niemeyer.

Ren, M. (2019) Why technology adoption succeeds or fails: an exploration from the perspective of intra-organizational legitimacy, *The Journal of Chinese Sociology*, 6(1): 1–26.

Richards, I.A. (1937) *Interpretation in Teaching*, London: Kegan Paul, Trench Trubner.

Riege, A. (2005) Three-dozen knowledge-sharing barriers managers must consider, *Journal of Knowledge Management*, 9(3): 18–35.

Riege, A. (2007) Actions to overcome knowledge transfer barriers in MNCs, *Journal of Knowledge Management*, 11(1): 48–67.

Riggs, W. and Von Hippel, E. (1994) Incentives to innovate and the sources of innovation: the case of scientific instruments, *Research Policy*, 23(4): 459–70.

Ring, P.S. and Van de Ven, A.H. (1994) Developmental processes of cooperative interorganizational relationships. *Academy of Management Review*, 19(1): 90–118.

Ringberg, T.V., Luna, D., Reihlen, M., and Peracchio, L.A. (2010) Bicultural-bilinguals: The effect of cultural frame switching on translation equivalence, *International Journal of Cross Cultural Management*, 10(1): 77–92.

Ringov, D.P., Liu, H., Jensen, R., and Szulanski, G. (2017) Adaptation and Unit Performance in Replicating Organizations, *Academy of Management Proceedings*, 1, p. 12258.

Riusala, K. and Smale, A. (2007) Predicting stickiness factors in the international transfer of knowledge through expatriates, *International Studies of Management & Organization*, 37(3): 16–43.

Rivkin, J.W. (2001) Reproducing knowledge: Replication without imitation at moderate complexity. *Organization Science*, 12(3): 274–93.

Roberts, N., Galluch, P. S., Dinger, M., and Grover, V. (2012) Absorptive capacity and information systems research: Review, synthesis, and directions for future research, *MIS Quarterly*, 36(2): 625–48.

Robinson, D. (1998a) Metaphrase, in M. Baker (ed.), *Routledge Encyclopedia of Translation Studies*, London: Routledge: 153–54.

Robinson, D. (1998b) Imitation, in M. Baker (ed.), *Routledge Encyclopedia of Translation Studies*, London: Routledge: 111–12.

Rosenstone, R. A. (1980) Learning from those "imitative" Japanese: Another side of the American experience in the Mikado's Empire, *The American Historical Review*, 85(3): 572–95.

Rosiello, A., Mastroeni, M., Castle, D., and Phillips, P.W. (2015) Clusters, technological districts and smart specialization: An empirical analysis of policy implementation challenges, *International Journal of Entrepreneurship and Innovation Management*, 19(5–6): 304–26.

Rothe-Neves, R. (2007) Notes on the concept of translator's competence, *Quaderns: Revista de Traducció*, 14: 125–38.

Rottenburg, R. (1996) When organizations travel: On intercultural translation, in B. Czarniawska and G. Sevón (eds.), *Translating Organizational Change*, Berlin: Walter de Gruyter: 191–240.

Rousseau, D.M. and McCarthy, S. (2007) Educating managers from an evidence-based perspective, *Academy of Management Learning & Education*, 6(1): 84–101.

Rouyre, A. and Fernandez, A.S. (2019) Managing knowledge sharing-protecting tensions in coupled innovation projects among several competitors, *California Management Review*, 62(1): 95–120.

Røvik, K.A. (1996) Deinstitutionalization and the logic of fashion, in B. Czarniawska and G. Sevón (eds.), *Translating Organizational Change*, Berlin: Walter de Gruyter: 139–72.

Røvik, K.A. (1998) *Moderne organisasjoner: Trender I Organisasjonsstenkningen ved Tusenårsskiftet* (Modern organizations: Trends in Organizational Thinking by the Millennium Turn), Bergen: Fagbokforlaget.

Røvik, K.A. (2002) The secrets of the winners: Management ideas that flow, in K. Sahlin-Andersson and L. Engwall (eds.), *The Expansion of Management Knowledge: Carriers, Ideas and Sources*, Stanford, CA, Stanford University Press: 113–44.

Røvik, K.A. (2014) *Reformideer og deres tornefulle vei inn i skolefeltet* (Circulating reform ideas and their paths to the educational field, in K.A. Røvik, T.V. Eilertsen and E. Moksnes Furu (eds.), *Reformideer i norsk skole* (Reform ideas in the Norwegian educational system), Oslo: Cappelen Damm Akademisk.

Røvik, K.A. (2007) *Trender og Translasjoner: Ideer som Former det 21. århundrets Organisasjon* (Trends and Translations: Ideas that Shape 21st-Century Organizations), Oslo: Universitetsforlaget.

Røvik, K.A. (2011) From fashion to virus: An alternative theory of organizations' handling of management ideas, *Organization Studies* 32(5): 631–53.

Røvik, K.A. (2012) Organisasjonsendring som organisasjonsgjøring (Organizational change as constructing organizations), *Magma*, 15(0812): 49–58.

Røvik, K.A. (2014) Translasjon - en alternativ doktrine for implementering, trans: Translation - an alternative implementation doctrine, in Røvik, K.A., Eilertsen, T.V., and Moksens Furu, E. (Eds.), *Reformideer i Norsk Skole* (trans: *Reform Ideas in the Norwegian Educational System*), 403–16, Oslo: Cappelen Damm Akademisk.

Røvik, K.A. (2016) Knowledge Transfer as Translation: Review and Elements of an Instrumental Theory, *International Journal of Management Reviews*, 18(3): 290–310.

Røvik, K.A. (2019) Instrumental understanding of management ideas, in A. Sturdy, S. Heusinkveld, T. Reay, and D. Strang (eds.), *The Oxford Handbook of Management Ideas*, Oxford: Oxford University Press: 120–38.

Røvik, K.A., Blindheim, B.T., and Klemsdal, L. (2021) Organisasjonsdesign som kompleks økologi (Organizational design as complex ecology), in B.T. Blindheim, L. Klemsdal, and K.A. Røvik (eds.), *Design av organisasjon* (Design of rganization), Oslo: Universitetsforlaget, 241–49.

Røvik, K.A. and Pettersen, H. (2014) Masterideer (Master-ideas), in K.A. Røvik, T.V. Eilertsen, and E. Mokses Furu (eds.), *Reformideer i Norsk Skole: Spredning, oversettelse og implementering* (Reform ideas in the Norwegian School Sector: Diffusion, translation and implementation), Oslo: Cappelen Damm: 53–86.

Rubel, P.G., and Rosman, A. (2003) *Translating Cultures: Perspectives on Translation and Anthropology*, London: Berg.

Ryle, G. (1945) Knowing how and knowing that: The presidential address, *Proceedings of the Aristotelian Society*, 46: 1–16.

Rynes, S.L. Bartunek, J.M., and Daft, R.L. (2001) Across the great divide: Knowledge creation and transfer between practitioners and academics, *Academy of Management Journal*, 44(2): 340–55.

Sackett, P.R. and Larson, J.R. (1990) Research strategies and tactics in industrial and organizational psychology, in M.D. Dunnette and L.M. Hough (eds.), *Handbook of Industrial and Organizational Psychology*, Palo Alto, CA: Consulting Psychologists Press: 419–89.

Sahlin, K. and Wedlin, L. (2008) Circulating ideas: Imitation, translation and editing, in R. Greenwood, C. Oliver, K. Sahlin, and R. Suddaby (eds.), *The SAGE Handbook of Organizational Institutionalism*, Los Angeles/London: Sage: 218–42.

Sahlin-Andersson, K. (1996) Imitation by editing success: the construction of organizational fields, in B. Czarniawska and G. Sevón (eds.), *Translating Organizational Change*, Berlin: Walter de Gruyter, 69–92.

Sahlin-Andersson, K. and Engwall, L. (2002) Carriers, flows and sources of management knowledge, in K. Sahlin-Andersson, and L. Engwall (eds.), *The Expansion of Management Knowledge—Carriers, flows, and Sources*, Stanford, CA: Stanford University Press: 3–32.

Saka, A. (2004) The cross-national diffusion of work systems: Translation of Japanese operations in the UK, *Organization Studies*, 25(2): 209–28.

Sakhdari, K. (2016) Absorptive capacity: review and research agenda, *Journal of Organisational Studies and Innovation*, 3(1): 34–50.

Salama-Carr, M. (1998) French tradition, in M. Baker (ed.), *Routledge Encyclopedia of Translation Studies*, London: Routledge: 409–17.

Sandberg, J. and Alvesson, M. (2021) Meanings of theory: Clarifying theory through typification, *Journal of Management Studies*, 58(2): 487–516.

Santoro, G., Vrontis, D., and Pastore, A. (2017) External knowledge sourcing and new product development: evidence from the Italian food and beverage industry, *British Food Journal*, 119 (11): 2373–87.

Santoro, M.D., and Bierly, P. (2006) Facilitators of knowledge transfer in university-industry collaborations: A knowledge-based perspective, *IEEE Transactions on Engineering Management* 53 (4): 495–507.

Sanwal, A. (2008) The myth of best practices, *Journal of Corporate Accounting & Finance*, 19(5): 51–60.

Sapir, E. (1929) /1949) The status of linguistics as a science. Reprinted, in *Selected Writings of Edward Sapir in Language, Culture, and Personality*, Berkeley and Los Angeles: University of California Press.

Schäffner, C. (1998) Skopos theory, in M. Baker (ed.), *Routledge Encyclopedia of Translation Studies*, London: Routledge: 235–38.

Schäffner, C. and Adab, B. (2000) *Developing Translation Competence*, Amsterdam: John Benjamins Publishing.

Schein, E.H. (1970) *Occupational Socialization in the Professions: The Case of Role Innovation*, Cambridge, MA: MIT.

Schein, E.H. (1985) Defining organizational culture, in J.M. Shafritz, J.S. Ott, and Y.S. Jang (eds.), *Classics of Organization Theory*, Belmont, CA: Thomson Wadsworth: 360–7.

Schein, E.H. (1990) Organizational culture, *American Psychological Association*, 45(2): 109–19.

Schein, E.H. (2010) *Organizational Culture and Leadership*, New York: John Wiley & Sons.

Scheuer, JD. (2006) Om oversættelse af oversættelsesbegrepet—en analyse af de skandinaviske ny-institutionalisters oversættelse af oversættelsesbegrepet, *Nordiske Organisasjonsstudier* (NOS), 4: 3–40.

Scheuer, J. D. (2021) *How Ideas Move: Theories and Models of Translation in Organizations*, London: Routledge.

Schilling, J. and Kluge, A. (2009) Barriers to organizational learning: An integration of theory and research, *International Journal of Management Reviews*, 11(3): 337–60.

Schlosser, E. (2001) *Fast food Nation: The Dark Side of the All-American Meal*, Boston, MA: Houghton Mifflin Harcourt.

Schminke, M. Ambrose, M.L., and Cropanzano, R.S. (2000) The effect of organizational structure on perceptions of procedural fairness, *Journal of Applied Psychology*, 85(2): 294–304.

Schmitt, A., Borzillo, S., and Probst, G. (2012) Don't let knowledge walk away: Knowledge retention during employee downsizing, *Management Learning*, 43(1): 53–74.

Schraeder, P.J. (2003) The state of the art in international democracy promotion: Results of a joint European-North American research network, *Democratization*, 10(2): 21–44.

Schumpeter, J.A. (1934) *The Theory of Economic Development*, London: Oxford University Press.

Schuster, M.A., McGlynn, E.A., and Brook, R.H. (1998) How good is the quality of health care in the United States? *The Milbank Quarterly*, 76(4): 517–63.

Schutz, A. (1962) Concept and theory formation in the social sciences, in A. Schutz: *Collected papers I*, Springer, Dordrecht: 48–66.

Schwartz, H. (1996) *The Culture of the Copy: Striking Likenesses, Unreasonable Facsimiles*, New York: Zone Books.

Scotchmer, S. (2004) *Innovation and Incentives*, Cambridge, MA: MIT Press.

Scott, W.R. (1987) The adolescence of institutional theory, *Administrative Science Quarterly*, 32(4): 493–511.

Scott, W.R. (1995) *Institutions and Organizations*. Thousand Oaks, CA, Sage.

Scott, W.R. and Davis, G.F. (2003) Networks in and Around Organization – Organizations and Organizing, New Jersey: Pearson Prentice Hall.

Seidler-de Alwis, R. and Hartmann, E. (2008) The use of tacit knowledge within innovative companies: knowledge management in innovative enterprises, *Journal of Knowledge Management*, 12 (1): 133–47.

Seleskovitch, D. (1978a) Language and cognition, in D. Gerver (ed.), *Language Interpretation and Communication*, Boston, MA: Springer: 333–41.

Seleskovitch, D. (1978b) *Interpreting for International Conferences*, Washington, DC: Pen and Booth.

Selmer, J., Chiu, R. K., and Shenkar, O. (2007) Cultural distance asymmetry in expatriate adjustment, *Cross Cultural Management: An International Journal*, 14(2): 150–60.

Selznick, P. (1949) *TVA and the Grass Roots*, Berkeley: University of California Press.

Serres, M. (1974/1982) *Hermes: Literature, Science, Philosophy*, Baltimore, MD: John Hopkins University Press.

Sevón, G. (1996) Organizational imitation in identity transformation, in B. Czarniawska and G. Sevón (eds.), *Translating Organizational Change*, Berlin: Walter de Gruyter: 49–67.

Shanon, B. (1992) Metaphor: From fixedness and selection to differentiation and creation. *Poetics Today*, 13: 659–85.

Shannon, C.E. (1948) A Mathematical Theory of Communication, *Bell System Technical Journal*, 27(4): 623–66.

Shannon, C.E. and Weaver, W. (1949) *The Mathematical Theory of Communication*, Urbana, IL: University of Illinois Press.

Sharma, G. and Bansal, P. (2020) Cocreating rigorous and relevant knowledge, *Academy of Management Journal*, 63(2): 386–410.

Shenhav, Y. (1999) *Manufacturing Rationality: The Engineering Foundations of the Managerial Revolution*, New York: Oxford University Press.

Shenkar, O., Tallman, S. B., Wang, H., and Wu, J. (2020) National culture and international business: A path forward, *Journal of International Business Studies*, 51 (8):1–18.

Shenkar, O. (2010) *Copycats: How Smart Companies Use Imitation to Gain a Strategic Edge*, Boston, MA: Harvard Business School Press.

Shenkar, O. (2001) Cultural distance revisited: Towards a more rigorous conceptualization and measurement of cultural differences. *Journal of International Business Studies*, 32(3): 519–35.

Shenkar, O., Luo, Y., and Yeheskel, O. (2008) From "distance" to "friction": Substituting metaphors and redirecting intercultural research, *Academy of Management Review*: 33(4): 905–23.

Shepherd, D. A., and Suddaby, R. (2017) Theory building: A review and integration, *Journal of Management*, 43(1): 59–86.

Sherman, L.W. (2009) Evidence and liberty: The promise of experimental criminology, *Criminology & Criminal Justice*, 9(1): 5–28.

Shils, E.A. and Finch, H.A. (1997) *The Methodology of the Social Sciences*, New York: Free Press.

Shreve, G.M. (2012) Bilingualism and translation, in Y. Gambier, and L. van Doorslaer (eds.), *Handbook of Translation*, Amsterdam: Benjamins: 1–6.

Sigala, M. and Chalkiti, K. (2007) Improving performance through tacit knowledge externalisation and utilisation: Preliminary findings from Greek hotels, *International Journal of Productivity and Performance Management*, 56(5/6): 456–83.

Simonin, B.L. (1999) Ambiguity and the process of knowledge transfer in strategic alliances, *Strategic Management Journal*, 20(7): 595–623.

Singh, J. (2005) Collaborative networks as determinants of knowledge diffusion patterns, *Management Science*, 51(5): 756–70.

Sjödin, D., Frishammar, J., and Thorgren, S. (2019) How individuals engage in the absorption of new external knowledge: A process model of absorptive capacity, *Journal of Product Innovation Management*, 36(3): 356–80.

Skogan, W.G. (2008) Why Reforms Fail, *Policing and Society*, 18(1): 25–37.

Slåtten, K. (2020) Personal og HR-funksjonen I Norge 1945 til 2020. En historisk studie av organisatoriske felt og institusjonelle logikker (The Personnel and HR-departments in Norway 1945–2020. An historical study of organizational fields and institutional logics). *Ph.D. thesis*. Department of Social Science, The Arctic University of Norway—Tromsø

Slavin, R.E. (2008) Perspectives on evidence-based research in education: What works? Issues in synthesizing educational program evaluations, *Educational Researcher*, 37(1): 5–14.

Snell-Hornby, M. (2006) *The Turns of Translations Studies: New Paradigms or Shifting Viewpoints?* Amsterdam: John Benjamins Pub.

Snellman, K.E. (2012) Window-dressers and Closet Conformists: Organizational decoupling revisited, *Academy of Management Proceedings* (1): p.14156.

Solli, R., P. Demediuk, and R. Sims, R. (2005) *The namesake: on best value and other reform marks*, Copenhagen: Liber & Copenhagen Business School Press.

Song, Y., Gnyawali, D.R., Srivastava, M.K., and Asgari, E. (2018) In search of precision in absorptive capacity research: A synthesis of the literature and consolidation of findings, *Journal of Management*, 44(6): 2343–74.

Sosnovskikh, S. (2017) Industrial clusters in Russia: The development of special economic zones and industrial parks, *Russian Journal of Economics*, 3(2): 174–99.

References

Souitaris, V. (2001) Strategic influences of technological innovation in Greece, *British Journal of Management*, 12(2): 131–47.

Spender, J.C. (1993) Competitive Advantage from Tacit Knowledge? Unpacking the Concept and its Strategic Implications, *Academy of Management Proceedings* (1): 37–41.

Spyridonidis, D., Currie, G., Heusinkveld, S., Strauss, K., and Sturdy, A. (2014) New developments in translation research, *British Journal of Management*, 16, 245–48.

Srivastava, S., Singh, S., and Dhir, S. (2020) Culture and International business research: A review and research agenda. *International Business Review*, 29(4):101709.

Stahl, G.K., Chua, C.H., Caligiuri, P., Cerdin, J.L., and Taniguchi, M. (2009) Predictors of turnover intentions in learning-driven and demand-driven international assignments: The role of repatriation concerns, satisfaction with company support, and perceived career advancement opportunities, *Human Resource Management*, 48(1): 89–109.

Stahl, G.K. and Sitkin, S.B. (2005) *Trust in Mergers & Acquisitions: Managing Culture and Human Resources*, Palo Alto, CA: Stanford Business Press: 82–102.

Stål, H.I. and Corvellec, H. (2018) A decoupling perspective on circular business model implementation: Illustrations from Swedish apparel, *Journal of Cleaner Production*, 171: 630–43.

Stamenković, D., Ichien, N., and Holyoak, K.J. (2019) Metaphor comprehension: An individual-differences approach, *Journal of Memory and Language*, 105 (April): 108–18.

Starkey, K. and Madan, P. (2001) Bridging the relevance gap: Aligning stakeholders in the future of management research, *British Journal of Management*, 12 (special issue): 3–26.

Stensaker, B. (2007) Quality as fashion: exploring the translation of a management idea into higher education, in D. Westerheijden, B. Stensaker, and M.J. Rosa (eds.), *Quality Assurance in Higher Education*, Dordrecht: Springer: 99–118.

Stevenson, W.B. and Gilly, M.C. (1991) Information processing and problem solving: The migration of problems through formal positions and networks of ties, *Academy of Management Journal*, 34(4): 918–28.

Stewart, W.D. (1935) *Mines, Machines and Men. [On the Condition of the Coal Industry.]*, London: PS King & Son.

Still, M.C. and Strang, D. (2009) Who does an elite organization emulate? *Administrative Science Quarterly*, 54(1): 58–89.

Stine, P. (1990) *Bible Translation and the Spread of the Church: The Last 200 Years*, Leiden, New York, Copenhagen: Brill.

Stock, G. N., Greis, N. P., and Fischer, W. A. (2001) Absorptive capacity and new product development, *The Journal of High Technology Management Research*, 12(1): 77–91.

Strang, D. and Macy, M.W. (2001) In search of excellence: Fads, success stories, and adaptive emulation, *American Journal of Sociology*, 107(1): 147–82.

Strang, D. and Meyer, J.W. (1993) Institutional conditions for diffusion, *Theory and society*, 22(4): 487–511.

Strang, D. and Still, M.C. (2006) Does ambiguity promote imitation, or hinder it? An empirical study of benchmarking teams, *European Management Review*, 3(2): 101–12.

Sturdy, A. (2011) Consultancy's consequences? A critical assessment of management consultancy's impact on management, *British Journal of Management*, 22(3): 517–30.

Sturdy, A., Werr, A., and Buono, A.F. (2009) The client in management consultancy research: Mapping the territory, *Scandinavian Journal of Management*, 25(3): 247–52.

Sturdy, A. and Wright, C. (2011) The active client: The boundary-spanning roles of internal consultants as gatekeepers, brokers and partners of their external counterparts, *Management Learning*, 42(5): 485–503.

Sturlusson, S. (1964) *Heimskringla: History of the Kings of Norway* (translated by L.M. Hollander), Texas: University of Texas Press.

Suddaby, R. (2010) Editor's comments: Construct clarity in theories of management and organization, *Academy of Management Review*, 35(3): 346–57.

Suddaby, R. and Greenwood, R. (2001) Colonizing knowledge: Commodification as a dynamic of jurisdictional expansion in professional service firms, *Human Relations*, 54(7): 933–53.

Suddaby, R., Hardy, C., and Huy, Q.N. (2011) Introduction to special topic forum: where are the new theories of organization? *The Academy of Management Review*, 36(2): 236–46.

Sultan, F. and Simpson, M.C. (2000) International service variants: airline passenger expectations and perceptions of service quality, *Journal of Services Marketing*, 14 (3): 188–216.

Sun, P.Y.T. and Scott, J.L. (2005) An investigation of barriers to knowledge transfer, *Journal of Knowledge Management*, 9(2): 75–90.

Sunaoshi, Y., Kotabe, M., and Murray, J. Y. (2005) How technology transfer really occurs on the factory floor: a case of a major Japanese automotive die manufacturer in the United States, *Journal of World Business*, 40(1): 57–70.

Szulanski, G. (1994) Intra-firm transfer of best practice project. Executive summary of the findings, *APQC-Report*, American Productivity & Quality Center, Houston, TX.

Szulanski, G. (1996) Exploring internal stickiness: Impediments to the transfer of best practice within the firm, *Strategic Management Journal*, 17(S2): 27–43.

Szulanski, G. (2000) The process of knowledge transfer: A diachronic analysis of stickiness, *Organizational Behavior and Human Decision Processes*, 82(1): 9–27.

Szulanski, G. (2003) *Sticky Knowledge: Barriers to Knowing in the Firm*, London: Sage.

Szulanski, G. and Cappetta, R. (2003) Stickiness: Conceptualizing, measuring, and predicting difficulties in the transfer of knowledge within organizations, in M. Easterby-Smith and M.A. Lyles (eds.), *The Blackwell Handbook of Organizational Learning and Knowledge Management*, Malden, M.A. & Oxford: Blackwell: 513–34.

Szulanski, G., Cappetta, R., and Jensen, R.J. (2004) When and how trustworthiness matters: Knowledge transfer and the moderating effect of causal ambiguity, *Organization Science*, 15(5): 600–13.

Szulanski, G. and Jensen, R. J. (2008) Growing through copying: The negative consequences of innovation on franchise network growth, *Research Policy*, 37(10): 1732–41.

Szulanski, G., Ringov, D., and Jensen, R.J. (2016) Overcoming stickiness: How the timing of knowledge transfer methods affects transfer difficulty, *Organization Science*, 27(2): 304–22.

Szulanski, G. and Winter, S. (2002) Getting it right the second time, *Harvard Business Review*, 80(1): 62–9.

Taddeo, R., Simboli, A., Ioppolo, G., and Morgante, A. (2017) Industrial symbiosis, networking and innovation: The potential role of innovation poles, *Sustainability*, 9(2): 169–86.

Tailby, S. (2011) Taylorism in the Mines? Technology, Work Organization and Management in British Coalmining before Nationalization, in M. Richardson and P. Nicholls (eds.), *A Business and Labour History of Britain*, London: Palgrave Macmillan: 155–81.

Tallman, S. and Chacar, A. S. (2011) Knowledge accumulation and dissemination in MNEs: a practice-based framework, *Journal of Management Studies*, 48(2): 278–304.

Tarde, G. (1903) *The Laws of Imitation*, New York: H. Holt.

Taussig, M. (1993) *Mimesis and Alterity: A particular History of the Senses*, New York: Routledge.

Tavares, M. F. F. (2020, Across establishments, within firms: worker's mobility, knowledge transfer and survival, *Journal for Labour Market Research*, 54(1): 1–19.

Taylor, F.W. (1911) *Shop Management*, New York: Harper & Brothers.

Teece, D.J. (1977) Technology transfer by multinational firms: The resource cost of transferring technological know-how, *The Economic Journal*, 87(346): 242–61.

Teece, D.J. (1981) The market for know-how and the efficient international transfer of technology, *The Annals of the American Academy of Political and Social Science*, 458(1): 81–96.

Teece, D. J., Pisano, G., and Shuen, A. (1997) Dynamic capabilities and strategic management, *Strategic Management Journal*, 18(7): 509–33.

Tell, F., Berggren, C., Brusoni, S, and Van de Ven, A. (2017) Managing knowledge integration across boundaries, in F. Tell, C. Berggren, S. Brusoni, and A. Van de Ven (eds.), *Managing Knowledge Integration across Boundaries*, Oxford, UK: Oxford University Press: 19–38.

Terry, F. (2000) Transport: beyond predict and provide. *What Works?*, in H.T.O. Davies, S.M. Nutley, and P.C. Smith (eds.), *What Works? Evidence-based Policy and Practice in Public Services*, Bristol: Policy Press: 187–205.

Tian, A.W. and Soo, C. (2018) Enriching individual absorptive capacity, *Personnel Review*, 47(5): 116–32.

Tidd, J. and Thuriaux-Alemán, B. (2016) Innovation management practices: cross-sectorial adoption, variation, and effectiveness, *R&D Management*, 46(S3): 1024–43.

Tillotson, J.E. (2008) Fast food—Ray Kroc and the dawning of the age of McDonald's, *Nutrition Today*, 43(3): 107–13.

Toby, R.P. (2007) The originality of the "copy": Mimesis and subversion in Hanegawa Tôei's Chôsenjin Ukie, in R. Cox (ed.), *The Culture of Copying in Japan, Critical and Historical Perspectives*, New York: Routledge: 83–122.

Todorova, G., and Durisin, B. (2007) Absorptive capacity: Valuing a reconceptualization, *Academy of Management Review*, 32(3): 774–86.

Tödtling, F. and Trippl, M. (2005) One size fits all?: Towards a differentiated regional innovation policy approach, *Research Policy*, 34(8): 1203–19.

Torfing, J. and Triantafillou, P. (2016) *Enhancing Public Innovation by Transforming Public Governance*, Cambridge: Cambridge University Press.

Torre, A. (2008) On the role played by temporary geographical proximity in knowledge transmission. *Regional Studies*, 42(6): 869–89.

Torsteinsen, H. (2006) Resultatenhetsmodellen i kommunal tjenesteproduksjon: instrument, symbol eller maktmiddel? *Ph.D. dissertation*, Department of Political Science, The Arctic University of Norway, Tromsø.

Toulmin, S. (1953/1967) *The Philosophy of Science*, London: Hutchinson and Co.

Tourangeau, R. and Sternberg, R.J. (1981) Aptness in metaphor, *Cognitive Psychology*, 13(1): 27–55.

Tourangeau, R. and Sternberg, R.J. (1982) Understanding and appreciating metaphors, *Cognition*, 11(3): 203–44.

Tourish, D. (2020) The triumph of nonsense in management studies, *Academy of Management Learning & Education*, 19(1): 99–109.

Toury, G. (1978) The nature and role of norms in translation, in *Literature and Translation: New Perspectives in Literary Studies*, Leuven: ACCO: 83–100.

Toury, G. (1980) *In Search of a Theory of Translation*. Porter Institute for Poetics and Semiotics: Tel Aviv University.

Toury, G. (1984) The notion of "native translator" and translation teaching, in W. Wilss and G. Thome (eds.), *Die Theorie des Ubersetzens und ihr Aufschusswert fur die Ubersetzungs und Dolmetschdidaktik*, Tübingen, Narr: 186–95.

Toury, G. (1985) A rationale for descriptive translation studies, in T. Hermans (ed.), *The Manipulation of Literature*, London: Croom Helm: 16–41.

Toury, G. (1986) Natural translation and the making of a native translator, *Textcontext*, 1: 11–29.

Toury, G. (1995) *Descriptive Translation Studies and Beyond*, Amsterdam: Benjamins.

Tracey, P., Dalpiaz, E., and Phillips, N. (2018) Fish out of water: Translation, legitimation, and new venture creation, *Academy of Management Journal*, 61(5): 1627–66.

Trist, E.L. and Bamforth, K.W. (1951) Some social and psychological consequences of the longwall method of coal-getting: An examination of the psychological situation and defences of a work group in relation to the social structure and technological content of the work system, *Human Relations*, 4(1): 3–38.

Trist, E.L., Higgin, G.W., Murray, H., and Pollock, A.B. (2013) *Organizational Choice: Capabilities of Groups at the Coal Face under Changing Technologies*, London: Routledge.

Tsai, W. (2001) Knowledge transfer in intraorganizational networks: Effects of network position and absorptive capacity on business unit innovation and performance, *Academy of Management Journal*, 44(5): 996–1004.

Tsai, W. (2002) Social structure of "coopetition" within a multiunit organization: Coordination, competition, and intraorganizational knowledge sharing, *Organization Science*, 13(2): 179–90.

Tsai, W. and Ghoshal, S. (1998) Social capital and value creation: The role of intrafirm networks. *Academy of Management Journal*, 41(4): 464–76.

Tsang, E.W. (2002) Acquiring knowledge by foreign partners from international joint ventures in a transition economy: Learning-by-doing and learning myopia. *Strategic Management Journal*, 23(9): 835–54.

Tsoukas, H. (1991) The missing link: A transformational view of metaphors in organizational science, *Academy of Management Review*, 16(3): 566–85.

Tsoukas, H. (1993) Analogical reasoning and knowledge generation in organization theory, *Organization Studies*, 14(3): 323–46.

Tucker, A.L., Nembhard, I.M., and Edmondson, A.C. (2007) Implementing new practices: An empirical study of organizational learning in hospital intensive care units, *Management Science*, 53(6): 894–907.

Tung, R.L. (1987) Expatriate assignments: Enhancing success and minimizing failure, *Academy of Management Perspectives*, 1(2): 117–25.

Tung, R. L., and Verbeke, A. (2010) Beyond Hofstede and GLOBE: Improving the quality of cross-cultural research, *Journal of International Business Studies*, 41(8): 1259–74.

Turkina, E. and Van Assche, A. (2018) Global connectedness and local innovation in industrial clusters, *Journal of International Business Studies*, 49(6): 706–28.

Urry, J. (2004) The "system" of automobility, *Theory, Culture & Society*, 21(4–5): 25–39.

Uzzi, B. (1996) The sources and consequences of embeddedness for the economic performance of organizations: The network effect, *American Sociological Review*, 61(4): 674–98.

Uzzi, B. and Lancaster, R. (2003) Relational embeddedness and learning: The case of bank loan managers and their clients, *Management Science*, 49(4): 383–99.

Valdés, C. (2017) Advertising translation, in C. Millán and F. Bartrina (eds.), *The Routledge Handbook of Translation Studies*, New York: Routledge, 303–16.

Van de Ven, A.H., and Ferry, D.L. (1980) *Measuring and assessing organizations*. New York: Wiley.

Van der Heiden, P., Pohl, C., Mansor, S., and van Genderen, J. (2016) Necessitated absorptive capacity and metaroutines in international technology transfer: A new model, *Journal of Engineering and Technology Management*, 41: 65–78.

Van Eijk, C. and Gascó, M. (2018) Unravelling the Co-Producers: Who are They and What Motivations do They Have?, in T. Brandsen, T. Steen, and B. Verschuere (eds.), *Co-production and Co-Creation: Engaging Citizens in Public Services*, New York: Routledge: 63–76.

Van Gils, M., Vissers, G., and De Wit, J. (2009) Selecting the right channel for knowledge transfer between industry and science: consider the R&D-activity, *European Journal of Innovation Management*, 12(4): 492–511.

Van Grinsven, M., Heusinkveld, S., and Cornelissen, J. (2016) Translating management concepts: Towards a typology of alternative approaches, *International Journal of Management Reviews*, 18(3): 271–89.

Van Maanen, E., and Schein, E.H. (1978) Toward a theory of organizational socialization, in B.M. Staw (ed.), *Research in Organizational Behaviour*, Greenwich, CT: JAI Press, 1: 209–64.

Van Veen, K., Bezemer, J., and Karsten, L. (2011) Diffusion, translation and the neglected role of managers in the fashion setting process: the case of MANS, *Management Learning*, 42 (2): 149–64.

Van Wijk, R., Jansen, J.J., and Lyles, M.A. (2008) Inter-and intra-organizational knowledge transfer: a meta-analytic review and assessment of its antecedents and consequences, *Journal of Management Studies*, 45(4): 830–53.

Varian, H.R. (2005) Copying and copyright, *Journal of Economic Perspectives*, 19(2): 121–38.

Veblen, T. (1914) *The Instinct of Workmanship and the State of Industrial Arts*, New York: The Macmillan Company.

Veenhoven, R. (1984) *Conditions of Happiness*, Dordrecht: D. Reidel Publishing.

Venuti, L. (1998) Strategies of translation, in M. Baker (ed.), *Routledge Encyclopedia of Translation Studies*, London: Routledge: 240–4.

Venuti, L., (1995) Translation, Authorship, Copyright, *The Translator*, 1 (1): 1–24.

Venuti, L. (1998) American tradition, in M. Baker (ed.), *The Routledge Encyclopedia of Translation Studies*, London and New York: Routledge: 305–16.

Venuti, L. (2012) *The Translation Studies Reader*, London: Routledge.

Venuti, L. (2017) *The Translator's Invisibility: A History of Translation*, London: Routledge.

Vermeer, H. (1986) Voraussetzungen für eine Translationstheorie—Einige Kapitel Kultur und Sprachtheorie; *Institut für Übersetzen und Dolmetschen*, Heidelberg: Selbstverlag.

Vermeer, H.J. (1978) Ein Rahmen für eine allgemeine Translationstheorie, *Lebende Sprachen*, 23(3): 99–102.

Vermeer, H.J. (1998) Didactics of translation, in M. Baker (ed.), *Routledge Encyclopaedia of Translation Studies*, London: Routledge: 60–3.

Vinay, J.P. and Darbelnet, J. (1958) Stylistique Comparée du Francais et de l-Anglais: Méthode de Traduction. Paris: Didier. (Translated and edited by Sager, J.C. and Hamel, M.J. (1995) Comparative Stylistics of French and English—*A Methodology for Translation*, Amsterdam: John Benjamins.

Vlaar, P.W. Van den Bosch, F.A., and Volberda, H.W. (2006) Coping with problems of understanding in interorganizational relationships: Using formalization as a means to make sense. *Organization Studies*, 27(11): 1617–38.

Vlajcic, D., Marzi, G., Caputo, A., and Dabic, M. (2019) The role of geographical distance on the relationship between cultural intelligence and knowledge transfer, *Business Process Management Journal*, 25(1): 104–25.

Volberda, H.W., Foss, N.J., and Lyles, M.A. (2010) Perspective—Absorbing the concept of absorptive capacity: How to realize its potential in the organization field, *Organization Science*, 21(4): 931–51.

Von Hippel, E. (1994) "Sticky information" and the locus of problem solving: implications for innovation, *Management Science*, 40(4): 429–39.

Von Krogh, G. (1998) Care in knowledge creation, *California Management Review*, 40(3): 133–153.

Von Krogh, G., Ichijo, K., and Nonaka, I. (2000) *Enabling knowledge creation: How to Unlock the Mystery of Tacit Knowledge and Release the Power of Innovation*, Oxford UK: Oxford University Press.

Waardenburg, L., Huysman, M., and Sergeeva, A.V. (2022) In the land of the blind, the one-eyed man is king: Knowledge brokerage in the age of learning algorithms, *Organization Science*, 33(1): 59–82.

Wæraas, A., and Sataøen, H.L. (2014) Trapped in conformity. Translating reputation management into practice, *Scandinavian Journal of Management Studies*, 30(2): 149–262.

Wagner, R.K. and Sternberg, R.J. (1987) Tacit knowledge in managerial success. *Journal of Business and Psychology*, 1(4): 301–12.

Wah, L. (1999) Making knowledge stick: No knowledge management program an succeed without a shift in corporate culture and that new culture must be woven into every business process, *Management Review*, 88(5): 24–33.

Waldorff, S. B. and Madsen, M. H. (2022) Translating to Maintain Existing Practices: Micro-tactics in the implementation of a new management concept, *Organization Studies*, 01708406221112475.

Walgenbach, P. (1997) Between "show business and galley": On the use of ISO 9000 standards in companies, *Paper presented at the SCANCOR/SCORE Seminar in Standardization*, at Arild, Sweden, September 18, 1997.

Walgenbach, P. and Hegele, C. (2001) What can an apple learn from an orange? Or: what do companies use benchmarking for? *Organization*, 8(1): 121–44.

Walker, H.A. and Cohen, B.P. (1985) Scope statements: Imperatives for evaluating theory, *American Sociological Review*, 50(3): 288–301.

Walsham, G. (1991) Organizational metaphors and information systems research, *European Journal of Information Systems*, 1(2): 83–94.

Walton, S. and Huey, J. (1993) *Sam Walton, Made in America: My Story*. New York: Bantam.

Wanberg, J., Javernick-Will, A., Taylor, J.E., and Chinowsky, P. (2015) The effects of organizational divisions on knowledge-sharing networks in multi-lateral communities of practice. *Engineering Project Organization Journal*, 5(2–3): 118–32.

Wang, C.L. and Ahmed, P.K. (2003) Structure and structural dimensions for knowledge-based organization, *Measuring Business Excellence*, 7(1): 51–62.

Wasserman, S. and Faust, K. (1994) *Social Network Analysis: Methods and Applications*, Cambridge: Cambridge University Press.

Weber, M. (1924) *Gesammelte aufsätze zur soziologie und sozialpolitik*, Tübingen: Mohr.

Weber, M. (1947) *The Theory of Social and Economic Organization*, New York: Oxford University Press.

Wedlin, L. and Sahlin, K. (2017) The imitation and translation of management ideas, in R. Greenwood, C. Oliver, T. Lawrence, and R.E. Meyer (eds.), *The SAGE Handbook on Organizational Institutionalism* (2nd ed.), London, UK: Sage: 102–27.

Wegner, D.M., Erber, R., and Raymond, P. (1991) Transactive memory in close relationships, *Journal of Personality and Social Psychology*, 61(6): 923–29.

Wellisz, S. (1953) Strikes in coal-mining, *The British Journal of Sociology*, 4(4): 346–66.

Wellstein, B. and Kieser, A. (2011) Trading "best practices"—a good practice? *Industrial and Corporate Change*, 20(3): 683–719.

Wenger, E.C. and Snyder, W.M. (2000) Communities of practice: The organizational frontier, *Harvard Business Review*, 78(1): 139–46.

Werr, A. and Stjernberg, T. (2003) Exploring management consulting firms as knowledge systems, *Organization Studies*, 24(6): 881–908.

Westney, D.E. (1987) *Imitation and Innovation: The Transfer of Western Organizational Patterns to Meiji Japan*, Cambridge, MA: Harvard University Press.

Westney D.E. (1993) Institutionalization theory and the multinational corporation, in S. Ghoshal and D.E. Westney (eds.), *Organization Theory and the Multinational Corporation*, New York: St. Martin's Press: 53–76.

Westney, D.E. and Piekkari, R. (2020) Reversing the translation flow: Moving organizational practices from Japan to the US, *Journal of Management Studies*, 57(1): 57–86.

Westney, D.E., Piekkari, R., Koskinen, K., and Tietze, S. (2022) Crossing borders and boundaries: Translation ecosystems in international business, *International Business Review*, 31(5): 102030.

Westphal, J.D. and Zajac, E.J. (2001) Decoupling policy from practice: The case of stock repurchase programs, *Administrative Science Quarterly*, 46(2): 202–28.

Whetten, D.A. (1989) What constitutes a theoretical contribution? *Academy of Management Review*, 14(4): 490–5.

Whetten, D.A., Felin, T., and King, B.G. (2009) The practice of theory borrowing in organizational studies: Current issues and future directions, *Journal of Management*, 35(3): 537–63.

Whitehead, L. (1996) *The International Dimensions of Democratization: Europe and the Americas*, Oxford, UK: Oxford University Press.

Whittle, A., Suhomlinova, O., and Mueller, F. (2010) Funnel of interest: the discursive translation of organizational change, *Journal of Applied Behavioral Science*, 46(1): 16–37.

Wickert, C., Post, C., Doh, J. P., Prescott, J. E., and Prencipe, A. (2021) Management research that makes a difference: Broadening the meaning of impact, *Journal of Management Studies*, 58(2): 297–320.

Willem, A. and Buelens, M. (2009) Knowledge sharing in inter-unit cooperative episodes: The impact of organizational structure dimensions. *International Journal of Information Management*, 29(2): 151–60.

Williams, B. (1985) *Ethics and the Limits of Philosophy*, London: Fontana Press.

Williams, C. (2007) Transfer in context: Replication and adaptation in knowledge transfer relationships, *Strategic Management Journal*, 28(9): 867–89.

Williams, J. and Chesterman, A. (2014) *The Map: A Beginner's Guide to Doing Research in Translation Studies*, London: Routledge.

Wilson, B. (2001) *Soft Systems Methodology, Conceptual Model Building and Its Contribution*, West Sussex: Wiley.

Wilss, W. (1982) *The Science of Translation: Problems and Methods*, Tübingen: Gunter Narr Verlag.

Wilss, W. (1996) *Knowledge and Skills in Translator Behavior*, Amsterdam: John Benjamins Publishing.

Wilss, W. (1998) Decision making in translation. In M. Baker (ed.), *Routledge Encyclopedia of Translation Studies*, London: Routledge: 57–60.

Winkless, L. (2022) *Sticky—The Secret Science of Surfaces*, London: Bloomsbury Sigma.

Winter, S.G. and Szulanski, G. (2001) Replication as strategy, *Organization Science*, 12(6): 730–43.

Winter, S.G. Szulanski, G., Ringov, D., and Jensen, R.J. (2012) Reproducing knowledge: Inaccurate replication and failure in franchise organizations, *Organization Science*, 23(3): 672–85.

Witt, U. (2016) *Rethinking Economic Evolution—Essays on Economic Change and its Theory*, Cheltenham, UK: Edward Elgar Publishing.

Witte, H. (1987) Die Kulturkompetenz des Translators: Theoretisch-abstrakter Begriff oder realisierbares Konzept? *TextConText*, 2 (2/3): 109–36.

Wollebæk, K. (1989) *Medarbeidersamtaler: Hvorfor og Hvordan? (Translated: Development Dialogue: Why and How?)*, Oslo: Universitetsforlaget.

Woodsworth, J. (1998) History of translation, *Routledge Encyclopedia of Translation Studies*, London/New York: Routledge, 100–6.

Worthy, J.C. (1950) Organizational structure and employee morale. *American Sociological Review*, 15(2): 169–79.
Wright, C. (2019) Thought leaders and followers. The impact of consultants and advisors on management ideas, in A. Sturdy, S. Heusinkveld, T. Reay, and D. Strang (eds.), *The Oxford Handbook of Management Ideas*, Oxford: Oxford University Press: 140–58.
Wu, H., Gu, X., Zhao, Y., and Liu, W. (2020) Research on the Relationship between Structural Hole Location, Knowledge Management and Cooperative Innovation Performance in Artificial Intelligence, *Knowledge Management Research & Practice*, 1–10.
Xie, X., Zou, H., and Qi, G. (2018) Knowledge absorptive capacity and innovation performance in high-tech companies: A multi-mediating analysis, *Journal of Business Research*, 88: 289–97.
Xu, D., and Shenkar, O. (2002) Institutional distance and the multinational enterprise, *Academy of Management Review*, 27(4): 608–18.
Xue, Y., Liang, H., Boulton, W.R., and Snyder, C.A. (2005) ERP implementation failures in China: Case studies with implications for ERP vendors, *International Journal of Production Economics*, 97(3): 279–95.
Yanow, D. (2004) Translating local knowledge at organizational peripheries, *British Journal of Management*, 15(S1): 9–25.
Yli-Renko, H., Autio, E., and Sapienza, H.J. (2001) Social capital, knowledge acquisition, and knowledge exploitation in young technology-based firms, *Strategic Management Journal*, 22(6–7): 587–613.
Yuqin Z, et al. (2011) A game between enterprise and employees about the tacit knowledge transfer and sharing. Paper presented to the international conference on applied physics and industrial engineering, *Physics Procedia*, 24: 1789–95.
Zahra, S.A., and George, G. (2002) Absorptive capacity: A review, reconceptualization, and extension, *Academy of Management Review*, 27(2): 185–203.
Zaltman, G., Duncan, R., and Holbek, J. (1973) *Innovations and organizations*. New York: John Wiley & Sons.
Zander, U., and Kogut, B. (1995) Knowledge and the speed of the transfer and imitation of organizational capabilities: An empirical test. *Organization Science*, 6(1): 76–92.
Zeng, J., Liu, Y., Wang, R., and Zhan, P. (2019) Absorptive capacity and regional innovation in China: An analysis of patent applications, 2000–2015, *Applied Spatial Analysis and Policy*, 12(4): 1031–49.
Zilber, T.B. (2006) The work of the symbolic in institutional processes: Translations of rational myths in Israeli high tech, *Academy of Management Journal*, 49(2): 281–303.
Zou, T., Ertug, G., and George, G. (2018) The capacity to innovate: A meta-analysis of absorptive capacity, *Innovation*, 20(2): 87–121.

Index

Note: As most entries refer to either knowledge transfer or translation these terms have been avoided wherever possible.

absorptive capacity 31–40, 44–45, 59t, 58, 123–124, 180, 181, 185–186, 201–202, 206–207
  ambiguities of antecedents 32–34
  ambiguities of outcomes 38–40
  ambiguous contents 35–38
  asset versus capability 34–35
  dynamic capability 35
  interconnectedness 37–38
  potential 35–36
  realized 35–36
  relative 37–38
  uncertainties 35–36
absorptive effort 36
absorptive knowledge base 36
absorptive process 36
abstracted skeleton model 99
acceleration of knowledge transfer 58
accidental modifications 166, 248–249
acquisition 37–38, 50–51
actor-network theory (ANT) 75, 90, 97
adaptations 83–84, 148–149, 164, 170–173
  contextual 186–187
addition 83–84, 175–176, 177f, 245t, 248
adequacy of translation 81
adherence to source 81–82, 107
adherence to target 81–82, 107
Agarwal, R. 7–8
airline cabin crews (case study) 117–119, 141–143
Alchian, A.A. 166
alteration 83–84, 170, 177f, 245t
  hybridization 170
  metamorphosis 170
alternative dimensions 36
ambiguities 35–38, 53–54, 56, 57–58
  of antecedents 32–34
  of outcomes 38–40
  see also causal ambiguity
analogies 69–76, 79, 98

causal 73
constitutive 73
heuristic 73
Ansari, S.M. 95–96
Antal, A.B. 125
antecedents 67–99
  barriers to translations 84–85
  borrowing 74–77
  competence 88–90
  decontextualization and contextualization 79–81
  domain of translation studies 78–79
  generic structure 98–99
  individual 33–34
  metaphors 70–73
  norms 81–83
  organizational 33–34, 90–98
  rules of translations 83–84
  sources to new theories of organizations 67–69
  translator 85–88
appropriateness, logic of 146–147
architecture of knowledge transfers 5–6
Argote, L. 115
Arthur Andersen 'Global Best Practice Database' 122–123
Ash, M.K. 126
asset versus capability 34–35
assimilation 35–39
augmentation 173
Austria 125
autonomy 199–200, 203–205
axiomatic knowledge 125

Baden-Fuller, C. 172
balancing acts 200
Bamforth, K 132–133, 139–140, 189–191
Barkhudarov, L.S. 83–84
Barnes, J.A. 40–41

barriers 5, 14, 17–19, 76–77b, 99, 178–182, 185, 193–196, 201–205, 207
  cultural 193–194, 205–206
  geographical distance 47–49, 58, 59t, 201–202, 206–207
  institutional 193–194, 207
  national 193–194, 207
  in organizational knowledge transfers 121
  to translations 84–85, 101b
  see also formal organizational structure
Bartlett, C.A. 28
Bassnett, S. 80–81, 84–85
Bauman, L.J 172–173
Baum, J.A. 7–8
benchmarking 122–124
Berger, P. 145–146
Berkman, U. 94
best practices 122–124
betweenness centrality 43
Bhagat, R.S. 31–32, 50–51
bible translation 78, 86
biculturalism 89–90, 108–109, 117, 220–221
bilingualism 88–90, 108–109, 117, 220–221, 223–225
Blakely, C.H. 10, 158–159
Blau, P.M. 152
blending 72, 99, 105–109
borders 5, 24–25, 27–28, 30–31, 69
  see also barriers
borrowing 74–77, 83–84, 148–149
  from outer domains 68
  generic structure 76–77
  horizontal 67–68
  saliency of domains 75–76
  vertical 67–68
boundaries 178–179
boundary-spanners 31
Bowden, R. 157–158
Brisset, A. 140–141
British coal-mining industry and knowledge transfer from United States 131–133, 137–140, 143–144, 186–191, 204–206, 208t, 248–249
  absenteeism 132–133, 189–190
  composite work groups 190–191
  configuring challenges 190
  contextual knowledge, lack of 189–190
  handgot system 131, 189–190
  isolated dependence 132
  learning processes, slow 190–191
  longwall method 131–132, 187, 188–190
  mechanization 187–188
  moral hazard 132–133
  productivity, low 132, 190, 204–205
  responsible autonomy, loss of 132–133
  strikes and stoppages 189–190, 204–205
Buelens, M. 26–27
Bunnell, T. 48–49
Burger King 185–187
Burns, T. 152
Burt, R. 43

Caimo, A. 28–29
Cairncross, F. 48
calque 83–84, 148–149
Caminade, M. 90
Campbell and Cochrane Collaboration 158
Canada 26–27, 139, 194
capability 42
capacity 2–3
Cardinal, L.B. 28–29
Carton, G. 213–214
causal ambiguity 53–54, 111, 112–114, 117–118, 120, 123–124, 141–143
cause-and-effect mechanisms 39, 109–110, 194, 199–200, 203–204, 248
centralization 28–29, 43, 44
chain affiliation 2–3
Chen, C.J. 26–29
China 167, 201–202
  copying 156–157, 160–161
  and happiness indices 194–197, 202, 204, 206–207, 208t
  Shanzhai 156–157, 160–161
chosen or taken for granted rules 159–161
Christensen, T. 30
Ciabuschi, F. 28–29
Cicero 78, 82, 83, 86, 164
clarity 56
closeness 74–75
clusters 47–49
Cochrane, A. 158
Cochrane Database for Systematic Reviews 158
code-switching 85–86
codification 55–57
Coe, N. 48–49
Coff, R.W. 55–56
cognitive pillar 52
cognitive processes 129, 221–223

Index

cognitive theory 33–34
Cohen, W. 31–34 35–36, 38, 39
cohesion 42
combining knowledge of source and
    recipient contexts 220–225
  bilingualism and biculturalism 220–221
  bilingualism as variable 223–225
  cognitive processes and
      competence 221–223
common causal schema 73
common knowledge 56–57
communication models 76–77
communication technology 48–49
communities of practice (CoPs) 30–31
comparative institutionalism 52
comparison phase 70–71
competence 1, 19, 88–90, 101b, 108–109,
    213–215, 221–223, 242–249
  contexts and deliberate usage 244–249
  modelling knowledge of
      contexts 242–244
  relational 111–112
  substitution 113
  technical 35–36
competitive advantage 54–56, 113–114
competitiveness 2, 5
complexity 6–7, 111–114, 119, 120–121, 125,
    128, 133–136, 141–144
conceptualizations 39, 69, 129–130, 137,
    143–144
concrete materialization processes 129
conditional knowledge 109–110, 125
configuration 129–130, 137–140, 143–144,
    190
connecting points 43
consequentiality, logic of 146–147
content of imports 69
contexts 98, 149–150, 202, 216–225,
    248–249
  combining knowledge of source and
      recipient contexts 220–225
  gaining knowledge 217–220
contextual adaptations 186–187
contextualization 16–19, 76–77, 79–81,
    96–98, 101b, 105–106, 109, 129–141,
    143–144, 179, 182
  configuration of new and existing
      practices 137–140
  inscribing new practice in target
      context 140–141

  orientation 96–97, 101b
  target organizational context 130–137
    complexity 133–136
    embeddedness 136–137
    explicitness 130–133
  see also de-contextualization
contextual knowledge, lack of 189–190
contingency theory 67–68
continuous translation 202
coordination challenges 12
copycats 86, 156–157, 160–161, 167–168,
    171, 235
copying 155–156, 160–163, 167–168, 171,
    177f, 228–234, 245t, 248–249
  China 156–157, 160–161
  exact 173
copyright 168
Cornelissen, J. 71–75 98, 105
creative artist 86
Crudup, A. 168–169
cultural adjustment 125
cultural barriers 207
cultural differences 84
cultural distance 47, 49–52, 58, 59t, 180,
    201–202, 206–207
cultural turn 80–82, 97
cultures
  national 50–52, 138
  reproducing 157–158
Cyert, R.M. 172–173
Czarniawska, B. 90 96–97

D'Adderio, L. 172–173
Darbelnet, J. 83–84, 148–149
Darwin, C. 167–168
Davenport 6–7
death of distance 47–49
deceleration 58
decentralization 28–29
decision-maker 87–88
declarative knowledge 109–110, 125
De Clercq, D. 26–27
decoding 14, 76–77
  see also contextualization
de-contextualization 16–19, 76–77, 79–81,
    96–98, 101b, 107–129, 141–143, 179,
    182
  airline cabin crews (case study) 117–119
  complexity 111–114
  embeddedness 114–116

de-contextualization (*Continued*)
  explicitness 116–117
  Norwegian stockfish production (case study) 119–121
  translatability 110–117
  translators 121–129
    expatriates 124–125
    insiders 126–129
    outsiders 122–124
deficient information 7–8
delayering 27–28
deliberate usage 225–242, 244–249
  scope conditions 225–234
democracy 3–5, 198, 199
Denmark 95, 201–202
  co-production in Aalborg 197–200, 202, 204, 206–207, 208*t*, 248
descriptive translation studies 78
de-territorialization of closeness 48–49
Dhanaraj, C. 57
differentiation 169
diffusion 90–91, 169
direct knowledge 6
direct transfer 49
dis-embedding 109, 115–116, 122, 141–143
dissimilarity/similarity 138
distance 46–53
  cultural 47, 49–52, 58, 59*t*, 180, 201–202, 206–207
  death of 47–49
  geographical 47–49, 58, 59*t*, 180, 201–202, 206–207
  high 58
  institutional 52–53, 58, 59*t*, 180, 201–202, 206–207
  low 58
  national 206–207
  physical 49
  power distance 50–51
  semantic 74–75
distortions to knowledge transfer 113–114
domain-interaction model 71–72, 74, 75–76, 98
domains 78–79
  primary 90–91
  secondary 90–91
  see also external domains
domestication 83, 87–88, 151, 200
Doty, D.H. 152–153

Durand, R. 73–75
Durisin, B. 36–37
Durkheim, E. 152
dyadic level 43–44
dynamic capability 35, 39–40

Easterby-Smith, M. 39–40
Eastern Europe 3–4
economic institutionalism 52
education sector 4–5, 9–10, 94–95, 156–158
effectiveness and efficiency 28–29, 159, 198–199
effortless-ness 117
ego networks 45
embeddedness 98, 114–116, 119, 121, 123–125, 128, 136–137, 141–144, 148–149
  high 121, 128
  low 128
  medium 128
  relational 57
emergent meaning 72
emotions 48–49
Empson, L. 30–31
enablers 181–182
encoding 14, 76–77
  see also decontextualization
equivalence 81–84, 148–149, 171
  connotative 81–82
  denotative 81–82
  dynamic 81–82
Etzioni, A. 152
European Union 3–5, 26–27
evidence movement, reproducing 158–159
expatriates 124–125, 141–143
experiential learning 248–249
explicitation 117, 175–176
explicit knowledge 54–57, 116–117
explicitness 116–117, 119, 130–133, 141–144
  low 121, 132–133
explicitness-tacitness variable 117–121
exploitation 35–38, 70–71
external domains 74–77, 99, 105–108, 145
  inspirations from 148–151
  see also organizational translation; translation studies
externalization 55
external knowledge acquisition 35–36

fashion 169
Faust, K. 40
fidelity 158–159, 161, 172–173
　high 9–10, 43–44
　low 10
　versus fit 170–171
Fink, G. 125
first-to-apply 161
first-to-invent 161
Ford fabric 131–132, 188–189, 204–205, 208*t*, 248–249
Fordism 187–188
foreignizing 83, 87–88, 151, 200
foreignness 168–169
formal organizational structure 24–31, 33–34, 59*t*, 180, 203–204, 206–207
　centralization 28–29, 43, 44
　decentralization 28–29
　formalization 25–27
　horizontal differentiation and integration 29–31
　vertical differentiation 27–29
R.H. Forrester 26–27
Foss, N.J. 152
foundational moment 167–168
France 83–85, 194
franchising 7–10, 161–162, 173, 200, 202
　franchisee 184–186, 202
　franchisor 184–185
　see also McDonald's
French/Scandinavian translation school 67, 74, 75
Frenkel, M. 94

Ganesh, L.S. 23
generic structure development 72, 76–77
Gentner, D. 69
geographical distance 47–49, 58, 59*t*, 180, 201–202, 206–207
geographic proximity 48–49
George, G. 35–37
Germany 83–84, 123–125, 164–165, 170, 174–175
Ghoshal, S. 28
Glick, W.H. 152–153
Govindarajan, V. 28–29, 31–32
Granovetter, M. 114
Grayson, C.J. 8
Gupta, A.K. 28–29, 31–32

habits and traditions of translations 148–149, 154, 167–170
Harré, R. 146
healthcare sector 4–5, 8–9, 40–41, 95, 127–128, 139, 158, 172–173
Hedlund, G. 56
Heeley, M. 35–36
Hermans, T. 82
Hofstede, G. 50–51, 231, 232, 240–241
Holmes, J. 78, 220–221
Holz-Mänttäri, J. 86–87
Horace 82
horizontal differentiation and integration 24–25, 27, 29–31
Horvat, D. 39–40
'how' question 39, 115–116
HRM systems 33–34
Huang, J.W. 26–29
Huet, T. 78
human-technology factor 111–112, 117–118, 141–143
hybridization 31, 170, 177*f*

Iacocca, L. 126
ideal types 152–155, 163–164, 171
ideas 91–93
images of translator 93–95, 101*b*
imitation 1–2, 56–57, 113, 155–156, 167–169
implicitation 174
inappropriate transformations of transferred practices 9–10
incommunicable knowledge 116–117
India 201–202
　see also Indo-Norwegian Project (INP) and Kerala fish industry
indirect transfer 49
individualism/collectivism 50–51
individual well-being and empowerment 198
Indo-Norwegian Project (INP) and Kerala fish industry 133–139, 143–144, 200–202, 205–206, 208*t*
industrial parks 47–48
Ingram, P. 7–8
innovation 1–2, 167–168, 171, 199–200
　poles 47–48
　potential 198
inscribing 129–130, 140–141, 143–144

insiders 126–129
institutional arrangements 138
institutional barriers 193–194, 207
institutional distance 52–53, 58, 59*t*, 180, 201–202, 206–207
institutionalism, organizational 52
instrumental theory 19
Intel Copy EXACT strategy 161–162
intellectual property rights 160–161, 168
interconnectedness 37–38
intercultural communicator 86–87
international joint ventures 57
interorganizational context 114–115
interorganizational diffusion 45–46
interorganizational knowledge transfers 5
interorganizational level 44–45
intra-organizational context 114
intra-organizational diffusion 45–46
intra-organizational knowledge transfers 35–36
intra-organizational level 44–45
intra-unit channels 30
invention 168
invention/innovation versus imitation-dichotomy 162
inventors 167
Isaac, G. 157–158
isolated dependence 132
Israel 94

Japan 5–6, 125, 167
  copying 160–162
  kata institution 160, 162–163
  organizational practices of car industry in United States 26–27, 93
  police system imported from France 164–166, 170
  postal system imported from UK 176
  public administration 4
  reproducing 155–157
  subsidiaries in United States 6–7
Jensen, R.J. 200, 233–234
Joerges, B. 96–97
joint ventures 50–51, 57
Jorem, K. 192–193
juxtapositions 106–109

Kaemper, E. 155–156
Kafouros, M. 74
Kedia, B.L. 31–32, 50–51

Kieser, A. 123–124, 214
Klausen, A.M. 134–137, 200–201
knowing how *see* procedural knowledge
knowing what *see* declarative knowledge
knowing who knows what *see* relational competence
knowing why and when *see* conditional knowledge
knowledge access challenges 12
knowledge-based view (KBV) 23
knowledge characteristics 53–57, 59*t*, 180
  evidence 56–57
  knowledge transferability 55–56
knowledge conversation 55
knowledge creation 13, 42
knowledge economy 13
knowledge management 13
knowledge processing routines 37–38
knowledge repository 14
knowledge source 14
knowledge transferability 55–56
Kogut, B. 50–51, 56–57, 112
Kostova, T. 52–53, 227–228, 233–234
Kroc, R. 159–160, 184–186, 202, 207
Krugman, P. 47–48
Kuhn, T. 15
Kumar, J.A. 23
Kwoma people (Papua New Guinea) 157–158

Lægreid, P. 30
Lane, P.J. 37–39
language differences 84
Larsson, I. 95
Latin America 3–4
Latour, B. 90–91, 93
Lean concept 95
learning processes, slow 190–191
Lefevere, A. 80–81
Leiner, L. 214
leveraging dilemma 25
Levinthal, D. 31–36, 38, 39
Levitt, B. 166
Liao, J. 35–36
Lichtenthaler, U. 39–40
link lengths 45–46
Lippmann, S.A. 53–54, 112–113
literal translation (metaphrase) 81, 83–84, 86, 148–149
Littler, C.R. 27–28

localization 140, 143–144
Lomi, A. 28–29
longitudinal approach 95, 101*b*
loose coupling 138, 143–144, 190
lost in translation 174–175, 195
Lubatkin, M. 37–38
Luckmann, T. 145–146

McDonald, D. 184–185
McDonald, M. 184–185
McDonald's 159–160, 184–186, 202, 206–207, 208*t*
McGrath, J.E. 115
Management by Objectives (MBO) 140–141, 193
Management by Results 192–193
management characteristics 33–34
Manipulation school 82, 97, 130, 164
man as rule-following agent 146
Mansfield, E. 112
March, J.G. 146–147, 172–173
Marx, K. 152
masculinity/femininity 50–51
Mavor, S. 188–189, 204–205
mediation 6
mediators 5–6, 107
MEDLINE 8–9
Meierewert, S. 125
mergers 30–31
metamorphosis 170, 177*f*
metaphors 68–77, 79, 98
  theory-confirming approach 70–71
  theory-generating approach 71–72
  theory quality beyond novelty 73
  transmission 178–179
meta-studies 158
methodological particularism 95–96
middle management 94–95
Miles, R.E. 152
mimeticism 155–156
Minkov, M. 240–241
Mintzberg, H. 152–153
misfit 138
missing implementation of transferred knowledge 8–9
modifying mode 17, 154, 170–176, 177*f*, 182–183, 197–201, 203–206, 238–242, 245*t*, 248–249
  addition 175–176

  Denmark and co-production in Aalborg 197–200, 202, 204
  failure 200–201
  omission 173–175
  operational translation rules 173
  research literature 171–173
  similarity 240–242
  translatability 238–240
modulation 83–84, 148–149
morale, low 132–133, 162
Moreland, R.L. 115–116
Morgan, G. 70–71, 73
Mortensen, N.M. 197–200, 241–242, 248
Mouricou, P. 213–214
Mowery, D.C. 39
multinational companies (MNCs) and subsidiaries 2, 28, 30–31, 55–56, 200

Nabokov, V. 81
national barriers 193–194, 207
national cultures 50–52, 138
national distance 206–207
nation-specific translation styles 148–149
nations, reproducing 155–157
Netherlands 8–9
network(s) 14, 125
  centrality 44–45
  characteristics 44–46
    ego networks 45
    network node position 44–45
    social relational network: tie strength 46
    whole network effects 45–46
  closure 45
  constraints 43
  density 44–46
  node position 44–45
  see also social networks
newness 167–169
Nida, E. 81–84
Nielsen, J.A. 95–97
node levels 43
Nonaka, I. 55
non-codified knowledge 49
normative pillar 52
norms of translation 81–83, 88–89, 101*b*, 107

306 Index

Norway 30, 201–202
    Confederation of Business and Industry (NHO) 165–166, 207
    Confederation of Trade Unions (LO) 165–166, 191–192, 207
    coworker dialogue based on American performance-appraisal and counselling (PAC) system 191–194, 202, 203, 206–207, 208*t*
    Development Dialogue based on American performance-appraisal systems 165–166, 170, 174–175
    educational sector 94–95
    healthcare sector 127–128, 175–176
    public sector organizations 140–141
    stockfish production (case study) 40–41, 119–121, 141–143
not-faithful translator 86
Novak, W. 126
novel theories 99
novelty 73, 167, 168–169, 171
    incentivizing 168
    real 168
    universal 168

object image of knowledge 18–19
Oddou, G. 125
O'Dell, C. 8
Olsen, J.P. 146
omission 83–84, 173–175, 177*f*, 245*t*
operationalizations 39
operational rules 154, 173, 182–183
opposite rule of radical translation 203
organizational institutionalism 52
organizational responsiveness 35–36
organizational routines 33–34
organizational structure 37–38, 201–202
organizational success 1–3
organizational translation 74, 90–98, 101*b*, 164
    contextualization orientation 96–97
    images of translator 93–95
    process orientation 95–96
    translation objects 92–93
    translation as transformation 97–98
Organization for Economic Cooperation and Development (OECD) 4–5
    innovation policy initiatives 47–48
organization and management (OMT) 67–68

Ortony, A. 75–76, 79, 99
Oswick, C. 67–68, 71
outbringers 126–127
outcome logics 198
outer domains *see* external domains
outsiders 122–124, 141–143
Özen, S. 94

Packard, D. 126
paradigmatic theories 69
patents 2, 38, 45–46, 50, 161, 168
patterns of behaviour 148, 151
person-embodied technology 50
Pertusa-Orgega, E.M. 26–27
Phelps, C. 40
physical distance 49
Piekkari, R. 93, 96–97, 220
Polanyi, K. 114
Polanyi, M. 54, 116–117
Popper, K.R. 163
Porter, M.E. 47–48, 152
Portugal 2–3
power distance 50–51
power imbalances 84–85
practice, concept of 109–110
Presley, E. 168–169
primary domain 90–91
principles and templates distinction 172
problem-solving capacity 164–165
procedural knowledge 109–110
process approach 122–123
process-embodied technology 50
process orientation 95–96, 101*b*, 107–108
process of transfer 76–77*b*, 99
product-embodied technology 50
productivity, low 132–133, 189, 190, 204–205
professional grief-process practice 127–128
propositional theories 69
pro-proximity view 47–48
public administrations 4–5, 63–64, 89, 107, 164–165, 233
Pym, A. 90, 171

quasi objects 91
Qur'an 85

Radaelli, G. 94–95
radical translation mode 17, 154, 163–171, 174–175, 177f, 182–183, 191–197, 203, 204, 235–238, 245t, 248–249
  accidental translations 166
  alteration 170
  calculated 164–166
  China and happiness indices 194–197, 202, 204
  fashion 169
  habitual translations 167–169
  Norwegian coworker dialogue based on American performance-appraisal and counselling (PAC) system 191–194, 202, 203
  novelty and templates for imitation 168–169
  risk avoidance 165–166
  similarity 237–238
  translatability 235–236
randomized controlled trials 158
Rank Xerox 161–162
Rashman, L. 8
rational calculations 182–183
rationalized knowledge management system 4–5
Reay, T. 129, 139
recipient organizational context 5
recipient units 76–77b, 99
recipient version 175–176
reciprocity 114
recognition 35–36
recontextualization 129
redistribution 114
reformulation 83–84
reframing 16–17
regularities 151
regulative pillar 52
reimagining idea that translators and translations make a difference 17–19
Reinhnold, S. 152
reinvention 172–173
relational competence 111–112
relational constructs *see* structural and relational constructs
relational knowledge 44, 125
relayering 27–28
relevance beyond business organizations 3–6
  architecture of knowledge transfers 5–6

renaming 140–141
repatriates 125
replacement 138–140, 143–144, 190
replication 170–171, 173
replication-adaptation pattern 151, 154
replication dilemma 171–173
replication strategy 159–160, 184–186, 202, 204–205, 207
reproducing-copying translation rule 183, 202
reproducing translation mode 17, 154, 155–163, 167, 177f, 182–191, 205, 228–234, 245t, 248–249
  British coal mines and American Taylorism 186–191, 204–205
  chosen or taken for granted rules 159–161
  copying 161–163
  cultures 157–158
  evidence movement 158–159
  McDonald's 184–186, 202
  nations 155–157
  similarity and copying 230–234
  translatability and copying 228–230
reproductions 167, 171
research-based evidence 158
research and development (R&D) 33–35, 37, 39
resource mobilization 198
responsible autonomy, loss of 132–133
re-territorialization 140–141
revealing modes and rules 17
revelatory insights 105
Ringov, D.P. 173
risk avoidance 165–166
rule-based complex response 147
rules of translation 83–84, 88–89, 101b, 108, 145–151, 182–183, 202
  addition 83–84, 175–176, 177f, 245t, 248
  blind application of 147
  editing 149–150
  explicit 147
  external domains 148–151
  formal rules 146
  informal rules 146
  macro level 146
  main pattern of outcomes 151
  meso level 146
  micro level 146
  non-matching and inappropriate 147
  omission 83–84, 173–175, 177f, 245t

rules of translation (*Continued*)
    search for 148
    sociology of 148
    uncodified 147
    see also alteration; copying; deliberate usage of translation rules
Rumelt, R.P. 53–54, 112–113
Ryle, G. 54

Sahlin-Andersson, K. 97, 149–150, 154, 174
Sahlin, K. 95
saliency imbalance of metaphors theory 99
salient features 75–76, 105–107
Sapir, E. 89
Scandinavia 15–16, 90
    see also Denmark; Norway; Sweden
Schumpeter, J.A. 47
science parks 47–48
scope conditions 225–234
    addition 245*t*
    alteration 245*t*
    copying 245*t*
    modifying mode 238–242, 245*t*
    omission 245*t*
    radical mode 235–238, 245*t*
        recipient and source 227–228
    reproducing mode 228–234, 245*t*
    similarity 245*t*
    source 227
    translatability 245*t*
Scott, W.R. 52, 152
search phase 70–71
secondary domain 90–91
Secord, P.F. 146
semantic distance 74–75
sensemaking theory 80
sensor capability 41
sequentiality 37, 172–173
Serres, M. 97
Sevón, G. 97
Shannon, C. 11
signal-transmission metaphor 11–13
silos 30
similarity 70–71, 138, 230–234, 245*t*
    and copying 230–234
        modifying mode 240–242
        radical mode 237–238
similes 69
Simon, H.A. 147
Simonin, B.L. 56–57

simple models, complex failures 10–13
Singh, H. 50–51
Singh, J. 45–46
Sitton-Kent, L. 94–95
situated knowledge 115
Sjödin, D. 39–40
Skopos theory 82–83, 97, 130, 164
Snell-Hornby, M. 86–87
Snow, C.C. 152
social capital 41–43, 125
social innovations programs 9–10
social mechanism 150
social networks 40–44, 59*t*, 58–63, 114, 179–180, 201–204
    knowledge-creation capability 42
    relational dimension 42
    sensor capability 41
    social capital 42
    storing capability 42
    structural dimension 42
    transfer capability 42
social relational network: tie strength 46
social relationships and kinships 114
social rule 145
social ties 125, 204–205
sociology of translation 15–16, 90, 97
Song, Y. 36, 38
source entity 99
source organizational context 5
sources to new theories of organizations 67–69
    borrowings from outer domains 68
    content of imports 69
source text 81–82
source unit 76–77*b*
Spain 26–27
specialized translation 89–90
speed of transfer process 8
Spender, J.C. 116–117
spin-out organizations 2–3
stakeholder theory 67–68
Stalker, G.M. 152
standardization 118, 131–132, 160, 184–185
standard operating procedure 147
state of the art 57–63
Stenberg, J-E. 192–193
'stickiness' 12–14, 18–19, 63–64, 123–124, 138, 179, 181–182
storing capability 42
strategies 83

strategizing 98
structural elements 44
structural holes 43, 45, 46
structural and relational constructs 43–44
    dyadic level 43–44
    node level 43
    whole network level 44
subject matter 89–90
subprocesses 122–123
substitution 83–84
subtraction 83–84, 173–175, 248
success and failures 6–13
success and failures, simple models, complex failures 10–13
Suddaby, R. 225–226
survival rates 2–3, 5, 52–53, 161–162
Sweden 56–57, 95
    research park in Stockholm modelled on Silicon Valley 149–150, 174
Szulanski, G. 8, 10, 17–18, 172, 178–179, 200, 233–234

tacit knowledge 43–44, 46, 48–49, 54–56, 116–117, 125, 175–176
tacitness 57, 130–131
Tailby, S. 188–189
Taiwan 26–27, 113–114
Takeuchi, H. 55
Tarde, G. 155–156
target organizational context 130–137
    complexity 133–136
    embeddedness 136–137
    explicitness 130–133
Taussig, M. 167–168
Tavares, M.F.F. 7–8
taxonomy 152–153
Taylor, F. 188
Taylorism 186–191, 204–206, 208t, 216, 248–249
    see also British coal-mining industry and knowledge transfer from United States
technical competence 35–36
technological districts 47–48
technological parks 47–48
technology-based practices 112
technopoles 47–48
templates 159–163, 168–169, 173, 174, 184–185, 198, 199–200, 248–249
text-context relationship 79–80

theories of knowledge transfers 13–15
theory-confirming approach 70–71
theory-generating approach 71–72
theory quality beyond novelty 73
Thuriaux-Alemán, B. 6–7
Tidd, J. 6–7
tie strength 43–44, 46
timing 140–141, 143–144
Todorova, G. 36–37
toning down 173–174, 248
Total Quality Management (TQM) 140–141
Toury, G. 81–83
trained incapacity 147, 204–205
trajectories 248–249
transactive memory 111–112
transactive memory system (TMS) network 115–116
transfer channels 76–77
transferees as translators 106–107
transfer image of knowledge flow 18–19
transferors 76–77
transformation 35–37, 97–98, 101b
translatability 110–117, 130, 141–144, 245t
    high 128–129
    low 121, 125, 128–129, 136
    modifying mode 238–240
    radical mode 235–236
translation 4, 18–19, 63–64, 181–182
translation ecologies 95
translation mode 17, 154
translation objects 92–93, 101b
translation performance 18–19, 181–187, 202, 205–206
    versus transfer barriers 206–207
translation studies 15–16, 67, 74, 98, 101b
translation theory 15–19, 23, 78
    see also antecedents of translation theory
translatorial action 86–87
translators 18–19, 85–88, 101b, 121–129, 182–183
    expatriates 124–125
    insiders 126–129
    outsiders 122–124
transmission metaphor 178–179
transposition 83–84, 148–149
trans-specialists 31
Trist, E. 132–133, 139–140, 189–191
trust 30–31, 43, 46, 125
Tsai, W. 28–29, 41, 44–45
Turkey 94

Tynsdale, W. 86
typologies as means of theorizing 152–153
typology of translation rules 153–155

uncertainties and absorptive capacity 35–36
uncertainty avoidance 50–51
unit-crossing transfer and sharing channels 30
United Kingdom 47, 164–165, 170, 194, 201–202
  see also British coal-mining industry and knowledge transfer from United States
United States 2–3, 8–9, 45–46, 50–51, 57, 112, 125, 161, 200, 201–202
unit of translation 80–81
untranslatability 84–85, 174
  cultural 84–85
  linguistic 84–85
  low 84–85

van Grinsven, M. 98
variation 6–7
  ideational 98
  structural 98
Veblen, T. 147
Venuti, L. 68
Vermeer, H. 82
vertical differentiation 25, 27–29
vertical structure (hierarchical coordination system) 24–25
Vinay, J.P. 83–84, 148–149

Volberda, H.W. 32
Von Hippel, E. 179

Walgenbach, P. 174–175
Walton, S. 126
Wanberg, J. 30
Wasserman, S. 40
Weaver, W. 11
weaving 138–139, 143–144, 190
Weber, M. 25–26, 152
Wedlin, L. 95
Wellisz, S. 189
Wellstein, B. 123–124
Westney, D.E. 4, 50, 93, 96–97, 164–166, 176, 220
'what' question 39
'where' question 114–115
Whetten, D.A. 67–68, 74–75, 226
whole network level 44–46
whole theories 69
Willem, A. 26–27
Williams, B. 55
Williams, C. 172–173
Wilss, W. 87–88
Winter, S.G. 7–10, 161–162, 172
wish rotation planning 127–128
Wollebæk, K. 192–194

X factor 14, 181

Zahra, S.A. 35–37
Zander, U. 56–57, 112
Zuni tribe (New Mexico) 157–158